CHARLES HENRY BROWNING

Born 5 August 1846
Died 4 June 1926

A biographical sketch appears on page 263.

By his organizations and writings, he laid a broad foundation for a popular interest in Old English family descents.

An acknowledgment of genuine friendship and wise counsel bestowed during an intimate association of many years, while the author was engaged with him in an extended study of the Great Charter.

MAGNA CHARTA

Part I The Romance of the Great Charter (1939)

Part II Pedigrees of the Barons (1942)

by

JOHN S. WURTS

of Hedgefield
Germantown, Pa.

Printed in the U. S. A.

This reprint March 1945
is referred to as
The Crown Edition

HERITAGE BOOKS
2024

HERITAGE BOOKS
AN IMPRINT OF HERITAGE BOOKS, INC.

Books, CDs, and more—Worldwide

For our listing of thousands of titles see our website
at
www.HeritageBooks.com

A Facsimile Reprint
Published 2024 by
HERITAGE BOOKS, INC.
Publishing Division
5810 Ruatan Street
Berwyn Heights, MD 20740

Originally published 1945
Brookfield Publishing Company
Founded by James B. Brookfield 1892
Mail Service Department
P. O. Box 4933, Philadelphia, Pa.

— Publisher's Notice —
In reprints such as this, it is often not possible to remove blemishes from the original. We feel the contents of this book warrant its reissue despite these blemishes and hope you will agree and read it with pleasure.

International Standard Book Number
Paperbound: 978-0-7884-3099-2

TABLE OF CONTENTS

	Page
The Romance	5
King John Surrendered	16
A List of the 25 Sureties	30
Dover Copy of Magna Charta	34
Lincoln Copy of Magna Charta	35
Pedigrees of the Barons, Chapter 1	39
Translation of Magna Charta, Chapter 26	137
Boadicea and the Druids, Chapter 27	149
Old King Cole	162
The Frankish Kings	164
Clovis and Magister Palatii	165
The Saxon Kings, Chapter 28	169
Alfred the Great	171
Charlemagne, Chapter 29	178
The Scottish Kings, Chapter 30	190
King Robert Bruce	193
The Normans, Chapter 31	194
William the Conqueror	195
Provence, Chapter 32	206
Castile, Chapter 33	211
King Edward I, Chapter 34	213
King Edward II	217
King Edward III, Chapter 35	218
The Order of the Garter, Chapter 36	220
The Original Knight Companions	224
Mr. and Mrs. Harry Cyrus Holloway	241
First Supplement	269
Second Supplement	285
Acknowledgment and Bibliography	32 and 290
The Grandin Family	293
Map of England and Wales	
Index	
Blank pages for personal data	

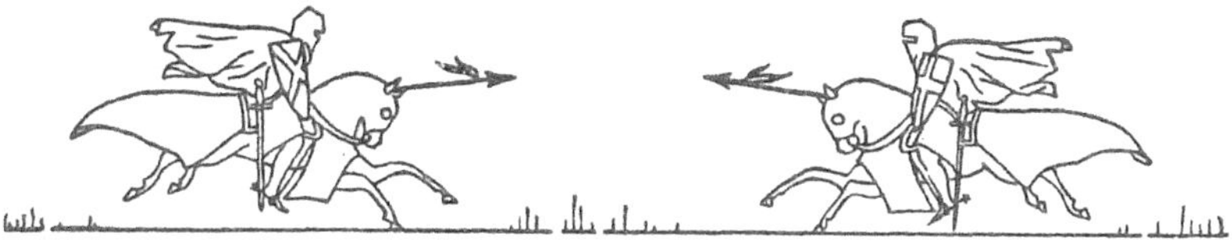

Part I

The Romance of The Great Charter

Remarks of John S. Wurts before
THE NATIONAL SOCIETY MAGNA CHARTA DAMES
Meeting Around the Original Magna Charta
In the British Pavilion, New York World's Fair, October 10, 1939
A portion of this message was broadcast over the radio from coast to coast.

THE ENGLISH-SPEAKING RACE was born free. It never had to purchase freedom from anyone, although it has time and again been faced by the necessity of keeping a tyrant from invading its freedom. Such a tyrant was King John, and Magna Charta was the price he paid for his arrogance and greed.

The story of Magna Charta is a Romance. A Romance in its highest sense is defined to be a blending of the **heroic,** the **marvelous** and the **mysterious,** and used in this sense, the word Romance exactly describes what I would say about this piece of parchment, around which we are gathered today.

The story of Magna Charta is indeed a Romance: It is a blending of the heroic, the marvelous and the mysterious, the full significance of which only the imagination can grasp. It is wonderful in its history. It transcends the ordinary. Hence it is a Romance. But who were the heroes? And what was their marvelous achievement?

In case we have forgotten our English history, let us be reminded that King John was a horrid person, an arbitrary and mercenary ruler, who threw people into dungeons at the drop of a hat. He married off wards of the Crown, young widows and pretty girls, to foreign adventurers and then collected a nice percentage of the wards' fortunes from their husbands. He had a tiresome habit of forcing the peasants to build bridges over streams he might wish to cross while hunting, and at one time he made the whole of England his own private game preserve, so that none of the starving peasantry could kill even a rabbit for supper. He greatly increased the royal taxes and replenished his exchequer with the confiscated property of the clergy. While "a king can do no wrong" he certainly can make mistakes.

While brave Richard the Lion Hearted was leading a crusade to the walls of Jerusalem, John vainly tried to usurp the crown, declaring falsely that King Richard was dead. Once when fighting in France, King John entertained his foes at dinner, then treacherously murdered them all and took their fortress and, when some years later Richard died, John indeed seized the throne, although Arthur, the son of his brother Geoffrey, was the rightful heir. Prince Arthur, aged 12, after a time of imprisonment was stabbed, presumably by John. Such treacherous success however, did not last long.

Shortly after John became King, in 1199, he quarrelled with the Pope who promptly laid an interdict upon his kingdom, prohibiting services in all the Churches and the administration of the sacraments. The Church bells were not rung. The dead were refused Christian burial. He then excommunicated all England. This lasted over six years, till it was lifted in June 1213, during which time no one had been rightly married, or buried and few baptized. Pope Innocent III found John hard to control, for he was always forgetting the "divine authority" of the Church.

Then the Pope deposed John, proclaimed him no longer

King, and set Philip of France to war against him. To checkmate Philip's invasion John, ignoring the deposing, made a gift to the Pope of all the realm, crown and revenue by written indenture dated Monday, 13 May 1213. But John at once received the crown back as the Pope's tenant and vassal, at a ferm or annual rental of a thousand marks for the whole kingdom, 700 for England and 300 for Ireland, payable semi-annually in advance to Master Pandulf the Pope's Delegate. The Pope then must protect John against Philip and instructs Philip to desist but, ignoring the Pope, Philip fights on.

KING JOHN

In writing the historic play "King John," it is rather remarkable that Shakespeare omitted, perhaps intentionally, to make any allusion whatever to that greatest event of King John's reign, the procuring from him the grant of Magna Charta. But the same writer, in the play "Henry VIII," also forbore mentioning any of the unpleasant features of that King's personal character. Nor did he mention that great event of his reign, the Reformation. However, the "King John" play has much to do with other affairs of the realm in which our Barons were concerned, and this introduced as characters, in the play, several of the prominent men of England and of France. Strange to say, only one of them, Roger Bigod, the Earl of Norfolk and Suffolk, was on the side of the Barons when they contended with King John for the Great Charter. The Earl has but a small part in the play. He came on and went off in four scenes and spoke only fifty words, and they never became a quotation from Shakespeare.

Instead, the dramatist could have better made an interesting farce, with amusing situations if he had more largely portrayed the state of public affairs in England. Through this act of surrender of his crown to the Pope, John brought about a remarkable condition in his realm, for thereupon the bond of feudalism in England was broken, and he was feudally extinct, when all feudal obligations to him ceased, and the Baronage died with him. Yet he did this with the consent of sixteen Earls, and many wealthy Barons, which may be understood as doing it without protest, as it may have been viewed as a harmless political measure, for the act protected England from threatened French invasion, since it made England taboo, it being now "Church property," and the French, being faithful to the Church, dare not trespass. And this scheme of defense and protection obtained for 150 years.

But what should most interest us, descendants of many of the Barons affected by John's act, is that the Barons did not do homage for their fees to the new lord paramount, the Pope, and hence, did not receive from him a renewal, by letters patent, of the Baronies. On the contrary the Pope, as the head of the fee, excommunicated them.

Under this condition, the Barons were only yeomen, or freeholders, or copy-holders of King John, now the freeholder of the Pope, and therefore, when the Barons met on Runnemede, they were outlaws against the Pope, the lord paramount, and the Pope's freeholder, John. Therefore these yeomen, erstwhile Barons of the realm, being now only sub-tenants, could not legislate, if that is what they did, as Barons, and the Magna Charta was without life or force and wholly invalid!

The Baronage, thus broken in 1213 (as far as feudal law was concerned, and it was still the supreme system) so remained for 150 years, while rent was paid annually to the Pope. The famous "Chronicle" of the monk, Matthew of Westminster (in printed volume II, page 116) gives the full text of the King's surrender to the Pope, and tells of John's reception of the realm as a freeholder, the feudatory of the Church of Rome, witnessed on Wednesday, 15 May 1213, by many prominent Englishmen. When their peculiar status after the surrender was fully recognized by the Barons they wished to know where they actually stood, and Magna Charta was in part to assure them, and it may be seen that in the introduction our Barons wrote themselves as "liberis hominibus regni nostri," the freemen of the kingdom. But they really were then only sub-tenants of John, the tenant in chief.

And they wrote of Earls and Barons holding "in chief by military service" of John. This was absurd. John was a tenant, paying rent, and the Earls and Barons were only his sub-tenants. And it was also absurd to say that John would for a certain purpose, "summon Earls and Great Barons of the realm singly by our letters." This was John's custom while lord paramount before 15 May 1213, but now he had no such right, having surrendered it to the Pope. Nor could there be Barons' Courts; and many other feudal prerogatives allowed Barons, became extinct or inoperative under this peculiar condition imposed upon England by John, and by His Majesty the Pope, who was in effect the real King of England.

It is interesting to note that the Nobles, ever ready to follow John's banner against any foe of England, now refused to fight for him abroad and because of this refusal, John's tyranny at home knew no bounds. At the battle of Bouvines on Sunday, 27 July 1214, John being utterly defeated, never again attempted to regain his Norman provinces.

For many years, the wretched people had been most unjustly oppressed; first they were despoiled of their possessions, then murdered. Those who had any property lost it by heavy taxes and unjust decrees. Justice was bought and sold; an heir and his land were disposed of to the highest bidder; permission to marry had to be purchased from the king; and the monarch demanded what taxes he thought fit to levy. All this reached its climax in the reign of John, a prince "utterly contemptible for his folly." We recall in particular his infamous conduct in Sherwood Forest toward Maid Page 77 Marion, Baron FitzWalter's daughter, whom he despoiled and caused to be poisoned. When to his exactions he added the debauchery of his Nobles' wives and daughters, the storm burst.

And a part of that storm broke on the walls of Colchester Castle. When the Barons learned that their King was raising forces for their repression, they each undertook the defense of a definite district of the country, in pursuit of which obligation it fell to the lot of Saire de Quincey, the first Earl of Winchester, to attack the Castle of Colchester. For John had had the forethought to dismiss the custodian of that fortress and give it into the charge of a Fleming upon whose faithfulness he could rely, besides sending from London a good supply of military engines and engineers. Notwithstanding that preparation, the Castle seems to have fallen an easy prey to de Quincey, who, however, was in turn attacked by the siege train which had been so successful in reducing Rochester Castle. The defense was stubborn, so stubborn that John himself came to direct the operations; but de Quincey held out for nearly two months, and then seems to have escaped safely to France.

As we contemplate the long struggle and the dramatic circumstances in which Magna Charta was secured, we instantly recall Stephen Langton, one of the noblest men of his time, a wise and learned ecclesiastic, who seemed specially raised up by Heaven to oppose and subdue the King. An English Cardinal was Stephen Langton, Archbishop of Canterbury, a true English Patriot for all that he was appointed by a foreign Pope without consultation of the English Church. He assembled the Barons in conference at the Abbey at Saint Edmunds-Bury to devise means to resist the impositions of King John. And here John reluctantly met them on Tuesday, 4 November 1214, but the Barons got nothing from him except his assurance that he most certainly expected them to pay the war tax he had levied. According to Matthew of Westminster, after the King left the Abbey, the Barons, declaring they had no faith in John's promises, were called to order by Stephen Langton. One by one they took a solemn oath on the high altar that they would stand united and not relinquish their efforts until they would compel the King to confirm their liberties or they would wage war against him to the death.

A rough draft containing the principal items they desired

ABBEY AT ST. EDMUNDSBURY

Bury St. Edmunds—"The Cradle of the Law"

had been prepared and this was submitted and approved by formal proceedings. John must consent to its proposals and confirm them by his seal or take the consequences. When shown to the King, his only reply was that as it was a great and difficult thing which they asked, he must have more time for its consideration. Roger of Wendover tells us that when John saw the Articles he swore by "God's teeth," his favorite oath, that he would never agree to such demands or any part of them.

To further delay the issue, the resourceful John, just before Easter 1215, announced that he was preparing for the Holy Crusade, when of course he would have it understood that he could not be disturbed for many months with even the matter of a Charter. During all this time there was general confusion throughout all England. The Barons had closed all courts. No man was even allowed to serve a writ in the king's name. John was deceived by his apparent successes. He underestimated the powers arrayed against him. The struggle was inevitable; to the modern mind the chief marvel is that it was so long delayed. The causes which led to the charter of English liberties were many, but they all had their root in the intolerable tyranny of the Norman kings.

Easter day, 19 April 1215, arrived and the Barons, who always kept their engagements, assembled according to their promise at Stamford in Lincolnshire, with a well-equipped army of more than two thousand knights. But as the place was not of his own selection John found it not convenient to meet them and sent word that he would await their coming at Oxford. But upon learning of their number, John decided not to attend there in person, sending instead two of his representatives, Stephen Langton and William Marshall, Earl Pembroke, who received the articles with the understanding that if the King still refused, the Barons would force his lingering consent by seizing his fortresses. When John received the Barons' Articles he replied, "They might as well ask for my Kingdom," completely ignoring the fact that he had already surrendered his Crown to the Pope. But indeed the only alternative was the loss of his Kingdom!

On Tuesday, 5 May 1215, the Barons chose Robert Fitz-Walter their leader, with the title of "Marshal of the Army of God and Holy Church." Theirs was a holy crusade against John to recover the liberties their forefathers had enjoyed and to restore the good old customs violated by a base and innovating king.

The towns of Exeter and Lincoln soon surrendered to the Baronial army. John, now at Windsor Castle, was informed that they were preparing to besiege the Castle and Tower of London, his strongest fortress, where they arrived Sunday, 24 May 1215. Of the Peers who had been neutral or faithful to the King, very few continued to side with him. Virtually powerless, with business of all kinds at a standstill, and with nearly his whole Baronage, and the majority of his subjects of all degrees in arms against him, he seems to have decided to surrender, at least for the time being. He finally called his Barons to a conference. They said, "then let the day be the 15th of June and the place Runnemede."

Runnemede is within sight of Windsor Castle and of St.

KING JOHN RELUCTANTLY YIELDS TO THE WILL OF THE PEOPLE

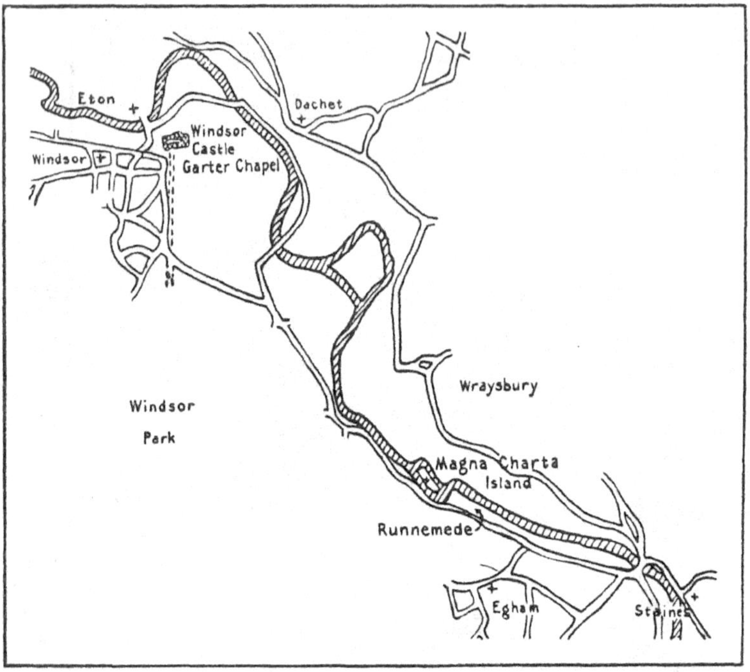

George's Chapel, the shrine of the Knights of the Garter, built by King Edward III about 1344. The towing-path, on the Surrey bank skirting the field of Runnemede, gives a beautiful five-mile ramble from Windsor to Staines. For ages the meadow called Runnemede has been crownland, and rented for pasturage, a portion being reserved in it for a racetrack, where the Egham races were run each year on a two-mile track in August and September, and this has been the only annual celebration on the historic field; but the events of 1215 are recalled by the racing for the "Magna Charta," the "Runnemede," and the "King John" stakes.

On the Dachet Road there is an old farm house, known as King John's hunting lodge, but having no more connection with King John than has the so-called Magna Charta Island, which lies off Wraysbury. At Ankerwyke House near Wraysbury still stands an immense yew tree, said to be older than the Magna Charta.

Of this wonder, William Thomas Fitzgerald, in 1807, wrote some lines beginning:

"What scenes have pass'd since first this ancient yew
In all the strength of youthful beauty grew!
Here patriot Barons might have musing stood,
And plann'd the Charter for their country's good.
And here, perhaps, from Runemede retir'd
The haughty JOHN, with secret vengence fired . . ."

Did King John ride out daily on horseback from Windsor Castle? Or did he travel four or five miles to the scene by boat? If we follow the latter route today, we pass under the turrets of the Royal Castle, and the grounds of Eton College, and drift in the shade of the huge riverside trees in Windsor Park. Navigation shall be free, says the Charter. A quaint thought that the young people now splashing round the bend of the river in bathing costumes or boating in summer dresses, should have a clause to themselves in Magna Charta. Presently we come to Runnemede, a long stretch of green meadow without hedges or fences, lying along the South bank at a curve in the River Thames, about thirty miles west of London. It is indeed a tranquil English scene. In the distance one can see a village and hear the tinkling of the cowbells.

At the tiny Norman church in the hamlet of Egham, Stephen Langton, the fearless Archbishop of Canterbury, gathered the Barons on a June day in 1215 to pray for strength to humble the arrogant King John. Today in the church at Egham may be seen the set of Barons' shields and plaques presented to it by The National Society Magna Charta Dames.

When it was proposed, a few years ago, to sell the field of Runnemede to the highest bidder, a great outcry was made. The former Cara Rogers, now Lady Fairhaven, a member of the Magna Charta Dames, an American girl, bought and presented to the British people the field of Runnemede as a memorial to her husband to be kept for all time as a sacred, historic spot.

On the day appointed, Trinity Monday, the 15th of June, 1215, King John met his Barons on the field of Runnemede, the ancient meadow of council. His followers were few because John's injustices and selfishness had increased his unpopularity beyond all bounds. With him were but a score of persons, most of whom despised him and were his advisors only in form. Encamped on the field of Runnemede more than two thousand Knights and Barons in arms awaited his coming.

We are told the Barons could at this time have demanded even more from John, for he now was in no position to refuse them anything they asked, but they seem from all that can be learned of them to have been an honorable set of men bent on having only what was just and right, and they simply remained firm to their first demands and asked no more.

The Barons had their demands carefully written on parchment. These John had seen seven months before. From what we know of John's character, he may have argued stubbornly for a time but at all events he now knew that he was there to yield, and that he was opposed by overwhelming force and so

KING JOHN SURRENDERED

Before the day passed he affixed his seal to the original but preliminary draft known as the "Articles of the Barons." The immediate forerunner of Magna Charta, these forty-nine articles contained the main principles of the Charter. The King has now promised to rule according to law. The King must keep the law and if he will not he may now be compelled to do so.

The undoubted original of the preliminary rough draft of Magna Charta, with a fragment of King John's seal in brown wax attached, may still be seen preserved in the British Museum. This supremely interesting original had been retained in the possession of King John. It was later captured by the Dauphin of France, reclaimed by the Protector, William Marshall, then Bishop Laud and later Dr. Warner had it, and thereafter it came into the more appreciative hands of Bishop Gilbert Burnet, the distinguished historian, an ancestor of Mrs. S. Fahs Smith. This priceless manuscript was later Pages 475, 600 owned by that Bishop's son's executor, whose daughter sold it, with proof of this chain of ownership, to the Earl of Stanhope, and he, in 1769, presented it to the British Museum, where this, the original preliminary draft, known as the "Forty-nine articles of the Barons," the forerunner of Magna Charta may now be seen.

The exact terms of the Charter itself were decided and engrossed during four subsequent days of negotiation, and it was on the 19th that the great seal was affixed to all copies. Doubtless, twenty-five duplicate originals were made, perhaps one for each of the Sureties. These were all dated back to the 15th of June, and duly sealed by the King. John didn't sign any of them with his autograph. As a matter of fact, he could neither read nor write, nor could the Barons, nor Knights, except a few, of whom was the noted Richard de Gilpin, the scholar. He was the Secretary and Adviser of Ivo de Talboys, Baron of Kendal, whom he accompanied to Runnemede. No one signed Magna Charta, it wasn't necessary as at common law sealing was sufficient to authenticate any formal document.

No doubt each of the twenty-five Surety Barons carried a copy home and had it read at the principal crossroads by order of the King, where the people swore by uplifted hand to support the Sureties in their determination to make the King keep all his promises.

The obligations written in the Charter constitute one of the very early examples of a company surety bond.

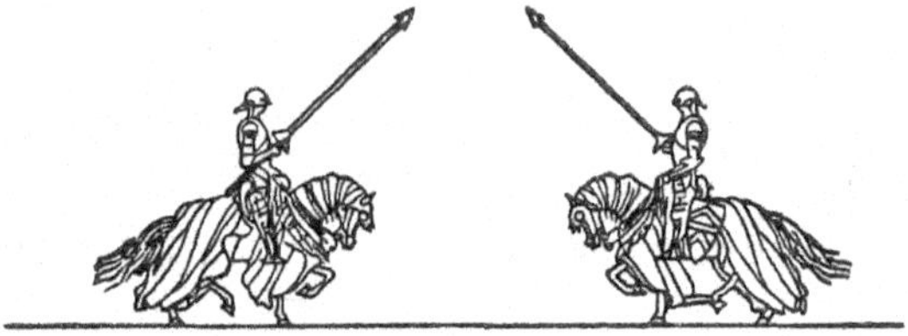

The first Magna Charta commemoration took place in the year 1215 when, by command of their Marshal, Robert, Lord FitzWalter, a great tournament in celebration of the granting of the Charter and the "Conclusion of peace betwixt the Kinge and his Barons" was held "near London in Staines Wood and at the town of Hounslow, on Monday, 29th June" 1215. And today, it is supremely fitting that such a group as the Magna Charta Dames should meet in this place around this original parchment to continue that fraternity, comradeship, and responsibility for others contemplated by the Charter, and to promote which this Society of Descendants has its reason for being.

Each year since 1909 the Magna Charta Dames have held celebrations in commemoration of this important event. As descendants they are deeply appreciative of the work accomplished by their Magna Charta ancestors and desire that the benefits flowing from The Great Charter might be more widely known and better understood.

We have supposed that at least twenty-five duplicate originals were made. Four original sealed copies of Magna Charta survive. The two in the British Museum were acquired with the library of that omnivorous collector of manuscripts, Sir Robert Cotton. It is said that for a few shillings he recovered one of them from a tailor when he was about to cut it into strips for measures. The other, found in Dover Castle, was later much damaged by a fire at the Cottonian Library over two centuries ago. The third copy is at Salisbury Cathedral where no doubt it has always been kept.

DOVER

WEMYS

SALISBURY

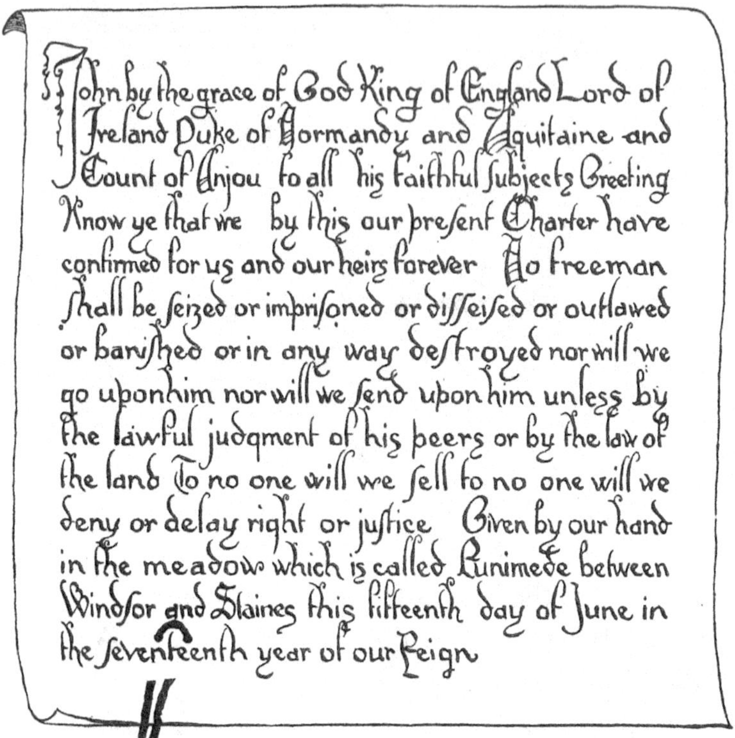

John by the grace of God King of England Lord of Ireland Duke of Normandy and Aquitaine and Count of Anjou to all his faithful subjects Greeting Know ye that we by this our present Charter have confirmed for us and our heirs forever No freeman shall be seized or imprisoned or disseised or outlawed or banished or in any way destroyed nor will we go upon him nor will we send upon him unless by the lawful judgment of his peers or by the law of the land To no one will we sell to no one will we deny or delay right or justice Given by our hand in the meadow which is called Runimede between Windsor and Staines this fifteenth day of June in the seventeenth year of our Reign

Pages 34, 35, 137

An illustration of the letters in which Magna Charta is written.

A free translation from the Latin, of the opening and closing sentences of the Great Charter of King John, together with its two most celebrated sections.

The one before us is the most perfect of the four originals surviving and is known as the Lincoln copy. It has been graciously lent by its owners, the Dean and Chapter of Lincoln Cathedral, and so far as we know, has been kept there since 1215. Probably Hugh, Bishop of Lincoln, brought it straight home from Runnemede after the sealing. Naturally, the Dean and Chapter have taken the most elaborate measures to preserve and protect their priceless treasure. LINCOLN

The whole Charter is as you see written on a single piece of sheepskin measuring 17½ x 18 inches. It is held between two sheets of heavy plate glass, and the bronze frame has been so fastened together that only the person who knows the secret of the screws can open it. It is indeed a priceless parchment, but the unseen benefits which it has brought to mankind are of even greater value. We have heard it stated on good authority that at the close of the World's Fair, this original Magna Charta will be placed for safe keeping in the Library of Congress at Washington. Page 35

If you understand medieval Latin and can interpret all the little quirks and flourishes by which the penman abbreviated his words, you will have no difficulty at all in reading Magna Charta. What kind of ink was used? Was it made from nut galls? Or was it cuttlefish ink? The cuttlefish or squid as you know is provided with a sac of black fluid to throw out and cloud the water enabling him to escape from his pursuers. What a contrast there is between the clear unfaded lettering more than seven hundred years old, and the faded endorsement you see on its margin made only 133 years ago.

Did John soon repent of his act? Did he think better of his bargain? Edmund Burke says of John that, without questioning in any part the terms of a treaty which he intended to observe in none, he agreed to everything the Barons thought fit to ask, hoping that the exorbitance of their demands would justify in the eyes of the world the breach of all his promises.

As a matter of fact, John did not keep his pledges made in Magna Charta and we are convinced he never intended to do so. Promptly on John's appeal, Pope Innocent III formally annulled the Charter and excommunicated the King's enemies and all disturbers of the peace. John with unexpected vigor then proceeded against the Barons who, under the terms of the Charter itself, immediately declared war upon the King who had been false to his promises, and the following spring Philip's son invaded England. A year and four months after Magna Charta had been secured, and while chaos reigned and the future seemed trembling in the balance, the struggle was brought to an end by the sudden death of John.

It happened in this way. After one of his masterful retreats from a far superior force, John was feasted by the Burghers of Lynn and at Swinestead Abbey, where the Monks set before him lampreys and cider and, partaking thereof gluttonously, he fell ill from acute indigestion. Suffering for nine days in great agony and fever, inflamed by this debauch, he was carried to Newark Castle where he died early in the morning, Tuesday, 19 October 1216, in the 49th year of his age. His body, at his desire, was honorably buried in the Cathedral of Worcester.

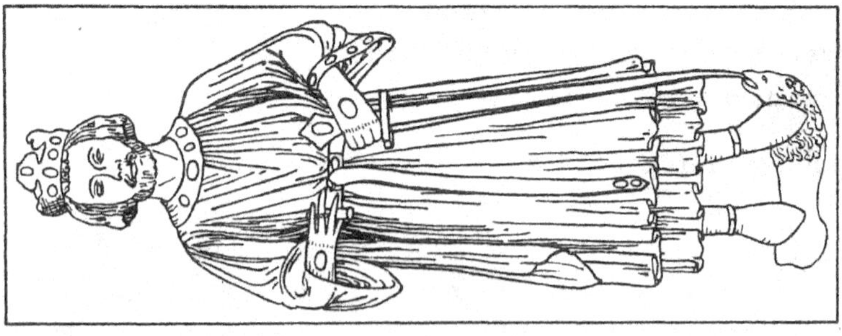

BRONZE EFFIGY AT THE TOMB OF KING JOHN

Did he really mean to keep the Charter? Was he sincere or only bluffing to gain time? His early death gives no positive answer to this question. Dying suddenly in the midst of his successes, John's death opened the way to a compromise and we now find all parties returning to allegiance to his youthful son, Henry III, then aged ten years, who was hastily crowned, with William Marshall, Lord Pembroke, as Regent and Protector. Although his son, the Surety, William Marshall, Jr., died without issue, the Protector William Marshall is, through his daughters, an ancestor of several of the Magna Charta Dames.

Page 103

The seal which John used was accidentally lost with all his treasure, when he was surprised by a rushing tide while crossing a dangerous quicksand called the Wash not very far from Wisbeach, only a few weeks before his death.

Magna Charta came at a time of great human achievements and in the midst of a generation that has to its credit some of the most enduring accomplishments of the race. That first half of the thirteenth century saw the rise of the great Gothic cathedrals, the development of the universities of Europe into the form which they practically retained ever since, and the creation of a literature in every country in Europe that still lives. A generation never does merely one thing well. It does all well or none. The after time has inherited more that is of enduring value for the race from that generation than perhaps from any other in human history.

We are living in a most important time in the history of our country. Our responsibility demands our best thought and effort. Shall we be indifferent to so great a need? At such a time as this it is surely a great privilege to be associated with persons of like mind in a work so truly worthwhile. We Americans are a thoughtful people, and careful thought makes for refinement and leads to good manners and gentle behavior. We all seek the well-being of our society and the influence it may have for the good of our beloved land, for righteousness and truth.

The Great Charter of Liberties has become The Mother of Constitutions! The liberties of half the civilized world are derived from Magna Charta! It is recognized as the basis of our laws, and of national liberty generally. That which before was vague is now made definite. Long standing customs, called Common Law, which had never before been reduced to writing, now for the first time become written law. **No taxation without representation!** Liberty is the keynote of the Charter. Liberty for all Englishmen! To have and to hold, to them and their heirs, for ever! The King is not above the law; the law is inviolable. Magna Charta places the king below the law.

Magna Charta is an expression in written words of the principles of human life which had been either grossly neglected or altogether forgotten by King John.

Magna Charta begins and ends with the declaration that the Church shall be free. All that there is in Magna Charta flows out of that.

"No free man shall be taken, or imprisoned, or dispossessed, or outlawed, or banished, or in any way destroyed, nor will we go upon him nor upon him send, except by the legal judgment of his peers or by the law of the land. To no one will we sell, to no one will we deny, or delay, right or justice." So read the celebrated 39th and 40th sections.

A Precedent for the Supreme Court

Section 61 authorized the election of the aforesaid twenty-five Surety Barons who should see that the provisions of the Charter were carried into effect. Their names are not recorded in the Magna Charta, but we learn them from Matthew Paris' "Chronica Majora."

These Sureties were astonishingly inter-related. Among them were several instances of father and son, of father-in-law and son-in-law, of brothers and of cousins. They had a common descent from Charlemagne. Four-fifths, or twenty of the twenty-five, were related in the degree of second cousin or nearer. Of these twenty-five Surety Barons only seventeen have descendants surviving to the present day and all seventeen are now represented by descendants in the membership of the Magna Charta Dames.

The most remarkable portion of section 61, if not of the whole charter, is that which grants unto the Barons, upon the failure of the King to keep his pledges, the right to distress and harass the King by any means in their power. In other words, they had permission to levy war upon their King, and commit other acts of high treason without, according to John's agreement, being guilty of any wrong. An amazing thing, legalized rebellion!

And the English spirit of fair play is crystallized in the final pronouncement of Magna Charta by which the Barons offered that all the concessions which the King made to them would in turn be passed on to their sub-tenants.

But the events which followed Magna Charta show that although the celebrated Charter had been truly and completely obtained from the reluctant John, it required constant vigilance on the part of the subject to maintain his prize unimpaired.

The triumphant success of the popular cause over the obstinacy of John, was a precedent to which the people have always delighted to refer. And we are their beneficiaries. It may be true that the Barons did not know or fully realize what they were moving toward, but they had a very clear and definite idea of what they were trying to get away from; and that was the arbitrary royal will.

Ours is a great heritage: Through seven and a quarter centuries, and down through some thirty generations, we trace the chain of events which binds Magna Charta to our celebration here today. Pioneer Americans inherited and brought across the sea the institutions of Old England. The unwritten Constitution of England was the constitution of these pioneers in the new world, and into the rights and benefits of Magna Charta they, our ancestors, entered as the lineal descendants of those free men of England to whom those rights and benefits had been assured forever.

God sifted a whole nation that he might send choice grain over into the wilderness.—William Stoughton, 1668.

The pursuit of genealogy illumines the past and becomes an inspiration for the future. - Diary, Good Friday, 6 April 1917 (the day on which the United States entered World War I).

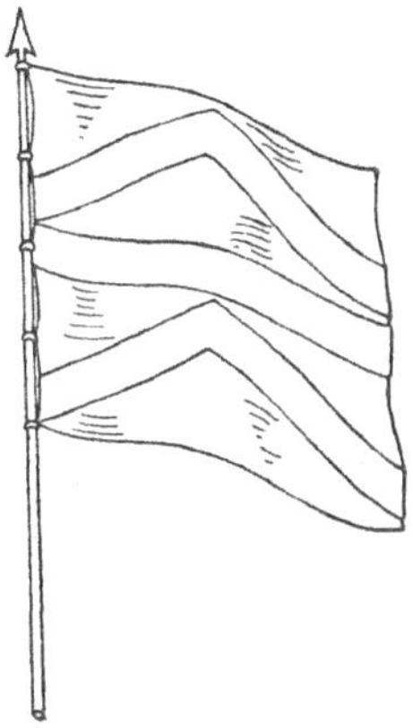

There is a most vital relationship, both by chain of events and by inheritance, between that striking scene at Runnemede in 1215 and this meeting here today, celebrating not only the anniversary of the Great Charter but also the 150th year since the inauguration of our first President, General George Washington.

If Magna Charta was, as has been sometimes said, a reactionary document, it was reactionary only in that it revived and confirmed liberties that had been forgotten and invaded by royal power. These liberties are part of man's nature and an attribute to human personality. To deny them, to hamper them, to invade them, is to install tyranny in the land. To take note of them, to build upon them and to appeal to them, is to open the door to that constructive progress whose limits are set only by the spiritual aspiration, the intellectual power and the moral earnestness of man.

The story of Magna Charta is indeed a Romance, a blending of the heroic, the marvelous, the mysterious!

(1) It is **heroic** in that it required the combined bravery of lords and people to withstand the treachery of John.

(2) It is **mysterious** in its causes, in exactly what happened and in its supreme benefit to mankind, and

(3) It is **marvelous,** in view of the resourcefulness of John, that the people ever accomplished their aim. John certainly was a remarkable man, not all good nor all bad, and that the Barons eventually got him to confirm the Great Charter is also remarkable.

Magna Charta asserts that great and eternal principle that each individual has inalienable rights, of which no government may deprive him, but to secure which all government exists.

Let all tyrants take note: Magna Charta has never been repealed.

Magna Charta guarantees freedom.

Freedom is the lesson which England has taught the world.

(The End)

BARON ROBERT FITZWALTER

The Twenty-five Renowned Sureties for the Observance of the Statutes contained in Magna Charta

*1. WILLIAM D'ALBINI,
Lord of Belvoir Castle, Leicestershire. d. 1236.

*2. ROGER BIGOD,
Earl of Norfolk (and Suffolk ?) d. 1220.

*3. HUGH BIGOD, The Earl of Norfolk's heir. d. 1225.

*4. HENRY DE BOHUN, Earl of Hereford. d. 1220.

*5. RICHARD DE CLARE, Earl of Hertford. d. 1217.

*6. GILBERT DE CLARE,
The Earl of Hertford's heir. d. 1230.

*7. JOHN FITZROBERT,
Lord of Warkworth Castle, Northumberland. d. 1240.

*8. ROBERT FITZWALTER,
Lord of Dunmow Castle, Essexshire. d. 1234.

9. WILLIAM DE FORTIBUS,
Earl of Albemarle. d. 1241. No great grand children.

10. WILLIAM DE HARDELL,
Mayor of London. d. after 1216. No known issue.

*11. WILLIAM DE HUNTINGFIELD,
A feudal baron in Suffolk. d. 1220.

*12. JOHN DE LACIE,
Lord of Halton Castle, Cheshire. d. 1240.

*13. WILLIAM DE LANVALLEI,
Lord of Stanway Castle, Essex. d. 1217.

*14. WILLIAM MALET,
Lord of Curry-Malet, Somersetshire. d. about 1217.

15. GEOFFREY DE MANDEVILLE,
Earl of Essex and Gloucester. d. 1216. No issue.

16. WILLIAM MARSHALL,
The Earl of Pembroke's heir. d. 1231. No issue.

17. ROGER DE MONTBEGON,
Lord of Horneby, Lancashire. d. 1226. No issue.

18. RICHARD DE MONTFICHET,
A feudal baron in Essex? d. after 1258. No issue.

*19. WILLIAM DE MOWBRAY,
Lord of Axholme Castle, Lincolnshire. d. 1223.

20. RICHARD DE PERCY,
A feudal baron of Yorkshire. d. 1244. No issue.

*21. SAIRE DE QUINCEY, Earl of Winchester. d. 1219.

*22. ROBERT DE ROOS,
Lord of Hamlake Castle, Yorkshire. d. 1226.

*23. GEOFFREY DE SAYE,
A feudal baron in Sussex? d. 1230.

*24. ROBERT DE VERE, Earl of Oxford. d. 1221.

25. EUSTACE DE VESCI, No issue surviving.
Lord of Alnwick, Northumberland. d. 1216.

---

* These are the 17 Sureties known to have descendants living to the present day. All 17 are now represented by descendants in the membership of the Magna Charta Dames.

ACKNOWLEDGMENT AND BIBLIOGRAPHY

This sketch has been presented as a contribution toward the seven hundred and twenty-fifth anniversary observance of the granting of Magna Charta. In its preparation the compiler has made a special use of the following books and articles and would here acknowledge his indebtedness to them:

The Great Charter. William Blackstone. 1759, &c.
Observations upon the Statutes. Daines Barrington, 1766.
Historical Treatise on the Feudal Law. Francis S. Sullivan, 1772.
Historical Essay on the Magna Charta. Richard Thomson, 1829.
Chartes des Libertes Anglaise. Charles Bémont, 1892.
The Magna Charta. Boyd C. Barrington, 1900.
Second Institute. Edward Coke, 1641, &c.
Magna Charta. A commentary. William S. McKechnie, 1905, 1914.
Magna Charta made in 9 Henry III. Edward Coke, 1684.
England under Angevin Kings. Kate Norgate.
John Lackland. Kate Norgate.
The Angevin Empire. James Henry Ramsay.
The Foundations of England, James Henry Ramsay.
The Constitutional History of England. William Stubbs.
Henry III and the Church. Abbot Gasquet.
History of Procedure in England. Melville M. Bigelow.
Feudal England. John H. Round.
Progress of the English Constitution. Edward Creasy.
History of the English Constitution. Rudolf Gneist.
English Constitutional History. Thomas P. Taswell-Langmead.
Chronica. Florence of Worcester.
Chronica. Henry of Huntingdon.
Sketches from English History. Arthur M. Wheeler, 1886.
A Child's History of England. Charles Dickens, 1868.
A Short History of the English People. John Richard Green, 1879.
History of England. Charles McLean Andrews, 1921.
A Student's History of England. Samuel R. Gardiner, 1898.
Magna Charta. (1215-1915). Nicholas Murray Butler.
Notes to Blackstone's Commentaries. Christian.
Coke Upon Littleton. Edward Coke, 1644.
Commentaries upon the Laws of England. William Blackstone, 1765.
Magna Charta Barons. Charles Henry Browning, 1898, 1915.
The Day We Celebrate. Henry Corneau Diller, 1915.
Magna Charta Defined. Elihu Root, 1915.
History of England. Cassel.
Statutes of the Realm. British Record Commission, 1810.
Select Statutes. George W. Prothero.
Chronica Majora. Matthew Paris. British Rolls Series.
Chronicon Anglicanum. (1235-1273). British Rolls Series.
Chronica (to 1201). Roger de Hoveden. British Rolls Series.
Chronica sive Flores Historiarum (to 1235). Roger of Wendover. Rolls Series.
Annals of Dunstable. Rolls Series.
Annals of Waverly. Rolls Series.
Memoriale. Walter of Coventry. Rolls Series.
Gesta Regum Anglorum. William of Malmesbury. Rolls Series.
Chronicon de Gesta Regum Angliae. Walter of Hemingburgh. Eng. His. Soc.
Gesta Regis Henry II. Rolls Series.
Select Charters. William Stubbs.

Chronica de rebus gestis Samsonis. Jocelyn of Brakelond. Camden Society.
Memorials of St. Dunstan. Rolls Series.
The Red Book of the Exchequer. Rolls Series
Testa de Neville. Record Commission Publication, 1807.
Foedera, Conventiones, etc. Thomas Rymer. Record Commiss. Publication.
Ancient Charters. Pipe Roll Society, vol. X.
Great Roll of the Pipe, temp. 12 Hen. II. Pipe Roll Society, vol. IX.
History and Antiquities of the Exchequer. Thomas Madox.
Firma Burgi. Thomas Madox.
Baronia Anglica. Thomas Madox.
De Legibus. Henry de Bracton. Rolls Series.
Political History of England. George B. Adams.
History of John, King of England. W. Prynne.
History of the Reign of John, King of England. J. Berington.
John, King of England. William Chadwick.
England, 1066-1215. George B. Adams.
England Under Normans and Angevins. H. W. C. Davis.
Simon de Montfort. Charles Bémont.
Geoffrey de Mandeville. John H. Round.
History of the Norman Conquest. E. A. Freeman, vols. I and II.
William the Conqueror and his companions. Planche.
Historical Works of Gervase of Canterbury. Rolls Series.
Gesta Stephani. Chronicals temp. Henry II. Rolls Series.
Archaeologia Cambrensis. 3d ser. vol. VIII.
Annals of Bury St. Edmund's. Harl. MS. 447. (Lieberman).
Annales Monastici. Rolls Series.
De Antiquis Legibus Liber. Camden Society Publication.
Calendar of English documents in France to 1206. London, 1899.
Calendar of Charter Rolls, 1226-1257. London, 1903, vol. I.
Calendar of Patent Rolls, 1232-1247. London, 1906, vol. I.
Close Rolls, 1227-1237. London, 1902-5-8, vols. I, II, III.
Flores Historiarum. Matthew of Westminster, (to 1307). Rolls Series.
Calendar of Inq. P.M., temp. Hen. III. London, 1904, vol. I.
Royal, and other letters, temp. Hen. III. Rolls Series.
Monasticon Anglicanum. Sir William Dugdale.
Chronicle of Robert of Gloucester. Rolls Series.
Political History of England. Longman.
Epochs of Modern History. Longman.
Mediaeval England. Mary Bateson.
The Making of England. John R. Green.
Royal Castles of England. H. C. Shelley.
Orderici Vitalis Historia Ecclesiastica. Paris, 1838-1855.
L'Art de Verifier les Dates des Faits Historiques.
Calendar of Papal Registers, 1198-1304. London, 1893, vol. I.
Rotuli Chartarum in Turri Londinensi asservati. 1199-1216. Rolls Series.
Rotuli Litterarum Clausarum in Turri Londinensi asservati. 1204-24.
Excerpta e Rotulis Finium. 1216-46. vol. I. Record Commission.
Rotuli Litterarum Patentium in Turri Londinensi asservati. 1201-1216. vol. I. (An itinerary of King John is appended to the Introduction.) British Record Commission, London, 1835.
Rotuli de Liberate ac de Misis et Praestitis regnante Johanne. London, 1844.
History of English Law. John Reeves.
A Constitutional History of the House of Lords. L. O. Pike.
The History of English Law. F. Pollock and F. W. Maitland.
A History of English Law. W. S. Holdsworth.
Two Principles of Magna Charta. G. Campbell Morgan, 1931.

A Photographic Reproduction of the Dover Copy.
The original is 14½ x 21½ inches.
The decorative shields have been added.

A Photographic Reproduction of the Lincoln Copy.
The original, 17½ x 18 inches, described on page 21, was exhibited at the New York World's Fair and is now on view at the Library of Congress in Washington.

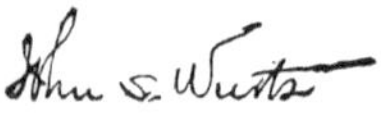

A biographical sketch appears on page 265.

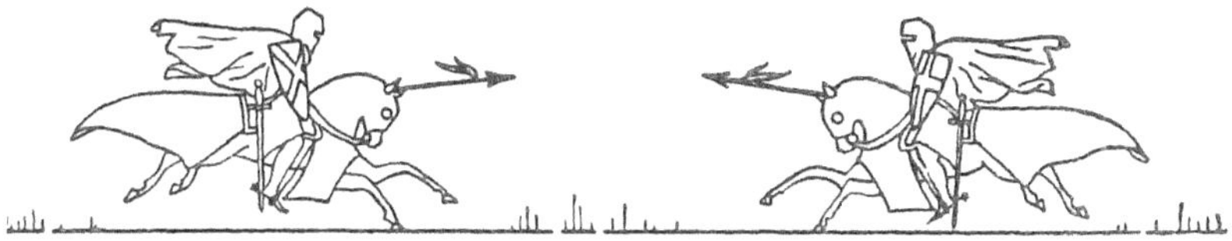

Part II

Pedigrees of the Barons

A List of the Surety Barons will be found at page 30

Roman numerals denote the generations preceding each Surety, whose descendants are numbered with Arabic numerals to denote the order of the children in each generation. For example, if read backwards, that is, from right to left, it is apparent that No. 461 552 is the second child of the fifth child of the fifth child of the eldest child of the sixth child of the fourth child of the head of the line.

Where there are more than nine children in a family, the letter x is used for the tenth child, y for the eleventh, z for the twelfth, and t f v s n and e for the thirteenth to eighteenth child respectively.

Because of the incompleteness of medieval records one cannot be sure that the children in these early families have been listed in the order of their birth.

Where a person's name is printed under only one Baron and King, it is *not* to be understood that such person is necessarily descended from *only* that one, for as a matter of fact most of the persons listed herein are descended from several Kings and Barons. In many cases parents and children, brothers and sisters and cousins having the same pedigree will be found intentionally listed under different Barons, as a means of recording a wider ancestry for the family in view.

Descendants' names arriving too late to be included herein will, at subscriber's request, be printed in the Supplement.

Part III will continue the pedigrees.

INTRODUCTION

It is certain everyone has ancestors, multitudes of them. It is not certain that a man will have surviving descendants. Family names frequently die out. In that connection it is interesting to note that no descendant in the male line of any Magna Charta Baron has for centuries sat in the House of Lords.

Most countries of the Old World have legends, as everyone knows, extending the genealogies of their heroes far back to earliest times, and these legends widely differ, some being so blended with mythology as to be quite uncertain; indeed, some of the claims made are wholly impossible.

As we consider ancient sources it is disappointing to find that the bards and monks and other contemporary historians do not agree in many of their details. This is true also of more modern pedigrees, making differing versions of the same ancestry, too few of which can at this late day be supported by original documents. Dates and places have often been too meagerly preserved to enable one now to form a fixed opinion as to the integrity of such pedigrees.

It is the task of the compiler to select the most fitting items from the material which is available. Such items the writer has endeavored to assemble and set forth in convenient form, as an aid to friends interested in pursuing these claims of long descent and, in the knowledge that to them it has brought real enjoyment, he has found much satisfaction.

This d'Albini family appears to be quite distinct from that of William d'Aubigny (d'Albini) Earl of Arundel, who was also present at Runnemede, but was not a Surety.

ALBINI

Chapter 1

William d'Albini

1st Baron of Belvoir.

A Surety for Magna Charta

Arms: Gules, a lion rampant or, armed and langued azure.

The following persons may claim descent from Baron d'Albini and the Emperor Charlemagne: Page 313

Her Majesty Queen Elizabeth
Edgar Wright Baird
Parker Baratta
Mary Harrison Bronson Wurts Barbour
William Thomas Baylies
Herbert Nathaniel Bayne
Celia Ellen Doane Bennett
Florence Wolcott Sanford Bissell
John H. Boogher
Pauline Davis Bowie
William Ernest Brackett, Jr.
Rena Brownell Smith Burnham
Frances Ann Ralston Butterfield
John Cadwalader
Winston Churchill
Elizabeth Hopkins Stewart Claflin
Almira Chew Poplar Collison
Mary Webster Buchey Comman
Martha Lenna Crary
Egerton Lafayette Crispin
Lulie Leigh Otey Darneal
Mary deS. Williams deMare
Gilbert Harry Doane
Louise Doolittle
Hubert Irénée duPont
Lillian Frances Eaton
Norma Anthony Edenton
Edgar Dudley Faries
William Innes Forbes
Helen Honeywell Fornof
William James Grandin
Anne Kaler Driesbach Henderson
Julia Rush Biddle Henry
Julia Crawford Hornor
Charles Jared Ingersoll
Dolores Nourse Johnson
The Princess Kaplanoff
George LeBoutillier
Rebecca Lamb Bolling Littlejohn
Eleanor Burroughs Morris Lloyd
Gertrude Smith Loveland
C. Kimball Lubbe
Marian Drake-Smith Maltby
Alan Douglas Merritt
Grace Meyer
Florence Cooley Miller
Isabella Ross Moen
Helen Hull Monnette
Almira Virginia Thompson Bramhall
Lawrence Johnson Morris
Howard Ross Nelson
Grace Mann Parker
George Stuart Patterson
Thomas Cotesworth Pinckney, Jr.
Mabel Hilliard Crispin Powers
Edna West Preuss
Nellie Cady Reimers
Samuel Bartram Richards
Agnes Peel Risher
Owen J. Roberts
Ellis Robins
Mary Lane Landis Scott
Randolph Scott
Rose Moss Scott
Mary Baird Shakespeare
Mary Williams Shoemaker
Flora Pearl Mitchell Smith
Lewis Stone Sorley
Elizabeth Fisher Wurts Spahr
Florence Morrison Spofford
Mary Glover Stacy
Louise McClure Tinsley Steinman
Anna Estes Hacker Strawbridge
John Stewart
Harold Leonard Stuart
Merritt Harrison Taylor
Mary Virginia Jackson Thiot
Helen Fowler Shaw Thomson
Marion Cooper Tull
Philip Van Culin
Henry Pepper Vaux
Maude May Coleman Walker
Anita Wetherill Warder
Elizabeth Fisher Washington
Thomas Washington
Mildred Genevieve Campbell Whitaker
Francis Churchill Williams
Alexina Robinson Wilson
Edith King Wilson
Lillian Mosher Winn
F. Dawson Winter
James Wilson Wister
Josephine Townsend Woolman
Edward Vanuxem Wurts
Ethel Denune Young
Laurens Carlington Young

I. Raoult de Toeni, Castellan of Tillieres Castle about 1014 to 1030, was the father of

II. ROBERT de TODENI, one of the Norman barons who came into England in 1066 as a standard bearer of Duke William; was the founder of this renowned, ancient family. For his distinguished services at Hastings, the victorious monarch rewarded him with the eighty lordships he possessed in twelve counties at the time of the first general survey of England. On one of his estates in Lincolnshire, near the border of Leicestershire, he erected a castle which he named Belvoir, from its commanding position, and this became his chief seat. He died in 1088, leaving by his wife Adela, a son

III. WILLIAM d'ALBINI, called the Briton, from having been born in England.

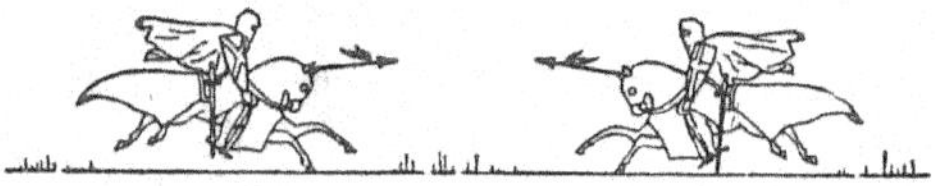

This feudal Baron was a soldier of distinction, and acquired great renown in the celebrated battle of Tenercheby, in Normandy, when he commanded the cavalry, for "by a charge of much spirit, he determined at once the fate of the day." The monk Matthew Paris records "in this encounter chiefly deserveth honour the most heroic William d'Albini, the Briton, who with his sword broke through the enemy and terminated the battle."

When he became a supporter of the cause of the Empress Maud, his castle of Belvoir, with all his great possessions, were seized by King Stephen, who presented them to Ranulphgerons de Meschines, the Earl of Chester.

William-Brito d'Albini died about 1155, leaving by his wife, Page 189 Maud, daughter of Simon St. Liz, see Chapter 29, an eldest son

IIII. WILLIAM-MESCHINES d'ALBINI, second Baron of Belvoir. He received back from Henry II, the castle of Belvoir, and the majority of the lordships confiscated by King Stephen. Dying in 1167, he was succeeded by his son

★ V. WILLIAM d'ALBINI, the Surety, lord of Belvoir Castle, third baron of this family. When his father died, he was in ward to King Henry II, and, in 1194, he was in the army of Richard I, in Normandy. Already a wealthy man at the time of the accession of John to the throne, he received several additional grants of great value. In 1201, when the Barons refused to attend their sovereign into France, King John demanded that their castles should be given up to him as security for their allegiance, beginning with William d'Albini of whom he claimed Belvoir Castle, instead of which d'Albini gave him his son, William, as a hostage.

He appears to have remained longer faithful to King John, as well as more moderate in his opposition to him, than most of the Barons, and did not join the insurgents until he could no longer with safety either remain neutral, or adhere to the King, for so late as January, 1214/15, he was one of King John's commissioners appointed for the safe-conduct of such as were traveling to his court, at Northampton.

After he joined the Barons' party, he entered with great spirit into their cause and was excommunicated; but, after having gained their point, he was looked upon with suspicion by the other Sureties because he did not attend the grand tournament in Staine's Wood, on 29 June 1215, to celebrate the victory, and it was not until after other Barons had alarmed him, that he fortified his castle at Belvoir, and joined them at London. But the sequel proves their suspicions were not well grounded. He was placed as governor of Rochester Castle, when, though he found it so utterly destitute of provisions as almost to induce his men to abandon it, he recruited and held it until famine and weakness, and watching, obliged them to surrender to the King. The siege having lasted three months, and his army being attended with considerable loss, King John ordered that all the nobles in the castle be hanged; but his chief counsellors resolutely opposing this sentence, William d'Albini and his son Odonel, with several other Barons, were merely committed to the custody of Peter de Mauley, and sent prisoners to Corfe and Nottingham Castles.

While d'Albini remained at Corfe, the King marched on Christmas morning, 1216, from Nottingham to Langar, near Belvoir Castle, and sent a summons to surrender. Upon this, Nicholas d'Albini, one of the Baron's sons, and a clerk in orders, delivered the keys to the King, asking only that his father should be mercifully treated. The fortress was then committed to the custody of Geoffrey and Oliver de Buteville. His liberty was gained only by William d'Albini's paying a fine to the king of six thousand marks (more than four thousand pounds), the sum being raised from his own lands by his wife. After King John's death, though he submitted himself to King Henry III, William d'Albini was forced to give his wife and son Nicholas as hostages for his allegiance; but in 1217 he was one of the King's commanders at the battle of Lincoln. He died at Offington, 1 May 1236, and his body was buried at Newstead, and "his heart under the wall, opposite the high-altar," at Belvoir Castle.

William d'Albini, the Surety, had no children by his second wife Agatha, daughter of William de Trusbut. By his first marriage to Margery, daughter of Odonel, Baron d'Umfraville, he had: 1 Robert; 2 Nicholas; 3 Odonel; all of whom died without issue, and

4 WILLIAM d'ALBINI, Jr., who also served in the Baronial Army. He married, first, Albreda, daughter of Henry, Lord Biseth, and dying in 1285, left a daughter, the sole heiress to the Surety, her grandfather,

41 ISABEL d'ALBINI, who died in 1301. This great heiress was a ward of the king and, 17 May 1244, Bernard de Savoy and Hugh Gifford were commanded to deliver her to her husband Robert de Roos, grandson of the Surety of that name, see Chapter Page 123 22. "But not," says Dugdale, "without a round computation, for there appears that both he and his wife in the 32nd of King Henry III were debtors to the king in no less the sum of £3285, 13s., 4d. and a palfrey; of which sum the king was then pleased to accept 200 marks a year until it should be paid."

BIGOD

Chapter 2

Roger Bigod

A Surety for Magna Charta

Arms: Or, a cross gules.

The following persons may claim descent from Baron Roger Bigod and King Ethelred II: Page 314

His Majesty King George VI
Frank Addison Augsbury, Jr.
Guilford Carlile Babcock
Anna Stanley Blatchley
Muriel Harmar Wurts-Dundas Boone
Wilmon Brewer
Helen Carpenter Brown
Henry Paul Busch
Jane Elise Dolph Campbell
E. Murton du Pont Carpenter
Marion Williams Pierce Carter
Edith Chesney
Georgia Vernon Sleeper Chubbuck
Maude Cook Clark
H. Ranney Corner
Marie Anthony Craighead
Charles Emmett Davidson
Flora Bogue Deming
Edwin Hooper Denby
Whittie Dickinson
Antoinette Ware Tatem Driscoll
Frances Maria Sweet Eaton
Mildred Colton Esty
Georgia Everett Perkins Fairchild
Alexander Carter Fergusson
Bertha Wurts Godwin
Ella Eustis Wister Haines
Charles Custis Harrison
Randall Groves Hay
Dixie Lee Cotton Herrin
Mayo Dyer Hersey
Annie Turner Hightower
Mary Warren Davis Holt
Arnold Harris Hord
Clara Morse Johnson
J. Gregory Johnston
Charles Conway Jones
Helen Hall Newbury Joy
Mate Almyra Medbury Lacy
Meade Burwell Laird
Belle Risdon Hinman Lammers
Maxwell Dwight Lathrop
Grace Royall Tyng Levis
Fanny Beulah Lippitt
Ethel Spencer Lloyd
Helen Davis Luke
Anne Nyce Kaler Marsh
Amy Rodick Willis
Mary Louise Earle McCain
Elsie Kebler Mercer
Lena Crissey Merz
Winifred Conwell Murray Milne
Marjorie Allen Montgomery
William Sawtell Muir
Barbara Kendig Mylin
Howard Ross Nelson
Jessie Cory Nott
Edna Gertrude Penniman
Bevan Aubrey Pennypacker
James De Wolf Perry
Grace Edna Vollnogle Phillips
Jessie Lincoln Randolph
John Bion Richards
Bushrod Washington Robbins
Dora Stuart McGill Scott
Frances Pepper Scott
Mary Lane Landis Scott
Margaret Cotton Skeen
Mary Delia Gregory Smith
Mary Carmally Spalding
Charles Vanuxem Sparhawk
Mamie Logan Stackhouse
Nellie Badders Stein
Joseph Janney Steinmetz
Dorothy Westervelt Taylor
H. Birchard Taylor
Louise Carroll Jackson Thomas
Mary Randolph Peaseley Thomas
Benjamin Chew Tilghman
Marguerite Elsie Valentine
Mary Vanuxem
Mary Grace Murray Verner
Prudence Sharpless Doyle Vollnogle
Jouett Lee Wallace
Martha Washington
Aubrey Herbert Weightman
Edith Bucknell Wetherill
Mary Virginia Saunders White
Mabel Ruth Owens Wilcox
Lester James Williams
Paul Frazer Williams
May Hartshorn Wood
Burkhardt Wurts
Dorothy Barrett Williams Wurts
Ethel Denune Young

The paternal ancestor of this Surety living at the time of the Norman conquest was

I. ROGER le BIGOD, who possessed six lordships in Essex and a hundred and seventeen in Suffolk beside many manors in Norfolk. We find of him that in 1103 he founded the Abbey of Whetford in Norfolk and that he was buried there four years later.

His wife was Adeliza, daughter of Hugh de Grantesmesnil, high steward of England. Their second son was

II. HUGH BIGOD. When his elder brother William was accidentally drowned, with the king's children in a shipwreck, in the 20th of King Henry I, and left no issue, Hugh succeeded as lord steward of the King's household to King Henry I. He was mainly instrumental in raising Stephen, Count of Boulogne, to the throne, and was rewarded by him with the earldom of East Angles, or Norfolk and Suffolk, about 1140. He was steadfast and faithful in his allegiance to King Stephen and continued to enjoy royal favor, being re-created Earl of Norfolk and Suffolk by Henry II, and obtaining a grant of the office of lord high steward of the kingdom, which his father had held. In 1177, as a Crusader, he made a pilgrimage to the Holy Land, and died in 23rd of King Henry II before March. Earl Hugh had by his wife Juliana Vere, daughter of Alberic de Vere and his wife Adeliza Clare, see Chapter 24, an eldest son Page 128

★ III. ROGER BIGOD, the Surety, born about 1150, who succeeded as second Earl of Norfolk and Suffolk. He was appointed in 1189, by King Richard, one of the ambassadors to Philip of France, for obtaining aid for the recovery of the Holy Land. In 1191, he was keeper of Hereford Castle. He was Chief Judge in the King's Court from 1195 to 1202. In 1200 he was sent by King John as one of his messengers to summon William the Lion, King of Scotland, to do homage to him in the parliament which was held at Lincoln, and subsequently attended King John into Poitou, but on his return he was won over to their cause by the rebel Barons and became one of the strongest advocates of the Charter of Liberty, for which he was excommunicated by Pope Innocent III. He died before August 1221, having married as his first wife Isabella, (Ida) daughter of Hameline Plantagenet, who was descended from the Earls of Warren, see Chapter 31, and they had 1 their eldest son, Page 204 IV Hugh Bigod, the Surety, see Chapter 3, p. 46 and 2 William who married Margaret, daughter of Robert de Sutton; 3 Thomas; 4 Margery, wife of William de Hastings, see later; 5 Adeliza, wife of Audley de Vere, Earl of Oxford who died without issue; 6 Mary, wife of Ralph FitzRobert of Middleham.

The fourth child as aforesaid of the Surety Roger Bigod was 4 Margery Bigod, who became the first wife of William de Hastings and they had a son

41 HENRY de HASTINGS, who owned extensive lands in six counties and married Ada, fourth daughter of David, Earl of Huntingdon and his wife Maud of Chester, see Chapter 30. Earl Henry died in 1249, leaving beside 412 Eleanor Hastings, wife of William Harcourt, a descendant of the Surety Saire de Quincey, see Chapter 21, a son and heir Page 112

411 HENRY de HASTINGS who married Eve (also called Joan) Cantilupe, descended from the Braos family, appearing in Chapter 5. He was known as Baron Hastings and died in 1268. His son and heir was Page 59

411 1 JOHN HASTINGS, 2nd Baron Hastings, and Baron of Bergavenny. He took an active part in the wars of King Edward I and in 1290 was one of the competitors for the crown of Scotland as grandson of Ada of Huntingdon. His first wife was Isabel, daughter of William de Valence, Earl of Pembroke and half brother of King Henry III. Issue.

Baron Hastings married second, Isabel Despencer, daughter of Hugh, Earl of Winchester. His death occurred in 1313. Issue.

(To be continued)

Chapter 39 Page 314

Chapter 3

Hugh Bigod

A Surety for Magna Charta

Arms: Or, a cross gules, a label of three points for difference.

See also Pedigrees D and O, pages 422 and 427.

The following persons may claim descent from Baron Hugh Bigod and the Emperor Vladimir: Page 427

Her Majesty Queen Mary
Irene Conway Artz
Caroline Banister Pryor Baker
Emily Barclay
Margaretta Wilson Bayard
Florence Harper Beadleston
Henry Edwin Beck
Charles Lathrop Bevan
Edyth Clements Shipley Britton
Helen Batte Carmine
Mabel Woodruff Porter Carter
Cummins Catherwood
Georgia Vernon Sleeper Chubbuck
Almira Little Peterson Colket
Anna Cuyler Hudson Condict
Mary Anderson Courtenay
H. Ranney Corner
Dwight Lathrop Crane
Sara Beekman Cregar
Helen Anderson Wilson Cresson
Tessa McPherson Dart
R. Clayton Dickinson
Etta Brown Dudley
Henrietta Irby Earle
Eleanor Alice Lawwill Felner
Jessie Gaither Fownes
Horace Binney Hare
A. Marjory Taylor Hardwick
Gail Elizabeth Sampson Hartman
Julia Vanuxem Hebard
William Worthington Herrick
Earle Dodge Holmes
Annie Lloyd Hord
Charles Lukens Huston
Albert Morse Johnson
Bertha B. Johnson
Franklin Chappel Jones
Jennie Farris Railey King
Harrie Hardwick Knox
Isabel Kruger
Charles Edgar Lathrop
George Haines Lathrop
Louise Margaret Karcher Leopold
Samuel Bunting Lewis
Graeme Lorimer
Elizabeth Scott Luce
Frances Henrietta Wilcox Glos
Belle Clay Lyons
Luella Wood Mackenzie
Cora Ellen Van de Mark Marsh
Barbara Emma Bullard McGee
Elsie FitzHugh McPherson McGill
Adelaide Newell Meek
Anna Menetta White Miller
Winifred Conwell Murray Milne
Lora Parsons Moore
Elizabeth Edge Armington Moulton
Ophelia Muir
Howard Ross Nelson
Mary Logan Orcutt
George Wharton Pepper
Grace Edna Vollnogle Phillips
Ida Lewis Pinkerton
Edith Robinson Porter
Lavinia Dandridge Richardson
Julia Johnston Robertson
Edward Robins
George Blight Robinson
Eleanor Stillman Gardner Rowe
Mary Lane Landis Scott
Russell Cecil Scott
Edwin Jaquett Sellers
Martha Reed Shoemaker
Benjamin Hallowell Shoemaker, 3d
Katherine Whitman Slayton
Claire Dashiell Ellegood Smith
Fannie Lawrence Steelman
Martha Jefferson Randolph Stevens
John Owen Strong
Minnie Antoinette Moore Tatem
Anita M. Steinmetz Taylor
Louise Carroll Jackson Thomas
Prudence Sharpless Doyle Vollnogle
Henrietta M. Washburn
Thomas R. Washington
Estelle Osborn Clark Watson
C. A. Heckscher Wetherill
Mary Virginia Saunders White
Susan Thurston Whitehead
Joseph E. Widener
Dorothea Wood
Laura Jay Wurts
Ethel Denune Young
Amy Rodick Willis

★ IV. HUGH BIGOD, son of the preceding Surety, and himself a Surety, was third Earl of Norfolk and Suffolk. He was born before 1195, and took part from the beginning in the Barons' Magna Charta proceedings. Not many particulars of this Baron's life have been preserved, as he enjoyed for only a few years the title of Earl of Norfolk and Suffolk, and his father's estates and honors, to which he had succeeded in the 5th of King Henry III. He died four years later, in February 1224/5, having married about 1212 Maud, a sister of the Surety William Marshall, see Chapter 16, and eldest daughter of William Marshall, the Protector. In her right William Marshall Hugh acquired the Earldom of Pembroke, and in this rank bore the royal sceptre at the coronation of King Richard I.

Hugh Bigod and his wife Maud Marshall had, among others:

1 ROGER BIGOD, who died without issue in 1270. He was fourth Earl and ward to Alexander, King of Scotland, and attained high reputation in all martial and warlike exercises. The most remarkable event in his life was his personal dispute with King Henry III, but by the interposing of the lords then present this heat soon passed over, so that shortly after he was, together with the Earl of Leicester and some others, sent on an embassy to the King of France, to treat with him for restoring some rights which he withheld from the king. Because his mother Maud was the eldest coheiress of William Marshall, to Roger was assigned the MARSHALSHIP of England, with the rights thereunto belonging. Roger Bigod married Isabel, sister of Alexander, King of Scotland, but died without issue in 1270, when all his titles and possessions devolved upon his nephew 21 Roger Bigod. Another son of Hugh Bigod and his wife Maud Marshall was

2 HUGH BIGOD, died 1266, an eminent lawyer appointed Chief Justice of England in 1257. He married first Joane, daughter of Robert Burnet and had two sons, 21 Roger and 22 John. Of these

21 ROGER BIGOD, was fifth Earl of Norfolk, and 2nd earl marshall of this family, and took a distinguished part in the wars of King Edward I. His lordship married, first, Aliva, daughter of Philip, Lord Basset, and widow of Hugh Despencer, slain at Evesham, and second, Joane, daughter of John de Avenne, Earl of Bayonne, but had no issue by either, and at his death in the 34th of King Edward I, (1306) the Earldom became extinct in the Bigod family, although his lordship was survived by his brother

22 JOHN BIGOD, his heir-at-law, whose right seems to have been so completely destroyed that he did not even inherit any of the great estates of his ancestors. He left a son

221 ROGER BIGOD of Lethingham, through whose children: 221 1 John, who died in 1389, and 221 2 Joan, wife of William de Chauncy, son of Sir Thomas de Chauncy, lord of the manor of Skirpenbeck, descent is traced to the present day. A third son of Hugh Bigod and his wife Maud Marshall was 3 Ralph Bigod who married Berta, daughter of Baron Furnival. He was the brother, not the father, of

Page 101 Page 88 4 ISABEL BIGOD, who became first the wife of Gilbert de Lacy, Lord of Meath in Ireland, whose parents were the renowned Walter de Laci and his wife Margaret Braos. Gilbert de Lacy had died during his father's lifetime in 1230 and Walter's only heiresses were his two granddaughters, children of this son Gilbert de Lacy and his wife Isabel Bigod. One of these

41 MARGERY LACY known also as Margaret, whose husband was John Verdon, had for her share of the inheritance the Castle of Webbeley. They had four sons and one daughter: the two eldest, 411 William and 412 John and the daughter 413 Agnes, dying without issue. The youngest son 415 Thomas had descendants surviving for a few generations in England, and the third son

414 THEOBALD de VERDON was Lord of the Moiety of Meath in Ireland. In the reign of King Edward I he held the office of constable of Ireland. His death occurred in 1309. The name of his wife was Margery and his eldest son 414 1 John, having died without issue in 1297, he was succeeded by his other son

414 2 THEOBALD de VERDON, as second Baron Verdon. In the 6th of King Edward II, he was consituted Justice of Ireland. His first wife was Maud, daughter of Edmund, Lord Mortimer of Wigmore. She died at Alveton Castle in the year 1315 and had two sons who died without issue and three daughters who married. His second wife was Elizabeth, daughter of Gilbert de Clare, Earl of Gloucester, a descendant of the Sureties Richard and Gilbert de Clare, see Chapter 6. Page 70 When she became the wife of Theobald de Verdon, she was the widow of John de Burgh, Earl of Ulster, and her third husband was Roger d'Amorie. By her, Theobald de Verdon had an only daughter 414 26 Isabel, who became the wife of Henry, Lord Ferrers of Groby. Theobald de Verdon died at Alveton Castle and was buried at Croxden in 1316, aged about 34 years. His grandmother's sister, the other daughter of 4 Isabel Bigod and her first husband Gilbert de Lacy was

42 MAUD LACY, who became the wife, first, of Peter de Geneva who had Ludlow Castle in her right. He died before 27 June 1249. In the 38th of King Henry III, Maud became the wife of Geoffrey de Genevill who had the Castle of Trim, co. Meath as part of her inheritance. He was born in or shortly after 1226 and soon after 1250 came into England from France. They had 421 Geoffrey de Geneville who died without issue during his father's lifetime; 423 Simon de Geneville, Lord of Culmullin, third son, who married Joan Fitz Leon and had three daughters as follows: 423 1 Matilda married to Baldwyn, Lord Slane; and 423 2 Elizabeth, wife of Sir William de Loundres, Baron of the Naas; and 423 3 Joan, whose husband was John Cusack. The second son of Geoffrey de Geneville and his wife 42 Maud Lacy, was

422 PETER de GENEVILLE who was second Baron but was never summoned to parliament. He married Joane, daughter of Hugh de Brune, Earl of Angolesme, as they had no sons, only three daughters: 422 1 Joane, wife of Roger Mortimer; and 422 2 Isabel Page 432 and 422 3 Beatrice, who were nuns at Aconbury, the barony of Geneville fell into abeyance among Peter's daughters.

4 ISABEL BIGOD was married, second, to John Fitz Geoffrey who was feudal lord of Berkhampstead and Kirtling manors, and of Shere, Fambridge and other estates, being sheriff of Yorkshire, and in 1246, Justice of Ireland. He died 23 November 1258. He had two sons: 43 John FitzJohn, who died without issue about 6 Nov. 1275, having married Margery, daughter of Philip Basset of Wycombe. She died before 29 October 1271. The second son was 44 Richard FitzJohn who also died while in Gascony, without issue, 5 August 1297. His wife was Emma, who died 26 January 1331/2. Of the daughters of John FitzGeoffrey and his wife Isabel Bigod: 45 Maud, died 16 or 18 April 1301 and was buried at the Grey Frairs', Worcester. Her first husband was Gerard de Furnivalle, lord of Hallamshire, who died without issue before 18 October Page 204 1261, and Maud was then married to William de Beauchamp, Earl of Warwick. He died at Elmley 5 or 9 June 1298; 46 Isabel, whose husband was Robert Vipount and they had 461 Isabel Vipount, married to Roger de Clifford, who died before his father Roger de Clifford, leaving a son 461 1 Robert de Clifford, who married Page 68 Maud Clare, a descendant of the Sureties Richard and Gilbert de

and had Robert, p. 115.

Clare, see Chapter 6, The other daughter of 46 Isabel FitzGeoffrey and her husband Robert Vipount was 462 Idonea who married first Roger Leybourne, and they had a son 462 1 William Leybourne. Idonea's second husband was John Cromwell, who died without issue; 47 Aveline FitzGeoffrey who died about 20 May 1274, having been married to Walter de Burgh, Earl of Ulster, who died 28 July 1271. Their son's wife is from the Surety William de Lanvallei, see Chapter 13; 48 Joan FitzGeoffrey, who died 4 April 1303. She was the wife of Theobald le Botiller of Thurles. He died at Arklow 26 September 1285, leaving two sons: 481 Theobald le Botiller who died without issue in 1299; and his brother 482 Edmund le Botiller who died in London 12 September 1321. Edmund's wife, whom he married in 1302, was Joan, daughter of John FitzThomas, Earl of Kildaire. Issue.

Page 93

Fitz. Geoffrey,

(To be continued)

Chapter 40 **Page** 317

BOHUN

Chapter 4

Henry de Bohun

A Surety for Magna Charta

Arms: Azure, a bend argent between two cottises and six lions rampant, or.

The following persons may claim descent from Baron Bohun and King David I: **Pages** 113, 192, 325

Bertha Brainerd Adams
Mary Carter Hartwell Adams
Elizabeth Rivers Bailey Bahl
Henry Liberty Bates
Grace Dutton Baylies
Charles Lathrop Bevan
Robert Pratt Bigelow
Florence Wolcott Sanford Bissell
Manning Pitts Brown
Hebe Duhring Bulley
Seth Bunker Capp
Ezra Patterson Carrell
Theodore Willard Case
Ozelah Badger Chappell
Elizabeth Brown Chew
George Sharpe Clarke
Mattie Willie Sale Conway
Adelaide Watts Crawford
Amelia Neville Oliver Crittenden
Genevieve Wolcott Whitehead Denison
Louis Ashton Dickinson
Grace Bailey Dunklee
Emily Quincy Atkinson Ellis
Walter Weston Folger
Alice Etta Lombard Fortson
Benjamin Sherman Fowler
Elizabeth Blake Gaylord
Charles A. Goodwin-Perkins
Natalie Fox Elkins Gribbel
Harry Waln Harrison
Emma Wilder Hast
Marie Elise Wilkinson Hodgkins
Robert Courtney King
John C. Knox
Julia Noble Shubrick Kothe
Charles Edgar Lathrop
Eunice Lathrope
Marianne Skelton Gibbs Layton
Harriet Rossiter Lewis
Genevieve Remsen Frantz Lohman
Harriette Hamilton Malley
Harriette Miller Malley
Lucretia Wiley McAdams
Gladys Redfield McPherson
Ellen Emmerich Mears
Mary Catharine Buck Miller
Allen Montgomery
Ellen Constance Walker Morse
Howard Ross Nelson
Ella Foy O'Gorman
Helen Shawmut O'Neill
Edith Dunham Parker
Grace Edna Vollnogle Phillips
Josiah Harmar Penniman
Henrietta Eleanor Wallis Perry
Margaret Bernardine Rheinberger
Ruth Ellsworth Richardson
Elizabeth May Leach Rixford
William Bowdoin Robins
Jay Besson Rudolphy
Julia Edwards Woodson Saunders
Ferne Fleming Savage
Frederic Robert Scott
Mary Lane Landis Scott
Francis Richmond Sears
Elizabeth West Schwinbeck
Helen Barnett Matthews Shirk
Dorothy Burns Wees Slaymaker
Helen King Smith
Katherine Bowen Smith
Pearl Pinkerton McClelland Snowden
Ralph Emerson Thompson
Harriet Helen Baylies Tilden
Roberta Keene Tubman
Louise Shurtleff Brown Verrill
Joanne Louise Viall
Prudence Sharpless Doyle Vollnogle
Effie Crouch Waite
Marion Porter Wales
George Buckley Warder
Elizabeth Reed Wurts Washburn
Agnes Harwood Washington
William Potter Wear
Mary Bahl Westerlind
Giles Price Wetherill
Marguerite Morton White
Peter A. B. Widener
Waldemar Wurts
Ethel Denune Young
Amy Rodick Willis

I. HUMPHREY de BOHUN, died abt. 1113, is said to have been a kinsman and companion in arms of William the Conqueror and is generally known as "Humphrey with the Beard." He was in possession of the lordship of Taterford in Norfolk and was succeeded by his son

Chapter 4

II. HUMPHREY de BOHUN, surnamed The Great. By command of King William Rufus, he married Maud, daughter of Edward d'Everux, progenitor of the ancient Earls of Salisbury, through which marriage he acquired large estates in Wiltshire, was sheriff of Wiltshire and Bearer of the royal standard in 1120, in the battle of Benneville in Normandy. He was succeeded by his son

III. HUMPHREY de BOHUN, who was steward and sewer to King Henry I. He married Margery, daughter of Milo de Gloucester, Earl of Hereford, Lord High Constable of England, whose charter was the earliest of express creation, the patent being dated in 1140. At the instigation of his father-in-law he espoused the cause of the Empress Maud and her son against King Stephen and was so faithful in his allegiance to the Empress that she, by her especial charter, granted him the office of steward and sewer both in Normandy and in England. In the 20th of King Henry II this Humphrey accompanied Richard de Lacy, Justiciar of England into Scotland with a strong army to waste the country. His death occurred 6th April 1187 and he was succeeded by his son

IV. HUMPHREY de BOHUN, Earl of Hereford and hereditary constable of England, who married Margaret of Huntingdon, see Chapter 30. Their eldest son was

Page 192

★ V. HENRY de BOHUN, the Surety, who was born before 1177. He became the first Earl of Hereford of this family, being so created by charter of King John, dated 28 April 1199; but the office of lord high constable of England he inherited from his father. As he took a prominent part with the Barons against King John, his lands were confiscated, but he received them again at the granting of Magna Charta. Having been excommunicated by the Pope, with the other Barons, he did not return to his allegiance on the decease of King John, but was one of the commanders in the army of Louis le Dauphin, at the battle of Lincoln, and was taken prisoner by William Marshall. After this defeat he joined Saire de Quincey, and other Magna Charta Barons in a pilgrimage to the Holy Land in 1220, and died on the passage, 1 June 1220. His body was brought home and buried in the chapter-house of Llanthony Abbey, in Gloucestershire.

Earl Henry married Maud, Fitz Geoffrey, daughter (by his first wife, Beatrix

Pages 100, 125

Saye) of Geoffrey FitzPiers, Baron de Mandeville, created in 1199 Earl of Essex and Justiciary of England, who died in 1212, and beside 2 Henry de Bohun who died young; and 3 Ralph de Bohun; and a daughter 4 Margery (who was married to Waleran, Earl of Warwick) they had a son and heir,

1 HUMPHREY de BOHUN, V second Earl of Hereford and Constable of England, born before 1208 and created Earl of Essex in 1228. He joined the Earl of Cornwall in his quarrel with the King in 1227. In 1237 he went on a pilgrimage to Santiago. He was appointed constable of Dover Castle 27 February 1238/9, which he surrendered 4 November 1241, and during these years was sheriff of Kent. In 1250 he was among those who took the Cross. On 18 December 1253, he and his elder son Humphrey had license to hunt hare, fox, cat, and other wild beasts in the forests of Bradon and Savernake, Wiltshire. In 1257 he was appointed to keep the marches between Montgomery and the land of the Earl of Gloucester. He was one of the fifteen chosen to advise the King on all points; he was also one of the twelve elected by the Barons to represent the community in three annual parliaments. In the struggle of 1263/4 he took the side of the King; was one of the keepers of the City of London, 9 October 1265. He married, first, Maud, daughter of Raoul, de Lusignan, Count of Eu in right of his wife Alice, and had 11 Humphrey, see below, and a daughter

12 ALICE BOHUN, whose husband was Ralph de Toni a lineal descendant of Ralph de Toni, Lord of Toni in Normandy, and one of the soldiers of Hastings. Issue.

11 HUMPHREY de BOHUN VI had a grant in 1254 as eldest son of Humphrey de Bohun, Earl of Hereford and Essex, of 80 marks a year. In 1257 he was among those who assisted his father to keep the marches between Montgomery and the land of the Earl of Gloucester, and in 1263 was ordered to join his father at Hereford to defend the lands and fortify the castles on the marches against Llywellyn. He joined the Barons against the King, and on 23 July 1264 had the custody of the Castle of Winchester, which he was ordered to surrender 3 June 1265. He fought at the Battle of Evesham, 4 August 1265, where he was taken prisoner, and died during his father's lifetime, 27 October 1265. He married, first,* Alianore, daughter of William de Braos of Brecknock, lord of Abergavenny, by Eve, sister of the Surety William Marshall, see Page 103 Chapter 16, and daughter of William Marshall, the Protector.

* His second wife was Joane Quincey, page 113.

Page 117 She was buried at Llanthony, in Gloucester. They had in addition to a daughter 112 Agnes, also known as Alianore, whose husband was Sir Robert de Ferrers of Chartley, a descendant of the Surety Page 97 Saire de Quincey, see Chapter 21; a son

111 HUMPHREY de BOHUN, VII Earl of Hereford and Essex, who was born about 1249. In 1297 he conducted the Princess Elizabeth and her husband, John, Count of Holland, on their journey from England, which Elizabeth his son later married. At the so-called parliament which met at Salisbury 24 February 1296/7 occurred the famous passage between the King and the Earls of Norfolk and Hereford, when the King was defied, the two Earls, one as marshal and the other as constable, refusing to do service in Gascony unless the King were present. They were deprived of their offices. Finally they came to London and practically dictated terms. The Earl of Hereford served in Scotland in 1298. He married in 1275, Maud, daughter of Enguerrand, Seigneur de Fiennes in Guisnes. Her death occurred before his, and she was buried at Walden in Essex. He died at Pleshey, 31 December 1298. Their son

111 1 HUMPHREY de BOHUN, VIII Earl of Hereford and Essex, and Constable of England, was born about 1276. He was at the marriage of Edward I to Queen Margaret at Canterbury, 9 September 1299. Serving in Scotland he was present at the siege of Carlaverock, 1 July 1300. In 1302, prior to his marriage with the King's daughter he surrendered his castles, towns, manors and lands in Essex, Herts, Middlesex, Hunts, Bucks, Wilts, Gloucester and Hereford and in Wales, and made a further surrender of his right, honour and dominion by virtue of the name of Earl in counties Hereford and Essex, as also of the constableship of England. After his marriage these were restored to him and his wife to be held as fully as he held them before quitclaiming to the King. He assisted in the execution of Piers de Gaveston in 1312, for which with others he was pardoned 16 October 1313. He fought at Bannockburn and was taken prisoner at Bethwell where he had retreated, having been betrayed by the Governor, Sir Walter Gilbertson. He was exchanged for Elizabeth, wife of Robert Bruce, King of Scotland. On 11 February 1315/6 he was appointed captain of all the forces against Llywellyn Bran in the land of Glamorgan. Summoned to attend the Council at Gloucester, he sent word he would not do so while Hugh Despenser, the younger, was in the King's comitive: he was then ordered to attend at Oxford, and preparing to attack the

said Despenser was ordered 1 May 1321, to abstain, but during May and June the lands of the Despensers were ravaged. In accordance with an agreement made in parliament, he received a pardon 20 August 1321. He married 14 November 1302, at Westminster, the Princess Elizabeth, widow of John, Count of Holland and Zealand, and daughter of King Edward I, see Chapter 34. The Princess Elizabeth was born 5 August 1282 at Rhudlan Castle, co. Carnarvon, died 5 May, 1316 and was buried at Walden Abbey. Bohun himself was killed at Boroughbridge, 16 March 1321/2 when endeavouring to force the bridge, and was buried in the church of the Friars Preachers at York. Of his five sons, lineages are traced through one son 111 11 William, see later, as well as, Pages 56, 130 through Humphrey's two daughters 111 12 Margaret, see later, and 111 13 Eleanor, also of whom later.

111 11 WILLIAM de BOHUN was a Knight of the Garter and was a person of great eminence in the turbulent times in which he lived, and one of the gallant heroes of Crecy. He was created Earl of Northampton, 17 March 1337, and from that period he appears as the constant companion in arms of the martial King Edward III and his son. William married Elizabeth, one of the daughters of Bartholomew Badlesmere and his wife Margaret Clare, a descendant of the Sureties Richard and Gilbert de Clare, see Chapter 6. They were the parents of a daughter 111 111 Elizabeth Bohun, who became the wife of Richard FitzAlan, a Knight of the Garter and a Page 132 descendant of the Surety Robert de Vere, see Chapter 24, and a son

111 112 HUMPHREY de BOHUN, IX second Earl of Northampton who succeeded his uncle of the same name in the Earldom of Hereford and Essex and as Lord High Constable of England he was a Knight of the Garter and a minor at the time of his succession in 1361 and was under the guardianship of Richard, Earl of Arundel. He did not, however, long enjoy his great accumulation of wealth and honor for he died in 1372 in the 32nd year of his age. He had married Joane FitzAlan the daughter of his late guardian the Earl of Arundel, a descendant of the Surety Robert de Vere, see Chapter 24, and they had two daughters 111 112 1 Alianore, wife of Thomas of Woodstock, Duke of Gloucester, sixth son of King Edward III, see Chapter 35, and 111 112 2 Mary, who became the wife of Henry of Bolingbroke, Earl of Derby, who afterward ascended the throne as King Henry IV.

111 1 Humphrey de Bohun and his wife Elizabeth Plantagenet had a daughter

111 12 MARGARET BOHUN, who became the wife of the renowned Hugh Courtenay, second earl of Devon. He distinguished himself in arms during the reign of King Edward III and died in Page 185 the year 1377. The family of Courtenay is of royal descent, the lineage being traced from King Henry I of France, see Chapter 29. Page 130 He descends also from the Surety, Robert de Vere, see Chapter 24.

111 1 Humphrey de Bohun and his wife Elizabeth Plantagenet had a second daughter

111 13 ELEANOR BOHUN, who was born in 1304 and was married, first in 1327 to James Butler, first Earl of Ormonde, and seventh of Butler. He was a descendant of the Sureties Roger and Hugh Bigod, see Chapter 3. He was a minor when his father died. Beside a son James Butler, page 93, they had a daughter

111 131 PETRONELLA BUTLER, who was married to Gilbert, third Baron Talbot, summoned to parliament from 14 August 1362 to 8 August 1385, and served under the Black Prince in the wars of France; and in the first of King Richard II was in the king's fleet at sea, with Michael de la Pole, admiral for the north. Issue.

111 13 Eleanor (Alianore) Bohun was married, second, to Thomas de Page 79 Dagworth, Lord Dagworth, and had a daughter 111 132 Eleanor, wife of Walter FitzWalter, a descendant of the Surety Robert Fitz-Walter, see Chapter 8.

(To be continued)

Chapter 41 Page 325

CLARE

Chapter 5

Richard de Clare

A Surety for Magna Charta

Arms: Or, three chevrons gules.

The following persons may claim descent from Baron Richard de Clare and King William the Conqueror: Pages 195, 329

Robert Livingston Acklen
Katharine Kellogg Adams
Cora Marguerite Stephens Anderson
Jane Virginia Hawkins Andrews
Elizabeth May Hicks Barrett
Mary Selma Pyle Stalfort Beach
Nellie Agnew Bechtel
Helen Bryant Below
Mae Conkling Benedict
Susan Montgomery Bland
Allison Douglass Williams Boutros
Ida Nail Bradley
Estelle Jane Brereton
Cordelia Ashlock Brown
Frank H. Bryant
Dean Winslow Buchan
Evelyn True Button
Sallie Johnston Byrd
George Allen Chandler
Rosa Pendleton Chiles
Mary Elizabeth Watson Clarke
Mary Anna Nixon Closson
Anna Cecelia Thompson Condit
Ella Moore Corbet
Blanche Stanley Cron
Emma Erskine Crosby
L. Effingham de Forest
Belle Kilby Denison
Emma McSwain Dial
Nellie Burnett Dickinson
Rufus Ebenezer Dickinson
Elizabeth Conway Doak
Dora White Browning Donner
Elizabeth Winslow Dulles
John Welsh Dulles
Ruth Larrabee Clay du Marais
Lotta Lavinia Edwards
Margaret Williams Elwell
Robert Ervien
Alice Garth Estill
Luela Bone Ettelson
Helen Huntly Thompson Frellsen
Eleanore Jane Fulton
Ida Janette Adams Garner
Leta Watts Gibbs
Eva Dorothy Payne Glass
Florence Grandin
Charles McClellan Gordon
Penelope Griffiss
Ellen Therese Dorrance Groves
Caro Bayard Hall
Anna Jenkins Ferris Hallowell
John Kearsley Mitchell Harrison
Lewis M. Hatch
Frank C. Irvine
Josephine Pearl Powers Kent
John Slack Keith
Ella Christina Kouwenbergh
Dwight Noble Lathrop
Charles Henry Leete
Elizabeth Allen Leslie
Clifton Lisle
Helen Harriet Hodge Lockwood
John Dudley Long
Douglas MacArthur
Hobart H. MacCubbin
Edwin Lockwood MacLean
Anna Baugh Maddock
Nancy Banks Mann
Katharine Martin
Thomas McKean
Betsy Morgan Fairweather Milham
Hazel Dean Mook
Alice Gertrude Probasco Mulford
Jennie Scudder Murray
Gene W. Nelson
Howard Ross Nelson
Samuel Davis Page
Cordelia Ayer Paine
Violet Leland Erskine Parish-Watson
Francis Pettit
Grace Edna Vollnogle Phillips
Mary Gordon Landon Pratt
Mary Turner Polk Pyle
Alice Grantham Rader
Florence West Rankin
Daisy A. Riehl
Anna Noel Rippey
George Pepper Robins
Susan Erskine Rogers
Olive Conover Rundstrom
Thomas B. Satterwhite
Emma Julia Scott
Mary Lane Landis Scott
Elizabeth Thorne Snow
Emma Breckinridge Squire
Mary Thompson Snowden Stansfield
Elizabeth King Sterritt
Dorothy Browning Rodgers Stewart
Marion Dibert Suppes
Adeline Sutherland Taggart
Beatrice Tassencourt
Nora Clark Tierney
Benjamin Franklin Tillson
Susan Vail-Cloud
Prudence Sharpless Doyle Vollnogle
Thomas Campbell Washington
Lucile Kilby Wayt
Webster King Wetherill
Franklin McGalliard Wolfe
Theodore Maximillian Wurts
Ethel Denune Young
William Dorr Wisner

Chapter 5

I. RICHARD FITZGILBERT, a lawyer and Chief Justice of England, born before 1035, was the founder of the House of Clare in England. He was the eldest son of Gislebert Crispin, Count of Eu, and Page 182 Brionne, a descendant of the Emperor Charlemagne, see Chapter 29. He accompanied Duke William into England, and later held one hundred seventy-six lordships or manors. One of these lordships was that of Clare, in co. Suffolk which, becoming his chief seat, caused him to be styled Richard de Clare, and his descendants known as Earls of Clare. He fell in a skirmish with the Welsh in 1090. He married Rohese, daughter of Walter Giffard de Bolebec, Page 75 and had in addition to Robert FitzRichard, see Chapter 8, and Alice Page 110 wife of William de Percie, see Chapter 20, a son

II. GILBERT de TONEBRUGE, second Earl of Clare, born before 1066. He appears to have joined in the rebellion against King William Rufus, and lost his castle of Tonebruge and, dying shortly afterwards, in 1114 or 1117, a munificent benefactor of the church, he was survived by his widow, Adeliza, daughter of Hugh, Count of Clermont, and his wife Marguerita. Their daughter Page 128 Adeliza, wife of Alberic de Vere, is mentioned in Chapter 24. Their eldest son

III. RICHARD FITZGILBERT de Clare, was born before 1105. He invaded Wales with an army and became lord of vast possessions there by power of his sword, but finally was slain in a skirmish with a few Welsh yeomen, near Abergavenny, 15 April, 1136. Richard married Adeliza, daughter of Ranulph de Meschines, Earl of Chester, who died in 1128. They were the parents of

IV. ROGER de CLARE, born before 1116, who succeeded his brother Gilbert when he died without issue in 1151. In 1164 he assisted with the Constitutions of Clarendon. This Earl who, from his munificence to the Church and his numerous acts of piety, was called the "good Earl of Hertford," died in 1173, leaving, by his wife Maud, daughter of James de St. Hillary, a son

★ V. RICHARD de CLARE, the Surety. He was 4th Earl of Hertford, but like his father and uncle was more generally known as EARL of CLARE. He was present at the coronation of King Richard I at Westminster, 3 September 1189, and of King John on 27 May, 1199. He sided with the Barons against King John, and his castle of Tonbridge was taken. On 9 November 1215, he was one of the commissioners on the part of the Barons to treat of peace with the King. On 4 March 1215/6 his lands in counties Cambridge, Norfolk, Suffolk, and Essex were granted to Robert de Betun; and he and his son were among the Barons excommunicated by the Pope in 1215. He died between 3 October and 28 November 1217. He married Amice,* Countess of Gloucester, second daughter of William FitzRobert, Earl of Gloucester, and his wife Hawise, daughter of Robert de Beaumont, Earl of Leicester. She died 1 January 1224/5. Among their children was

* called Amicia Meullent, pages 167, 185

1 JOAN CLARE, who became the wife of Rhys-gryd, Lord of Ystrad Tyni who died in the year 1234. Joan was perhaps his second wife, and they had

11 RHYS MECHYLL de DINEFUR who became Lord of Landovery Castle and died in the year 1224. His wife was Matilda Braos and they were the parents of 111 Rhys Fychn who died in 1271.

Another daughter of Richard de Clare, the Surety, was

2 MAUD CLARE, whose first husband was Roger, Baron Lacie, Lord of the Castles of Halton and Pontefract and they were Page
the parents of John de Lacie, the Surety, see Chapter 12. Maud 89
Clare was married, second,° to William de Braos who was starved to death with his mother at Windsor Castle. He was the son of William de Braos and Maud St. Walerie, his wife, who had another son, Reginald, great grandfather of Joan Cantilupe, wife of Henry Page
de Hastings, see Chapter 2. Maud Clare and her husband William 45
de Braos were the parents of

21 JOHN de BRAOS, surnamed Tadody, who had been privately nursed by a Welsh woman, at Gower. This John had grants of lands from King Henry III, and held also the Barony of Brembye, in Sussex, where he died in 1231, by a fall from his horse, his foot remaining in the stirrup. It is stated that he married Page
Margaret, daughter of Llewellyn, Prince of Wales, by whom he had 435
an eldest son 211 William, see later; and

212 RICHARD de BRAOS, Lord of Stainten Manor, whose daughter

212 1 MARGARET BRAOS was married to Roger, 2nd Baron Coleville of Bytham Castle, and they had

° (This second marriage is according to Burke; but according to Surrey County History, Maud, wife of William de Braos, was widow of Roger de Clare and daughter of Ralph de Fay, Lord of Bramley.)

212 11 ALICE COLEVILLE, whose husband John de Gernon was Lord of Lexton, in Essex. They had a son

212 111 JOHN de GERNON, Lord of Lexton and Lees through whom descent is traced to the present day.

The eldest son of 21 John de Braos and wife Margaret, was

211 WILLIAM de BRAOS, who in the 41st of King Henry III, when Llewellyn ap Griffith menaced the marches of Wales with a great army, was commanded by the king to defend his own marches about Gower. He died in 1290, leaving by Isabel Clare, his first wife, a son,

211 1 WILLIAM de BRAOS, who, in the 22nd of King Edward I, had summons to attend the king with other great men, to advise regarding the important affairs of the realm. For several years afterwards he appears to have been constantly engaged in the wars, and always distinguished himself. Lord Braos married Aliva, daughter of Thomas de Moulton, and had

Page 109 211 11 ALIVA BRAOS, known also as Alice, who became the wife of John de Mowbray, great grandson of William de Mowbray, the Surety, see Chapter 19.

In addition to his two daughters, 1 Joan and 2 Maud, Richard de Clare, the Surety, had a son: VI Gilbert de Clare, the Surety, see Chapter 6. Page 61

(To be continued)

Chapter 42 Page 329

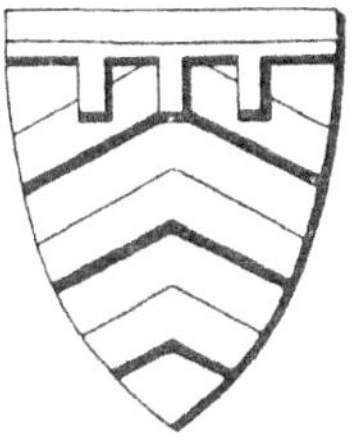

CLARE

Chapter 6

Gilbert de Clare

A Surety for Magna Charta

Arms: Or, three chevrons gules, a label of three points for difference.

See also Pedigree C, page 421.

The following persons may claim descent from Baron Gilbert de Clare and King Louis I: Pages 167, 188, 332

Zillah Bostwick Agerton
Sarah Brinton Audenried
Laura Thomson Barrow
James Culver Bierbower
Charles Garrard Bierbower
Mabel Iredell Prettyman Biggs
Florence Wolcott Sanford Bissell
Helen Kerr Blackmer
Elizabeth St ayman Bonham
William Gibbons Bramham
Sara Frances Smith Conlon
Mildred Merrill Hoge Conway
Virginia Ingram Corbin
Harriet Janney Doan
Mary Frances Foley Dudley
Bessie Duval Dunn
Norvell Cox Dunstan
Mildred Letitia Egger
Robert Ervien
Sara Sullivan Ervin
Luela Bone Ettelson
Eleanore Jane Fulton
Juliet Hite Gallaher
Eleanor Kendall Gibson
Janet Whitcomb Gill
Eva Dorothy Payne Glass
Emily Godley
Dora Ethel Jack Gunnett
Mary W. Huston Haines
William Penn Gaskell Hall
Anna Jenkins Ferris Hallowell
Rose Breckinridge Hamblen
Jean Barclay Penn-Gaskell Hancock
Charles Willing Hare
Maude Blaine-Dickson Harris
Olive DeLoche Dobbins Hatcher
Camilla Hammond Boone Herbert
Harry Gibbs Clay Hill
Roberta Stockton Benton Horton
Katharine Kennard Hutchins
Mary Etta Bartley Ivy
Agnes Gordon Paden Jarden
Charles Conway Jones
William Neely Keith
Hattie Terrell Ketchum
Elizabeth Maria New Kennedy
Helen Irvine Kennedy
Luella Pugh Knott
Lucretia Wiley McAdams
George Irving Laing
Henry Ridgway Lathrop
Electra Pearl Baker Long
Dorothy A. McKinney
Emily Pleasants Johnson Megee
Owen Meredith
David Ralph Millard
Mary DeCamp Banks Moore
Randal Morgan
Roland S. Morris
Howard Ross Nelson
William Byrd Page
Grace Hambleton Ober Palmer
Mary Cousins Parry
William M. Pettit
Grace Edna Vollnogle Phillips
Anne Carrington Martin Porcher
Neva Lamb Parvis Richardson
Armour Richardson
Theodore Roosevelt
Raymond Southack Ross
G. Ridgely Sappington
Louisa Pierpont Morgan Satterlee
Kathleen Wilson Seyburn
Mary Lane Landis Scott
Elizabeth Vanuxem Kennedy Slaughter
Elizabeth Thorne Snow
Frances Polk Pyle Stalfort
Elizabeth Bailey Strong
R. Livingston Sullivan
Lucy Nelson Taliaferro
Anne Powell Tarver
Mary Scott Ferguson Taylor
Mary Craik Davis Temple
Nancy Scott Thomas
Katharine Rogers Torrence
Prudence Sharpless Doyle Vollnogle
Dorothy DeLand Walden
George Lafayette Washington
Rose Pettus Weaver
Abel Proctor Wetherill
Mary Virginia Saunders White
Robert Wilberforce
Donald Henderson Williams
Lillard Witherspoon
Eleanor Worthington
Charles Stewart Wurts
Ethel Denune Young
William Dorr Wisner

★ VI. GILBERT de CLARE, himself a Surety, and son of Richard de Clare the preceding Surety. was born about the year 1180. In June 1202 he was entrusted with the lands of Harfleur and Mostrevilliers. He was one of the Barons still opposing the arbitrary proceedings of the crown, who championed Louis le Dauphin, fighting at Lincoln under the baronial banner, and was taken prisoner by William Marshall, whose daughter he later married. He led an army against the Welsh in 1228 and captured Morgan Gam, who was released the next year. Being engaged in an expedition to Brittany, he died on his way back at Penros in that duchy, 25 October 1230. His body was conveyed by way of Plymouth and Cranbourn to Tewkesbury. He was buried there before the high altar, Page 103 10 November 1230, a monument being erected by his widow, Isabella, sister of William Marshall, the Surety, see Chapter 16, and daughter of William Marshall, the Protector. He had married Isabella Marshall on 9 October 1217 and she died 17 January 1239/40. Their children were 2 Agnes (Rose) Clare, who became the wife of Roger Page 108 de Mowbray, grandson of the Surety William de Mowbray, see Chapter 19. Another daughter was

3 ISABEL CLARE, who was born 2 November 1226 and was Page 192 living 10 July 1264. In May 1240 she was married to Robert Bruce, son and heir of Robert Bruce, lord of Annandale and his wife Isabel, second daughter of David, Earl of Huntingdon, see Chapter 30. He succeeded his father in 1245 and his mother in 1251. On 19 April 1267 he, together with his son, swore fealty to the King and Prince Edward. His second wife, whom he married before 10 May 1275, was Christian, daughter of William d'Irevy. Robert Bruce died at Lochmaben Castle and was buried 17 April 1295 in Guisborough Priory. His descent from King Malcolm III appears Page 193 in Chapter 30. In addition to their son 31 John Bruce, whose grandson 311 1 Robert Bruce married Isabel Stewart and had 311 11 Robert Bruce from whom descend the Earls of Elgin and Kincardin, Robert Bruce and his wife 3 Isabel Clare had a daughter

32 CHRISTIANA BRUCE, whose first husband was Gretney, Earl of Mar. Their daughter

321 ELENE was married to John Menteth, and they had a daughter

321 1 CHRISTIANA MENTETH, who was married to Edward Keith, and their daughter

321 11 JANET KEITH, became the wife of Thomas Erskine, son of Robert Erskine and his wife, Beatrix Lindsay. Issue.

32 CHRISTIANA BRUCE was married, second, to Patrick Dunbar, who took an active part in Scottish politics, and was one of the leaders of the English party. His surprisal of the Castle of Edinburgh delivered Alexander III and his Queen from the Comyns. He was, after the death of that monarch, one of the Regents of Scotland and one of the Seven Earls of Scotland—a distinct body separate from the rest of the estates of the Kingdom. The Earl of Dunbar died in 1289, aged seventy-six, leaving by Christiana, his wife who founded "ane house of religione in ye toune of Dunbar," a son

322 PATRICK DUNBAR, surnamed "Black Beard," and styled also Earl of March, who swore fealty to Edward I of England and was a steadfast adherent of the English interest, but his wife, Marjory Comyn, daughter of Alexander Comyn, Earl of Buchan, sided with the opposite party, and held the castle of Dunbar for Baliol, until forced to surrender it to Edward, in 1296. In 1298, the Earl of March was appointed the king's Lieutenant in Scotland, and in 1300 was at the siege of Carlaverock. By Marjory, his wife, he had 322 2 Alexander (who had 322 21 Patrick Dunbar, died 1356, husband of 332 12 Isabel, youngest daughter of 332 1 Thomas Randolph) and

322 1 PATRICK DUNBAR, who was with his father at Carlaverock; and, after the battle of Bannockburn, gave refuge to Edward II, in his Castle of Dunbar, and secured the king's escape in a fishing boat to England. Making peace, however, with Robert Bruce, he signed the letter to the Pope in 1320, was appointed Governor of Berwick Castle, and held that fortress against Edward III, until the defeat of the Scots at Halidon Hill necessitated its surrender. Not long after, his Countess, known in history as "Black Agnes," his cousin, and daughter of the renowned Regent of Scotland, Thomas Randolph, Earl of Moray, see later, and grandniece of Bruce, defended in the absence of her husband, in January 1337/8, the Castle of Dunbar against the English, under the Earl of Salisbury, during a fierce and determined siege of nineteen weeks, and at length forced the Earl to abandon the attempt. This gallant resistance of the Countess of Dunbar is memorable in Scottish annals, and has given subject to many a minstrel's song. "Black Agnes" became eventually heiress of her brother, John Randolph, 3rd Earl of Moray, and her husband added the Earldom of Moray to his other dignities. They had a daughter

322 11 AGNES DUNBAR, whose husband was James Douglas, Lord Dalkeith and Liddesdale. Issue.

Chapter 6

The son of Robert Bruce and his wife, 3 Isabel Clare was

33 ROBERT BRUCE, born in July, 1243, Lord of Annandale. He married, first, in 1271, Margaret, in her own right Countess of Carrick. After his first wife's death, he resigned the Earldom of Carrick to his son. He was summoned to attend the King at Salisbury, 26 January 1296/7. He married, second, Alianore and, dying shortly before 4 April 1304, aged 60, he was buried in the Abbey of Holm Cultram. Of his children

331 EDWARD BRUCE, was crowned King of Ireland in 1316 and was killed at the battle of Dundalk in 1318. He had

331 1 ALEXANDER BRUCE, Earl of Carrick, whose daughter

331 11 ELEANOR BRUCE, was married to William Cunynghame of Kilmaurs on whom King David II conferred the Earldom of Carrick in 1361 in right of his wife. Through their son 331 111 William Cunynghame descent is traced to the present day.

33 ROBERT BRUCE and Margaret his wife had in addition to their son 331 Edward, several daughters, among whom was

332 ISABELLA, whose first husband was Thomas Randolph, high Chamberlain of Scotland. They had

332 1 THOMAS RANDOLPH, Earl of Moray, Regent of Scotland, whose youngest daughter 332 12 Isabel married 322 21 Patrick Dunbar, and whose eldest daughter

332 11 AGNES RANDOLPH was married to her cousin 322 1 Patrick Dunbar, Earl of March, see above.

Another daughter of 33 Robert Bruce and his wife Margaret Carrick was

333 MATILDA BRUCE, who became the wife of Hugh, Earl of Ross, and they had

333 1 WILLIAM LESLIE, 6th Earl of Ross, who married as his second wife, a daughter of David Graham of Montrose and had

333 11 MARGARET LESLIE, wife of David Hamilton of Cadyou, who died in the year 1374. They were the parents of

333 111 DAVID HAMILTON of Cadyou, who died before 14 May 1392. His wife was Johannetta, daughter of Robert de Keith, Great Marshall of Scotland in 1324. Issue.

Robert Bruce and his wife Margaret Carrick were the parents also of

334 MARY BRUCE, whose first husband was Neil Campbell, also known as Nigel, who was knighted by King Alexander III toward the close of that monarch's reign. He joined Robert Bruce in 1296, and the king granted to Neil and his wife, and to their only son 334 1 John, all the lands which belonged to David de Strathbogie, Earl of Atholl. Mary Bruce was Neil's third wife and she was married, second, in 1316, after her first husband's death, to Alexander Fraser, Great Chamberlain of Scotland. Beside her son 334 1 John Campbell of Moulin, Mary Bruce had a son

334 2 JOHN FRASER, laird of Aberbothnot, who was the father of

334 21 MARGARET FRASER, wife of William Keith, great Marshal of Scotland. Issue.

The most celebrated child of 33 Robert Bruce and his wife Margaret Carrick was, of course, Page 193

335 KING ROBERT BRUCE, who was born 11 July 1274 at Writtle, Essex, and on 25 March 1306 was crowned King of Scotland, see also Chapter 30. He was the eldest of three brothers, and seven sisters, whose marriages with some of the leading families of Scotland proved an important element of his success. His earliest years were passed at the Castle of Turnberry, where his mother resided; but as he grew older, his father, who considered himself an English baron, thought proper that he should be removed to the English Court. The friendship between King Edward I and the Earl of Carrick induced the former to adopt the Earl's son; so that the confiding monarch trained up his mortal enemy in the use of those arts and weapons which were one day to be turned against him.

Bruce died in his fifty-fifth year, 7 June 1329, and was buried in the abbey-church of Dumfermline, as he had desired. By his first wife, Isabel, daughter of Donald, 10th Earl of Mar, he had an only daughter, 335 1 Marjory, see later. By his second wife, Elizabeth (Ellen) Burgh, see Chapter 13, he had four children: 335 2 David, who succeeded him and d.s.p.; 335 6 John, d.y.; 335 3 Margaret, married to William, Earl of Sutherland; 335 4 Matilda, who was married to Thomas Isaacs; Bruce had also Elizabeth, who became the wife of Walter Oliphant of Cask. Page 93

In the prime of his life Bruce has been described as "upwards of six feet high; his shoulders broad, his chest full and open; the cheekbones strong and prominent, and the muscles of the back and neck of great size and thickness; his hair curled short over a broad forehead, and the general expression of his face was calm and cheerful, yet when he pleased, he could assume a character of stern command."

335 King Robert Bruce and his first wife, Isabel, as stated above, were the parents of

335 1 MARJORY BRUCE, who died 2 March 1315/16, she was heiress to the Scottish crown and in 1315 became the wife of Walter Stewart, died 9 April 1326, son of James, Lord High Steward of Scotland and Egidia Burgh his wife. Walter and Marjory had

KING ROBERT II

335 11 ROBERT, who in 1371 ascended the throne of Scotland as King Robert II, and was ancestor of the long line of Stuart kings, see Chapter 30.

Page 193

Gilbert de Clare, the Surety, had in addition to his daughters, a son

4 WILLIAM de CLARE, whose daughter 41 Elizabeth Clare, was the wife of Ralph de Rockley and they had 411 Anne Rockley, wife of Henry, 3rd Baron Grey of Wilton Castle, a descendant of the Surety Saire de Quincey, see Chapter 21.

Page 119
Page 112

The eldest son and successor to Gilbert de Clare, the Surety, was

1 RICHARD de CLARE, Earl of Gloucester and Hertford, born 4 August, 1222. A year after he became of age, he was in an expedition against the Welsh. Through his mother he inherited a fifth part of the Marshall estates, including Kilkenny and other lordships in Ireland. He joined in the Barons' letter to the Pope in 1246 against the exactions of the Curia in England. He was among those in opposition to the King's half-brothers, who in 1247 visited England, where they were very unpopular, but afterwards he was reconciled to them. On 20 April, 1248, he had letters of protection for going over seas on a pilgrimage. At Christmas 1248, he kept his Court with great splendour on the Welsh border. In the next year he went on a pilgrimage to St. Edmund at Pontigny, returning in June. In 1252 he observed Easter at Tewkesbury, and then went

across the seas to restore the honour of his brother William, who had been badly worsted in a tournament and had lost all his arms and horses. The Earl is said to have succeeded in recovering all, and to have returned home with great credit, and in September he was present at the "Round Table" tournament at Walden. In August 1252/3 the King crossed over to Gascony with his army, and to his great indignation the Earl refused to accompany him and went to Ireland instead. In August 1255 he and John Maunsel were sent to Edinburgh by the King to find out the truth regarding reports which had reached the King that his son-in-law, Alexander, King of Scotland, was being coerced by Robert de Roos and John Baliol. If possible, they were to bring the young King and Queen to him. The Earl and his companion, pretending to be two of Roos's knights, obtained entry to Edinburgh Castle, and gradually introduced their attendants, so that they had a force sufficient for their defence. They gained access to the Scottish Queen, who made her complaints to them that she and her husband had been kept apart. They threatened Roos with dire punishments, so that he promised to go to the King. Meanwhile the Scottish magnates, indignant at their castle of Edinburgh's being in English hands, proposed to besiege it, but they desisted when they found they would be besieging their King and Queen. The King of Scotland apparently travelled South with the Earl, for on 24 September they were with King Henry III at Newminster, Northumberland. In July 1258 he fell ill, being poisoned with his brother William, as it was supposed, by his steward, Walter de Scotenay. He recovered, but his brother died.

Richard died at John de Griol's manor of Asbenfield in Waltham, near Canterbury, 15 July 1262, it being rumored that he had been poisoned at the table of Piers of Savoy. On the following Monday he was carried to Canterbury where a mass for the dead was sung, after which his body was taken to the canons' church at Tonbridge and interred in the choir. Thence it was taken to Tewkesbury and buried 28 July 1262, with great solemnity in the presence of two bishops and eight abbots in the presbytery, at his father's right hand. His first wife was Margaret, daughter of Hubert de Burgh, Earl of Kent. She died in November, 1237, and he married, second, on or Page 90
before 25 January 1237/8, Maud, daughter of the Surety John de Lacie, see Chapter 12. She, who had the manor of Clare and the manor and castle of Usk and other lands for her dower, erected a splendid tomb for her late husband at Tewkesbury and was living in 1287, but she died before 10 March 1288/9. Their second son was

12 THOMAS de CLARE, governor of the city of London in the first of King Edward I. He was killed in the battle of Ireland fourteen years later, (1286) leaving by his wife Julian, not Amy, daughter of Sir Maurice FitzMaurice, Lord Justice of Ireland, a third, but only surviving son: 123 Thomas de Clare; and two daughters, 125 Maud, see later; and 124 Margaret Clare, the wife of Bartholomew Badlesmere who succeeded his father in 1301, being then aged twenty-six years. He was in the Scottish wars in 1303/4 and was governor of Bristol Castle in 1307. Beside their son 124 1 Giles, Bartholomew Badlesmere and his wife Margaret Clare were the parents of four Page 124 daughters: 124 2 Margery, wife of William de Roos, a descendant of the Surety Robert de Roos, see Chapter 22; 124 3 Maud, wife Page 133 of John de Vere, a descendant of the Surety Robert de Vere, see Page 320 Chapter 24; 124 4 Elizabeth, wife first of Edmund de Mortimer, a descendant of the Sureties Roger and Hugh Bigod, see Chapter 3; Page 55 (and wife second, of William de Bohun, a Knight of the Garter and a descendant of the Surety Henry de Bohun, see Chapter 4); and 124 5 Margaret, wife of John de Tibetot, a descendant of the Surety Robert de Roos, see Chapter 22. Page 124

The second daughter of 12 Thomas de Clare and his wife Julian FitzMaurice was

Page 49 125 MAUD CLARE, whose husband was Robert de Clifford. He participated in the Scottish wars of King Edward I and had a principal command in the English army. He was killed in the following reign at the battle of Bannockburn. He was a descendant of the Sureties Roger and Hugh Bigod, see Chapter 3.

The elder son of 1 Richard de Clare and his wife Maud Lacie was

11 GILBERT de CLARE, Earl of Gloucester and Hertford, "the Red Earl," born 2 September 1243, at Christchurch, Hants. Being under age at his father's death, he was a ward of Humphrey de Bohun, Earl of Hereford. In April 1264 he led the massacre of the Jews at Canterbury, as Simon de Montfort had done in London. His castles of Kingston and Tonbridge were taken by the King, who, however, allowed his Countess, who was in the latter, to go free because she was his niece; and on 12 May he and Montfort were denounced as traitors. Two days later, just before the battle of Lewes, on 14 May, Montfort knighted the Earl and his brother Thomas. The Earl commanded the second line of the battle

and took the King prisoner, having hamstrung his horse. As Prince Edward had also been captured, Montfort and the Earl were now supreme. On 20 October following, however, the Earl and his associates were excommunicated by the Papal Legate and his lands placed under an interdict.

In the following month, by which time they had obtained possession of Gloucester and Bristol, the Prince and the Earl were proclaimed to be rebels. They at once entered on an active campaign, the Earl, in order to prevent Montfort's escape, destroying the ships at Bristol and the Bridge over the Severn. He shared the Prince's victory at Kenilworth on 16 July, and in the battle of Evesham, 4 August, in which Montfort was slain, commanded the second division and contributed largely to the victory. The castle of Abergavenny was committed to his charge on 25 October and on the 29th the honour of Brecknock was added. On 24 June 1268 he took the Cross at Northampton, and at Michaelmas his disputes with Llewelyn were submitted to arbitration, but without a final settlement. At the end of the year 1268 he refused to obey the King's summons to attend parliament, alleging that, owing to the constant inroads of Llewelyn, his Welsh estates needed his presence for their defense. At the death of Henry III, 16 November 1272, the Earl took the lead in swearing fealty to Edward I, who was then in Sicily on his return from the Crusade. The next day, with the Archbishop of York, he entered London and proclaimed peace to all, Christians and Jews, and for the first time, secured the acknowledgment of the right of the King's eldest son to succeed to the throne immediately. Thereafter he was joint Guardian of England, during the King's absence, and on his arrival in England, in August 1274, entertained him at Tonbridge Castle. On 3 July, 1290 the Earl gave a great banquet at Clerkenwell to celebrate his marriage with the Princess Joan in the previous May. Thereafter he and she are said to have taken the Cross and set out for the Holy Land, but in September he signed the Barons' letter to the Pope, and on 2 November surrendered to the King his claim to the advowson of the bishopric of Llandaff. In the next year, 1291, his quarrels with the Earl of Hereford about Brecknock culminated in a private war between them. Both were imprisoned by the King, and the Earl of Gloucester, as the aggressor, was fined 10,000 marks, and the Earl of Hereford 1,000 marks. He died at Monmouth Castle on 7 December, 1295, and was buried at Tewkesbury, on the left side of his grandfather Gilbert. The Earl married, first, in the spring of 1253, Alice, daughter of Hugh le Brun, Count of La Marche and Angouleme, and his wife, Yolande, daughter of Pierre Mauclerk.

Earl Gilbert's second wife, whom he married in 1290, when he was about 47 years of age, was Joan of Acre, Countess of Gloucester and Hertford, born at Acre in Palestine probably early in 1272. She was the second daughter of King Edward I, by his wife Eleanor of Castile, see Chapter 34. She was first betrothed to Herman, son of the King of Germany, who died in 1282.

After Earl Gilbert's death, to her father's great displeasure, she married clandestinely, in the early part of May 1297, Ralph de Monthermer, a member of the late Earl's household. On 29 January, 1296/7 the escheator was ordered to take into his hand all the lands, goods and chattels of Joan, Countess of Gloucester, from which it might be inferred that the King suspecting her intentions with regard to Monthermer, sought to coerce her to abandon the marriage by degradation and loss of estates. On 16 March the King gave his assent to her marriage with Amadeus of Savoy, and therefore must have been ignorant of her marriage, if it had already taken place, and on 12 May it was ordered that Joan should have reasonable allowance for herself and children. It would seem that by 3 July the King had discovered Joan's marriage with Monthermer, for he took her lands into his own hand, but by 31 July, when he certainly knew of the marriage, he appears to have been partly mollified, for her lands were restored, except Tonbridge. She died 23 April, 1307, and was buried in the Austin Friars' church at Clare in Suffolk, aged 35.

She and her first husband, 11 Gilbert de Clare had several children, among whom were 111 Alianore, who was married first
Page 438 in 1337 to Hugh Despencer, son of Hugh Despencer and his wife Isabel Beauchamp, and, second, to William, Lord Zouche de Mortimer; 112 Margaret, who was married, first, to Piers Gaveston,
Page 94 Earl of Cornwall, second, to Hugh Audley; 113 Elizabeth, who became the wife, first, of John de Burgh, a descendant of the
Page 48 Surety William de Lanvallei, see Chapter 13; and, second, of Theobald de Verdon, a descendant of the Sureties Roger and Hugh Bigod, see Chapter 3; and, third, of Roger d'Amory, by whom she had two daughters 113 1 Elizabeth Amory, wife of John, Lord Bardolph and 113 2 Alianore Amory, wife of John de Raleigh.

(To be continued) Page 332

FITZ ROBERT

Chapter 7

John FitzRobert

A Surety for Magna Charta

Arms: Or, two chevrons gules

See also Pedigrees H and N, pages 424 and 427.

The following persons may claim descent from Baron FitzRobert and the Emperor Hugh Capet: Page 184, 341

Mary Taylor Williams Archer
Bertha Richardson Baton
Louise Post Beardsley
Clara Louise King Bowdry
Sophie Meredith Boyce
Zolita Lillian Rogers Bray
William T. Carpenter
Harriet Addison Bayne Castle
Russell L. Cecil
James M. Cecil
Ouina Mary Pegram Childress
Linda Lee Wallace Colgate
Henry Hill Collins
John H. Converse
Coltilde Florance Cohen Crawford
Marie Girvin Owens Crerar
Ambrose Winston Deatrick
Mariane Wood Diaz
Miriam Gardner Reed Robinson Dingley
Elsie Taylor Ford Draper
William Joseph Duval
William Newbold Ely
Harriet Overton Woodward Ennis
Marion FitzRandolph
Alice Urquhart Fewell
Susan Stadiger Hanna Foote
John Gill, 7th
John C. Gilpin
Florence Isabel Preston Graves
Anna Jenkins Ferris Hallowell
Mattie Scruggs Hanger
William Wurts Harmar
Frederick Vanuxem Hebard
Anna Scattergood Hoag
Mary Warren Davis Holt
Emily Gilpin Hopkinson
Marie Lovett Jewett
Nettie Browning Danforth Kinnison
Mary Martin Knight
Henry Lewis d'Invilliers Levick
Charles Edward Greenough
Harriette Miller Malley
Idella Gribbel McCurdy
Alice Davis Miller
Ethel Haynes Miller
Louise Davis Lawrence Miller
John Kearsley Mitchell
Josephine La Coste Neilson
Lois Bath Newcombe
Elizabeth Spencer Norton
John Hooker Packard
Oliver Randolph Parry
Anthony J. Drexel Paul
Josephine Lyons Pemberton
Elizabeth Eggleston Stone Perrow
Tunstall Barker Perry
Grace Edna Vollnogle Phillips
Frances Jackson Pickett
Anna Thornton Key Fort Pipes
Elsa Neide Brooke Pridgen
Martha Bess Hall Probert
Jane Watson Rockey
Anna Rossiter Kones Roelker
Emma Louise Cone Rust
Elizabeth Barnett Cecil Scott
Mary Lane Landis Scott
Wharton Sinkler
Katherine Bowen Smith
Eleanor Brooke Perry Stiefel
Maud Tilghman
Theodora Van de Mark
Louisa Vanuxem
Prudence Sharpless Doyle Vollnogle
Jouett Lee Wallace
Hannah Fairfax Washington
Cary Nelson Weisiger, Jr.
Alice Tracy Welch
Harry Bond Wilmer
Courtney Warner Halsey Wurts
Lucien I. Yeomans
Ethel Denune Young
Amy Rodick Willis

The first known paternal ancester of this Surety was

I. JOHN de BURGO. He was feudal lord of Tourborough, or Tonsburgh in Normandy and was commanding general in the Norman army of William the Conqueror, and for his services he was appointed governor of the chief burghs or towns in Normandy, and was also the titular Earl of Comyn. His son

II. EUSTACHE de BURGO, lord of Tonsburgh, was the father of

III. JOHN-MONOCULUS "One Eye" de BURGO, governor of Bamburgh Castle, Northumberland, for Henry 1, brother of Serle de Burgo, who erected Knaresborough Castle. He had by his wife Magdalen, said to have been an aunt of King Stephen of England,

IV. EUSTACHE FITZJOHN de BURGO, or Burgh, feudal lord of Knaresborough Castle, as heir to his uncle Serle. He was one of the wealthiest of the feudal lords, through his marriages with two heiresses, and was one of the most powerful and influential of the northern feudal barons, and a favorite of King Henry I. Page 135 He married, first, Beatrix, the heiress of the de Vesci family, of Alnwick Castle, and had by her a son William de Vesci, and married, second, Agnes, daughter and heiress of William Fitznigel, feudal lord of Halton Castle, constable of Chester, by whom he had

V. RICHARD (Robert) FITZEUSTACE, feudal baron of Halton Castle and constable of Chester. He married Albreda Page 88 Lisours, daughter of Robert (Eudo) de Lisours and his wife Albreda, called also Aubreye, sister of Henry de Lacie, lord of Pontfract Castle, Yorks, and they had

VI. ROGER FITZRICHARD, third son, who was granted by King Henry II the lordship of Warkworth, in Northumberland. He married Alice also called Adeliza, widow of Henry of Essex, lord Page 128 of Raleigh, and daughter of Alberic de Vere, great high chamberlain of England, see Chapter 24. They had an only son

VII. ROBERT FITZROGER. He was thrice high sheriff of each of the counties of Northumberland, Norfolk, and Suffolk. In the early proceedings of the barons in the matter of Magna Charta, this rich baron, although indebted to King John for immense territorial possessions, sided with the barons, but under apprehension of confiscation and other visitations of royal vengeance, he was induced to return to his allegiance. He married Margaret, only child of William de Cheney, lord of Horsford, Norfolk and dying in 1240, was succeeded by his only son

★ VIII. JOHN FITZROBERT, the Surety. At the time of the meeting of the barons at Saint Edmundsbury, this baron was still loyal to King John, and was, with John Marshall, joint governor of the castles of Norwich and Oxford, but subsequently he joined in the insurrection, and took such a prominent part that his lands were seized by the king, and confiscated. Returning to his allegiance in the next reign, his castles and vast estates were returned to him and he was constituted by King Henry III, high sheriff of county Northumberland and governor of New-Castle-upon-Tyne.

He died in the same year as his father, 1240. The monk, Matthew Paris, records: "In this year died John FitzRobert, a man of noble birth, and one of the chief barons of the northern provinces of England." FitzRobert had by his wife Ada Baliol, a son 2 Hugh FitzJohn, father of 21 John of Eure, as well as a son 3 Robert FitzJohn and his successor

1 ROGER FITZJOHN, lord of Warkworth and Clavering, who married Isabel and died in 1249. Their son

11 ROBERT FITZROGER (Clavering) became eminent in the Scottish wars of King Edward I, particularly in the battle of Falkirk, and other memorable conflicts. He married Margaret Zouche and beside their son 111 John, see later, had a daughter

112 ANASTASIA FITZROBERT, who was known also as Euphemia Clavering and who became the wife of Ralph de Neville. He was in the wars of France in the time of King Edward I, and in those of Scotland in the next reign. It is said, however, that he little minded secular business, but devoted the principal part of his time to conversation with the canons of Merton and Coverham, upon whom he bestowed some considerable grants.

Beside their daughter 112 Anastasia FitzRobert, 11 Robert FitzRoger and his wife Margaret Zouche had a son

111 JOHN FITZROBERT of Costessey, Norfolk, afterwards of Clavering, son and heir aged forty-four at the time of his father's death. He distinguished himself in the French and Scottish wars. He married in 1278 at the age of twelve, and she under thirteen, Hawise, daughter of Robert de Tibetot. He died without male issue in 1331/2, before 23 January at Aynhoe, Northants. His widow died before 14 April 1345.

111 1 EVE FITZROBERT, their daughter who was aged forty and more at her mother's death, was married, first, when very young, to Thomas Audley, son of Nicholas Audley, who died in the lifetime of his father and without issue, 16 January 1307/8. She was married, second, before 2 December 1308, to Thomas de Ufford, who was slain at Bannockburn 24 June 1314. Issue.

Ralph de Neville and his wife 112 Anastasia FitzRobert, had a son and heir

112 1 RALPH de NEVILL, second Baron, who in the time of his father was retained by indenture to serve the Lord Henry Percy for life, in peace and war, against all men except the king. In the

7th of King Edward III, Lord Nevill was one of the commissioners sent into Scotland, there to see that the covenants between Edward de Baliol, King of Scots, and his royal master, were ratified by the parliament of that kingdom. He died in 1367, and was buried in the church of Durham. His wife was Alice, daughter of Hugh Audley, and widow of Ralph, Lord Greystock, died 1323. Alice died in 1374. Among the six sons and five daughters of Ralph de Neville and his wife Alice Audley were 112 11 Margaret, wife of Henry Percy, Earl of Northumberland and

112 12 JOHN de NEVILL, third baron, who, when scarcely five years of age, was carried by his father to witness the battle of Durham, and was knighted some years afterwards when in arms near Paris. During the remainder of King Edward's reign he was constantly in active service either in France or Scotland, and was made a Knight of the Garter. He married, first, Maud, daughter of Henry, Lord Percy, by whom he had two sons and three daughters. He died at Newcastle 17 October 1388, and was buried in the south side of the nave of Durham Cathedral. Among his children by his first wife were 112 121 Ralph, his successor, see later; 112 122 Thomas, who married Joane, only daughter and heiress of William de Furnival; 112 123 Alice, who became the wife of William, Lord Deincourt a descendant of the Surety Robert de Roos, see Chapter 22. Page 124

112 12 John de Nevill's second wife was Elizabeth, daughter and heiress of William, Lord Latimer, a Knight of the Garter, and they had a son 112 124 John, and daughters 112 125 Elizabeth and 112 126 Margaret. At his death he was succeeded by his eldest son

112 121 RALPH de NEVILL, fourth baron, who, in the 21st of King Richard II was made constable of the Tower of London, and shortly afterwards advanced by the parliament to the dignity of Earl of Westmoreland. The Earl was afterwards governor of the town and castle of Carlisle, warden of the West Marshes towards Scotland, and governor of Roxborough. He was also a Knight of the Garter, and died in 1425. He married, first, Margaret, daughter of Hugh, Earl Stafford, K. G., and a descendant of the Page 219 Sureties Richard and Gilbert de Clare, see Chapter 6. Issue.

112 121 Ralph de Nevill's second wife was Joan Beaufort, daughter of John of Gaunt, K. G. and granddaughter of King Edward III, see Chapter 35. Issue.

(To be continued) Page 341

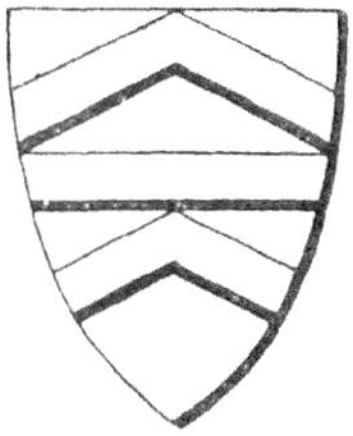

FITZ WALTER

Chapter 8

Robert FitzWalter

A Surety for Magna Charta

Arms: Or, a fess between two chevronels, gules.

See also Pedigrees E and P, pages 422 and 428.

The following persons may claim descent from Baron FitzWalter and King Cadwal ader: Pages 349, 434

Bird Allen
Horace Waters Avery
Louise Tice Palmer Beebe
Harry Clark Boden
Ellon Brooke Culver Bowen
Clarence Cresson Brinton
Alice Higgins Buttolph
Ellen Chase
Laurence Clark
John Lyman Cox
Brinton Coxe
Sarah Wood Crary
Edith Elizabeth Hatch Davenport
Adelaide Milton de Groot
Guilford Dudley
Margaret Williams Elwell
Stanwood E. Flitner
Myrtilla Malvina Pierce Frissell
Maud Chatfield Gerth
Arthington Gilpin
Elizabeth Grandin
Ada Gordon Gray
Clement Acton Griscom
Anna Jenkins Ferris Hallowell
Cornelia Thomas Hamlin
Laura Hammond
William M. Hannay
Florence McLean Knowles Harris
Luteola Gibbs Hawley
Dayton Edwards Herrick
Edward Hopkinson
Archibald Chetwode Kains
Meta Gilpin Kent
Ruth Ann Gans King
Mabel Levan Kutz
Delinda E. Stoll Lanterman
John Gardiner Lennig
Annie Rees Locke
Gilpin Lovering
Dorothy Yorke Beaman Mackenzie
Ada Florence Spring Maddox
Elizabeth Rogers Woodworth Marble
Clara Gardner Miller
Hardgrove Spofford Norris
Jennie Gardner O'Boyle
Edith Cox Page
Jessie Allen Page
Roy Clifford Smith Park
Edith Weir Perry
Anne Beatrice Lamborn Polk
Caroline Chester Knickerbacker Porter
Beverley Randolph Potter
Vesta L. Price
Emily Maria Eaton Rainey
Daniel L. Ransom
Edna Veazey Shaw Reeves
Alice Blackburn Rhodes
Gertrude Gilpin Oliver Richards
Mary Da Costa Brick Ringe
Katharine May Hammond Roberts
Alexander Calt Robinson
Alline Burleson Hartson Rogers
Alfred Garrett Scattergood
Edna Elizabeth Webb Schuh
Carrie Triplett Taliaferro Scott
Mary Lane Landis Scott
Hoxie Harrison Smith
Annie Chapman Stephenson
Mary Gould Woodhull Stevens
Margaret Tullidge Sturr
Helen Herron Taft
Ada Louise Taylor
Leonard Moorhead Thomas
Eliza Middleton Fox Tilghman
Juliet Stanton Adee Townshend
Fannie Long Walsh
Carolyn Chase Warren
S. Brinton Wharton
Susan Thurston Whitehead
Jane Welles May Woodroe
Lydia Rowland Woolman
Anne Bronson Wurts
Norman Wurts
Anna Brinton Coxe Yarnall
Ethel Denune Young
Charles Edward Greenough

I. RICHARD FITZGILBERT, first lord of Clare, and his wife Lady Rohese had, beside Gilbert de Tonebruge, who appears in Chapters 5 and 29, another son Page 58

II. ROBERT FITZRICHARD, steward to King Henry I. He

obtained from that monarch the barony of Dunmow, in Essex, and dying about 1134, had by his wife, Maud, "Lady of Bradham", died 1140, daughter of Simon de St. Liz, page 189, a son

III. WALTER FITZROBERT, second lord of Dunmow Castle, eldest son. In the controversy between the Earl of Moreton, brother of King Richard I, and the Bishop of Ely, Walter adhered to the bishop, and was given the custody of the Castle of Eye, in Suffolk. He married, first, Maud, who died in 1140, daughter of Richard de Lucie and sister of Geoffrey, Bishop of Winchester. With her he had the lordship of Disce, in Norfolk. He married, second, Margaret and, dying in 1198, was succeeded by his eldest son,

★ IV. ROBERT FITZWALTER, the Surety, third lord of Dunmow Castle, leader of the Magna Charta Barons and their army, styled "Marshal of the Army of God and the Holy Church." The first public act recorded of this subsequently important Baron who was standardbearer of the city of London, conveys at first a bad impression of him. It is recorded that "in 5th. John, 1203, Robert FitzWalter, being trusted, together with Saire de Quincey, also a Surety, to keep the Castle of Ruil, in France, delivered it up to the King of that realm as soon as he came before it with an army." This appears to imply not less of disloyalty than of cowardice; but a short time proved to which of these motives it was to be assigned. At that time the Barons, not only those abroad, were preparing to compel King John to keep his promises in the matter of the proposed statutes, and several conspiracies to this end were discovered, wherein Robert FitzWalter was materially concerned. On the discovery of his "treasonable practices," FitzWalter, with his wife and children, sought refuge in France; but in the following year, 1213, his friends persuaded him to return home and, with the other Barons, he was reconciled to King John. But this friendship was only of short duration, for soon it was discovered that he was still plotting against the King in the interests of reform in the government, so his residence in London, the Castle of Baynard, was, in consequence, almost entirely destroyed, and the hatred between John and FitzWalter was violent in the greatest degree. His lands were seized, which course effectually secured him to the discontented barons and the people. The active spirit of FitzWalter made him a desirable leader for their party, and he was selected as one of the commissioners to treat of a composure of differences at a meeting at Erith Church and subsequently was elected their leader.

After the granting of Magna Charta, when King John endeavored to elude his promises, FitzWalter was one of the committee of the baronial party which went to France to invite the Dauphin to accept the throne of England, and on this prince's coming, he, with William de Mandeville and William de Huntingfield, the Sureties, reduced the counties of Essex and Suffolk to the authority of the Dauphin. Upon the accession of Henry III, FitzWalter, then a prisoner, with the majority of the rebel Barons, finding the Dauphin a useless political factor, dropped him, and returned to their allegiance, and engaged to ship him back to France. In 1218, although a prisoner, he was allowed to assume the cross and join a crusade, when he took part in the famous siege of Damietta, returned home, and died a peaceful death in 1234, and was buried before the high-altar of Dunmow Priory. Nothwithstanding his enmity to Kings John and Henry III, and the frequent confiscations of his property, FitzWalter died in 1234/5 possessed of an extensive estate. The monk Matthew Paris, records: "In the same year (1234/5) at the advent of our Lord, Robert FitzWalter, a baron of illustrious race, and renowned in feats of arms, went the way of all flesh." His first wife was Gunora, daughter of Robert, second lord de Valoines, and he married, second, Roese, who survived him. By his first wife, FitzWalter had 2 Matilda the Fair, called "Maid Marion," said to have been poisoned by King John, see page 9; and

I WALTER FITZROBERT, eldest son and successor, who in the 24th of King Henry III paid into the exchequer a fine of 300 marks for livery of his lands, and eighteen years later had a military summons to march against the Welsh. He died shortly before 10 April 1258 having married Ida, daughter of William Longesepee, Earl of Salisbury. In addition to a daughter 12 Ela, see later, they had a son and heir

11 ROBERT FITZWALTER of Woodham Walter, who was born at Henham, Essex, in 1247, proved his age in 1268, and was knighted in 1274. On 4 July 1275 he had license to sell Baynard's Castle to the Archbishop of Canterbury. He accompanied the King to France in May 1286, and was appointed constable of Hadleigh Castle, Essex, in July 1289/90. He was at the siege of Carlaverock in July 1300, and on the King's service in Scotland in 1303 and 1306. On 9 October 1306 he had a pardon for all debts to the King, and in April 1310 he was about to go to Jerusalem with Alice, his wife, and was again going on pilgrimage

beyond seas in February 1316/7. He married, first, Devorgille, daughter of John de Burgh, and Cecily, his wife, daughter of John de Baliol, of Barnard Castle, co. Durham. Robert's wife, who was aged twenty-four in 1280, died in 1284 and was buried in Dunmow Priory. He married, second, in 1289, in the King's Chapel at Westminster, Alianore, daughter of Robert de Ferrers, of Chartley, co. Stafford, sometime Earl of Derby, by his second wife, Alianore, daughter of Humphrey de Bohun, of Kimbolton, Hunts. Alianore was buried in Dunmow Priory. He married, third, in May 1308, Alice, widow of Warin Del Isle and by her had a daughter 114 Christian, see later. He died 18 January 1325/6. His son and heir apparent was

111 WALTER FITZROBERT, who was the only son by his first wife, Devorgille Burgh. He was born in 1275 and married at Woodham, Joan, daughter of John Engaine. He died in 1293 leaving an only son

111 1 ROBERT FITZWALTER, who was born 1291, and died in childhood.

11 ROBERT FITZWALTER by his second wife Alianore Page 117 Ferrers, had 113 Ida, who became the wife of Robert de la Warde, mother of 113 1 Joan, wife of Hugh de Meynell, and a son

112 ROBERT FITZWALTER of Woodham Walter, who was aged twenty-five and more at his father's death. He married Joan. daughter of Thomas de Multon and his wife Eleanor, daughter of Richard de Burgh, a descendant of the Surety William de Page 94 Lanvallei, see Chapter 13. He died 6 May 1328. His widow, Joan Multon, who was aged thirty in 1334, died 16 June 1363, and was buried in Dunmow Priory. Robert FitzWalter and his wife Joan Multon were the parents of

112 1 JOHN FITZWALTER, aged thirteen and more at his father's death. He served continuously, in the retinue of the Prince of Wales, from the King's arrival at La Hogue, 12 July 1346, till his return to England. He married Alianore, daughter of Henry de Percy, of Alnwick, Northumberland and his wife Idonea, daughter of Robert de Clifford, Lord of Westmoreland. She predeceased him, and he died 18 October 1361. Both were buried in Dunmow Priory. Page 133 In addition to their daughter 112 11 Alice FitzWalter, wife of Aubrey de Vere, a descendant of the Surety Robert de Vere, see Chapter 24, they had

112 12 WALTER FITZWALTER, born and baptized at Henham, 31 May 1345. He accompanied Robert Knolles in his raid into the North of France in July 1370 in which expedition, or soon afterwards, he was captured by the French. In Nov. 1375, in order to pay for his ransom, he mortgaged his Castle of Egremont and all his lands. He was Marshal of the army of the Earl of Buckingham in his raid from Calais into Brittany, July 1380 to April 1381, and was at the siege of Nantes. He was Admiral of the Fleet towards the Northern parts, in December 1382. He married, first, in June 1362, Alianore, daughter of Thomas de Dagworth Page 56
and his wife Alianore, daughter of Humphrey de Bohun, a descendant of the Surety Henry de Bohun, see Chapter 4. She, who was living 29 November 1375, was buried in Dunmow Priory. He married, second, before 27 June 1385, Philippe, second daughter of John de Mohun, of Dunster, Somerset. His widow, for whom, as Lady FitzWalter, robes of the Garter were provided in 1390, died without issue 17 July 1431, and was buried in the Chapel of St. Nicholas, in Westminster Abbey.

11 Robert FitzWalter had by his third wife Alice Del Isle, a daughter

114 CHRISTIANA FITZWALTER, who became the wife of John Marshall who died in the 12th of King Edward I. They had

114 1 WILLIAM MARSHALL who, in the 34th of King Edward I was in the wars of Scotland and died the following year, being succeeded by his son, 114 11 John Marshall who died two years later, leaving as his heir his sister

114 12 HAWISE MARSHALL, who was wife of Robert, Lord Morley. Issue.

Walter FitzRobert and his wife Ida Longesepee had, beside their son 11 Robert FitzWalter, a daughter

12 ELA FITZWALTER, who became the wife of William Odingsells of Maxstoke, Warwick, died 1295, Justiciar of Ireland, and they had, 121 Edmund, born about 1273; 123 Alice, who died before 1320, the wife of Maurice de Caunton and mother of 123 1 William, 123 2 David and 123 3 Edmund de Caunton; 124 Ela, the wife of Peter FitzJames MacPhiores; 122 Ida the eldest daughter, see later; and the youngest daughter

125 MARGARET ODINGSELLS, aged eighteen years on 15 May 1295. Her first husband was John de Grey, son and heir of Robert de Grey of Rotherfield, died 1295, and his wife Joan, daughter of Thomas de Valoines. John was an executor of Edmund, Earl of Cornwall, and was present at the siege of Carlaverock. He died in 1311, leaving by Margaret, his wife, a son

125 1 JOHN de GREY, who was born at Rotherfield, 9 October and baptized 1 November, 1300, in the church there. About the year 1331, Geoffrey le Scrope, who made the King's speech, declared that Monsieur John de Grey of Rotherfield and Monsieur William de la Zouche of Ashby, then at variance, were commanded to do no violence, but nevertheless hot words passed between them in the presence of the King and his Council and Grey put his hand to his knife and partly drew it. Both had been sent to prison, and Zouche had been released on bail till this parliament. Grey had been given into the custody of William de Clinton, and was present in that custody. He appears to have been pardoned not long after. He was made a Knight of the Garter, at the institution of that Order, and was steward of the household, certainly from 1350 to 1356. He died at Rotherfield, 1 September 1359. For his second wife Lord Grey married Avice (whose descent from Robert de Marmyon, a Magna Charta Baron but not one of the 25 Sureties, is as follows:

ROBERT de MARMYON, lord Fountney in Normandy, married Amice, the daughter of Jerneygan FitzHugh. "Being in arms with the rebellious Barons, he obtained letters of safe conduct for coming in to King John, to make his peace. He again, however, took up arms in the baronial cause, in the ensuing reign, along with his brother William, and appears to have held out to the last."

Robert de Marmion and Amice his wife were the parents of William de Marmion who married Lora, daughter of Reese de Dover and had John de Marmion who, dying in 1322, left a son John de Marmion, who died in 1335, having married Lady Maude Furnival; they had a daughter, Avice, who married John, first Lord Grey of Rotherfield, as aforesaid.) They had

125 11 ROBERT de GREY, who died without male issue about the year 1367, having married Lora, who died in 1369, a younger daughter of Herbert de St. Quentin of Brandesburton in Holderness, and had:

125 111 ELIZABETH MARMION, born about the year 1363, died in 1427, who married Henry, third Lord FitzHugh of

Ravensworth in Richmondshire, born about 1358, and a Knight of the Garter. He was nominated about the year 1409. In the eighth year of King Henry IV's reign he was accredited upon an important mission to Denmark, and in five years afterward he was again commissioned upon affairs of Scotland. On the coronation of Henry V, Lord FitzHugh was appointed constable of England.

It is said that he travelled more than once to Jerusalem and to Cairo. On his return he fought with the Saracens and the Turks. With the help of the knights of Rhodes, he built a fortress there called St. Peter's Castle. He died in 1424. Issue.

The eldest daughter of William Odingsells and his wife 12 Ela FitzWalter, was

122 IDA ODINGSELLS, born about the year 1270, and living as late as 1 March 1321/2. She was married, about 1290, to John de Clinton of Amington. He was born about the year 1258, the second son of Thomas de Clinton and his wife Maud, daughter of Ralph Bracebridge of Kinsbury, co. Warwick. John de Clinton served, or was called upon to serve, in the Scottish and French wars. He appears to have been Knight of the Shire for co. Warwick in 1300, and was Constable of Wallingford Castle in 1308, dying late in 1310. His widow accompanied the Queen Consort to France in 1312/3. They were the parents of 122 1 William de Clinton, Earl of Huntingdon, and of

122 2 JOHN de CLINTON, Lord Clinton, who was born in, or shortly before, the year 1300. He fought in the Battle of Boroughbridge in 1321 and was knighted in 1324. His wife whom he married before 24 February 1328/9 was Margery, daughter of William Corbet of Chaddesley, co. Worcester. She survived him and was living as late as May 1343. They had a son

122 21 JOHN de CLINTON, who was born not later than March 1325/6 as he was aged 28 years when he became heir to his uncle William de Clinton, 25 August 1354. The following year he served in the French wars and in 1356 was at the battle of Poitiers. The year 1380 found him once more in the wars of France. From 1390 to September 1397 he was Constable of Warwick Castle. Page
His first wife, whom he married about the year 1350, was Idonea, 126
daughter of Geoffrey de Saye and a descendant of the Surety of the same name, see Chapter 23. His death occurred 6 September 1398. Issue.

(To be continued)

Page 349

FORTIBUS

Chapter 9

William de Fortibus

A Surety for Magna Charta

No great-grandchildren

•

Arms: Gules, a cross patonce vair

Born 1193 or 4 ? died 1241, age 21 in 1215.

I. WILLIAM de FORTIBUS, constituted by Richard the Lion-hearted, one of the admirals of the fleet in which this king soon afterwards sailed towards Jerusalem, died in 1194. His widow Hawyse married, third, Baldwin de Bethune, Earl of the Isle of Wight, who died without issue in 1212. William and Hawyse Aumale his wife had a daughter, Alice and a son

★ II. WILLIAM de FORTIBUS, the youngest of the Magna Charta Sureties. He became of age in 1214/15, when King John confirmed to him all the lands which accrued to him by inheritance from his mother, and he succeeded in her right as Earl of Albemarle.

Although at first on the side of the barons, this Surety deserted them and joined King John in his expedition into the north of England, so marked by destruction. For his services the king granted Page 103 him all the lands belonging to his sister Alice, then wife of William Marshall, Jr., the Surety, see Chapter 16, and constituted him, in 1218, governor of the Castles of Rockingham in Northamptonshire, Sauvey in Leicestershire, and Botham in Lincolnshire, with strict command to destroy all the houses, parks and possessions of those barons who were in arms against the king. In the reign of King Henry III, this nobleman fought under the royal banner at the battle of Lincoln, and shared largely in the spoils of victory. He was alternately for and against the Charter and being opposed by the king, his submission was only accomplished by excommunication. In 1230, he was one of the commanders of the royal troops in Normandy, and having set out on a pilgrimage to the Holy Land, he died on the Mediterranean Sea, 29 March 1241. Of William de Fortibus, the monk Matthew Paris wrote: "As the weather was at this time (1241) favorable, William de Fortibus, Earl of Albemarle, a bold knight (and other knights named), took leave of their friends, and commending themselves to the prayers of the religious men, set out in great pomp on their way towards Jerusalem and, embarking at the Mediterranean Sea, in the autumn, sailed forth on their voyage across the sea. 1241: Among the English nobles who died in this year, was William de Forbes (sic), Earl of Albemarle who, when on his pilgrimage, was taken ill in the Mediterranean Sea, and being unable to eat, endured protracted sufferings for eight days, and on Friday, next before Easter, on which day Christ on the cross resigned his spirit to His Father, he, in a like manner, resigned his spirit to Christ." He married Aveline, sister of Richard, Baron de Montfichet, the Surety, see Chapter 18, and had 1 William de Fortibus, Count d'Aumale, whose only child, 11 Aveline, Countess of Holderness, and Countess of Devon and of the Isle of Wight, married as his first wife, Edmund Plantagenet, a son of King Henry III, see Chapter 31, and died without issue. This Surety had also two other sons, 2 John de Fortibus, who died in his father's lifetime without issue, and 3 Thomas de Fortibus, who survived his father, but also died without issue.

Page 105

HARDELL

Chapter 10

William de Hardell

A Surety for Magna Charta

No known issue

Arms: Vert, a fesse flory and counterflory, or

This Surety was the mayor of the city of London at the time of the insurrection of the barons. Very likely he induced the citizens to deliver up one of the entrances to the city, called Aldgate, to the barons, through which they entered on Sunday morning, 17 May 1215, while the people were at mass.

There is no evidence that he was a feudal baron, or one by tenure, and being a civil officer of so early a period, there is some doubt as to the arms attributed to him. He served as sheriff of the city of London in 1207, and was the first mayor of the city by popular election, in 1215, by consent of King John. It was with his installation that were begun the "Ridings", or Lord Mayor's Shows, when the candidate was obliged by royal command to ride in state to Westminster, where the royal palace was situated and the judges sat, to be presented to the king for his approval.

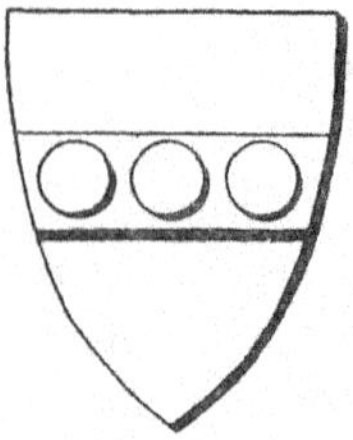

HUNTINGFIELD

Chapter 11

William de Huntingfield

A Surety for Magna Charta

Arms: Or, on a fess gules three plates argent

The following persons may claim descent from Baron Huntingfield and King Edward III:

Susie de Lorenzi
Robert Graham Dun Douglas
Ruth Lincoln Woodbury Draper
Winifred Sears Freiot
Josephine Brown Green
Catharine Dittmar Hohn
Jessie May Tillson Link
Margaret Currie Maywood
Minerva Lester Power
Evelyn Douglas Prime
Eva Hanson Thornton
Sarah Louise Jones Waller

The earliest recorded paternal ancestor of this Surety was

I. ROGER de HUNTINGFIELD, who held the manor of Huntingfield, co. Suffolk, as undertenant of Robert Malet in the time of King Henry I. His son and heir

II. WILLIAM de HUNTINGFIELD, with the consent of his son Roger, gave the whole Isle of Mendham, co. Suffolk, and divers other lands, to the monks of Castle Acre, co. Norfolk, thus founding the Cluniac Priory of Mendham during the reign of King Stephen. He died in 1155 and his wife Sibyl, in 1189. They had a son

III. ROGER de HUNTINGFIELD, who in 1199 gave 200 marks for land in Norfolk and Suffolk. He and his wife, Alice Senlis, died in 1204, leaving a son,

★ IV. WILLIAM de HUNTINGFIELD, the Surety. He married Isabel Gressinghall, widow of Osmond de Stuteville. He was made constable of Dover Castle in the 5th of King John, and as hostages for his loyalty to the king, delivered up his son and daughter, the former to remain with the Earl of Arundel, the latter with Earl Ferrers.

He was one of five wardens of the Ports of Norfolk and Suffolk from 1210 to 1212 and the following year he was one of the itinerant justices at Lincoln, and was high sheriff of Norfolk and Suffolk until the end of 1214. He witnessed King John's grant of freedom of election to churches in 1214. He was governor of Sauvey Castle, in Leicestershire, when he joined the cause of the barons in arms against King John, and was excommunicated by the Pope, and his lands given to Nicholas de Haya. Very likely the cause of the protectors' severity toward Huntingfield was that he was one of those who plotted to have the Dauphin come to England and, after the landing, was very active in reducing the courts of Essex and Suffolk to his authority. He fought at Lincoln, 20 May 1217, and was taken prisoner by the King's forces. William had a daughter 2 Alice Huntingfield, who was married twice, but the name of her first husband has not been preserved. Her father paid to the king a fine of "six fair Norway Goshawks," in the 15th of King John, for permission to marry Alice, his daughter, then a widow, to Richard de Solers. William de Huntingfield, the Surety, died in 1220, leaving a son

I ROGER de HUNTINGFIELD, who died in or before 10 July 1257, having married, as his second wife Joan, died before 7 September 1297, daughter of William de Hobrugg. They had

II WILLIAM de HUNTINGFIELD, of Huntingfield and Mendham, Suffolk; and other estates, who was born 24 August 1237. He sided against the king in the Barons' War. From 1263 to 1287 he was summoned for military service and to attend King Edward I at Shrewsbury 28 June 1283. He married Emma, who died in 1264, the daughter of John de Grey of Shirland, Derby and his first wife Emma, daughter of Geoffrey de Glanville. William de Huntingfield died before 2 November 1290, possibly in 1283. Their son was

III ROGER de HUNTINGFIELD, whose seal is appended to the Barons' Letter to the Pope in 1300. He married in 1277 Joyce, daughter of John d'Engaine of Laxston in Northamptonshire, whose wife was Joan, daughter and heiress of Gilbert de Greinville. Roger de Huntingfield died 20 November 1302. It is probable that Joyce, his wife, died in 1312. Their son was III I William de Huntingfield, whose only son, III II Roger, had a son III III William, born 1330, died without issue, and therefore the Barony became extinct. The next heir of his grandfather 111 1 William de Huntingfield, was found to be the grandfather's daughter 111 12 Eleanor, the younger William's aunt, who was married to John de Norwich, brother of William's mother Cicely, Cicely and John being children of Judge Walter de Norwich.

As 111 12 Eleanor Huntingfield, wife of John de Norwich, died without issue, Blanche Norwich was certainly not her daughter; therefore there can be no descendants of Baron Huntingfield through the Norwich family. The inheritance passed to the descendants of

111 2 JOAN HUNTINGFIELD, daughter of Roger de Huntingfield and his wife Joyce Engaine. Joan became the wife of Richard, Lord Basset of Great Weldon, Northamptonshire, son of Ralph Basset and his wife Alianora, daughter of Henry Wade. On 26 January 1296/7 he was summoned to attend King Edward I at Salisbury. On 24 June 1314 he was taken prisoner at the battle of Bannockburn, and died before 18 October of that year. Beside sons 111 21 Richard and 111 22 Roger Basset, Joan Huntingfield and her husband, Richard Basset, were the parents of

111 23 RALPH BASSET, 1st Lord Basset of Weldon born in 1300 at Huntingfield and was baptized in the church there. His wife was Joan Sturdon of Winterbourne, co. Gloucester. He died before 4 May 1341 and his widow later married Robert de Fourneux. The eldest son, 111 231 Richard Basset, died without issue before his father and the second son, 111 232 Ralph Basset, became 2nd Lord Basset of Great Weldon. His wife was Joane de la Pole and they had a son 111 232 1 Ralph Basset, whose son, 111 232 11 Richard Basset, died without issue 9 January 1399. This Richard's heirs were the children of his grandfather's sisters Joan and Eleanor, daughters of 111 23 Ralph Basset and his wife Joan Sturdon. Of these: 111 233 Joan Basset, became the wife of Thomas Aylesbury of Milton Keynes, co. Bucks. Issue. Her sister 111 234 Alianore Basset, who died in 1388, was married to John Knyvett, died 1381, of Wynwick in Northamptonshire, Lord Chancellor of England, Chief Justice of the king's bench, Executor of the will of King Edward III. He was son of Richard Knyvett by Joan his wife and a great-great-grandson of John Knyvett, ruler of Southwick. Issue.

(To be continued) Page 355

LACIE

Chapter 12

John de Lacie

A Surety for Magna Charta

Arms: Or, a lion rampant purpure

See also Pedigree M, page 426.

The following persons may claim descent from Baron Lacie and King Malcolm Canmore: Pages 191, 357

Miriam Jay Wurts Andrus
Margaretta Wilson Bayard
Mary Louise Wolcott Beardsley
Doris Wolcott Bissell Bigelow
Florence Wolcott Sanford Bissell
Mida Collins Blake
William Gibbons Bramham
Ione Brown Brewer
Mary Brooke Burt
Ray Webb Chatterton
Bertha Lewis Clark
George Norwood Comly
Lena Ruby Conable
Oliver Reeve Cope, Jr.
Elizabeth Craig
Martha Lenna Crary
Marion Josephine Fitts Davis
Julia V. Dickinson Dial
George Dallas Dixon
Mary Stretch Irick Drexel
Edmund McAshan Dupree
Ida Frances Jack Eckel
Alverta Bird Ellis
Dorothy Leib Harrison Eustis
Florence Ford Fenno
Anne Helene Gardiner Fulstow
Eleanor Goodenough Gray
Joseph Ridgway Grundy
Elizabeth A. Hall
George Leib Harrison
Marie Louise Harrison
Jessica Lauvenia Hawthorne
William Wade Hinshaw
George de Benneville Keim
Frederick Wilkinson Kilbourne
Margaret Antoinette Lennig
Rose Lawton Douglas Lewis
Elizabeth Sites Macke
Ada Florence Spring Maddox
Frank Hoy Mancill
Alice May Brown McDermott
Gertrude Evangeline Dunham Miller
Mary Elizabeth Sadler Morgan
Ralph Morgan
Bessie Dutton Murray
George Craghead Gregory
Lucretia Wiley McAdams
Georgiana Groot Murray
Harriet Williams Myers
Barbara Kendig Mylin
Howard Ross Nelson
Mary Elizabeth Moody Northen
Clarissa Starling Peterson
Nathaniel Allan Pettit
Grace Edna Vollnogle Phillips
Edgar Allen Poe
Thaddeus Rich
Mary Peabody Leavenworth Riddle
Henry Reed Robins
William Ives Rutter
Sara Farnsworth Sadler
Grace Emily Smith Scofield
Mary Lane Landis Scott
William Lord Sexton
Alice Harroun Shaw
Mary Eva Moore Sherrerd
Sarah Harrison Simms
W. Gregory Smith
Ely John Smith
Edith Abercrombie Snow
Mattie Hotchkiss Stewart
Henry Grafton Story
Nora Clark Tierney
Lucile Brakenridge Till
Celeste Heckscher Troth
Mary Vanuxem Wurts Tunis
Anna Louise Hubbell Vanderwerf
Prudence Sharpless Doyle Vollnogle
Mabel Shaw Walker
Lawrence Washington
Pendleton Watmough
Margaret Stuart Grattan Weaver
Francis Macomb Wetherill
Herbert Wheeler
Edward Wiener
Edward Shippen Willing
Estelle McGalliard Wolfe
Frances Blue Woodson
Leonie Augusta Tilghman Work
William Lawrence Ross Wurts
Natalie Doughty Wurts
Ethel Denune Young

Living at the time of William the Conqueror was

ILBERT de LACI, whom King William presented with the castle and town of Brokenbridge, co. York, which he afterwards named "Pontfract", and he also possessed other vast territorial grants, at the time of the general survey having nearly 164 lordships. Of his two sons, Robert and Hugh, the elder,

ROBERT de LACIE, also known as Robert de Pontfract, attaching himself to the interest of Robert Curthose after the death of Rufus, he and his son Ilbert were expelled from the realm by King Henry I and the honour of Pontfract bestowed upon Henry Travers. When this Henry was mortally wounded by one of his servants and caused himself to be shorn a monk and so died three days later, the king gave the honour to Guy de la Val, who held it until the time of King Stephen when, it is stated, Robert de Lacie's son Ilbert de Lacie, by the special favour of King Stephen, re-obtained his barony of Pontfract, and was ever afterwards one of the most loyal adherents to that monarch. Ilbert's wife was
Page 186 Alice, daughter of Gilbert de Gant, and upon his death without issue he was succeeded by his brother

HENRY de LACIE, who was received into favor by the Empress and her son King Henry II and had full restitution of Pontfract and all his other lands in England and Normandy. He was succeeded by his son Robert who died without issue in 1193. Henry's sister

I. ALBREDA, called also Aubreye, married Robert (Eudo) son of Fulk de Lisours and had

II. ALBREDA LISOURS, who became the wife of Richard (Robert) FitzEustace, feudal baron of Halton Castle and constable of Chester. She inherited from her first cousin Robert de Lacie the
Page 72 Barony of Pontfract and all his other lands, under pretence of a grant from Henry de Lacie, her uncle. Her son John FitzEustace became heir to the said Robert de Lacie, assuming that surname and inheriting as

III. JOHN de LACIE the Baronies of Halton and Pontfract. He was constable of Chester and his wife Alice was daughter of Geoffrey de Mandeville. Lacie died in the year 1190 while in the Holy Land, and was succeeded by his eldest son

IV. ROGER de LACIE, constable of Chester. Under the banner of Richard the Lionhearted, Roger assisted at the siege of Acon in 1192.

About this time Ranulph, Earl of Chester, having entered Wales at the head of some forces, was compelled to shut himself up in the Castle of Rothelan, and found it necessary to send for aid to Roger, the constable. Hugh Lupus, the 1st Earl of Chester, in his charter of foundation of the abbey of St. Werberg at Chester, had given a privilege to the frequenters of the Chester fair "that they should not be apprehended for theft, or any other offence during the time of the fair, unless the crime was committed therein". Thus the fair was of course made the resort of thieves and vagabonds from all parts of the country. When Roger de Lacie as constable marched to the relief of the Earl, he took with him a great company of people which he had collected at the fair, consisting of minstrels and loose characters of all descriptions, forming altogether so numerous a body that the besiegers of the Castle, at their approach, mistaking them for soldiers, immediately surrendered. For this timely service the Earl of Chester conferred upon Baron Lacie and his heirs, the patronage of all the minstrels in those parts, which patronage the constable transferred to his steward, Dutton, and his heirs. Roger de Lacie died in 1211, leaving by his wife Maud, Page 59 daughter of Richard de Clare, the Surety, see Chapter 5, a son

V. JOHN de LACIE, the Surety, seventh Baron of Halton Castle, and hereditary constable of Chester. He was one of the earliest who took up arms at the time of Magna Charta, and was also appointed to see that the new statutes were properly carried into effect and observed in the counties of York and Nottingham. He was excommunicated by the Pope. Upon the accession of King Henry III he joined a party of noblemen and made a pilgrimage to the Holy Land, and did good service at the Siege of Damietta.

In 1232 he was made Earl of Lincoln and in 1240, governor of Chester and Beeston Castles. He died 22 July 1240, and was buried in the Cistercian Abbey of Stanlaw, in co. Chester. The monk Matthew Paris, records: "On the 22nd of July, in this year (1240), which was St. Magdalen's Day, John, Earl of Lincoln, after suffering from a long illness went the way of all flesh." His first wife was Alice, daughter of Gilbert d'Aquila, but by her had no issue. She died in 1215 and he married, second, after his marked gallantry Page 113 at the siege of Damietta, Margaret, the only daughter and heiress of Robert de Quincey, a fellow crusader, who died in the Holy Land, eldest son of the Surety Saire de Quincey, see Chapter 21. John, Earl of Lincoln, had three children by Lady Margaret, who survived him and was married, second, to Walter Marshal, Earl

Page 67 of Pembroke. Of these the elder daughter 2 Maud was given in marriage to Richard de Clare, sixth Earl of Hertford, as mentioned in Chapter 6; 3 Idonea, the younger daughter was married, first, to Geoffrey de Dutton and, second, to Roger de Camville, see later. Both daughters were in the 27th of King Henry III removed to Windsor Castle there to be educated with the King's own daughters. The son of John de Lacie and his wife Margaret Quincey,

1 EDMUND de LACIE, presumed to be 2nd Earl of Lincoln, died before his mother. His wife was Alice, daughter of the Marquess of Saluces, in Italy, and cousin of the queen. Edmund died in 1257, leaving three children: 12 John, 13 Margaret, who became the wife of George de Cantilupe, Baron of Bergavenny, and

11 HENRY de LACIE, 3rd Earl of Lincoln who, having married Margaret, daughter and co-heiress of William de Longesepee, son of William, Earl of Salisbury, became in right of his wife, Earl of Salisbury. Baron Lacie was one of the most eminent noblemen of the period in which he lived, and was in favour with King Edward I, taking a distinguished part in the Welsh Wars. He took part in the wars of France, Gascony and Scotland, and when King Edward II marched into Scotland, the Earl of Lincoln was constituted governor of England during the King's absence. His death occurred in 1312 "at his mansion house, called Lincoln's Inn, in the suburbs of London, which he himself had erected, in that place, where the Black-friars habitation anciently stood." His only daughter was

111 ALICE LACIE, whose first husband was Thomas Plantagenet, Earl of Lancaster, said to have in her right become Earl of Lincoln. She was married, second, to Eubold le Strange and, third, to Hugh le Frenes. She died without issue in 1348, when the honours of Lincoln and Salisbury became extinct in the family of Lacie.

3 IDONEA LACIE, also called Alice, the second daughter of the Surety John de Lacie, was a minor and ward of King Henry III after the year 1240, and was married to Geoffrey de Dutton, third feudal baron of Nether Tabley manor, and of Warburton manor, Cheshire. They had two sons: 32 Thomas, of whom later, and

31 GEOFFREY de DUTTON, who was his heir and who succeeded to the manors of Nether Tabley, Warburton, Westhale, and other estates. He died in 1277, having been twice married. By his first wife, whose name has not been preserved, he had a daughter

311 MARGARET DUTTON who, when she became the wife of Robert de Denbeigh about the year 1270/1, received a portion of Nether Tabley manor and the whole of the manor of Westhale. Her husband died without issue in 1276 and the following year she became the wife of Nicholas de Leycester, a knight and steward, to Henry, 3rd Earl of Lincoln. He died about the year 1295. They were the parents of

311 1 ROGER de LEYCESTER, who was lord of Nether Tabley and Westhale manors. In 1296 he obtained the release for the balance of Nether Tabley from his uncle, Peter de Dutton. He made his home at Westhale manor house, where he died 1349/50. He was apparently married twice and had either by wife "Joyce" or by wife "Isabel," a son

311 11 NICHOLAS de LEYCESTER, his heir, who was feudal lord or Baron by tenure of the manors of Nether Tabley, Westhale, Heile and others, in Cheshire. He died about the year 1352, having married about 1322, Mary, daughter of William de Mobberley of Cheshire. Issue.

The second son of Geoffrey de Dutton and his wife 3 Idonea Lacie, was

32 THOMAS de DUTTON, of Clayton, and lord of Thelwell and other manors. He was the father of

321 RANDLE DUTTON de CLAYTON, lord of Thelwell, Clayton and other manors. He had

321 1 HENRY de CLAYTON, lord of Clayton and Thelwell manors, who died after 1348 and left a son

321 11 THOMAS de CLAYTON, lord of Clayton and Thelwell manors, who died in 1426. Issue.

(To be continued) Page 357

LANVALLEI

Chapter 13

William de Lanvallei

A Surety for Magna Charta

Arms: Gules, a lion passant or

The following persons may claim descent from Baron Lanvallei and King Duncan: Pages 191, 359

Jeannette Tillotson Acklen
George Garland Allen
Marie d'Arcy Logan Todd Appleton
Helen Moore Falkner Arndt
Lulu Gray Auld
Alethea Burroughs Avery
Alice Crane Bigelow
Dorothy Phillips Booth
Florence Broughton Morey Brown
Carrick Hume Buck
Elizabeth Millar Bullard
William Aylett Callaway
Francis Dayton Canfield
Agnes Atkinson Mayo Carter
Charles Robert Churchill
Curtis Livingston Clay
Martin Withington Clement
Evelyn Joynes Coit
Eliza Robinson Coleman
Esther Stevenson Nicholas Cooper
Mabel Julia Curtiss
Elizabeth Daniel
Josephine Kern Dodge
Sallie Hume Douglas
Louise Crittenden Earll
Mabel Bayard Kane Fox
Emily Finch Gilbert
Clara Gordon
Frank Samuel Grandin
Helen Spottswood Turner Henderson
Wallace McLauren Henry
Lucien Beverley Howry
Edgar Erskine Hume
Jessamine Spear Johnson
Catherine Lindsay Smith Knorr
Charlotte Augusta Brown Lea
Clara Gladys Leonard Lednum
Edna Ruth Trapp Starling
Catherine Mumford Lennig
Mary Thomas Burkhalter Little
William Filler Lutz
Barbara Ann Mangam
Jennie Marie Webster Mangam
Bertha Smith Marsh
Margaret Giltner Jones Merchant
Josephine Adams Perry Morgan
Isabel Wurts Page
Katharine Wright Dunn Pagon
Celestine Page Bowie Pepper
Minnie Livingston Radcliffe
Almira Chandler Williams Rich
Mildred Handy Ritchie
Marion Morgan Richardson Robertson
Henrietta Strong Wurts Ruxton
Mary Lane Landis Scott
George Grant Snowden
Jennie Laura Heath Stoll
Joseph Clifford Taylor
Charles Wickliffe Throckmorton
Harriette Bailey Norton Tilton
Josephine Mason Torrence
Joseph B. Townsend
The Princess Troubetzkoy
Florence Van Rensselaer
Ella Elizabeth Dimmick Walters
Helen Carpenter Washburn
Anne Madison Washington
Charles Willing
Anne VanMeter Wilson
Elizabeth Browning Donner Winsor
Edward Randolph Wood
Gertrude Houston Woodward
Lionel Wurts
Thomas Howe Childs Wurts
Ethel Denune Young

William de Lanvallei, died 1211, married Hawise and had

★ WILLIAM de LANVALLEI, the Surety, was governor of Colchester Castle in 1215, when he joined with the Barons. In 1212, Alan Basset of Wycombe, in Bucks, father of Philip Basset, Chief Justice of England, who is named in Magna Charta as one of the king's liegemen, gave the king two hundred marks and "an excellent palfrey" that his daughter Hawise might be married to William de Lanvallei. He died in 1217. They had an only daughter

1 HAWISE LANVALLEI, died in 1249, who became the wife of John de Burgh, son of Beatrix Warren and her husband Hubert de

Burgh, one of the most eminent and conspicuous nobles of his time. John and his wife Hawise were the parents of

11 JOHN de BURGH, who married Cecily Baliol. He died in the 8th of King Edward I, leaving the extensive manors and estates which he inherited from his father and mother to his daughters one of whom was 111 Devorgille, first wife of Robert FitzWalter, see Chapter 8; another was 112 Hawise, who became the wife of Robert Greslei, see later; and the third was

113 MARGARET BURGH, married 27 February 1280/81 to Richard de Burgh, Earl of Ulster, who was born in 1259 and died 29 July 1326. She died about the year 1303. He was the son of Walter de Burgh, Earl of Ulster, who died 28 July 1271, and his wife Aveline (Fitz John) FitzGeoffrey, died about 20 May 1274, and was buried at Dunmow Priory, the daughter of John FitzGeoffrey and Isabel Bigod his wife, see Chapter 3. Of the children of Richard de Burgh and his wife Margaret Burgh, 113 1 Elizabeth Burgh, became the wife of Robert Bruce, see Chapter 6; 113 2 Joan Burgh, was married first to Thomas FitzGerald, 2nd Earl of Kildare and had 113 21 Maurice FitzGerald, 4th Earl of Kildare, who died in 1390. Issue. Joan's second husband was John, Baron Darcy, and she was his second wife. When King Edward III ascended the throne, Darcy was appointed sheriff of Yorkshire, governor of the Castle at York and re-constituted Justice of Ireland, to which latter post, with the government of the country, he was re-appointed the following year. He was for a time constable of the Tower of London and steward of the king's household. In the 11th of King Edward III he was accredited ambassador to the courts of France and Scotland. He attained honors at the Battle of Crecy. King Edward III finally appointed him Justice of Ireland and constable of the Tower for life. By his first wife, Emeline, daughter and coheiress of Walter Heron, Darcy had a son and heir John Darcy, husband of Elizabeth Meinill, and by his second wife, Joan Burgh, he had beside a son 113 22 William, a daughter

Page 65

Page 193

113 23 ELIZABETH DARCY, who became the wife of James (Butler) 2nd Earl of Ormonde, called "The Noble Earl," because of his being the great-grandson of King Edward I. He was appointed Lord Justice of Ireland. He was the son of James, first Earl of Ormonde and his wife Eleanor Bohun, see Chapter 4. Issue.

Page 56

113 3 ELEANOR BURGH, third daughter of Richard de Burgh and his wife 113 Margaret Burgh, was married to Thomas de

Multon who died in 1321. Beside a son 113 31 John, they had three daughters, 113 32 Elizabeth, wife of Walter de Bermichan; 113 33 Margaret, wife of Thomas de Lucy; and 113 34 Joan, who was married to Robert FitzWalter, see Chapter 8. Page 78

113 6 KATHERINE BURGH, daughter of Richard de Burgh and his wife Margaret, was married to Morice FitzThomas, see Chapter 21. Page 117

Richard de Burgh and his wife 113 Margaret Burgh had beside their daughters, two sons, 113 4 Walter and 113 5 John. Of these

113 4 WALTER de BURGH died without male issue in the year 1302, leaving a daughter

113 41 AGATHA BURGH, who was married to John de Grenville, and they had a daughter

113 411 NICHOLA GRENVILLE, wife of Reginald de Hampton. Issue. Among their descendants was William Shakespeare.

113 5 JOHN de BURGH, the other son of Richard de Burgh and his wife 113 Margaret Burgh, married Elizabeth Clare, a descendant of the Sureties Richard and Gilbert de Clare, see Chapter 6. Page 70 He was Earl of Ulster and Baron of Connaught and of Trim, dying at Galway 18 June 1313. Elizabeth, his wife, was born at Tewksbury 16 September 1295 and died 4 November 1360. They were married at Waltham Abbey 30 September 1308, and were the parents of

113 51 WILLIAM de BURGH, Earl of Ulster, Baron of Connaught and Trim, who was murdered by his own followers in 1333. His wife Maud, was the daughter of Henry, Earl of Lancaster, see Chapter 31. Page 203

112 HAWISE BURGH, daughter of John de Burgh and his wife Cecily Baliol, was married to Robert Greslei. He was made Baron de Greslei of Ringston and died in the year 1283, being succeeded by his son 112 1 Thomas, who died without issue in 1347 and the estates were then inherited by his sister,

112 2 JOAN GRESLEI, who became the wife of John, Baron de la Warre, K. C. B. son of Roger. In the 20th of King Edward III John was in the van of the Black Prince at the Battle of Crecy. His death occurred in 1347. Issue.

(To be continued) Page 359

MALET

Chapter 14

William Malet

A Surety for Magna Charta

Arms: Gules, a lion rampant or, debruised with a bendlet ermine

This Malet lineage agrees with that given in "The Genealogist's Magazine" for June 1939 and is a revision of the line as set forth by Turton (1928) and by Crispin (1938).

See also Pedigree L, page 425.

The following persons may claim descent from Baron Malet and King Clovis:
Pages 206, 363

Charles Biddle Atlee
Leila Perone Austin
Daisy Scott Ball
Mary Rogers Lyons Brown
Charles Shepard Bryan
Patrick Henry Callaway
Esther Maria Lewis Chapin
Elizabeth Livingston Steele Childs
Emma Josephine Armitage Cory
Mary Gwynne Anderson Crocker
Joey Denton
Mary Malvina Pettis Dille
Helen Peterson Greene Dodge
Jane Blanche Hammitt Dolan
Hiram Kennedy Douglass
Sara Sullivan Ervin
Annie Ball Field
Lucile James Coleman Forsythe
Ethel Bell Goodell Freeman
Mae Jewett Frye
Errol C. Gilkey
Frances Gordon-Smith
Esther Miller Fleming Graham
Mary Gloster Graham
Genevieve Sprigg Ludlow Griscom
Margaret Ridgway Grundy
Frances Russell Tyng Harrison
Charles Wolcott Henry
Mary Elizabeth Hewett
John Woodman Higgins
Ella Willard Higgons
Grace Annie Hill
Hazel Kirk Stocker Hoggett
Ethel Elaine Holton
Hilton Ira Jones
Waldine Zimpleman Kopperl
Elizabeth Cunningham Leupold
Lucile Cary Lowry
George Craghead Gregory
Belle Clay Lyons
Charles Harrison Mann
Edna Haynes McCormick
Margaret Giltner Jones Merchant
Florence Thiot Milner
Lora Parsons Moore
Ellen Harwood Rich Morton
Howard Ross Nelson
Charlotte Neal Pettigrew
Grace Edna Vollnogle Phillips
Mary Emma Leach Safford
Ella May Schermerhorn
Mary Lane Landis Scott
Harriet Letitia Valentine Selden
Grace Greenwood Cochran Sherard
Lillian Whiting Shirer
Mellcene Thurman Smith
Lucy Neville Mitchell Smith
Margaret Fisher Sullivan
Malvina May Scott Sykes
Margaret Hale Thomas
Louise Akerly Floyd-Jones Thorn
Prudence Sharpless Doyle Vollnogle
Myrtle Daspit Warrington
George Augustine Washington
Glenn Hylton Wayne
Alice Tracy Welch
John Wells
Arthur Rindge Wendell
Avis Stanbury Newcombe Fairbanks
Bertha R. Wiggin
Charlotte Lansing Parker Wilson
Leila Morse Wilson
Lottie Gertrude Woods
Annie Smith Wright
Pierre Jay Wurts
Ethel Denune Young
Irene Taggart Young

The earliest recorded paternal ancestor of this Surety was

I. WILLIAM, LORD MALET, a Norman Baron, one of the generals and companions of William the Conqueror, said to have been the brother of King Harold's wife, and to have been entrusted with the guard of Harold's body after he had been slain on the battlefield. After the conquest he was made governor of York Castle and was slain in its defense about 1071. His wife was Hesilia Crispin, by whom he had two sons and a daughter Beatrice. One son was Robert, the other Gilbert. In a deed which Gilbert witnessed Beatrice gave the village of Rending Fieldam to the monks of St. Peter of Eye. Her husband was William de Arches. Robert, Lord Malet, son of William, was great chamberlain of England under King Henry I. He was also Lord of Eye in Suffolk, and was banished and disinherited, and William's other son

II. GILBERT MALET, left a son

III. ROBERT MALET, who before 1130 acquired the barony of Curry Malet in co. Somerset. He died before 1155, leaving a son

IV. WILLIAM MALET, baron of Curry Malet, who had other estates as well, in Sussex, Surrey, Kent and Suffolk. He was steward to King Henry II and died in 1169/70. His son

V. GILBERT MALET, was also steward to King Henry II and baron of Curry Malet. His wife was Alice, daughter of Ralph Picot, sheriff of Kent and they had, with other sons,

★ VI. WILLIAM MALET, the Surety, who was mentioned in 1194 as a minor, in connection with an expedition made that year into Normandy. His principal estate was Curry-Malet. From 1210 to 1214 he was sheriff of the counties of Somerset and Dorset. When he joined with the Barons against King John and became one of the Sureties his lands in four counties were confiscated and given to his son in law Hugh de Vivonia, and to his father in law Thomas Basset, and Malet was excommunicated by the Pope in 1216. He was also fined two thousand marks, but this remained unpaid until after his death, and at that time one thousand marks were remitted, being found due to him for military service to King John in Poitou. It is interesting to note that there were five contemporary relatives named William Malet, and they all held lands in England or in Jersey. He died about 1217, having married Mabel, also called Alice, daughter of Thomas Basset of Headington. She survived him and was married, second, to John Biset. The Surety had two sons who died during their father's lifetime, 1 Hugh, whose descendants did not survive; 2 William, who d.s.p.; and three daughters: 3 Mabel, wife of Hugh de Vivonia, see later; 5 Bertha, who never married, and

4 HAWISE MALET who was married, first, to Hugh de Poyntz, who died 4 April 1220 and their son 41 Nicholas de Poyntz died in 1272. Hawise's second husband was Robert de Muscegros, of Berwain and Norton. He died 29 January 1253/4. Beside a daughter 42 Mabel, Lady of Finborough, who was living 17 May 1271, Robert and his wife Hawise had a son

43 JOHN de MUSCEGROS, born 10 August 1232, died 8 May 1275, of Charlton, Norton, and other estates, who married Cecily, Lady of Bicknor, Taynton and Longford, died 10 August 1301, daughter of William Avenel of Bicknor, born about November 1202, died 21 April 1236, and his wife Aline, living at the time of her husband's death. John and Cecily were the parents of

431 ROBERT de MUSCEGROS, aged 23 and more in 1275. He was also of Charlton and Norton, and died 27 December 1280. His wife Agnes was living 9 May 1281. Their daughter

431 1 HAWISE MUSCEGROS, was born 21 December 1276, and was living as late as 24 June 1340. Her first husband, William de Mortemer of Bridgewater died without issue 30 June 1297. She Page 117 was married, second, to John de Ferrers born at Cardiff 20 June 1271, died 1324, of Southoe and Keyston, son of Robert de Ferrers, died 1279, a descendant of the Surety Saire de Quincey, see Chapter 21; and his wife Agnes Bohun also called Alianore, Page 54 a descendant of the Surety Henry de Bohun, see Chapter 4. For her third husband, Hawise was married to Sir John de Bures, who died at Boddington 22 December 1350, leaving a daughter

431 11 KATHERINE BURES, Lady of Boddington and Longford, aged 35 and more in 1350/1 and living in October 1355. Before 21 May 1329 she was married to Giles de Beauchamp of Powick, who died 12 October 1361. Issue.

3 MABEL MALET, the other daughter of the Surety William Malet and his wife Alice Basset, became the wife of Hugh de Vivonia, baron of Chewton and steward of Poitou, who held West Kington in 1214. Of their children, were 31 John, who died without issue in 1314; 32 William, who married Maud Ferrers, see later; and

33 HELEWYSE VIVONIA, who was married to Walter de Wahull, son of Saiher de Wahull, who died in 1250. His death occurred in 1269, when he was succeeded by his son

Chapter 14

331 JOHN de WAHULL, who became of age in 1269. In the 22nd of King Edward I, he had a military summons to march into Gascony and later had a similar summons to march against the Welsh, but within two years he died, in 1295. His wife was Agnes, daughter of Sir Henry Pinckeney, of Weldon Pinckeney. Their son was

331 1 THOMAS de WAHULL, who had the manors of Wahull, co. Bedford, and Pateshill, co. Northampton when he died in 1304. By his wife Hawise, daughter of Henry Praers, he left a son and heir

331 11 JOHN de WAHULL an infant at the time of his father's death. He married Isabella and died in the 10th of King Edward III. Their elder son, 331 111 John's, line ended with his two granddaughters, 311 111 11 Elizabeth and 331 111 12 Eleanor, who died without leaving issue. Their youngest son was

331 112 NICHOLAS de WAHULL, who married Margaret, daughter and heiress of John Foxcote, and died in the 12th of King Henry IV. Beside a son 331 112 2 Richard and daughters 331 112 3 Edith and 331 112 4 Margaret, Nicholas and his wife, Margaret, had an elder son and heir

331 112 1 THOMAS de WAHULL, who died in the 9th of King Henry V, having married Elizabeth, sister and heiress of Thomas Chetwode, and had two sons: 331 112 11 Thomas and 331 112 12 William. Issue.

32 WILLIAM de VIVONIA de FORTIBUS, son of Mabel Malet and her husband Hugh de Vivonia, married Maud Ferrers, and had four daughters: 321 Sybil, wife of Guy de Roche Chinard; 322 Mabel, wife of Fulk de L'Orty; 323 Joan, married to Reynold FitzPiers, see later; and

324 CECILY, heiress to her cousin John. She was married to John de Beauchamp who died in 1283. In the 5th of King Edward I he was made governor of the Castles of Caermerdin and Cardigan. They had a son

324 1 JOHN de BEAUCHAMP. He took part in the wars of Scotland and soon after, in the 14th of King Edward II, he succeeded to the very extensive landed possessions of his mother, in cos. Dorset, Wilts, Surrey and Cambridge. Two years afterward he

was made governor of the Castle of Bridgewater. He died in the year 1336, and was succeeded by his son

324 11 JOHN de BEAUCHAMP, 2nd Lord Beauchamp of Hacche. He died in 1343, having taken part in the French wars of King Edward III. Issue.

323 JOAN VIVONIA, daughter of William de Vivonia, and wife of Reynold de FitzPiers, died before 1314, some time after her husband, leaving several children, among whom was 323 1 John FitzReynold, the ancestor of the FitzHerberts; 323 2 Peter FitzReynold, who was born about 1275 and died in 1323. As heir to his cousin John de Vivonia he held half of West Kington, as did his aunt Cecily, wife of John de Beauchamp. He and his wife Ela were the parents of 323 21 Roger FitzPeter, called also Roger Martel. Issue.

Reynold FitzPiers and his wife 323 Joan Vivonia had also a daughter:

323 3 ELEANOR FITZPIERS, who became the wife of William Martin. He fought in the Scottish wars and was summoned to parliament as a Baron from 23 June 1295 to 10 October 1325. Of the children of William Martin and his wife Eleanor, only one daughter left issue:

323 31 JOAN MARTIN who, as widow of Henry de Lacie, Earl of Lincoln, was married without license, in 1312, to Nicholas Audley of Heleigh, co. Stafford, born 11 November 1289. He died in 1316, shortly before 9 December, at the age of 27 years. His widow died before 1 August 1322. Issue.

(To be continued) Page 363

MANDEVILLE

Chapter 15

Geoffrey de Mandeville

A Surety for Magna Charta

No issue

Arms: Quarterly, or and gules, an escarbuncle sable

Living at the time of William the Conqueror was

I. GEOFFREY de MAGNAVILLA, who obtained as his share of the spoils of the Norman conquest many valuable manors in a dozen English counties, and seated himself at Waldene. He was made constable of the Tower of London for life.

II. WILLIAM de MANDEVILLE, Keeper of the Tower of London, died 1130, married Margaret, daughter of Eudo de Rie, dapifer (steward) to King William, and had Geoffrey and

III. BEATRIX MANDEVILLE, who was married, first, to Lord Hugh de Talbot, from whom she was divorced, and second, to Lord
Page 125 William de Saye. They had Geoffrey de Saye, father of the Surety of that name, see Chapter 23, and

IIII. WILLIAM de SAYE, eldest son, who died in his father's lifetime leaving two daughters: Maud (wife of William de Borland) and

Page 52 V. BEATRIX SAYE, who was married (as his first wife) to Geoffrey FitzPiers, or Peter, who became Baron Mandeville, in right of his wife. He was made justiciar of England by King Richard, and created 27 May 1199 Earl of Essex by King John, dying 14 October 1213. He had a daughter Maud, wife of Henry de Bohun, the Surety, see Chapter 4, a son William de Mandeville, Earl of Essex, and their other son was

★ VI. GEOFFREY de MANDEVILLE, the Surety. Upon the payment to King John of twenty thousand marks, he obtained in 1214, license to marry Avisa, or Isabella, daughter of William, Count of Meullent, which lady had first been the wife of King John himself, but was repudiated in 1200 on account of consanguinity, both being great-grandchildren of King Henry I.

Her second husband, having died two years after their marriage, Isabella was promised in marriage to Hubert de Burgh, but this was not accomplished and she died without issue. In right of his wife, Geoffrey de Mandeville became Earl of Gloucester, and was placed in full possession of all the liberties belonging to this earldom, and the lordship of Glamorgan, in Wales. He was one of the wealthiest of the barons opposed to King John, and for adhering to them he was excommunicated, but lived only a short time, as in February

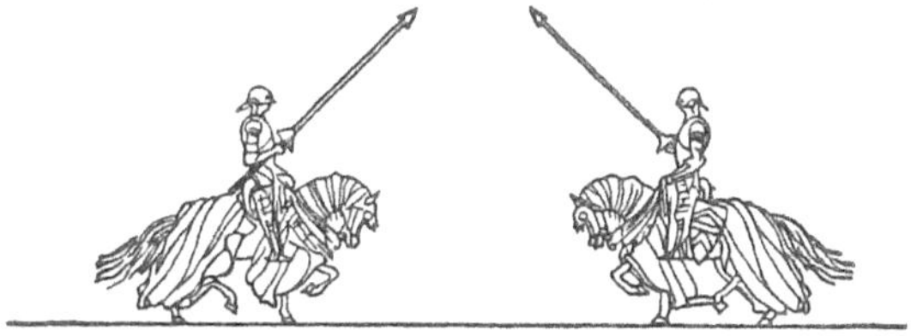

1216, he was mortally wounded at a tournament in London and, dying on the 23rd, without issue, was interred in the priory of the Holy Trinity, in the suburbs of the city. He was succeeded by his brother, William de Mandeville, who also took the part of the barons, and maintained it even after the death of King John, being one of those who then assisted Louis of France in the siege of Berkhamstead Castle, occupied by the King's forces. William died without issue 8 January 1227, when the earldom of Essex devolved upon his sister, Maud Bohun, Countess of Hereford, while the lands which he inherited passed to his half brother, John FitzGeoffrey whose wife was Isabel Bigod, widow of Gilbert de Lacy and daughter of Hugh Bigod, the Surety, see Chapter 3. Page 48

MARSHALL

Chapter 16

William Marshall

A Surety for Magna Charta

No issue

Arms: Party per pale or and vert, a lion rampant gules, armed and langued azure.

See also Pedigrees F and Q, pages 422 and 428.

I. GILBERT le MARESCHAL, earliest recorded paternal ancestor of this Surety, died about 1130, leaving a son

II. JOHN MARESCHAL, who died 1164, having married Sibilla, daughter of Walter d'Enreux, and his wife Sibilla Chaworth. Their son was

III. WILLIAM MARSHALL, the famous Lord Pembroke, regent and protector of the kingdom, who was born before 1153, died 14 May 1219 and married in August 1189, Isabel, second cousin of Richard de Clare the Surety and daughter of Richard de Clare, Earl of Pembroke called "Strongbow." Earl William was constable of Chichester Castle and sheriff of Gloucestershire. Their son

★ IV. WILLIAM MARSHALL, the Surety, was sometimes as strenuous a supporter of the baronial cause as his father was of the royal interests; consequently he was excommunicated by the Pope. When the Dauphin came to London, he was one of the prominent men who recognized him as King of England. Upon the death of King John, the protector procured the consent of the barons to the coronation of young Henry, requiring the allegiance of the barons, including his own son, William. In 1223/4 he returned from Ireland and gained a great victory over Prince Llewellyn and the Welsh, who had taken in his absence two of his castles, and was made governor of the Castles of Caerdigan and Caermarthen, and in 1230, captain-general of all the king's forces in Bretagne. William Marshall succeeded as the second Earl of Pembroke, and died 24 April 1231, very wealthy but he had no issue by either of his two Page 82 wives: (1) Alice, step-daughter of Baldwin de Bethune, and (2) Princess Alianore Plantagenet, who survived him, a daughter of King John, whom he married 23 April 1224. He was buried near his father, in the Knights' New Temple, London, where his tomb may be seen. Of Earl William's five sisters:

1. Sibilla Marshall, was married as in Chapter 21, to William de Ferrers, Earl of Derby. Issue. Page 114

2. Maud Marshall, was married, as in Chapter 3, to Hugh Bigod, the Surety. Issue. Page 47

3. Isabella Marshall, was married as in Chapter 6, to Gilbert de Clare, the Surety. Issue. Page 62

4. Eve Marshall, died 1246, was married to William, sixth Baron Braos, of Brecknock Castle. Issue. Page 53

5. Joan Marshall, died 1247, was married to Warine, lord of Montchensi. Their daughter, Joan, married William le Brune, Count of Valence, created Earl of Pembroke in 1264. Issue.

See also Pedigree F, page 422.

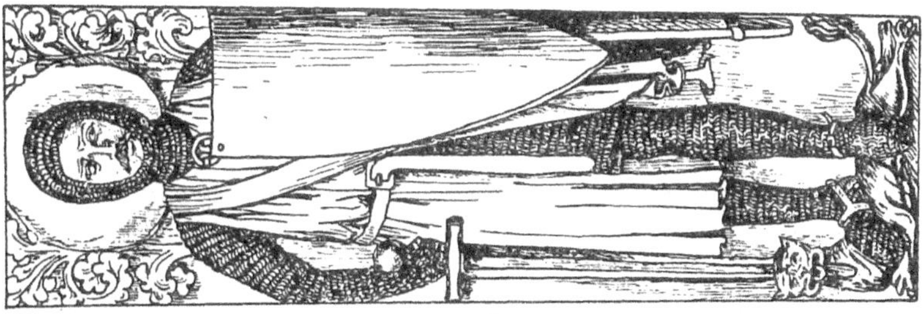

TOMB OF WILLIAM MARSHALL THE PROTECTOR, TEMPLE CHURCH, LONDON

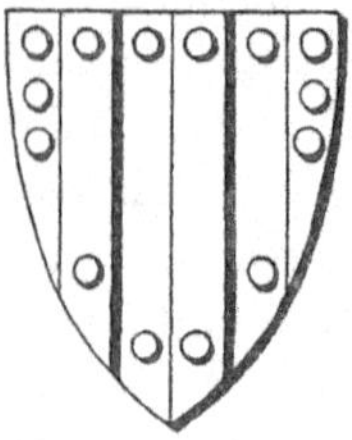

MONTBEGON

Chapter 17

Roger de Montbegon

A Surety for Magna Charta

No Issue

Arms: Paly of six, argent and gules, fourteen roundles in orle, countercharged.

★ ROGER de MONTBEGON, the Surety, was the successor of Adam de Monte Begonis, whose principal lands were in Lincolnshire, and he was apparently the son of this Adam, by his wife, Maud FitzSwaine. During the imprisonment of Richard I in Germany, Roger de Montbegon seems to have favored Prince John's designs on the throne, since he was one of those who held out the castle of Nottingham against the Bishop of Durham, but when the king on his return advanced to besiege that fortress, he came out and submitted himself, without firing an arrow. In the barons' proceedings to procure the Charter of Liberty from King John, he took a prominent part and was one of the parties to the covenant for surrendering the city and Tower of London into the hands of the barons, although several lordships were granted or confirmed to him by King John as late as 1215/16. There is however, no reason to doubt his original loyalty to the cause of the barons, for when he took up arms against the king, his possessions were seized and given to Oliver d'Albini, while he himself was excommunicated, with the other barons, by the Pope. Roger de Montbegon died in 1225/6, having had no issue by his wife Olivia whom he married about 1200, widow of Robert St. John. When he died, his Castle of Horneby, in Lancashire, was given by the king to John de Warren, Earl of Surrey; but Henry de Montbegon, being found heir to Roger, recovered it. Roger deserted the barons, nevertheless, before Magna Charta was confirmed a year, and Roger de Mowbray was substituted
Page 107 for him among the Sureties. He was a younger brother of the Surety William de Mowbray, see Chapter 19, and died in 1217/18 not having married, when his elder brother, William, succeeded to his estate. The armorial ensigns of Roger de Mowbray are extant in the south aisle of Westminster Abbey, as he was one of its benefactors.

MONTFICHET

Chapter 18

Richard de Montfichet

A Surety for Magna Charta

No Issue

Arms: Gules, three chevrons, or

I. RICHARD de MONTFICHET, royal forester of Essex, and keeper of the king's houses at Havering and elsewhere in the forests, or royal preserves, of Essex, died in the 5th of King John, leaving a son

II. RICHARD de MONTFICHET, the Surety, who was under age at the time of his father's death, and his wardship was committed to Roger de Lacie, constable of Chester. As he did not become of age until the spring of 1215, his first public act appears to have been that of joining the baronial party in arms against the king. The next year he went with the Surety, *Robert FitzWalter, into France to solicit aid, and continued one of the most enthusiastic of the barons until he was taken prisoner at Lincoln. Even after he was released he attended a tournament of the barons at Blithe, in the 7th of King Henry III, contrary to the king's, that is, the protector's prohibition, for which his lands were seized. He later made peace with the king and was, in 1236/7, constituted justice of the king's forests or game parks, in nineteen counties of England, and in 1241/2 was made sheriff of Essex and governor of Hertford Castle. He appears to have been the last survivor of the Sureties. Page 31

Richard de Montfichet died without issue never having married, and after 1258 his lands were divided among his three sisters, one of whom was Aveline, wife of William de Fortibus, the Magna Charta Surety, see Chapter 9. Page 83

MOWBRAY

Chapter 19

William de Mowbray

A Surety for Magna Charta

Arms: Gules, a lion rampant, argent

The following persons may claim descent from Baron Mowbray and King Louis II:

Annie Lee Steele Adams
Marjorie K. Gilmour Allison
Philip Meredith Allen
Alice Simms Anderson
Franklin Bache
Matilda Phillips Jones Badger
Martha Jane Barnett
Elizabeth Smith Beaty
Anna Randolph Wurts Bissell
Oswald Chew
Annie Hill Childs
Harrison Conaway
Ross K. Cook
Esther Stevenson Nicholas Cooper
Luretta Brigham Crissey
Anna Mosier Day
E. Carter Delano
The Countess de Trampe
Thomas Munroe Dobbins
Charles W. Fairfax
Berthania Elizabeth Weatherby Flick
Mary Large Fox
Cora Viola Bailey Harper
John Scott Harrison, 4th
Anna Howell Lloyd Hayward
Helen Spottswood Turner Henderson
Juliet Field Heyl
Samuel Frederic Houston
Mary Hannah Stoddard Johnston
Mary Kingsbury Shackford Johnston
Emma Foote Kirk
Florence Calvert Kuhn
Amy Elizabeth Mason Lansing
Helen Bixby Smith McClinton
Ella Friend Mielziner
Meribah Irwin Stearns Moore
Edna Ruth Trapp Starling
Susan Elizabeth McCoy Myers
Gene Wellington Nelson
Howard Ross Nelson
Edith Crozier Packer
Harriet Church Rhodes
William H. Ridgway
Ruth Bent Sapp
Helen Isabel Chickering Scott
Edwin Van Dusen Selden
Bertha Davis Separk
Sarah Billings Smith Seydel
William Dusenbery Sherrerd
Joseph Grundy Shryock
Mary Miller Smiser
Mary Carmally Spalding
Rachel Cooper Reeve Spear
Mary Bogert Steward
Paul Stinchfield
Candace Richey Strawn
Carolina V. Sudler
Blanche Emily Schutt Torreyson
Trabue Van Culin
Ellen Isham Schutt Wallis
Constance Key Wandel
Simons Vander Horst Waring, Jr.
Francis Ryland Washington
Mabel Minerva Dalrymple Waters
Elsie Webber
Mary Elizabeth Webber
Herbert Wheeler
Purl Parker Wightman
May Kirby Williamson
George Edward Wilson
Susan Lillard Witherspoon
Robert Kennedy Wurts
Ethel Denune Young

I. NELE d' AUBIGNY, younger son of Roger and brother of William, came into England with William the Conqueror and obtained several lordships after the battle at Hastings. After the battle of Tenercheby in 1106 the King granted him the English lands of

Robert de Stuteville. During the Norman rebellion Nele, with his brother William, remained faithful to King Henry I and fought for him at the victory over the French King at Bremule on 20 August 1119. He had a grant of Montbrai or Mowbray and the other forfeited lands in Normandy of Robert de Mowbray, Earl of Northumberland, whose former wife Maud he married after 1107, but had no issue. She was the daughter of Richard de Laigle, second baron d'Aquila. He married, second, in June 1118, Gundred, sister of Hugh and daughter of Gerard de Gourney, who died 1096, and his wife Edith, daughter of William, first Earl of Surrey. Nele d'Aubigny died about 26 November 1129 and by his second wife left a son

II. ROGER de MOWBRAY, a minor at his father's death, eldest son who, succeeding to the lands of Mumbray or Mowbray, thus came to be known by the surname de Mowbray. In 1138, though still young, he took part in the expedition against the Scots which culminated in the battle of the Standard. At the battle of Lincoln in Feb. 1140/1 he fought for Stephen and was taken prisoner. In 1147 he took part in the second Crusade. At about Easter 1186, again as a Crusader, he arrived in Jerusalem. In the battle of Hittin, 4 July 1187, he was taken prisoner and the following year was ransomed by the Templars, but died 1188, in Palestine or on the way home. His wife was Alice, widow of Ilbert de Lacy, and they had

III. NELE de MOWBRAY, second baron, who was present at the council of Clarendon in January 1163/4, and who joined with his father in the rebellion of 1173. In the 3rd of King Richard I he assumed the cross and set out for Palestine but, while on the journey, died at Acre in 1191.

He married before March 1170, Mabel who died about 1203. They had (beside Roger de Mowbray the Substitute Surety, page 104) another son

★ IV. WILLIAM de MOWBRAY, the Surety, who became of age in 1194/5. He was early embittered against King John by being compelled by him to surrender the barony of Frontboeuf, which Henry I had conferred upon his great-grandfather, Sir Nigel d'Aubigny. This was probably because Mowbray, upon the accession of King John was tardy in pledging his allegiance, and at length only swore fealty upon condition that "the king should render to every man his right." At the breaking out of the baronial war he was governor of York Castle, and it is not surprising that he at once sided with the barons against King John, and was one of the most forward of them.

He was a party to the "Covenant for holding the city and Tower of London," and one of those whom the Pope excommunicated. He continued in arms after the death of King John, and in the battle of Lincoln was taken prisoner, when his lands were confiscated and bestowed upon William Marshall, Jr., the Surety, but he was subsequently allowed to redeem them. After this he attached himself to King Henry III. He died in 1223/24, at his castle in the Isle of Axholme, and was buried in the Abbey of Newburgh in Yorkshire. He married Avice d'Albini, and their children were 1 Nigel, 2 Roger and 3 Joan. Of these

3 JOAN MOWBRAY, in 1257/8 became the second wife of John de Warren, Earl of Surrey, who had children only by his first wife, Alice le Brun, see Chapter 31. Page 205

1 NIGEL de MOWBRAY married Maud, died before 6 October 1240, the daughter of Roger de Camvil, but they had no children and dying in 1228, he was succeeded by his brother

2 ROGER de MOWBRAY, a minor at the time of his brother's death. He received several military summonses to attend King Henry III into Scotland and Wales. He married Maud, daughter of William de Beauchamp of Bedford and died in 1266. His widow died before April 1273, having become the wife of Roger le Strange. They had a son 21 Roger, see later; and a daughter

22 ELIZABETH MOWBRAY, wife of Adam de Newmarch who joined the baronial standard in the time of King Henry III and was summoned to Parliament as a Baron after the Battle of Lewes by the lords who at that time usurped the government. He was later made a prisoner and compounded for his estates under the Dictum of Kenilworth. Issue.

21 ROGER de MOWBRAY the son of Roger de Mowbray and his wife Maud Beauchamp, took part in the wars of Wales and Gascony. His wife was Rose Clare, also known as Agnes, a de-
Page 62 scendant of the Sureties Richard and Gilbert de Clare, see Chapter 6. Lord Roger died in 1298, leaving two sons: 211 Alexander who went to Scotland, and

212 JOHN de MOWBRAY, 2nd Baron Mowbray, who while yet a minor was actively engaged in the wars of Scotland and in consideration of these services he was given all his lands before he became of age. Being sheriff of Yorkshire and governor of the City of York in the 6th of King Edward II, he was then commanded to seize upon Henry dePercy, a great Baron of the north, because Percy had allowed Piers de Gaveston, Earl of Cornwall, to escape from Scarborough Castle, when he had undertaken to keep him in safety. When he took part in the insurrection of Thomas, Earl of Lancaster, he was with him and others imprisoned at the Battle of Boroughbridge, and immediately hanged at York, in the year 1321, when his lands were seized by the crown, and Aliva, his widow, Page 60 with her son, were imprisoned in the Tower of London. She was the daughter of William de Braos and his wife Aliva Multon and had property in her own right, some of which she conferred upon Hugh le Despencer, Earl of Winchester, in order to relieve her desperate situation. For her second husband Lady Mowbray was married to one de Peshale, Knight, and she died in the 5th of King Edward III. Her son

212 1 JOHN de MOWBRAY, became 3rd Baron and was in great favour with King Edward III, being his constant companion in arms through the years, the king having given him his lands before he was of full age, in recognition of the splendid services rendered by his predecessors. Mowbray assisted at the siege of Nantes and the raising of the siege of Aguillon. In the 20th of King Edward III he was at the Battle of Durham, and he was for a time governor of Berwick-upon-Tweed. His first wife was Joan, daughter Page 203 of Henry, Earl of Lancaster, see Chapter 31. They had a son John who succeeded, and a daughter 212 12 Alianore, who became the third wife of Roger, Lord la Warre, born 1326, died 1370. Alianore has been presumed to have been the daughter of her brother John de Mowbray, but this pedigree has been amended. Issue.

(To be continued)

Page 367

PERCY

Chapter 20

Richard de Percy

A Surety for Magna Charta

No Issue

Arms: Or, a lion rampant azure

GEFFRY, Signeur de Percie of Lower Normandy, was the father of

See also Pedigree J, page 424.

I. WILLIAM de PERCIE, who accompanied William the Conqueror into England in 1066, was called "William with the Whiskers." He accompanied Duke Robert in the first crusade, and died in 1096/7 at Mountjoy, near Jerusalem, having married Emma la Port, of a Saxon family, whose lands were among those bestowed upon him by the Conqueror. "he wedded hyr that was very heire to them," and they had

II. ALAN de PERCIE, eldest son, and heir to his father's feudal rights. He married Emma, daughter of Gilbert de Gand, feudal lord of Folkingham, son of Baldwin VI, eighth Count of Flanders and Artois, and a nephew of Maud, queen consort of William the Conqueror. Their son was

III. WILLIAM de PERCIE, third feudal baron of this family, who married Alice, daughter of Richard FitzGilbert de Clare, see Chapter 5, and had a daughter,

Page 58

IV. AGNES PERCIE. She was married to Josceline, Count of Louvaine and Brabant, fourth Baron de Percie, in right of his wife, who was the brother of Queen Adelicia, second wife of Henry I, King of England. They had two sons: Henry and

★ V. RICHARD de PERCY, the Surety, who, after the decease without issue of his aunt, the "Countess of Warwick," entered into her share of the Percy inheritance. He was one of the first of the powerful lords who took up arms against King John in the cause of "a constitutional government," and was excommunicated by the Pope. He died without issue about 1244.

QUINCEY

Chapter 21

Saire de Quincey

A Surety for Magna Charta

Arms: Or, a fess gules, a label 8 points azure

The following persons may claim descent from Baron Quincey and King Alfred the Great: **Pages** *171, 371*

Arthur Adams
Jane Potter Mengel Allen
Anna M. S. Anable
Sara A. Anable
Jane Virginia Hawkins Andrews
Laura Ann Andrews
Alida May Kelsey Babcock
Bertha Crosley Ball
Lydia Corrie Austin Beutel
Nellie Howe Blood
Estelle Jane Brereton
Hazel Coffin Brown
Juanita Read Harmar Brown
Grace L. Brooke
Elizabeth Irene Winslow Buchan
Lydia Leaming Smith Busch
Margaret Scruggs Carruth
Mary Conner Bass Cole
Beryl Goodwin Coulson
Rebecca Warren Tinkham Cramer
Whittie Dickinson
Mary Quincy Allen Dixon
Benjamin Davis Doane
Russell Duane
Mary Elizabeth Coulson Dye
Lillian Frances Eaton
Berenice Long Eckel
Edgar Hanks Evans
Alice Bates McFadden Eyre
Florence Weeks Faithorn
Hannah Miller Ferriss Ferguson
William Thomas Fluker
Joseph McMahon Foster
Henry Bowerman Fuller
Florence Alice Jayne Gates
Ruth Lillian Giddings
Erna Malvina Sawyer Goodman
Sarah Woodbury Sylvester Hedge Godwin
Conrad Harrison Goodwin
Carl Raymond Gray, Jr.
Mary Cooper Johnson Griest
Harriet Amelia Meikle Harris
Elma Paul Harvey
Henry Reed Hatfield
Daniel Francis Hazen
Josephine Neff Hill
Agnes Foote Hoard
Thomas Leiper Hodge
Nettie Reeder Haines Holt
Evelyn May Roberts Hopkins
Minnie M. Coin Hussong
Lenette Ellison Ford Jeanes
Katie Eliza Fowler Johnson
John Clark Jones, 3d
Estelle Capp Jost
A. Atwater Kent
Susan Abigail Johnson Kimball
Eldora Mindwell Kirkhuff
Bessie Place Knight
Alma Bromley Kruger
Ida Fensley Soule Kuhn
Jeannette Landon
Alvin H. Lane
Elizabeth Selden Lane
Lulie Margaret Hughey Lane
Meredith Biddle Leach
Orah Burgess Leet
Daniel Clark Lewis
George Craghead Gregory
Fanny Beulah Lippitt
Randolph Scott Dewey Lockwood
David Brainerd Lyman, III
Parmelee Lyman
George Norbury Mackenzie
Cora Ellen Van de Mark Marsh
Edward Bennett Mathews
Virginia Shackelford Bostick McArthur
Elizabeth Collins McCoy
Margaret J. Crenshaw McElroy
Annah Colket French McKaig
Emma Marion McPheeters
Florence Lenora Hazen Miller
Adelia Ball Morris
Maria Lydia Bennett Morris
Maud Burr Morris
Jonathan Cilley Neff
Flora Elsie Sheldon Nelson
Howard Ross Nelson
Janet Ann Nelson
Amelia Day Campbell Parker
Mary Williamson Parrent
Grace Edna Vollnogle Phillips
Ida Lewis Pinkerton
Nellie Cady Reimers
Emmy Scott Dewey Roberts
Arthur de Berdt Robins
Virginia Berkley Bowie Schoenfeld
Mary Lane Landis Scott
Evelyn Gilliam Traylor Semones
Frances May Seamans
Mary Edith Coffin Sisson
Emily Ellsworth Ford Skeel
James Somers Smith
Laura Chattin Smith
Gertrude Clough Smither
Jeannette Lowrie Childs Speer
Mary Estella Wade Spining
Elizabeth Doan Sprague
Blanche Powell Spring
John E. Stansfield
Helen Cleveland Varian Steele
Susan A. Sterne
Earle Talbot
Emilia Houghton Telford
Carrie Frances Benjamin Thomas
Augusta True
Prudence Sharpless Doyle Vollnogle
Buckner Ashby Wallingford
Leona L. Walker
Edith Nevill Ward
Paul Carruth Washburn
William Lanier Washington
Margaret Stuart Grattan Weaver
Annie Early Wheeler
Grace Dyer Manton Wheeler
Tristram Coffin Whitaker
Rachel Cidinna Wilkins
Jane Cranston Williams
Iona Berry Wilson
John Graham Wilson
Mary Alice Morgan Wilson
Ethel Lytle Whall Woodbridge
Hiram Baxter Worth
Albert Wurts
Louisa Vanuxem Wurts
Ethel Denune Young
Zara Lydia Ruhm Frierson
Lucretia Wiley McAdams

I. RICHARD de QUINCEY had

II. ROBERT de QUINCEY who married (2) Orabilis and had

III. SAIRE de QUINCEY the Surety, born before 1154, a Baron present at Lincoln when William the Lion, of Scotland, did homage to the English monarch in October 1200. He obtained large grants and immunities from King John, and was created Earl of Winchester, 2 March 1207, having been, in 1203, governor of the castle of Ruil, in Normandy. To him is credited the re-writing of Magna Charta from the Charter of King Henry I and the Saxon code. Opposing the King's concession to the Pope's legate, he was bitterly hated by King John. He was one of the Barons to whom the city and Tower of London were resigned, and was excommunicated with the other barons the following year. He was sent, with Robert FitzWalter, the Surety, by the other Barons. to invite the Dauphin of France to assume the crown of England, and, even after the death of King John, he kept a strong garrison in Mountsorell Castle, in behalf of Prince Louis. When the Barons, being greatly outnumbered, were defeated by the troops of King Henry III, Saire de Quincey with many others was made prisoner and his estates forfeited. In the following October his immense estates were restored upon his submission. In 1218, the Earl of Winchester went with the Earls of Chester and Arundel to the Holy Land, assisted at the siege of Damietta, 1219, and died 3 November in the same
Page 185 year on the way to Jerusalem. His wife Margaret was daughter of Robert de Bellomont and his wife Petronella Grantmesnil, and was descended from the Emperor Charlemagne, see Chapter 29. Among their children were: 1 Hawise Quincey, who became the wife
Page 129 of Hugh de Vere, son of the Surety Robert de Vere, see Chapter 24. Another daughter,

2 ARABELLA QUINCEY became the wife of Richard de Harcourt, of Stanton Harcourt and Ellenhall, and through his marriage with her he acquired the manor of Bosworth. His death occurred in 1258 and they had a son

21 WILLIAM de HARCOURT. By his first wife Alice, daughter of Roger la Zouche, William had two daughters: 211 Margaret, who died without issue, wife of Sir John Cantelupe, and 212 Arabella, who was married to Sir Fulke Pembrugge. By his second
Page 192 wife Eleanor, daughter of Henry, Lord Hastings and his wife Ada of Huntingdon, see Chapter 30, William had an only son

213 RICHARD de HARCOURT, who died in 1293. Margaret his wife was daughter of John Beke, Lord of Eresby, co. Lincoln. Their elder son

213 1 JOHN de HARCOURT who died in 1330 was knighted 22 May 1306. His first wife, Eleanor, daughter of 432 Eudo Page 119 la Zouche, was also descended from Saire de Quincey, and she bore him a son 213 11 William. John de Harcourt's second wife, Alice, was daughter of Peter Corbett of Causcastle, Salop. Issue.

Saire de Quincey and his wife Margaret Bellomont had also three sons: 4 Roger, who succeeded his father and two sons 3 and 5 named Robert, the second of the name being termed "the younger." Of these, the elder

3 ROBERT de QUINCEY, the eldest son, died in the Holy Land, having married Hawise, daughter of Hugh Keveliok, Earl of Chester, by whom he had an only daughter

31 MARGARET QUINCEY, who was married to the Surety JOHN de LACIE, see Chapter 12. Page 89

5 ROBERT de QUINCEY "the younger," married Helen, eldest daughter of Llewelyn the Great, Prince of North Wales, and widow of John Scot, Earl of Huntingdon. Robert's death occurred in 1257, in the tournament at Blie. They had three daughters: 51 Anne, who became a nun; 52 Joane, married to Humphrey de Bohun, the younger; and

53 MARGARET QUINCEY, wife of Baldwin Wake, a feudal lord who died in 1282. They had

531 JOHN WAKE, who was summoned to Parliament as a Baron 1 October 1295.

The second son of Saire de Quincey and Margaret Bellomont his wife, was

4 ROGER de QUINCEY, who held his father's estates while his brother 3 Robert was absent in the Holy Land, and succeeded as Earl of Winchester in 1235. In the same year, in right of his wife, Helen MacDonal, daughter of Alan MacDonal, Lord of Galloway, and his wife Margaret, daughter of Prince David, a Page 192 grandson of King David I of Scotland, see Chapter 30, Roger became lord high constable of Scotland. By Helen he had only three daughters: 41 Margaret, wife of William de Ferrers, 7th Earl of Derby; 42 Elizabeth, wife of Alexander Comyn, 2nd Earl of

Page 119 Buchan; and 43 Ela, also called Elena, wife of Alan, 4th Baron la Zouche of Ashby. Earl Roger's second wife, Maud, Countess of Pembroke, was daughter of Humphrey de Bohun, Earl of Hereford and Essex. His third wife was Alianore, daughter of William de Ferrers, 6th Earl of Derby, who survived him and became the wife of Roger Leybourne. Roger's arms were: gules, seven mascles or, three, three, and one. Upon his death, 25 April 1264, the earldom became extinct, and his possessions devolved upon his daughters, the eldest of whom, as stated previously, was

41 MARGARET QUINCEY, wife of William de Ferrers, 7th Earl of Derby, who brought to her husband the Manor and Barony of Groby. From his youth he had suffered greatly with the gout, and therefore had to be carried from place to place in a chariot. He lost his life by being thrown, through the heedlessness of his driver, over the bridge of St. Neots, co. Huntingdon, in 1254. He was the elder son of William de Ferrers, 6th Earl of Derby, and his wife Agnes of Chester. William the 7th Earl had married first Page 103 Sibilla, one of the daughters of William Marshall, Earl of Pembroke, and by her he had seven daughters. By his second wife, 41 Margaret Quincey, Earl William had two sons and two daughters: 411 Robert de Ferrers, his successor, see later; 412 William, who married Joan Despencer, see later; 413 Agnes, and

414 JOAN FERRERS, who died 19 March 1309/10 and was buried at St. Augustine's, Bristol. In 1267 she was married to Thomas de Berkeley, feudal Lord of Berkeley, who "may bee called Thomas the Wise", born at Berkeley in 1245. He was present at the bloody battle and defeat of the Scots at Falkirk 22 July 1298, and in July of 1300 at the siege of Carlaverock. Taken prisoner at the Battle of Bannockburn, 24 June 1314, he paid a large sum for his ransom. As a statesman he had important duties, being in June 1292 on the Commission to examine the claims to the Crown of Scotland, and in January 1296 on an Embassy to France, and to Pope Clement V in July 1307. He died 23 July 1321, at Berkeley, aged about 76. Beside their daughter 414 2 Margaret, who became the wife of Thomas FitzMorice, see later, Thomas de Berkeley and his wife Joan Ferrers were the parents of

414 1 MAURICE de BERKELEY, Lord de Berkeley, who "may bee called Maurice the Magnanimous", who is said to have been born in April 1281, but more probably in 1271. He dis-

tinguished himself in the Scottish wars from 1295 to 1318, and was present at the siege of Carlaverock in July 1300. Within six months of his father's death he was sent prisoner to Wallingford Castle, 20 January 1321/2, where he died about four years later. His first wife, whom he married in 1289 when both were very young, was Page 119 Eve, daughter of 432 Eudo la Zouche, also descended from the Surety Saire de Quincey. She died 5 December 1314 and was buried in Portbury Church, Somerset. His second wife, Isabel, whom he married about 1316 was born 10 March 1262/3, a daughter of Gilbert de Clare, Earl of Gloucester, by his first wife, Alice le Brun, not his second wife, Joan of Acre, see Chapter 6, but Isabel died without issue in 1333. Lord Maurice died, as aforesaid, 31 May 1326, and was buried at Wallingford, but later was removed to St. Augustine's, Bristol. By his first wife he had a daughter 414 11 Isabel, see later; and a son

414 12 THOMAS de BERKELEY, Lord Berkeley, who "may bee called Thomas the Ritch". On 4 April 1327 he was made Joint Custodian of the deposed King Edward II, whom he "curteously received" the next day at Berkeley Castle, but being commanded to deliver over the government thereof to his fellow custodians, he left there to go to Bradley "with heavy cheere perceiving what violence was intended". As an accessory to the murder of the deposed King, he was tried by a jury of 12 knights in the 4th of King Edward III, but was acquitted. His first wife, Margaret, whom he married on or shortly before 25 July 1320, was daughter of Roger Mortimer, Earl of March, and his wife Joan Geneville. Page 49 Margaret died 5 May 1337, when less than 30 years of age, and was buried at St. Augustine's, Bristol. For his second wife, Thomas married at Charfield, co. Gloucester, on 30 May 1347, Katharine, daughter of John Clivedon and his wife Emma. Lord Thomas died 27 October 1385 in the 69th year of his age, and was buried in Berkeley Church. His widow died 13 March 1385, and is also buried there. Issue.

414 1 Maurice de Berkeley and his wife Eve Zouche had a daughter, as stated previously,

414 11 ISABEL BERKELEY, who in 1328 was married to Robert de Clifford, born in 1305, died 20 May 1344, a descendant of the Sureties Richard and Gilbert de Clare, see Chapter 6. Her second husband was Thomas Musgrave, one of the commanders in the van of the English army that entirely defeated

David, King of Scotland at Durham, in the 20th of King Edward III. Later he was made sheriff of Yorkshire and governor of the castle of York. The barony was not continued in his descendants, nor were any of them deemed barons of the realm. Issue.

Thomas de Berkeley and his wife 414 Joan Ferrers, were the parents of

414 2 MARGARET BERKELEY who was married before 7 February 1283/4 to Thomas FitzMorice, called "the Crooked Heir," son of Morice FitzJohn and his wife Maud de Barry. Born about April 1261 he came to England in 1282 and appears to have remained there constantly until February 1291/2. He was summoned for military service from 29 June 1294 to 17 May 1297, holding the position of Keeper of Ireland from 19 April to 2 December 1295, and received the salary of Justiciar. His death occurred on 4 June 1298 at Knockainy, co. Limerick, and was buried in the Dominican Friary at Tralee. His widow, Margaret Berkeley, was married, second, before 5 April 1299 to Reynold Rosel. They were both living 4 May 1320. Of the children of Thomas FitzMorice and Margaret Berkeley were: 414 21 Thomas FitzThomas, who died young without marrying, and

414 22 MORICE FITZTHOMAS, who in 1325 was admonished for refusing to obey the Justiciar and, having quarrelled with the Earl of Ulster, peace was made between them in a Parliament at Dublin in March 1329. On 10 July 1344 he was summoned for military service in France. The Earl absented himself from a Parliament held in Dublin, in June 1345, whereupon the Justiciar, Ralph d'Ufford, seized his lands into the King's hand, and besieged and took his castles. FitzThomas escaped and could not be found and his lands were therefore forfeited. He was excepted from pardon on 12 May 1346, but on 28 June he received a special protection in order that he might come to England to answer his accusers before the King. On 20 July the Justiciar was ordered to send him to England and he embarked at Youghal with his wife and two sons on 13 September, the King making him an allowance of 20 shillings a day from the time he reached England. For more than a year he remained in custody, and was released on 18 February 1347/8. Finally on 28 November 1349 he was admitted to the King's grace, pardoned for all treasons, but he was required to leave his two sons there as hostages during the King's pleasure. Returning to Ireland about May 1350, he received, on 16 Septem-

ber 1351, a special protection against his enemies there. In May 1355 he was again in England and on 8 July 1355 he was appointed Justiciar of Ireland, which office he held until his death. Page 94

His first wife, Katherine, whom he married 5 August 1312, was daughter of Richard de Burgh, Earl of Ulster, and his wife Margaret, see Chapter 13. She died about 1 November 1331 at Dublin, and his second wife Margaret, was daughter of Conor O'Brien of Thomond. He married a third time, before 20 April 1344, Aveline, probably the daughter of Nicholas FitzMorice of Kerry. Morice FitzThomas died 25 January 1355/6 in Dublin Castle and was buried in the Dominican Friary at Tralee. His widow was living as late as 14 March 1358/9. Issue.

As stated previously, William de Ferrers and his wife 41 Margaret Quincey had a son and successor,

411 ROBERT de FERRERS, who was born about 1239. When the Barons' War broke out in 1263 he seized three of Prince Edward's castles. The following year he captured Worcester and destroyed the town. In the next few months Prince Edward retaliated by wasting his lands and demolishing Tutbury Castle. On 24 December 1264 he was summoned to Parliament, where he was accused of various trespasses and was sent to the Tower by Earl Simon, his lands being taken into the King's hand. Once again he was fully pardoned and admitted to the King's grace on 5 December 1265. By his first wife, Mary, daughter of Hugues le Brun, Earl Robert had no male issue. About 26 June 1269 he married his second wife Alianore, daughter of Humphrey de Bohun and his first wife, Alianore Braos, see Chapter 4. He died in 1279. His Page 54 widow died 20 February 1313/4. Of their children were 411 1 Alianore, wife of Robert FitzWalter, see Chapter 8, and Page 78

411 2 JOHN de FERRERS, who was born at Cardiff June 1271. In 1297 he was the principal supporter of the Earls of Hereford and Norfolk in their quarrel with the King. He was unsuccessful in his attempts to regain the lands which had been forfeited by his father's rebellion. John was in Scotland on the King's service in 1298 and in 1303, and was constable of the army of Scotland in 1306. He was given the custody of Gloucester Castle for a term, beginning 24 September 1311. He married, between 2 February 1297/8 and 13 September 1300, Hawise, daughter of Robert Page 97 de Muscegros, a descendant of the Surety William Malet, see Chapter 14. In August 1312 John died in Gascony, probably of poison, at the age of 41 years. Issue.

Chapter 21

The second son of William de Ferrers, 7th Earl of Derby, and his wife 41 Margaret Quincey,

412 WILLIAM FERRERS, obtained as a gift from his mother the manor of Groby in Leicestershire, whereupon he assumed the arms of the de Quincey family. He died in 1288, having married first, Joan, daughter of Hugh Despencer and second, Eleanor, daughter of Matthew Lovaine. His children, all by his first wife, were: 412 1 Anne, wife of John, Lord Grey of Wilton, see later; and

412 2 WILLIAM FERRERS who was active in the wars of Scotland during the reigns of Edward I and Edward II, dying in 1325, His wife was Margaret daughter of John, 2nd lord Segrave, and they had two sons and a daughter: 412 23 Anne, wife of Edward Despencer, a descendant of the Sureties Richard and Gilbert de Clare, see Chapter 6; 412 22 Thomas, and the eldest

412 21 HENRY FERRERS, 2nd Baron Ferrers of Groby. He took an active part in the wars of King Edward III in Scotland and in France and in consequence acquired very large territorial possessions, by grants from the crown, in recognition of his services. His wife, Isabel, fourth daughter of Theobald de Verdon, and a descendant of the Sureties Richard and Gilbert de Clare, see Chapter 6, and through her he obtained lands in Ireland. They had, beside 412 211 William, successor to his father, a son 412 212 Ralph, who married Joan, daughter of Richard, Baron Grey, of Codner; and two daughters, 412 213 Philippa, married to Guy de Beauchamp, son of Thomas, and 412 214 Elizabeth, wife of David, Earl of Athol. Lord Henry died in 1343. Issue.

412 William Ferrers and his wife Joan Despencer had a daughter, as previously mentioned:

412 1 ANNE FERRERS, who was married as his first wife, to John, Lord Grey, of Wilton. In the 10th of King Edward II he was constituted Justice of North Wales, and Governor of the Castle of Caernarvon. When he died in 1323, Lord John had, among other possessions, the manor of Eston Grey, in Wilts, and the Castle of Ruthyn, in North Wales. His son 412 11 Henry, was his first wife's child, as was his daughter 412 12 Maud, wife of Sir John Norville. His second wife was Maud, daughter of Ralph, Lord Basset, by whom he had another son, Roger, Lord Grey of Ruthyn. The elder son and successor

412 11 HENRY de GREY, 3rd Baron, being abroad at the time of his father's death, could not come to claim his inheritance as soon as, according to custom, he should have done. King Edward III therefore, in the first year of his reign, in consideration of de Grey's eminent services, remitted him a debt he owed to the exchequer. Henry married Anne, daughter of Ralph de Rockley, Page 66 and a descendant of the Sureties Richard and Gilbert de Clare, see Chapter 6. He died in 1342 and was succeeded by his only son

412 111 REGINALD de GREY, died 1370 fourth baron, whose wife was Maude, daughter of John Botetourt. Issue.

Among the children of 4 Roger de Quincey was a daughter

43 ELA QUINCEY, also called Elena, who died in the year Page 114 1296. She became the wife of Alan la Zouche, who was son of Roger and descended from the Earls of Brittany. In the 26th of King Henry III he had a military summons to attend the King into France. He was later made justice itinerant for the counties of Southampton, Buckingham, and Northampton. When the arbitration was made between King Henry II and the barons by King Louis of France, Zouche was one of the Sureties on behalf of the King. Three years later he was constituted constable of the Tower of London, and Governor of the Castle at Northampton. He was violently assaulted and severely wounded at Westminster Hall, in 1268, by John, Earl of Warren and Surrey, because of a dispute arising from a question of some landed property. His son 431 Roger, who was with him, was also wounded. A year later Alan la Zouche died. Among his children by his wife Ela Quincey were 431 Roger, his successor, see later; 433 Robert; and

432 EUDO la ZOUCHE, living in 1273, whose wife was Milicent, daughter of William de Cantilupe and his wife Eva Braos. Her brother was George de Cantilupe of Bergavenny, and Milicent had previously been married to John de Montalt. Beside their son 432 1 William la Zouche who succeeded and had 432 11 Eudo la Zouche, who had 432 111 William, they had daughters: 432 2 Eleanor Zouche, wife of 213 1 John Harcourt, also a descendant Page 113 of Saire de Quincey, see above; 432 3 Lucy Zouche, wife of Thomas de Greene; 432 4 Eve Zouche, wife of 414 1 Maurice de Berkeley, also a descendant of Saire de Quincey, see above. Page 114

Alan la Zouche's eldest son and successor

431 ROGER la ZOUCHE, married Ela, daughter of Stephen Longesepee and his wife Emeline of Ulster, son of William, Earl of Salisbury. He died in the year 1285, being succeeded by his son

431 1 ALAN la ZOUCHE, born in 1267, died 1314, who distinguished himself in the wars of Gascony and Scotland during the reign of King Edward I. In 1311 he was made governor of Rockingham Castle in Northamptonshire and steward of Rockingham Forest. His wife was Eleanor, daughter of Nicholas de Segrave and they had three daughters: 431 13 Elizabeth, the youngest, a nun at Brewood, co. Stafford; 431 12 Ellen, who was married first, to Nicholas St. Maur, and second, to Alan de Charlton; and

431 11 MAUD ZOUCHE, who became the wife of Robert de Holand, of a family of great antiquity in the county of Lancaster. Robert was secretary to Thomas, Earl of Lancaster, to whom he owed his advancement. In the 15th of King Edward II, at the insurrection of Earl Thomas, his former master, Robert promised him all the aid in his power; but he was not able to fulfill his engagement, and Lancaster was forced to escape to the North and was finally taken prisoner at Boroughbridge, whereupon Lord Holand gave himself up to the King at Derby and was taken prisoner to Dover Castle. He was accordingly held in great disfavor by the people, for his duplicity, and when he was again made prisoner, in the year 1328, in a wood near Henley Park, towards Windsor, he was beheaded and his head sent to Henry, Earl of Lancaster. Robert de Holand and his wife 431 11 Maud Zouche were the parents of four sons and two daughters: 431 111 Robert, 431 112 Thomas, 431 113 Alan and 431 114 Otho; (Otes) 431 115 Jane, was married to Sir Edumund Talbot; and 431 116 p. 237 Mary, married to Sir John Tempest. Issue.

(To be continued)

Chapter 51 Page 371

ROOS

Chapter 22

Robert de Roos

A Surety for Magna Charta

Arms: Gules, three water-bougets argent, two and one

The following persons may claim descent from Baron Roos and King Donald I: Page 389

Caroline Taliaferro Anderson
Katherine Clark Pendleton Arrington
Mabel Rogers Baird
Ann Parker Baratta
Anne Wister Barclay
Alice C. Tillinghast Bartlett
Katharine Geddes Benedict
Owen Biddle
Florence Wolcott Sanford Bissell
Marion McDowell Brackett
Olive Walton Jones Brown
Christine Louise Martin Bruer
Richard McCall Cadwalader
Virginia Marshall Clopton
Dike Cooley
Floy Johnston Coil
Douglas Errol Collins
Jay Cooke
Louise Norvell Jones Cox
Jane Penn Crispin
Susie deLorenzi
Mary Elizabeth Doolittle
Mary Sue Brookes Douglass
Mary Richard Chichester duPont
Harriet Overton Woodward Ennis
Alma Imogene Fennell
Joseph Mickle Fox
Nancy Washington Fuller
Garrard Glenn
Elizabeth Southall Clarke Gordon
Elliot Culver Grandin
Elizabeth Dawson Hacker
Minerva Beazley Hart
Juliet Hammond
Lillian Van Culin Harper
Virginia Barbara Smith Hawkins
Joseph Welles Henderson
Mary Louise High
Nema Whitcomb Holloway
Roland Mather Hooker
Blanche Louise Hoopes
Edward Marston Hussong
Julia Ann Getty Jewett
The Princess Kaplanoff
Sarah Louise Kimball
Nettie Browning Danforth Kinnison
Rosa Packard Laird
Philip Le Boutillier
Irene Miller
Nathalie Tucker Powers Miller
Rose Cecilia Poplar Montgomery
Frances Biddle Williams Morgan
Effingham Buckley Morris
Mary Winder Morris
Howard Ross Nelson
Boies Penrose
Katharine Risher Randall
Laura May Wiatt Richardson
Marion Morgan Richardson Robertson
Mary Routh Ellis Robins
Roberta Driscoll Rooke
Eleanor Stillman Gardner Rowe
Benjamin Rush
John Morin Scott
Mary Lane Landis Scott
Fannie May Scoville
Mary Griswold Hall Selby
Frances Smith Shrednick
Margaret Throckmorton Sisson
Mary Wynne deMare Smith
Vernon Rogers Siems Smith
Louise McClure Tinsley Steinman
Marion Yorke Lawrence Symmes
Fannie Smith Tams
Edith Page Harrison Taylor
Anna Laura Driscoll Thomson
George K. Throckmorton
Susan Starling Towles
William T. Van Culin
Eleanor Wurts Wallace
Louisa A. Johnson Waring
George Steptoe Washington
Rebecca Emmet Dashiel Whitham
Elizabeth Robinson Wilson
Anne Elise Roane Winter
Owen Wister
Dorothy Williams Wurts
John Jay Wurts
Ethel Denune Young
William Dorr Wisner

The recorded paternal ancestry of this Surety begins with his great grandfather

I. PETER de ROOS, a feudal baron of the Lordship of Roos in the time of King Henry I. His wife was Adeline, a sister of the renowned Walter d'Espec. He died in 1157, leaving a son

II. ROBERT de ROOS, second lord of Hamlake Manor in the North Riding of Yorkshire. He married Sybell Valoines whose second husband was Ralph d'Albini. Robert died about 1160; his son

III. EVERARD de ROOS, was a minor at the time of his father's death. He was in ward to Ranulph de Glanvil. His wife was Rose, otherwise known as Roysia, daughter of William de Trusbut, Lord of Watre in Holderness, and when her brothers died without issue, she became co-heiress to her father's estate, in the East Riding of Yorkshire, which estate was eventually inherited by her descendants, the Lords Roos. Everard de Roos was evidently a man of considerable importance in the period in which he lived, as in the year 1176 we find him paying what was then a very large sum, £526 as a fine for his lands, and four years later £100 more to have possession of those held by the Earl of Albemarle. He died about the year 1186, when he was succeeded by the older of his two sons,

★ IV. ROBERT de ROOS of Fursan, the Surety, fourth baron of Hamlake Manor, who was born in 1177. In 1197, when only twenty years of age, while he was with the King in Normandy, he was arrested, for what offence it does not appear and committed to the custody of Hugh de Chaumont, but Chaumont, trusting his prisoner to William de Spiney, the latter allowed him to escape out of the Castle of Bonville. King Richard thereupon hanged Spiney and collected a fine of twelve hundred marks, about eight hundred pounds, from Roos' guardian as the price of his continued freedom.

Upon the accession of King John, this monarch, to conciliate him gave young Roos the whole barony of his great-grandmother's father, Walter d'Espec. About the 14th of King John, Robert assumed the habit of a monk, whereupon the custody of all his lands and Castle Werke, were committed to Philip d'Ulcote but Roos did not long continue a recluse, as in about a year he was executing the office of high sheriff of co. Cumberland. At the beginning of the struggle of the barons for a constitutional government, he at first sided with King John, and in consequence obtained some valuable grants from the crown, and was made governor of Carlisle, but he was later won over by the barons. He returned to his allegiance in the reign of King Henry III, for in 1217-18 his manors were restored to him, and although he was a witness to the second Great Charter and the Forest Charter, of 1224, he seems to have been in favor with the king.

He erected the Castles of Helmesley, or Hamlake, in Yorkshire, and of Werke, in Northumberland, and was a member of the Order of Knights Templar. He died in 1226-7, and was buried "in his proper habit" in the Knights' Church, or the New Temple in London, where his tomb may be seen. His effigy is described by Gough, in "Sepulchral Monuments," as "The most elegant of all the figures in the Temple Church, representing a comely young knight in mail, and a flowing mantle with a kind of cowl; his hair neatly curled at the sides; his crown appears shaved. His hands are elevated in a praying posture, and on his left arm is a short, pointed shield charged with three water-bougets. He had on his left side a long sword, and the armor of his legs, which are crossed, has a ridge, or a seam up the front, continued over the knee. At his feet is a lion, and the whole figure measures six feet two inches." Robert de Roos had by his wife Isabel daughter of William the Lion, King of Scotland and widow of Robert Bruce, see Chapter 30, a younger son 2 Robert de Roos, who was Chief Justice of the Forests of six counties and was prominent in the affairs of his day. His sons were 21 Robert de Roos and 22 William de Roos.

Robert de Roos the Surety and Isabel his wife, had a younger son 3 William de Roos, termed "of Ingmanthorpe." Their eldest son was

1 WILLIAM de ROOS, fifth baron of Hamlake Castle by tenure, who in the lifetime of his father was an active supporter of the baronial cause and was made prisoner at the battle of Lincoln by the Royalists. He was later released and delivered up to his father. When the two sisters of his grandmother, Rose Trusbut, died without issue, he became sole heir of the baronial estates of Trusbut in Watre. His death occurred in 1258. His wife was Lucia, daughter of Reginald FitzPiers of Blewleveny in Wales, by whom he had, beside a son, 12 Peter de Roos and a daughter 13 Alice, wife of John Comyn,

11 ROBERT de ROOS, eldest son, of Hamlake Castle. He took an active part against the king and was one of the first Barons after the battle of Lewes in 1264 to be summoned to the Parliament which was called by the barons in the king's name. During the lifetime of his father Robert de Roos married Isabel, granddaughter of the Surety William d'Albini, see Chapter 1. Roos must later have gained royal favor to some extent, for he then had permission to place a new embattled wall around the Castle of Belvoir. He died 16 June 1285. Of his children: 113 Isabel became the wife, first, of Walter de Fauconberge and, second, of Marmaduke Thweng, and through her daughter 113 1 Alice Thweng, who was married to Roger Kryton, descendants survive to the present day; 112

Page 42

Robert de Roos, through whose son 112 1 Sacer de Roos, many present day persons descend. It is, however, through the eldest son that the majority of the lineages are traced. He was

111 WILLIAM de ROOS born in the year 1255. He was one of the competitors for the Scottish Crown in the year 1296 through his grandmother Isabel, natural daughter of William the Lion, King of Scotland. When William found that his kinsman Robert de Roos, then Lord of Werke, was planning to deliver up that Castle to the Scots, he informed the king who sent him a thousand men to defend that place, but the Scots attacking this force, cut it to pieces. King Edward I himself then advanced from Newcastle-Upon-Tyne, soon took the Fort and appointed Lord Roos its governor. Roos married Maud, also called Matilda, one of the daughters of John de Vaux, and died in 1316. Of their children,

111 1 WILLIAM de ROOS was his successor. In the 5th of King Edward II he was one of the commissioners appointed to negotiate peace with King Robert Bruce of Scotland. He died 16 February 1342/3. His wife was Margery Badlesmere a descendant of the Sureties Richard and Gilbert de Clare, see Chapter 6. They had, among others: 111 11 William; 111 12 Thomas, who married Beatrice Stafford and had 111 121 William de Roos, seventh Baron Roos and Lord Treasurer of England. He was a Knight of the Garter under King Henry IV. Of his (Thomas') daughters through whom descent may be traced are 111 122 Margaret Roos, wife of Reynold de Gray; and 111 123 Elizabeth Roos, wife of Thomas Clifford a descendant of the Sureties Roger and Hugh Bigod, see Chapter 3. 111 1 William de Roos who married Margery Badlesmere had the following daughters: 111 13 Maud Roos who became the wife of John de Wells, a descendant of the Sureties Roger and Hugh Bigod, see Chapter 3; 111 14 Alice Roos, who married Nicholas, Lord Meinill of Wherlton Castle, whose only daughter was 111 141 Elizabeth Meinill, the wife, first, of John, second Baron D'Arcy and, second, of Peter, sixth Baron Mauley. 111 15 Milicent Roos, whose husband was William, Lord d'Eyncourt, and they had a son 111 151 William d'Eyncourt. Issue. Page 74

111 William de Roos who married Maud Vaux had a daughter, 111 2 Agnes Roos, also known as Anne, who was married to Payne de Tibetot, son of Robert and through their son 111 21 John, second Baron Tibetot who married Margaret Badlesmere a descendant of the Sureties Richard and Gilbert de Clare, see Chapter 6, and through their daughter, Auda Tibetot, wife of John Mohun, lineages are traced to the present day. Page 68

Chapter 52 (To be continued) Page 389

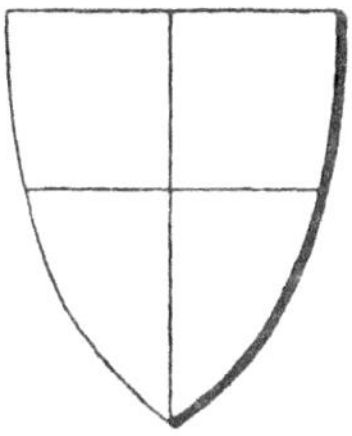

SAYE

Chapter 23

Geoffrey de Saye

A Surety for Magna Charta

Arms: Quarterly, or and gules

The following persons may claim descent from Baron Saye and King Kenneth: Pages 191, 396

Isabelle Strong Allen
Sara Wilson Allen
Emma Wilson Anderson
Cornelia Simrall Anderson Atherton
Lena Grandin Baldwin
Maria Wurts Muir Ballentine
Mary Mays Beatty
Marguerite duPont Ortiz Boden
Frances Claypool Boone
William Gibbons Bramham
Jessie Alma Mellichamp Brunson
Nancy Pierce Busch
The Princess Cantacuzene
Laura Hoe Carter
Anna Tyler Lovering Christopher
Frances Elliott Clark
Frances Dallam Blandy Claypool
Mary Alice Rodhouse Collins
Grace Clark Curry
Eleanor Marine Dashiell
Madeleine Schuyler de Miège
Allison Dodd
Eleuthèra Bradford duPont
Ruth Ballard Fullinweider
Edith Howard Bennet Gardner
Charles Edward Greenough
Axel Henry Gren
Marion Grant Baylies Hooper
Ellen Newbold Cooke Jacobs
Katherine Hague Laubach
Helen Kline LeFavour
Blanche Evelyn Baldwin McGaw
Maude Songer McKnight
William Morton Muir
William Warren Orcutt
Florence Paul Patton
Marian Frazer Harris Perry
Alice Blackburn Rhodes
Helen Avery Robinson, Jr.
Ida Josephine Hyde Sexton
Katharine Bullard Cotton Sparks
Harriet Frances Barnes Stuart
Margaretta P. Suermondt
Alice Righton Taylor
Clarice Paterson Taylor
Alice Elizabeth Trabue
Maude Van Heusen
Virginia Fairfield Watson
Edith Ross Parker Weston
Cornelia De Camp Williams
John S. Wurts, Jr.
Ethel Denune Young

The earliest known paternal ancestor of this Surety was

I. WILLIAM de SAYE, who came into England with William the Conqueror. He had a son

II. WILLIAM de SAYE, whose son was

III. WILLIAM de SAYE, who married Beatrix, only daughter of William de Mandeville, Earl of Essex. Her mother was Margaret, only daughter of Eudo, steward for Normandy. The eldest son of William de Saye and his wife Beatrix, was William, ancestor of the Surety Geoffrey de Mandeville, see Chapter 15, and of Maud, wife of the Surety Henry de Bohun, see Chapter 4. The second son Page 100 Page 52

IV. GEOFFREY de SAYE, was one of the Barons chosen to take the ransom for King Richard I. He died in 1214. His wife Lettice was sister of Wakeline Maminot. They were the parents of

★ V. GEOFFREY de SAYE, the Surety. He was in arms with the other barons against the king and consequently his extensive lands and possessions in ten counties were seized and were given to Peter de Crohim. Returning to his allegiance in the reign of King Henry III, after the expulsion of the Dauphin, he had full restitution. His death occurred in Gascoign, 24 October 1230. His first wife was Alice, daughter of William de Cheyney. Their son was

I WILLIAM de SAYE, who was constituted governor of Rochester Castle in the year 1260. He died in 1272 and was succeeded by his son

II WILLIAM de SAYE, who with others had summons in the 22nd of King Edward III to advise with the king upon the most important affairs of the realm. He died in 1295, leaving a son 111 Geoffrey, see later; and a daughter 112, who became the wife of John, Baron Sudley and died without issue in 1336. It is thus apparent that there can be no descendants of the Surety, Geoffrey de Saye through the Sudley family.

111 GEOFFREY de SAYE, who died in 1322 was only fourteen years of age when his father William, died. His wardship was given to William Leyburne in order that he might marry Idonea, this William's daughter. She was a descendant of the Sureties Roger and Hugh Bigod, see Chapter 3. Beside a daughter Juliana who became the first wife of Roger de Northwode, and left descendants, Geoffrey and Idonea had a son

111 1 GEOFFREY de SAYE, who became second Baron Saye and was summoned to Parliament from the year 1342 to 1353. In the 10th of King Edward III he was constituted Admiral of the king's fleet from the mouth of the Thames westward. From this time Lord Saye was constantly employed in the wars of France and Flanders and proved most gallant. He died in 1359, having married Maud, daughter of Guy de Beauchamp, Earl of Warwick.

In addition to two sons: 111 12 Thomas and 111 13 John, and a daughter 111 14 Elizabeth, all of whom died without issue, Geoffrey de Saye and his wife Maud Beauchamp were the parents of the following children: 111 11 William de Saye, third Baron Saye; 111 15 Idonea Saye, who became the wife of John Clinton of Maxtock, county Warwick, a descendant of the Surety Robert FitzWalter, see Chapter 8; 111 16 Joane Saye, who became the wife, first, of William Fiennes. Issue. Her second husband was Stephen de Valoines.

Page 81

Chapter 53 (To be continued) Page 396

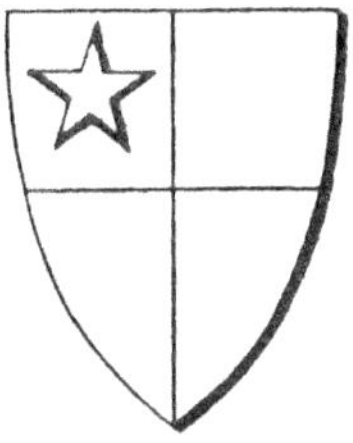

VERE

Chapter 24

Robert de Vere

A Surety for Magna Charta

Arms: Quarterly, gules and or, in the first quarter a mullet, argent

See also Pedigree K, page 424.

The following persons may claim descent from Baron Vere and King Egbert: Pages 170, 398

Josephine Parry Amos
Helen Gray Bush Anderson
Anna Hough Parsons Appleman
Matilda Phillips Jones Badger
Jane Hyde Hall Battle
Hermion Beatrice Behr
Clara M. Green Bell
Mary Camp Benenson
Florence Wolcott Sanford Bissell
Harold King Bowen
Helen McGill Hamilton Bryan
Williamson Buckman
Rosalie Dennis Cooke Carpenter
Mary Amanda Conway Cashman
Stanley G. Child
Eleanor Bedford Wilkins Cooch
Sarah Wood Crary
Caleb Cresson
John Welsh Croskey
Dorothy Shelby Siems de Peyster
Margaret Dod Williams Doane
William Boone Douglass
Matilda Letitia Dorsey Egger
Caroline Moore Rayburn Elliott
Lucy Lane Erwin
Lincoln Eyre
Eleanor Alice Lawwill Felner
Cynthia Eaton Ferres
Emma Davis Robins Gibson
Frances Roller Grattan
Robert B. Haines, 3d
The Right Honourable Viscount Halifax
Meredith Hanna
Evangeline Lukens Harvey
Olive Harriet Harwood
Anna Vanuxem Wurts Hill
Thura Helen Truax Hires
Ella Syrene Holbrook
Augusta True Button Jameson
Charles Francis Jenkins
Howard Cooper Johnson
John Clark Jones, Jr.
Livingston E. Jones
The Princess Kaplanoff
Blanche Gladys Mayers Knowles
Ellis Lewis
Elizabeth Jones Evans Lindsey
Marie Macneil of Barra
Adde Mercer McCall
Marie Aull Wilson McWatters
Lillian K. Moore
Mary Sabine Levick Neilson
Howard Ross Nelson
Janet Ann Nelson
Jessie Bath Newcombe
Clara Audrea Sibley Paine
Carrie Isabel Knous Parker
Thomas Lea Perot
Marion Louise Dewoody Pettigrew
Grace Edna Vollnogle Phillips
Anna Thornton Key Fort Pipes
Lucy Thomas Powell
Evan Randolph
Alice Blackburn Rhodes
Dorothy Cotton Rice
Mary Lane Landis Scott
Kathleen Moore Wilson Seyburn
Howard Merrill Shelley
Mary Louise Shirk
Margaret Rubinkam Slack
Georgine Northrop Wetherill Smith
Jennie Vene Smith
Gladys Louise Higgons Snyder
Richard P. South
Blanche Whaley Spain
Olivia Sproat Sparhawk
Anne Bronson Robins Starin
Heath Steele
Leila Anderson Stilson
Lucy Frances Higgins Stiness
Dorothy Tarwater
Louis de Puy Vail
Ada Eliza Osborn Viall
Prudence Sharpless Doyle Vollnogle
Samuel Walter Washington
Charlotte Dungan Way
Samuel Price Wetherill
F. Edythe Horney Whitaker
Florence Katharine Sharples Whitridge
Julia M. Barker Wiggins
Marshall Williams
Gilberta Elizabeth Woodhull
Davis Page Wurts
Ethel Denune Young
Margaret Shippen Buckley Zantzinger
Charles Edward Greenough

The family of de Vere, the noblest in England and indeed, as Englishmen love to say, "the noblest in all Europe," derive their title through an uninterrupted male descent from a time when the Nevilles and Percys enjoyed only a local celebrity and when even the great name of Plantagenet had not yet been heard in England.

Chapter 24

We are all familiar with Alfred, Lord Tennyson's advice to Lady Clara Vere de Vere:

"A simple maiden in her flower
   Is worth a hundred coats-of-arms.

   The daughter of a hundred earls,
. . . you fix'd a vacant stare
And slew him with your noble birth.

Trust me, Clara Vere de Vere
   From yon blue heavens above us bent
The gardner Adam and his wife
   Smile at the claims of long descent.
Howe'er it be, it seems to me,
   'T is only noble to be good.
Kind hearts are more than coronets,
  And simple faith than Norman blood."

I. Alphonso, Count de Ghesnes appears to be the earliest known paternal ancestor of this Surety. His son

II. Alberic de Vere, Count Aubrey, "Sanglier," married before 1039 Beatrix de Ghent daughter of Henry and his wife Sibylla and they had

Page 72 III. Alberic de Vere who died in 1140. He, being in high favor with King Henry I, was constituted great high chamberlain of the Kingdom in 1133, to hold the same in fee to himself and heirs. In 5 Stephen, 1140, while a joint sheriff of several counties, Page 44 with Richard Basset, Justiciary of England, he was slain in a Page 58 popular tumult at London. He married Adeliza, also called Alice, daughter of Gilbert de Tonebruge, see Chapter 5, and granddaughter of Hugh, Count of Clermont and his wife Marguerita, Page 186 see Chapter 29. Their eldest son was

IV. AUBREY de VERE, born before 1120, third Baron by tenure, of Kensington, Count of Ghisnes. For his fidelity to the Empress Maud, he was confirmed by her in his inheritance and all his father's possessions. He was given also the choice of several earldoms, and selected that of Oxford, and was so created by King Henry II in 1155, and died in 1194. He married first, Eufamia, daughter of William le Cantilupe, by whom he had no issue, and married secondly, Lucia, daughter of Henry de Essex, and they had

★ V. ROBERT de VERE, the Surety, second son, who succeeded and became heir to his brother, Aubrey de Vere, who died without issue before September, 1214, reputed to be one of the "evil councillors" of King John. Although hereditary lord great chamberlain of the kingdom, Robert pursued a different course in politics from that of his brother, and was one of the principal Barons in arms against King John, a party to that covenant which resigned to the Barons the custody of the city and tower of London, and one of those excommunicated by the Pope. In the beginning of the reign of King Henry III, having made his peace with that young monarch after the battle of Lincoln, he was received into his favor, and was appointed one of the judges in the Court of King's Bench, but died a few months afterwards, 25 October 1221 and was buried in the priory of Hatfield, Broad Oak, in Essex. His wife was Isabel, who died 3 February 1245, daughter of Hugh, second Baron de Bolebec, in Northumberland who died in 1261, and had:

1 HUGH de VERE, fourth Earl of Oxford, and Baron de Bolebec, great chamberlain of England, born about 1210, died December 1263. He married, after 11 February 1223, Hawise, first daughter of Saire de Quincey, the Surety, see Chapter 21. They were the parents of 11 Robert de Vere, see later; 12 Aubrey de Vere; 13 Richard de Vere; 14 Margaret Vere, married to Hugh de Cressi; 15 Maud Vere; and

Page 112

16 ISABEL VERE who became the wife of John de Courtenay, a feudal Baron of Oakhampton, of a most illustrious ancestry through the Courtenay and Redvers families, his father being Robert de Courtenay Viscount of Devonshire and governor of the Castle of Exeter. Baron Robert died 26 July 1242, having married Mary, youngest daughter of William de Redvers, surnamed Vernon, 6th Earl of Devon, an adherent to King John. John de Courtenay and his wife 16 Isabel Vere had an only son

161 HUGH de COURTENAY, Baron of Oakhampton, who married Eleanor, daughter of Hugh Despencer, and his wife Aliva Basset and died 28 February 1291. They had two daughters: 161 1 Egelina, wife of Robert Scales, and 161 2 Avelina, whose husband was a Gifford, and a son

161 3 HUGH de COURTENAY, 1st Earl of Devon and Baron of Oakhampton. Having distinguished himself in the Scottish wars

of King Edward I he was one of 300 persons of eminence knighted by him at Westminster and during the reign of King Edward II he was made a knight-banneret. In 1292 he married Agnes, daughter of John, the lord St. John of Basing, and died in 1340, being succeeded by his son 161 32 Hugh, see later. Their other children were the eldest son 161 31 John, Abbot of Tavistock; 161 33 Robert, of Moreton, who died young; 161 34 Thomas, of Southpole, who married Muriel, daughter of John Moels; 161 35 Eleanor, married to Henry, Lord Grey of Codner; and 161 36 Elizabeth, wife of Lord Lisle. The second son, and successor

Pages 56,439

161 32 HUGH de COURTENAY, 2nd Earl of Devon, was born 12 July 1303. On 11 August 1325 he married Margaret Bohun, daughter of Humphrey, Lord High Constable of England and his wife Elizabeth Plantagenet, see Chapter 4. His wife died 16 December 1391. They were the parents of nine daughters and eight sons. Earl Hugh served in the Scottish and French wars. In 1352 he was Joint Warden of Devon and Cornwall, and Chief Warden of Devon in 1373. His death occurred 2 May 1377, when he was aged 73 years, and he was buried in Exeter Cathedral, where his widow was also buried. Issue.

The eldest son of 1 Hugh de Vere and his wife Hawise Quincey, was, as has been said,

11 ROBERT de VERE, 5th Earl of Oxford and 6th great chamberlain. A few days before the Battle of Evesham he, in supporting young Hugh de Montfort, Earl of Leicester, was among those who were surprised with him at Kenilworth, and taken prisoner, but he made his peace soon afterward, under the "Dictum of Kenilworth," and King Edward I sent him against the Welsh. He died 2 September 1296. His wife whom he married before 22 February 1252 and who died 7 September 1317, was Alice, daughter of Gilbert de Saunford, Chamberlain in fee to Eleanor, Queen of King Henry III. Among their children were: 111 Robert de Vere, who died without issue; 112 Alphonso de Vere, see later; 113 Hugh, Baron Vere, who died without issue; 114 Lora Vere, who became the wife of Reginald de Argentine, see later, and

115 JOAN VERE who became the wife of William de Warren, killed 15 December 1285, in a tournament at Croydon, in his father's lifetime. He was the son of John de Warren, Earl of Warren and Surrey and his first wife, Alice le Brun. When he died

he left, beside a daughter 115 1 Alice Warren, wife of Edmund FitzAlan, Earl of Arundel, see later, a posthumous son

115 2 JOHN de WARREN, surnamed Plantagenet, Earl of Warren and Surrey. In the 34th of King Edward I, when Prince Edward was knighted with great solemnity, Earl John with 200 other noblemen of distinction had the honour of knighthood conferred upon him. The king made him a free grant of the castle and honour of Peke in Derbyshire, with the whole forest of High Peke, to hold during his life. In the 5th of King Edward II he and the Earl of Pembroke besieged Piers Gaveston in Scarborough Castle and forced him to surrender. Later he was one of those who surrounded the Castle of Pontefract when it was held by Thomas, Earl of Lancaster, and his followers, and was among those who sat in judgment upon him and condemned him to death. He died 30 June 1347, at the age of 61 years. By his first wife, Joane, daughter of the Count of Barre, he had no children. By Maud Nerford he had three sons and three daughters as follows: 115 21 John de Warren; 115 22 William de Warren; 115 23 Thomas de Warren; 115 24 Joan, of Basing; 115 25 Catherine, wife of Robert Heveningham; and 115 26 Isabel Warren. He later married Johanna, eldest daughter and heiress of Malise, 7th Earl of Strathern in Scotland, and had a grant of that earldom from Edward Baliol.

William de Warren and his wife 115 Joan Vere had, as has been said, a daughter

115 1 ALICE WARREN who in 1305 was married to Edmund FitzAlan, Earl of Arundel, born 1 May 1285 in the Castle of Marlborough. On 9 November 1306 he was summoned to Parliament as Earl of Arundel, and took part in the Scottish wars of that year. On 25 February 1307/8 he officiated as "Pincerna" at the coronation of Edward II. For a long while he was in opposition to the King, and was violent against Piers Gaveston, who had beaten him in a tournament. However, in 1231 he changed sides and thereafter was one of the few nobles who adhered to the King. Having been captured in Shropshire by the Queen's party, Edmund was, without trial, beheaded at Hereford, 17 November 1326, in his forty-second year. He was subsequently attainted, when his estates and honours became forfeited. His widow, Alice Warren was living in 1330, but died before 23 May 1338. Among their children were: 115 11 Richard FitzAlan, his successor, see later; 115 12 Edmund FitzAlan who married Sibil, daughter of William

Montacute, Earl of Salisbury, and had one daughter, 115 121 Alice FitzAlan, married to Leonard, Lord Carew; 115 13 Alice FitzAlan, wife of John de Bohun, Earl of Hereford; 115 14 Jane FitzAlan, married to Warine Gerrard, Lord L'Isle; and 115 15 Alaive FitzAlan.

The eldest son and successor of Edmund FitzAlan and his wife 115 1 Alice Warren, was

115 11 RICHARD FITZALAN, Earl of Arundel, who succeeded on 30 June 1347. This Richard, called "Copped Hat," was born about 1313. He was made Justiciar of North Wales for life in 1334, Governor of Carnarvon Castle in 1339, and Sheriff of Shropshire for life in 1345. He took a distinguished part in the wars with France, was Admiral of the West, 1340/41 and 1345/47, commanded the second division at the battle of Crecy, and was at the fall of Calais in 1347. He died 24 January, 1375/6 at Arundel, in his 70th year and was buried at Lewes. His first wife whom he married 9 February 1320 was Isabel, daughter of Hugh Despenser the younger, and his wife Alianore Clare, see Chapter 6. They had a daughter 115 111 Philippa, married to Richard Sergeaux, of Cornwall. In 1344 he obtained a papal mandate for the annulment of this marriage on the ground of his minority and of his never Page 203 having willingly consented to the match. His second wife was Lady Eleanor Plantagenet whose descent from the distinguished family of Beauchamp is found in Chapter 31. They had three sons and four daughters as follows: 115 112 Richard FitzAlan, 10th Earl Page 55 of Arundel, K. G., who married Elizabeth Bohun; 115 113 John FitzAlan, Marshal of England, married Eleanor Maltravers; 115 114 Thomas FitzAlan, called Arundel, Archbishop of York and of Canterbury, and Lord High Chancellor of England; 115 115 Joane FitzAlan, married to Humphrey de Bohun; 115 116 Alice FitzAlan, married to Thomas Holand, Earl of Kent, K. G.; 115 117 *Mary FitzAlan married to John, 4th Baron Strange of Blackmere; and 115 118 Eleanor, wife of Robert d'Ufford.

The second son of 11 Robert de Vere and his wife Alice Saunford,

112 ALPHONSO de VERE, married Jane, daughter of Richard Foliot, and they had a son

112 1 JOHN de VERE who succeeded as 7th Earl of Oxford and 8th Great Chamberlain, when his Uncle Robert de Vere died

* A footnote in Volume I of the New Complete Peerage, page 244, places the above 117 Mary (Isabel) as child of the first wife and names an eldest son Edmund, who

without issue. Earl John was a person of great military renown in the reign of King Edward III, being only eighteen years of age when he succeeded to the earldom, and soon afterwards he was with the army in Scotland, where he remained for some time. At the assault upon the Castle of Pellegrue, he was taken prisoner in his tent, but was soon afterward exchanged for the Viscount of Bonquentyne. Thereupon he marched with the Earl of Derby to Attveroche, which was being besieged by the French, and relieved it. "But about the feast of the Blessed Virgin" writes Dugdale, "returning out of Brittany, he was by tempest cast upon the coast of Connaught, in Ireland, where he and all his company suffered much misery from the barbarous people there, who pillaged them of all they had." Returning to France soon after this episode, de Vere spent nearly all the remainder of his life in the wars of that country, being one of the heroes of Crecy, and one of those in command at Poitiers. He died while in the English army encamped before the walls of Rheims, 24 January 1360, it is said from fatigue and exposure. His wife was Maud, sister and heiress of Giles, Lord Badlesmere, and widow of Robert FitzPayn, and they had 112 11 Page
Thomas de Vere, his successor; 112 12 Aubrey de Vere who 78
married Alice FitzWalter, a descendant of the Surety, Robert FitzWalter, see Chapter 8. 112 13 John de Vere, who died without issue; and a daughter 112 14 Margaret who became the wife, first, of Nicholas Lovain, second, of Henry, Lord Beaumont, and third, of John Devereux. Issue.

11 Robert de Vere and his wife Alice Saunford had, with others, as stated above, a daughter

114 LORA VERE, whose husband was Reginald de Argentine, a nobleman having large estates in counties Cambridge, Norfolk, Suffolk and Hertford, which he inherited from his father Giles de Argentine. Dying in 1307, he was succeeded by his son

114 1 JOHN de ARGENTINE, 2nd Baron, whose first wife, Joane, by whom he had three daughters, was daughter of Roger Bryan, Lord of Throcking, Herts. His second wife was Agnes, daughter and heiress of William Bereford of Burton, co. Leicester and when he died in the 12th of King Edward II he was succeeded by their only son 114 14 John, see later. His daughters were: 114 11 Joane, co-heiress of her mother, who became the wife of John le Boteler, and had 114 111 Edward le Boteler; 114 13 Dionysia, third daughter, co-heiress of her mother; and

114 12 ELIZABETH ARGENTINE, wife of John's brother, William le Boteler, and they had 114 121 Elizabeth Boteler, who was married to Piers de Dutton. 114 1 John de Argentine's only son, the child of his second marriage, was

114 14 JOHN de ARGENTINE, who was only six months of age when he succeeded to his father's estates. He was 3rd Baron Argentine, and was knighted in the 4th of King Edward III, but was not summoned to parliament. He died in 1382/3, leaving by his wife Margaret, daughter of Robert D'Arcy of Stretton, three daughters: 114 141 Maud, wife of Sir Eudo FitzWarren; 114 142 Joan, wife of Bartholomew Naunton; and 114 143 Elizabeth, married to Baldwin St. George. Issue.

(To be continued)

Chapter 54 **Page** 398

VESCI

Chapter 25

Eustace de Vesci

A Surety for Magna Charta

No great-great-grandchildren

Arms: Gules, a cross argent

I. YVO de VESCI with William the Conqueror came into England in 1066. His son

II. JOHN de VESCI, married Ada, also called Beatrix, daughter of William de Tyson. Their only child was

Page 71

III. BEATRIX VESCI who was married, to Eustacius (Eustache) FitzJohn de Burgo, killed in 1157, leaving an eldest son

IV. WILLIAM FITZJOHN de VESCI, who inherited many manors and was high sheriff of Northumberland and Lancashire. He assisted in repelling an invasion of the Scots, and captured their king in the battle of Alnwick. Dying in 1184 William, by his wife Burga, daughter of William, fourth Baron de Stuteville, who died in 1203, left a son

V. EUSTACE de VESCI, the Surety, a feudal lord of Alnwick Castle, in Northumberland. He became of age in 1190 and in 1199, was sent by King John as one of the ambassadors to King William the Lion, of Scotland, one of whose daughters he had married but shortly he became intimately connected with the rise and progress of the baronial cause. In 1212, he and Robert FitzWalter, the Surety, upon being required to give security for their faithful allegiance, fled to Scotland. His English possessions were seized, and his castle of Alnwick was ordered to be destroyed, but this was not done. This order and other factors so embittered de Vesci that he became the most persistent of the king's enemies, and a principal leader in the insurrection, and took a prominent part in all their conventions, in the endeavor to obtain a revival of the laws of Edward the Confessor. He was one of the barons to whom the city and tower of London were committed; was excommunicated, and was one of those who urged the Dauphin to come to England. In attending his brother-in-law, Alexander, King of Scots, to welcome Prince Louis, and to do him homage for that kingdom in 1216, they passed Bernard Castle, in Yorkshire, which displayed the royal banner. Approaching too near, to see if it could be captured, Eustace de Vesci was mortally wounded by one of the garrison.

He married Margaret, a natural daughter of King William the Lion of Scotland, and had

1 William de Vesci, eldest son, lord of Alnwick Castle who died in 1253. He married, first, Isabel, daughter of William Longesepee, Earl of Salisbury and, second, Agnes, daughter of William de Ferrers, seventh Earl of Derby and by the latter had two sons 11 John de Vesci, lord of Knapton, who married twice, but died without issue in 1289, and 12 William de Vesci, lord of Kildare, in Ireland, first Baron Vesci, who died in 1297, whose only legitimate son, 121 John de Vesci, married but died without issue in his father's lifetime.

Isabel Vesci who married William, Lord Wells, was not, as has been supposed, the daughter of the Surety's grandson William, since, on William's death, the Surety's estates were given to the heirs of the Surety's father, which would not have been the case had the Surety himself left any lineal descendants surviving to that day.

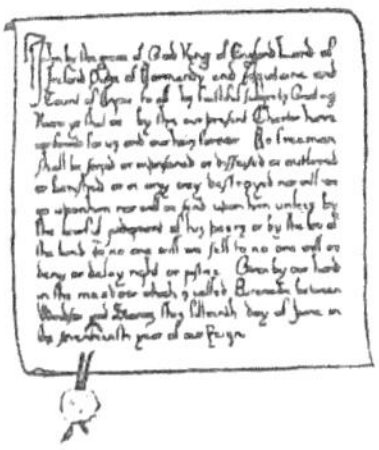

Chapter 26

An English Translation

As everyone knows, Magna Charta was written in Latin, medieval Latin, see page 21, and has been many times translated into English and other languages. It has no paragraph divisions in the original but is here divided into sixty-three numbered sections for convenient reference.

MAGNA CHARTA

The Great Charter of King John
Granted 15 June 1215

Page 20

John, by the grace of God, King of England, Lord of Ireland, Duke of Normandy and Aquitaine, and Earl of Anjou: To the Archbishops, Bishops, Abbots, Earls, Barons, Justiciaries, Foresters, Sheriffs, Reves, Ministers, and all Bailiffs and others, his faithful subjects, Greeting. Know ye that We, in the presence of God, and for the health of Our soul, and the souls of Our ancestors and heirs, to the honour of God, and the exaltation of Holy Church, and amendment of Our kingdom, by the advice of Our reverend Fathers, Stephen, Archbishop of Canterbury, Primate of all England and Cardinal of the Holy Roman Church; Henry, Archbishop of Dublin; William of London; Peter of Winchester, Jocelin of Bath and Glastonbury, Hugh of Lincoln, Walter of Worcester, William of Coventry, Benedict of Rochester, Bishops; and Master Pandulph, the Pope's subdeacon and familar; Brother Aymeric, Master of the Knights of the Temple in England; and the noble persons, William Marshal, Earl of Pembroke; William, Earl of Salisbury; William, Earl of Warren; William, Earl of Arundel; Alan de Galloway, Constable of Scotland; Warin Fitz-Gerald, Hubert de Burgh, Seneschal of Poictou, Peter Fitz-Herbert, Hugo de Neville, Matthew Fitz-Herbert, Thomas Basset, Alan Basset, Philip Daubeney, Robert de Roppelay, John Marshal, John Fitz-Hugh, and others, our liegemen, have, in the first place, granted to God, and by this Our present Charter confirmed for Us and Our heirs for ever:

1. That the Church of England shall be free and enjoy all her rights in their integrity and her liberties untouched. And that We will this so to be observed appears from the fact that We of Our mere and free will, before the outbreak of the dissensions between Us and Our Barons, granted, confirmed, and procured to be confirmed by Pope Innocent III., the freedom of elections which is considered most important and necessary to the English Church, which Charter We will both keep Ourself and will it to be so kept by Our heirs for ever.

2. We have also granted to all the free men of Our Kingdom, for Us and Our heirs for ever, all the liberties underwritten, to have and to hold to them and their heirs of Us and Our heirs. If any of Our Earls, Barons, or others who hold of Us in chief by Knight's service, shall die, and at the time of his death his heir shall be of full age and owe a relief, he shall have his inheritance by ancient relief; to wit, the heir or heirs of an Earl of an entire Earl's Barony, £100; the heir or heirs of a Baron of an entire Barony, £100; the heir or heirs of a Knight of an entire Knight's fee, 100s. at the most; and he that oweth less shall give less, according to the ancient custom of fees.

3. If, however, the heir of any such shall be under age and in ward, he shall, when he comes of age, have his inheritance without relief or fine.

4. The guardian of the land of any such heir so under age shall take therefrom reasonable issues, customs, and services only, and that without destruction and waste of men or property; and if We shall have committed the custody of any such land to the Sheriff or any other person who ought to be answerable to Us for the issues thereof, and he commit destruction or waste upon the ward-lands, We will take an emend from him, and the land shall be committed to two lawful and discreet men of that fee, who shall be answerable for the issues to Us or to whomsoever We shall have assigned them. And if We shall give or sell the wardship of any such land to any one, and he commit destruction or waste upon it, he shall lose the wardship, which shall be committed to two lawful and discreet men of that fee, who shall, in like manner, be answerable unto Us as hath been aforesaid.

5. But the guardian, so long as he shall have the custody of the land, shall keep up and maintain the houses, parks, fish ponds, pools, mills, and other things pertaining thereto, out of the issues of the same, and shall restore the whole to the heir when he comes of age, stocked with ploughs and wainage according as the season may require and the issues of the land can reasonably bear.

6. Heirs shall be married without disparagement, to which end the marriage shall be made known to the heir's nearest of kin before it be contracted.

7. A widow, after the death of her husband, shall immediately and without difficulty have her marriage portion and inheritance, nor shall she give anything for her marriage portion, dower, or inheritance which her husband and herself held on the day of his death; and she may remain in her husband's house for forty days after his death, within which time her dower shall be assigned to her.

8. No widow shall be distrained to marry so long as she has a mind to live without a husband; provided, however, that she give security that she will not marry without Our assent if she holds of Us, or that of the lord of whom she holds, if she hold of another.

9. Neither We nor Our bailiffs shall seize any land or rent for any debt so long as the debtor's chattels are sufficient to discharge the same; nor shall the debtor's sureties be distrained so long as the chief debtor hath sufficient to pay the debt, and if he fail in the payment thereof, not having wherewithal to discharge it, then the sureties shall answer it, and, if they will, shall hold the debtor's lands and rents until satisfaction of the debt which they have paid for him be made them, unless the chief debtor can show himself to be quit thereof against them.

10. If any one shall have borrowed money from the Jews, more or less, and die before the debt be satisfied, no interest shall be taken upon such debt so long as the heir be under age, of whomsoever he may hold; and if the debt shall fall into Our hands We will only take the chattel mentioned in the Bond.

11. And if any one die indebted to the Jews his wife shall have her dower and pay nothing of that debt; and if the children of the said deceased be left under age they shall have necessaries provided for them according to the condition of the deceased, and the debt shall be paid out of the residue, saving the lord's service; and so shall it be done with regard to debts owed to other persons than Jews.

12. No scutage or aid shall be imposed in Our kingdom unless by common council thereof, except to ransom Our person, make Our eldest son a knight, and once to marry Our eldest daughter, and for this a reasonable aid only shall be paid. So shall it be with regard to aids from the City of London.

13. And the City of London shall have all her ancient liberties and free customs, both by land and water. Moreover We will and grant that all other cities, boroughs, towns, and ports shall have all their liberties and free customs.

14. And for obtaining the common council of the kingdom concerning the assessment of aids other than in the three cases aforesaid or of scutage, We will cause to be summoned, severally by our letters, the Archbishops, Bishops, Abbots, Earls and great Barons; and in addition We will also cause to be summoned, generally, by Our sheriffs and bailiffs, all those who hold of Us in chief, to meet at a certain day, to wit, at the end of forty days at least, and at a certain place; and in all letters of such summons We will explain the cause thereof, and the summons being thus made the business shall proceed on the day appointed, according to the advice of those who shall be present, notwithstanding that the whole number of persons summoned shall not have come.

15. We will not, for the future, grant permission to any man to levy an aid upon his free men, except to ransom his person, make his eldest son a knight, and once to marry his eldest daughter, for which a reasonable aid only shall be levied.

16. No man shall be distrained to perform more service for a knight's fee or other free tenement than is due therefrom.

17. Common pleas shall not follow our Court, but be holden in some certain place.

18. Recognisances of Novel Disseisin, Mort d'Ancestor, and Darrein Presentment shall be taken in their proper counties only, and in this wise;—We Ourself, or, if We be absent from the realm, Our Chief Justiciary, shall send two justiciaries through each county four times a year, who, together with four knights elected out of each shire by the people thereof, shall hold the said assizes on the day and in the place aforesaid.

19. And if the said assizes cannot be held on the day appointed, so many of the knights and freeholders as shall have been present

thereat on that day shall remain as will be sufficient for the administration of justice, according as the business to be done be greater or less.

20. A free man shall not be amerced for a small fault, but according to the measure thereof, and for a great crime according to its magnitude, in proportion to his degree; and in like manner a merchant in proportion to his merchandise, and a villein in proportion to his wainage if he should fall under Our mercy; and none of the said amercements shall be imposed unless by the oath of honest men of the venue.

21. Earls and Barons shall only be amerced by their peers in proportion to the measure of the offence.

22. No clerk shall be amerced for his lay tenement, except after the manner of the other persons aforesaid, and not according to the value of his ecclesiastical benefice.

23. Neither shall any vill or person be distrained to make bridges over rivers, but they who are bound to do so by ancient custom and law.

24. No sheriff, constable, coroners, or other Our bailiffs shall hold pleas of Our Crown.

25. All counties, hundreds, tithings, and wapentakes shall stand at the old ferms, without any increased rent, except Our demesne manors.

26. If any one die holding a lay fee of Us, and the sheriff or Our baliff show Our letters patent of summons touching the debt due to Us from the deceased, it shall be lawful to such sheriff or bailiff to attach and register the chattels of the deceased found in the lay fee to the value of that debt, by view of lawful men, so that nothing be removed therefrom until Our whole debt be paid; and the residue shall be given up to the executors to carry out the will of the deceased. And if there be nothing due from him to Us, all his chattels shall remain to the deceased, saving to his wife and children their reasonable shares.

27. If any free man shall die intestate his chattels shall be distributed by the hands of his nearest kinsfolk and friends by view of the Church, saving to every one the debts due to him from the deceased.

28. No constable or other Our bailiff shall take corn or other chattels of any man without immediate payment for the same, unless he hath a voluntary respite of payment from the seller.

29. No constable shall distrain any knight to give money for castle-guard, if he will perform it either in his proper person or by some other fit man, if he himself be prevented from so doing by reasonable cause; and, if We lead or send him into the army, he shall be quit of castle-guard for the time he shall remain in the army by Our command.

30. No sheriff or other Our bailiff, or any other man, shall take the horses or carts of any free man for carriage except with his consent.

31. Neither shall We or Our bailiffs take another man's timber for Our castles or other uses, unless with the consent of the owner thereof.

32. We will only retain the lands of persons convicted of felony for a year and a day, after which they shall be restored to the Lords of the fees.

33. From henceforth all weirs shall be entirely removed from the Thames and Medway, and throughout England, except upon the sea coast.

34. The writ called "Praecipe" shall not for the future issue to any one of any tenement whereby a free man may lose his court.

35. There shall be one measure of wine throughout Our kingdom, and one of ale, and one measure of corn, to wit, the London quarter, and one breadth of dyed cloth, russetts and haberjects, to wit, two ells within the selvages. And as with measures so shall it be also with weights.

36. From henceforth nothing shall be given for a writ of inquisition upon life or limbs, but it shall be granted gratis, and shall not be denied.

37. If any one hold of Us by fee-farm, socage or burgage, and hold land of another by knight's service, We will not have the wardship of his heir, or the land which belongs to another man's fee, by reason of that fee-farm, socage or burgage; nor will We have the wardship of such fee-farm, socage, or burgage, unless such fee-farm owe knight's service. We will not have the wardship of any man's heir, or the land which he holds of another by knight's

service, by reason of any petty serjeanty which he holds of Us by service of rendering Us daggers, arrows, or the like.

38. No bailiff shall for the future put any man to trial upon his simple accusation without producing credible witnesses to the truth thereof.

39. No free man shall be taken, or imprisoned, or disseised, or outlawed, or banished, or in any way destroyed, nor will We go upon him, nor will We send upon him except by the lawful judgment of his peers or by the law of the land.

40. To none will We sell, to none will We deny, to none will We delay, right or justice.

41. All merchants shall have safe conduct to go and come out of and into England, and to stay in and travel through England by land and water for purchase or sale, without maltolt, by ancient and just customs, except in time of war, or if they belong to a country at war with Us. And if any such be found in Our dominion at the outbreak of war, they shall be attached, without injury to their persons or goods, until it be known to Us or Our Chief Justiciary, after what sort Our merchants are treated who shall be found to be at that time in the country at war with Us, and if they be safe there then these shall be so also with Us.

42. It shall be lawful in future, unless in time of war, for any one to leave and return to Our kingdom safely and securely by land and water, saving his fealty to Us, for any short period, for the common benefit of the realm, except prisoners and outlaws according to the law of the land, people of the country at war with Us, and merchants who shall be dealt with as is aforesaid.

43. If any one die holding of any escheat, as of the honour of Wallingford, Nottingham, Boulogne, Lancaster, or other escheats which are in Our hands and are baronies, his heir shall not give any relief or do any service to Us other than he would owe to the baron if such barony should have been in the hands of a baron, and We will hold it in the same manner in which the baron held it.

44. Persons dwelling without the forest shall not for the future come before Our justiciaries of the forest by common summons, unless they be impleaded or are bail for any person or persons attached for breach of forest-laws.

45. We will only appoint such men to be justiciaries, constables, sheriffs, or bailiffs as know the law of the land and will keep it well.

46. All barons, founders of abbies by charters of English kings or ancient tenure, shall have the custody of the same during vacancy as is due.

47. All forests which have been afforested in Our time shall be forthwith disafforested, and so shall it be done with regard to rivers which have been placed in fence in Our time.

48. All evil customs concerning forests and warrens, foresters, warreners, sheriffs, and their officers, rivers and their conservators, shall be immediately inquired into in each county by twelve sworn knights of such shire, who must be elected by honest men thereof, and within forty days after making the inquisition they shall be altogether and irrevocably abolished, the matter having been previously brought to Our knowledge or that of Our Chief Justiciary if We Ourself shall not be in England.

49. We will immediately give up all hostages and charters delivered to Us by the English for the security of peace and the performance of loyal service.

50. We will entirely remove from their bailiwicks the kinsmen of Gerard de Atyes, so that henceforth they shall hold no bailiwick in England, Engelard de Cygoyney, Andrew, Peter, and Gyon de Cancelles, Gyon de Cygoyney, Ralph de Martiny and his brothers, Philip Marc and his brothers, and Ralph his grandson, and all their followers.

51. And directly after the restoration of peace We will dismiss out of our kingdom all foreign soldiers, bowmen, serving men, and mercenaries, who come with horses and arms to the nuisance thereof.

A Precedent for the Supreme Court

52. If any one shall have been disseised or deprived by Us, without the legal judgment of his peers, of lands, castles, liberties, or rights, We will instantly restore the same, and if any dispute shall arise thereupon, the matter shall be decided by judgment of the twenty-five barons mentioned below for the security of peace. With regard to all those things, however, whereof any person shall have been disseised or deprived, without the legal judgment of his peers, by King Henry Our Father, or Our Brother King Richard, and which remain in Our hands or are held by others under Our war-

The King, like Congress, could make the laws, but the Barons, like the Supreme Court, would interpret them.

ranty, We will have respite thereof till the term commonly allowed to the crusaders, except as to those matters on which a plea shall have arisen, or an inquisition have been taken by Our command prior to Our assumption of the Cross, and immediately after Our return from Our pilgrimage, or if by chance We should remain behind from it We will do full justice therein.

53. We will likewise have the same respite and in like manner shall justice be done with respect to forests to be disafforested or let alone, which Henry Our Father or Richard Our Brother afforested, and to wardships of lands belonging to another's fee, which We have hitherto held by reason of the fee which some person has held of Us by knight's service, and to abbies founded in another's fee than Our own, whereto the lord of that fee asserts his right. And when We return from Our pilgrimage, or if We remain behind therefrom, We will forthwith do full justice to the complainants in these matters.

54. No one shall be taken or imprisoned upon a woman's appeal for the death of any other person than her husband.

55. All fines unjustly and unlawfully made with Us, and all amercements levied unjustly and against the law of the land, shall be entirely condoned or the matter settled by judgment of the twenty-five barons of whom mention is made below, for the security of peace, or the majority of them, together with the aforesaid Stephen, Archbishop of Canterbury, if he himself can be present, and any others whom he may wish to summon for the purpose, and if he cannot be present the business shall nevertheless proceed without him. Provided that if any one or more of the said twenty-five barons be interested in a plaint of this kind, he or they shall be set aside, as to this particular judgment, and another or others elected and sworn by the rest of the said barons for this purpose only, be substituted in his or their stead.

56. If We have disseised or deprived the Welsh of lands, liberties or other things, without legal judgment of their peers, in England or Wales, they shall instantly be restored to them, and if a dispute shall arise thereon the question shall be determined on the Marches by judgment of their peers according to the law of England with regard to English tenements, the law of Wales respecting Welsh tenements, and the law of the Marches as to tenements in the Marches. The same shall the Welsh do to Us and Ours.

57. But with regard to all those things whereof any Welshman shall have been disseised or deprived, without legal judgment of his peers, by King Henry Our Father or Our Brother King Richard, and which We hold in Our hands or others hold under Our warranty, We will have respite thereof till the term commonly allowed to the crusaders, except as to those matters whereon a plea shall have arisen or an inquisition have been taken by Our command prior to Our assumption of the Cross, and immediately after Our return from Our pilgrimage, or if by chance We should remain behind from it We will do full justice therein, according to the laws of the Welsh and the parts aforesaid.

58. We will immediately give up the son of Llewellyn and all the Welsh hostages, and the charters which were delivered to Us for the security of peace.

59. We will do the same with regard to Alexander, King of the Scots, in the matter of giving up his sisters and hostages, and of his liberties and rights, as We would with regard to Our other barons of England, unless it should appear by the charters which We hold of William his father, late King of the Scots, that it ought to be otherwise, and this shall be done by judgment of his peers in Our Court.

60. All which customs and liberties aforesaid, which We have granted to be enjoyed, as far as in Us lies, by Our people throughout Our kingdom, let all Our subjects, clerks and laymen, observe, as far as in them lies, towards their dependents.

61. And whereas We, for the honour of God and the amendment of Our realm, and in order the better to allay the discord arisen between Us and Our barons, have granted all these things aforesaid, We, willing that they be for ever enjoyed wholly and in lasting strength, do give and grant to Our subjects the following security, to wit, that the barons shall elect any twenty-five barons of the kingdom at will, who shall, with their utmost power, keep, hold, and cause to be holden the peace and liberties which We have granted unto them, and by this Our present Charter confirmed, so that, for instance, if We, Our Justiciary, bailiffs, or any of Our ministers, offend in any respect against any man, or shall transgress any of these articles of peace or security, and the offence be brought before four of the said five and twenty barons, those four barons shall come before Us, or Our Chief Justiciary if We are out of the

kingdom, declaring the offence, and shall demand speedy amends for the same. And if We or in case of Our being out of the kingdom, Our Chief Justiciary, fail to afford redress within the space of forty days from the time the case was brought before Us or Our Chief Justiciary, the aforesaid four barons shall refer the matter to the rest of the twenty-five barons, who, together with the commonalty of the whole county, shall distrain and distress Us to the utmost of their power, to wit, by capture of Our castles, lands, possessions, and all other possible means, until compensation be made according to their decision, saving Our person and that of Our Queen and children, and as soon as that be done they shall return to their former allegiance. Any one whatsoever in the kingdom may take oath that, for the accomplishment of the aforesaid matters, he will obey the orders of the said twenty-five barons, and distress Us to the utmost of his power; and We give public and free leave to every one wishing to take such oath to do so, and to none will We deny the same.

62. Moreover We will compel all such of Our subjects who shall decline to swear to, and together with the said twenty-five barons to distrain and distress Us of their own free will and accord, to do so by Our command as is aforesaid. And if any one of the twenty-five barons shall die or leave the country, or be in any way hindered from executing the said office, the rest of the said twenty-five barons shall choose another in his stead, at their discretion, who shall be sworn in like manner as the others. And in all cases which are referred to the said twenty-five barons to execute, and in which a difference shall arise among them, supposing them all to be present, or that all who have been summoned are unwilling or unable to appear, the verdict of the majority shall be considered as firm and binding as if the whole number should have been of one mind. And the aforesaid twenty-five shall swear to keep faithfully all the aforesaid articles, and, to the best of their power, cause them to be kept by others. And we will not procure, either by Ourself or any other, anything from any man whereby any of the said concessions or liberties may be revoked or abated; and if any such procurement be made let it be null and void; it shall never be made use of either by Us or any other. We have also wholly remitted and condoned all ill-will, wrath, and malice which have arisen between Us and Our subjects, clerks and laymen, during the disputes, to and with all men; and We have moreover fully remitted, and as far as in Us lies, wholly condoned to and with all clerks

and laymen all trespasses made in consequence of the said disputes from Easter in the sixteenth year of Our reign till the restoration of peace; and, over and above this, We have caused to be made in their behalf letters patent by testimony of Stephen, Archbishop of Canterbury, Henry, Archbishop of Dublin, the Bishops above mentioned, and Master Pandulph, upon the security and concession aforesaid.

63. Wherefore We will, and firmly charge, that the Church of England be free, and that all men in Our Kingdom have and hold all the aforesaid liberties, rights, and concessions, well and peaceably, freely, quietly, fully, and wholly, to them and their heirs, of Us and Our heirs, in all things and places for ever, as is aforesaid. It is moreover sworn, as well on Our part as on the part of the Barons, that all these matters aforesaid shall be kept in good faith and without evil subtilty. Witness the above-mentioned Prelates and Nobles and many others. Given by Our hand in the meadow which is called Runnemede between Windsor and Staines, on the Fifteenth day of June in the Seventeenth year of Our reign.

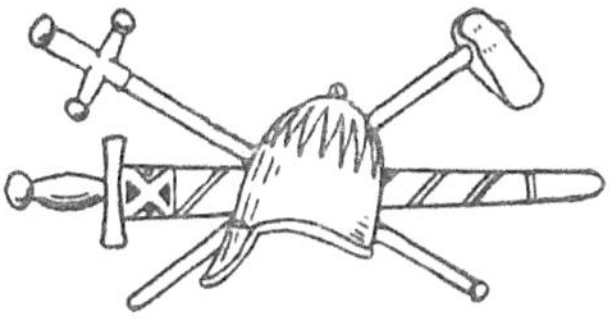

Chapter 27

Queen Boadicea

45 Generations to King Edward III

Rule Britannia! Britannia rules the waves! Britons never shall be slaves! Thus sang James Thompson two hundred years ago.

Sad indeed is the lament of the Ancient Briton: "We dwelt in a goodly land. We were peaceful and happy. By and by the Romans came and brought us new laws and a strange religion. Then the Romans went and the Saxons came, and the Danes came, and all manner of strange and fierce people landed on the eastern shores of Britain. With beguiling words they entered our homes and with loving protestations they married our daughters. But soon, alas so soon! they trampled out our hearth fires and despoiled our altars; and they set up kingdoms and kingships among us and now the shepherd and the husbandman of the Cymry and the great and Sovereign Lords of the Cymry are gone, even the speech of our fathers has passed from us and the songs of our childhood are forgotten. Once happy Britain has become the home of strangers!"

Knowledge of noble ancestry should be an incentive to noble living.—Diary, 18 June 1897.

Chapter 27

THE DRUIDS

Before the Days of Abraham

Druidism was introduced into England more than two thousand years before Christ by Hu Gadarn, the Mighty, the first colonizer of Britain and for many generations Boadicea's people had been Druids. The whole population of southern England, including the eastern coast inhabited by the Iceni, was under the control of the Druidical priesthood consisting of three orders: (1) The Druids, the guardians and interpreters of the laws and the religious guides and instructors of youth and the judges of the people. (2) The Eubates, the working clergy who performed all the rites, and (3) The Bards, whose duty it was to preserve in verse the memory of any remarkable event, to celebrate the triumph of their heroes and, by their exhortation and songs, excite the chiefs and people to deeds of courage and daring on the day of battle.

Notwithstanding its many errors, its terrible idolatry, superstition and cruel practices, Druidism had some points in its favor. For example it made the immortality of the soul the basis of all its teaching, holding it to be the principal incentive for a righteous life. The defence of one's country in a just war was a high virtue in its system. Yet for a people of such remarkable civilization and culture, their conduct was barbarous and cruel. Druidism declined and at last disappeared because although it taught forgiveness and love, it lacked the power to perform these virtues. Christianity supplied this power and Druidism vanished, not however until it had accomplished its special mission, the preservation in Western Europe of the idea of the unity and trinity of God and in extension of this principle it employed the triads, or trinities of life and worship, of which many hundreds were taught.

There is touching beauty in many of these ancient Druidic and later Welsh triads, for example:

There are three obligations of every man: Justice, love, humility.

There are three rights of every man: Life, freedom, achievement.

There are three duties of every man: Worship God; Be just to all men; Die for your country.

Believe in God who made thee; Love God who saved thee; Fear God who will judge thee.

Three persons have the claims of brothers and sisters: The widow; the orphan; the stranger.

There were in ancient Britain no less than forty Druidic universities which were also the capitals of the forty tribes, the originals of the modern counties, which preserve for the most part the ancient tribal limits. In these universities was a total enrollment of sixty thousand souls, among whom were included the young nobility of Britain. It required twenty years' attendance at college to master the circle of Druidic knowledge, for they taught all that was known concerning natural philosophy, astronomy, arithmetic, botany, geometry, law, medicine, poetry, oratory and natural theology. Well informed on all known subjects were the graduates of a Druid university.

Caesar records in his commentaries that they instructed their pupils in the movements of the heavenly bodies and the grandeur of the universe. Their knowledge of mathematics must have been considerable, since they applied it to the measurement of the earth and stars. In mechanics they were equally advanced, judging from the huge monuments which remain. Of these the most remarkable

STONEHENGE RESTORED

in England is Stonehenge (hanging stones) on Salisbury plain, consisting of 139 enormous blocks from five to twenty-two feet high, arranged in a circle. This Druidic temple and cairn is now nearly 3500 years old; older than the Ten Commandments!

In the clan times, the preservation of a pedigree was necessary to maintain all that was valuable in blood, station and property. Without a pedigree a man was an outlaw; he had no clan, consequently no legal rights or standing. Genealogies were guarded with extreme jealousy and recorded with painful exactitude by the herald-bards of each clan. On the public reception into the clan of a child at the age of fifteen, his family genealogy was proclaimed, and all challengers of it commanded to come forward. By the common law every Briton held as his birthright ten acres of land. I am indebted to Dr. G. Campbell Morgan and Dr. R. Wynn Morgan for the above and for much of the following.

THE ORDER OF DRUIDS

No one could be a candidate for the Order who could not prove his descent from nine successive generations of free forefathers. No slave could be a Druid; becoming one, he forfeited his Order and privileges. Here is one of the chief reasons for the long, stubborn and finally successful resistance to the Roman armies. They never conquered the island. It was not until A.D. 120, and then only by treaty, that Britain became a part of the Roman dominions, the Britons retaining their kings, their laws and their property, in return promising to furnish three legions for the defense of the common empire.

The ancient British slogan:
Y Gwir Yn Erbyn Y Byd.
"The truth against the world"

Every congress was opened with the words "The country is above the king." Generally speaking the authority and the influence of the Druids were as popular as they were great. The extreme penalty lodged in their hands and the one most dreaded was that of excommunication. The terror it inspired is proof that it was not abused and but rarely resorted to. Woe to the unfortunate upon whom this awful sentence fell. He was now no longer considered a human being. Like the beast of the forest his life was at the mercy of anyone who chose to take it. He had no more civil rights and could neither inherit land nor sue for the recovery of debts. Everyone was at liberty to spoil his property. None could feed or aid him, and even his nearest kin fled from him in horror and aversion.

It was thus performed: After a year and a day's allowance for the offender to make amends, if he failed to do so he was brought before the congress and the Sword of the Tribe was unsheathed against the offender by name. His name was then erased from the tribal and family genealogies, his badge taken, his sword broken, his head shaved and the executioner drew blood from his forehead and, pouring it on his head exclaimed "the blood of this accursed man be on his own head." His forehead then branded, he was led forth, the herald proclaiming "this man hath no name nor family nor tribe. Henceforth let no man touch him nor speak to him, nor eye look upon him, nor hand bury him, and let perpetual darkness be upon him." Unable to sustain such horrors, worse than death, the excommunicated crawled away to become an unburied skeleton.

Clad in white and wearing ornaments of gold, they celebrated their mystic rites in the depths of the forest. Groves of oak were their chosen retreats. The Druids held the mistletoe in highest veneration, and when found growing upon the oak it represented man, a creature entirely dependent on God for support and yet with an individual existence and will of his own. Marriage to one woman was early established among the Britons. They treated their wives with a respect which could only have existed amongst a people where marriage elevated woman to a level with man, and often they were willingly governed by the widows of their kings who, in more than one instance, conducted them to battle.

CAESAR'S FIRST INVASION

Caesar found the people living in a very primitive state depending for support upon their farms, flocks and herds. Their houses were rather rudely built, formed of wicker and plastered with mud; and their cities consisted of a number of these huts ranged without order, and surrounded by a deep ditch.

The costume of the ancient Britons was equally primitive, being made from the spoils of the chase. Tertullian informs us, that in preparing for war, they were accustomed to throw off these skins and display with pride their tall, muscular bodies, tattooed in deep blue lines, as the British sailors still do. They cast off all superfluous clothing to fight, a thing which the British school boy continues to do and no other nation does. These immemorial usages, rooted in something much deeper than taste or imagination, continue the memory of the true-blue ancient Britons.

They were a handsome athletic race, wearing their hair long, and the moustache upon the upper lip also long and flowing; and scanty as their numbers were, might have always bid defiance to the Romans or any other invaders, had they not been divided by internal factions. Such was the country and such the condition of its inhabitants when Julius Caesar, the greatest man Rome has ever produced, undertook its conquest.

His first invasion occurred on 5 August B.C. 55. Eighty vessels from Calais and eighteen galleys of cavalry sailed from a distant port at about the same time. The troops landed at Deal; a considerable force of the Britons under Caswallon resisted the attack but the disciplined Romans overcame them. The eighteen galleys with cavalry were driven back on shore by a severe storm and the same night under a full moon at the equinox, the tide rose to an unusual height and destroyed many of Caesar's transports. After campaigning fifty-five days, in which time Caesar failed to advance beyond seven miles from the coast, they attacked his camp, a thing without precedent, and he fled with his army by night, taking hostages with him.

Although the Senate at Rome ordered a thanksgiving of twenty days for the triumph of the Roman army, the first expedition against the island cannot be regarded in any other light than a failure.

ANOTHER INVASION

The second invasion took place the year following and lasted four months. On 10 May B.C. 54, more than a thousand ships, carrying five legions and two thousand horsemen, easily landed at Ryde. The Britons overcome, retreated to the woods, where it was impossible for the Roman legions to follow. The next morning, just as the victorious leader was about to follow in pursuit, news arrived from the camp that a violent tempest had seriously damaged the fleet. Many vessels were wrecked and others rendered unfit for service. Julius Caesar was General-in-chief of the Roman armies. After four months of the most desperate fighting, the furthest point Caesar had penetrated from the coast was seventy miles, and having repaired his ships, he decided to pass the winter on the continent. Accordingly, on 25 September, after imposing an annual tribute upon Britain and exacting more hostages, Caesar again took his departure, by night. Leaving not a Roman soldier behind, Caesar flees with all his army, the one which afterwards completed the conquest of the world. Caesar cannot be said to have conquered the island. Although victorious in practically all battles, he made no permanent settlement. More than one classic writer has borne witness to the superb bravery of the ancient Britons, and for nearly a century after, no Roman ventured to set hostile foot upon the island. This dual repulsion of the Romans by the Britons remains unparalleled in history.

He found the English tough in their resistance, as Napoleon did, many centuries later, when he said they were such unreasonable fellows that they never knew when they were beaten. They never did know, and never will!

LATER ATTEMPTS

It is true that 24 years later, in B.C. 30, a third attempt was made to invade Britain. The Emperor Augustus moved half the Page 162 forces of the Empire to the Channel. Cynvelin (Cymbeline), who was educated in Rome by the same Emperor, concentrated his army at Dover. A British fleet, commanded by Bran, swept the Channel. British diplomacy triumphed and the Emperor abandoned his designs. Later invasions were accompanied with only limited success.

In A.D. 42 the Romans prepared to invade England with a large well-equipped fleet, but the Roman army refused to embark and mutinied, saying "We will march anywhere *in* the world, but not *out* of it," whereupon Narcissus was despatched from Rome, declaring he would himself lead them into Britain, where two days later the army landed. King Caradoc headed the British army between the Kentish hills and the Thames, Britain matched in arms against the world, but the odours of elephants imported by the Romans so frightened the horses of the British chariots that Caradoc suffered defeat and a treaty followed.

On the recall of Plautius (who had married Gladys, a sister of Caradoc) a truce was concluded for six months during which Caradoc visited Rome. When shown the public buildings, he said, "It is singular a people possessed of such magnificence at home should envy me my soldier's tent in Britain." After his return he was betrayed by Aregwedd, Queen of the Brigantes, and while asleep as a guest in her palace, was seized and sent as a prisoner to Rome in A.D. 52. "Rome trembled when she saw the Briton, though fast in chains." Caradoc's speech before the Roman Senate is familiar to all. With great calm the hero of forty battles, great in arms, still greater in chains, stood before the court and said:

"Had my government in Britain been directed solely with a view to the preservation of my hereditary domains or the aggrandizement of my own family, I might long since have entered this city an ally, not a prisoner; nor would you have disdained for a friend a king descended from illustrious ancestors and the sovereign of many nations. My present condition, stript of its former majesty, is as adverse to me as it is a cause of triumph to you. What then? I was lord of men, horses, arms and wealth: what wonder if at your demand I refused to resign them? Does it follow that, because the Romans aspire to universal dominion, every nation is to accept the vassalage they would impose? I am now in your power: betrayed, not conquered. Had I, like others, yielded without resistance, where would have been the name of Caradoc? And where your glory? Oblivion would have buried both in the same tomb. Bid me live, and I shall survive for ever in history as one example at least of Roman clemency."

The life of Caradoc was spared on condition of his never again bearing arms against Rome. A residence of seven years at Rome was imposed upon him, and while here Gladys, his daughter, was adopted by the Emperor Claudius and became Claudia Britannica. In her seventeenth year, A.D. 53, she married Rufus Pudens, a wealthy Roman senator, and she alone of a large family group died a natural death, before any of her children, in A.D. 97. (See No. 37 below.) With their two sons and two daughters they were instructed in the Christian faith by St. Paul and within a short time, around the year 100, all these except the mother, suffered martyrdom in Rome under Nero, who at age 16 succeeded Claudius as emperor on 28 September A.D. 53.

BOADICEA'S HUSBAND

Prasutagus had for many years under the Claudian treaty been the faithful ally of Rome. He was ruler of the Iceni, inhabitants of the land now comprising the counties of Norfolk and Suffolk, and in part Cambridgeshire and Huntingdonshire. The capital was Venta, now Winchester.

After a war of about forty years, waged by the Emperors Claudius, Nero and Domitian, much of the Icenian land was subject to Roman authority. Prasutagus, thinking to protect his Queen, Boadicea, and their daughters, made the Emperor Nero coheir with them of his great wealth. The outcome was not as planned, for at his death in A.D. 61 the Roman officers took complete possession of the palace, giving up the princesses to the licentious brutality of the soldiers, and humiliating the Queen by a public scourging. Stung to madness by the wrongs which most nearly affect womanhood, Boadicea leads 120 thousand men to battle. The sense of injury has changed her whole nature and she lives only for revenge. At Leicester she ascended the general's tribunal. Her long golden tresses reached nearly to her knees. In her hand she carried a spear. Her manner calm, her voice deep and pitiless, she thus in part addressed the Britons:

QUEEN BOADICEA EXHORTING HER COUNTRYMEN

"I rule not over beasts of burden as are the effeminate nations of the East, nor over tradesmen and traffickers, nor like the man-woman Nero, over slaves; but I rule over Britons, little versed in craftiness and diplomacy, it is true, but born and trained to war; men who in the cause of liberty willingly risk their lives, their lands and property. Queen of such a race, I implore your aid for freedom, for victory! Never let a foreigner bear rule over me or my country-men! Never let slavery reign in this island!"

Attacking their oppressors, they burned London, Colchester and other cities. Some say her army had now increased to 230 thousand men. Seventy to eighty thousand on each side were killed. These valiant Icenians were finally defeated by the Romans under Sentonius Paulinus in A.D. 62, and rather than fall into the hands of the invaders, Boadicea took her own life with a poisoned dagger, and is buried in Flintshire.

Chapter 27

BOADICEA, in latin "Victoria," is described in the records as "cousin" of Caradoc and his sister Gladys.

One of her daughters, whose name has not been preserved, Dr. Anderson tells us, became the wife of Meric, whom the Romans Page 162 called Marius. He was son of Arviragus, King of Britain, and his wife Venissa Julia, daughter of Tiberius Claudius Caesar, Emperor of Rome, who was grandson of Mark Anthony.

Marius died A.D. 125. His remarkably long ancestry has been preserved in the ancient Welsh records.

King Caradoc's birth-book or pedigree register records his own as well as others' descent from "clari majores" illustrious ancestors, through thirty-six generations from Aedd Mawr and runs as follows:

1. AEDD MAWR, King Edward the Great, who appears to have lived about 1300 B.C., the time of Boaz and Ruth, had a son

2. Brydain who settled in the island at an early date and being a great legislator as well as a warrior, according to tradition gave his name to the entire island, which has since been corrupted into Britain. His son

3. Annyn Tro was the father of

4. Selys Hen whose line of descendants continues as follows:

5. Brwt

6. Cymryw

7. Ithon

8. Gweyrydd

9. Peredur

10. Llyfeinydd

11. Teuged

12. Llarian, in whose day London was a considerable town,

having been founded B.C. 1020, or earlier as some hold, at least 270 years before the founding of Rome.

13. Ithel

14. Enir Fardd

15. Calchwynydd

16. Llywarch

17. Idwal

18. Rhun

19. Bleddyn

20. Morgan

21. Berwyn

22. Ceraint Feddw, an irreclaimable drunkard, deposed by his subjects for setting fire just before harvest to the cornfields of Siluria, now Monmouthshire.

23. Brywlais

24. Alafon

25. Anyn

26. Dingad

27. Greidiol

28. Ceraint

29. Meirion

30. Arch

31. Caid, the register continues, had

32. Ceri

33. Baran.

[Caswallon was king at the time of the first invasion. The antagonist of Caesar, he successfully repulsed the armies of the ablest general of antiquity, the conquerors of Europe, Asia and Africa. He continued to reign after the invasion seven years.]

34. Llyr (King Lear). He was educated in Rome by Augustus Caesar. Among the "wise sayings" recorded by the Bards we find this attributed to Llyr: "No folly but ends in misery." He was the father of

35. Bran, King of Siluria, and commander of the British fleet. In the year A.D. 36 he resigned the crown to his son Caradoc and became Arch-Druid of the college of Siluria, where he remained some years until called upon to be a hostage for his son. During his seven years in Rome he became the first *royal* convert to Christianity, and was baptized by the Apostle Paul, as was his son Caradoc and the latter's two sons, Cyllinus and Cynon. Henceforth he is known as Bran the Blessed Sovereign. "He was the first to bring the faith of Christ to the Cymry." His recorded proverb is: "There is no good apart from God." He introduced the use of vellum into Britain. His son

36. CARADOC (Caractacus) was King of Siluria (Monmouthshire, etc.), where he died. He was born at Trevan, Llanilid, in Glamorganshire. His valiant services to his country have been told in connection with the attempted invasions of the island. The Bards record his wise saying: "Oppression persisted in brings on death." He had three sons, Cyllin (Cyllinus), Lleyn (Linus) and Cynon, and two daughters, Eurgain and Gladys (Claudia).

37. St. Cyllin, King of Siluria, son of Caradoc, was sainted by the early Church of Britain. "He first of the Cymry gave infants names, for before names were not given except to adults, and then from something characteristic in their bodies, minds or manners."
Page 156
His brother Linus the Martyr, his sister Claudia and her husband Rufus Pudens aided the Apostle Paul in the Christian Church in Rome, as recorded in II Timothy 4:21 and Romans 16:13.*

38. Prince Coel, son of Cyllin, was living A.D. 120. (Dr. Anderson makes him identical with King Coel, son of Marius, of whom later, but this is evidently a misapprehension.) Prince Coel was the father of

39. King Lleuver Mawr, of whom later, the second Blessed Sovereign (Cadwallader was the third).

* Rufus Pudens and St. Paul are shown to be half brothers: children of the same mother, they had different fathers.

"His mother and mine." She thus appears to have been the mother of an elder son, Paul, by a Hebrew husband, and a younger son, Rufus, by a second marriage with a Roman Christian.

CONTEMPORANEOUS EVENTS

AUGUSTUS OCTAVIUS CAESAR, called Caesar Augustus in St. Luke 2, verse 1, the first Roman Emperor, was the successor and grandnephew of Julius Caesar. During his reign and at a moment of universal peace when "no war nor battle sound was heard the world around," there was born in Bethlehem among the hills of Judea, One whose influence on the future of the world was destined to outshine the influence of all the warriors and emperors the world has ever seen. JESUS was born among the lowly, and the rushing, seething Roman world knew nothing of the event. But the time was coming when all history would be reckoned by so many years before or after the birth of Christ. "He came unto His own things and His own people received Him not." Said they, "We will not have this Man to reign over us," and He was put to death under a pretense of religious and civil law. His disciples bore witness to the fact that He rose from the dead and they eagerly devoted their lives, even unto death, to proclaiming the Good News. No wonder that thousands of converts soon joined them. Nor was the new way to succeed by force, but by persuasion and conviction. Saint Paul, a Roman citizen, became the chief instrument in carrying the new religion to the Roman dominions, near and far. It was not long before the converts were made to suffer terrible persecutions. The first of these was in the time of Nero, who to divert suspicion from himself accused the Christians of setting fire to the City of Rome. Nero was one of the wickedest men who ever sat upon a throne and instead of trying to stop the fire is said to have fiddled and danced while Rome burned. Tacitus tells us that a great many Christians were put to death. Some were crucified, some were devoured by wild beasts and some were covered with pitch and set on fire to light the public places at night, "yea, they were stoned, they were sawn asunder, were slain with the sword; they wandered about in sheepskins and goatskins; in deserts, and in mountains, and in dens and caves of the earth." With the universal decline of private virtue, the mighty Roman Empire inevitably decayed, but Christianity survived all the terrific persecutions and within three centuries became the religion fostered and promoted by the State.

No civilization has ever survived a moral breakdown.

Capoir, was father of Manogan who married and had

BELI (Heli) THE GREAT, died B. C. 72, leaving two sons, Caswallon and his brother Lud.

LUD, died B. C. 62 (son of Beli) was father of

(A) TENUANTIUS, described as "a gentle ruler," who had

(B) Cynvelin (Cymbeline) King of Britain. He was educated in Rome by Augustus Caesar, and later forestalled the third invasion of the island. His eleventh son

(C) ARVIRAGUS, King of Britain, lived in Avalon, the renowned enemy of Rome, called cousin of King Caradoc, as stated Page 158 above married Venissa, and their son

(D) Meric (Marius) King of Britain, married the daughter of Boadicea (Victoria). They had a daughter (E) Eurgen, of whom later, and a son Coel, who became King of Britain in 125. OLD Page 190 KING COLE was "a merry old soul," educated in Rome, built Colchester (Coel-Castra) and died A.D. 170, see Chapter 30.

For the Frankish kings descended from King Cole, see page 164. Dr. Morgan continues:

(E) Eurgen was the mother of

(F) Gladys who became the wife of:

39. Lleuver Mawr (Lucius the Great) a great grandson of Caradoc. He was baptized at Winchester by his father's first cousin St. Timothy, who suffered martyrdom at age 90 on 22 August A.D. 139. When in A.D. 170 Lucius succeeded to the throne of Britain he became the first Christian *king* in the world. He founded the first church at Llandaff and changed the established religion of Britain from Druidism to Christianity. He died in 181 leaving an only recorded child, a daughter

40. Gladys who became the wife of Cadvan of Cambria, Prince of Wales. Their daughter

41. Strada "the Fair," married Coel, a later king of Colchester, living A.D. 232, whose parentage is not stated. They were the parents of

42. Helen "of the Cross." The arms of Colchester were "a cross with three crowns." She was born 248, died 328, and became the wife of Constantius I, afterward Emperor of Rome and, in right of

his wife, King of Britain. He was born 242 and died 306. Their son

43. CONSTANTINE THE GREAT, born 265, died 336. Of British birth and education, he is known as the first Christian *Emperor*. With a British army he set out to put down the persecution of Christians forever. The greatest of all Roman Emperors, he annexed Britain to the Roman Empire and founded Constantinople.

In 325 he assembled the Council, which he attended in person, at Nicea in Bithynia, Asia Minor, which formulated the Nicene Creed. The following edict of Constantine clearly sets forth the standards of his life: "We call God to witness, the Saviour of all men, that in assuming the government we are influenced solely by these two considerations—the uniting of the empire in one faith, and the restoration of peace to a world rent in pieces by the insanity of religious persecution." According to Dr. Anderson, he married Fausta and had three sons, Constantine II, Constantius II and Constans I.

These uncertain descents are as recorded by Plantagenet-Harrison and Dr. Anderson.

His eldest son, Constantine II, was the father of Uther Pendragon, who became King of Britain in 498. The latter's son, KING ARTHUR, one of the Nine Worthies, succeeded his father in the year 516 at the age of 15, repulsed the invading Saxons and died 21 May 542. He is most popularly known in connection with his fabulous Knights of the Round Table. In a sumptuous tomb at Glastonbury, he rests beside his wife Guinevere.

44. Constantius II, second son of Constantine the Great, married Fausta and died in 360. Their son

45. Constantius III, who married Placida and died in 421, had

46. Valentinian III, died in 455, whose line of descendants continues as follows:

47. Eudoxia became the wife of Hunneric who died in 480

48. Hilderic, King of the Vandals in 525

49. Hilda, wife of Frode VII, who died in 548

50. Halfdan, King of Denmark

51. Ivar Vidfadma, King of Denmark and Sweden in 660

52. Roric Slingeband, King of Denmark and Sweden in 700

53. Harald Hildetand, King of Denmark and Sweden in 725

54. Sigurd Ring, living in 750

55. Rayner Lodbrok, King of Denmark and Sweden, who died in 794, having married Aslanga

56. Sigurd Snodoye, King of Denmark and Sweden, died in 830

57. Horda Knut, King of Denmark, died in 850

58. Frotho, King of Denmark, died in 875

59. Gorm Enske who married Sida and died in 890

60. Harold Parcus, King of Denmark, whose wife was Elgiva, daughter of Ethelred I, King of England, a brother of King Alfred the Great

61. Gorm del Gammel, King of Denmark, who died in 931. His wife was Thyra

62. Harald Blaatand, King of Denmark, who died in 981

63. Lady Gunnora, wife of Richard I, third Duke of Normandy, born 933, died 996. They had (beside their son Richard II, see later) a son

Page 194 64. Robert d'Evereux, the Archbishop, who died in 1087

65. Richard, Count d'Evereux, who died in 1067

66. Agnes Evereux, who became the wife of Simon I de Montfort

67. Bertrade Montfort, wife of Fulk IV, Count d'Anjou, born 1043, died 1109

Fulk's descent from Old King Cole is as follows:

THE FRANKISH KINGS

Pages 162, 190 OLD KING COLE, son of Marius (D) above, was the father of

101. Athildis, wife of Marcomir IV, King of Franconia, who died 149. They had

102. Clodomir IV, King of the Franks, died 166. His wife was Hasilda, daughter of the King of the Rugij. The lineal descent continues as follows:

103. King Farabert, died 186

104. King Sunno, died 213
105. King Hilderic, died 253
106. King Bartherus, died 272
107. King Clodius III, died 298
108. King Walter, died 306
109. King Dagobert, died 317
110. Genebald I, Duke of the East Franks, who died 350
111. King Dagobert, died 379
112. King Clodius I, died 389
113. King Marcomir, died 404
114. King Pharamond, who married Argotta, daughter of Genebald

115. King Clodio married Basina de Thuringia and died 455

116. Sigermerus I, who married the daughter of Ferreolus Tonantius

117. Ferreolus, who married Deuteria, a Roman lady

118. Ausbert, who died 570, having married Blithildes, daughter of Clothaire I, King of France (and his wife Ingonde) and granddaughter of CLOVIS THE GREAT, King of France, born 466, baptized at Rheims 496, and died 511, and his wife St. Clothilde of Burgundy, "the Girl of the French Vineyards." It was she who led him to embrace Christianity, and 3000 of his followers Page 206 were baptised in a single day. When Clovis first listened to the story of Christ's crucifixion, he was so moved that he cried "If I had been there with my valiant Franks I would have avenged Him."

Ausbert and Blithildes were the parents of

119. Arnoul, Bishop of Metz, died 601, who married Oda de Savoy, and had

120. St. Arnolph, Bishop of Metz, died 641, who married Lady Dodo, and had

121. Anchises, married Begga of Brabant, who died 698. They had

122. Pepin d'Heristal, Mayor of the Palace, died 714, who married Alpais.

MAGISTER PALATII

The royal successors of Clovis were woefully inefficient. They left the rule of the kingdom to their Mayors of the Palace, and only showed themselves to the people once a year, at the March parliament, when, adorned with crowns and their fair hair flowing loose to their waists, they rode on a car drawn by oxen. As they did little but eat and drink and enjoy themselves, they went by the name of the sluggard kings, all power being in the hands of the Mayors of the Palace. Among these mayors, Pepin of Heristal made himself conspicuous. His home was near Spa, in the pretty woodland country about Liege. He made the office hereditary in his family. His heroic son

123. Charles Martel, the Hammer, Mayor of the Palace, King of France, was still more famous because, in the decisive battle of Tours in 732 he utterly routed the Arabs who had conquered Spain and the south of France. Charles Martel married Rotrude and died in 741. His sons

124. Pepin the Short and Karlomann, succeeded him, but Karlomann resigned his authority into his brother's hands and, tired of fighting, entered a monastery. Pepin had much to do; the Saxons,

Pepin the Short

Bavarians and Arabs were all menacing or revolting, and he had to rush from one part of the kingdom to another, defending its frontiers, and getting no help from the stupid sluggard king, at Paris. At last, impatient of the farce, he sent this question to the Pope: "Who is king, he who governs or he who wears the crown?" "He who governs, of course," answered the Pope. "That is myself," said the little man with a great will; "so the sluggards shall go to sleep forever," and he sent the last of them, Childeric III, into a monastery. Then his nobles put their shields together, and the little man was seated on a chair, on their shields, and with him thus, shouting and raising their shields as high as they could, they marched three times, round the parliament, and then, by St. Boniface, he was anointed Archbishop of Metz, A.D. 752. Pepin did not forget that he owed a debt of gratitude to the Pope for the answer he had given to his question, and when, shortly after, the Pope sent to complain of the trouble occasioned by the Lombards, Pepin crossed the Alps, punished the Lombards, took from them all their territory about Rome and gave it to the Pope "to belong to him and to the bishops of Rome forever. That was the beginning of the Papal sovereignty. The States of the Church, as they were called, remained under the sovereignty of the Popes until 1871." Pepin le Bref, King of France, died in 768, leaving by his wife Bertha of Laon two sons, Charlemagne and Carloman. The latter died a few years later and then, with the consent of the great nobles, Charlemagne, Charles the Great, became king.

125. CHARLEMAGNE, the greatest figure of the Middle Ages, Page 178
see Chapter 29, by his wife Hildegarde of Suabia, born 757, died 30 April 782, had a son

126. Louis I, the Debonaire, see Chapter 29; who by his second Page 188
wife Judith, daughter of Guelph, Count of Andech and Bavaria, and his wife Edith of Saxony, was father of Gisela, grandmother of Duke Burkhardt who died 911, from whom descended Ulrich von Uerikon, Swiss knight, born 1259. Gisela was also the ancestress of Hugh Capet, King of France and of Amicia, wife of Richard de Page 59
Clare, the Surety. Louis I by his first wife Ermengarde, who died 818, daughter of Ingram, Count of Hasbania, was father of

127. Lothaire, Earl of Germany, who married Ermengarde of Alsace, and had

128. Ermengarde, who was the wife of Gislebert. The lineal descent continues:

129. Regnier I, Count of Hainault, died 916, who married Albreda

130. Gislebert, Duke of Lorraine, married Gerberga and died 930

131. Albreda of Lorraine, wife of Renaud, Count de Roucy, who died 973

132. Ermentrude Roucy, wife of Alberic II, Count de Macon, who died 975

133. Beatrice Macon, wife of Geoffrey I de Gastinois

134. Geoffrey II de Gastinois married Ermengarde d'Anjou

Page 164 135. Fulk IV, Count d'Anjou, born 1043, died 1109, married Bertrade de Montfort, No. 67 above, and had

68. Fulk V, Count d'Anjou, born 1092, died 1144, married Ermengarde du Maine who died 1126. They were the parents of

Page 192 69. GEOFFREY PLANTAGENET, born 1113, died 1151, who married Matilda of England, born 1103, died 1167, a great great great granddaughter of Richard I, Duke of Normandy (and his wife Lady Gunnora, No. 63 above), as follows: Richard I's son

Page 194 533. Richard II, Duke of Normandy, died in 1026, having married Judith de Bretagne, who died in 1018. Their son

534. Robert of Normandy who by Herleve de Falaise had

Page 195 535. WILLIAM THE CONQUEROR, born 1027, died 1086, see later, who married Maud of Flanders, died 1083, and had

536. Henry I, King of England, born in 1070, died in 1135, whose wife, Matilda of Scotland, was born in 1082 and died in 1118. She was the daughter of Malcolm III Canmore. Henry and Matilda had

537. Matilda of England, wife of Geoffrey Plantagenet, No. 69 above, and they had

70. Henry II, King of England, married Eleanor of Aquitaine

71. John, King of England, married Isabel de Taillefer

72. Henry III, King of England, married Eleanor of Provence

73. Edward I, King of England, married Eleanor of Castile, see Chapter 34 Page 213

74. Edward II, King of England, married Isabel of France, see Chapter 34 Page 217

75. Edward III, King of England, married Philippa of Hainault, see Chapter 35 Page 218

Egbert King of West Saxons
Died 839

Chapter 28

The Saxon Royal Line

201. CERDIC, a patriarch of the Blood Royal of Saxony, Page 163
landed in Hampshire in 495 and in 519 gained a great victory at Charford. He was first crowned king of the West Saxons when the renowned King Arthur, who had his castle on the steep coast of Cornwall, and whose ancestry is given in Chapter 27, yielded to him the section of country now known as Hampshire and Somerset. In 520, being unable to extend his rule west of the Avon and defeated at Badbury, co. Dorset, Cerdic withdrew. Ten years later he conquered the Isle of Wight. He died in 534.
His son Creoda was father or brother of

202. CYNRIC, who had greatly distinguished himself in the wars of his father. He fought a great battle in 552 against the Britons, but his reign was a comparatively peaceful one. He died in 560. His son

203. CEOLIN, succeeded his father and greatly enlarged his kingdom. He was the father of

204. CUTHWINE, who was slain in battle against the Scots in 581. He was the father of

205. CUTHA, second son, who had

206. CEOLWALD, father of

207. CENRED, who had

208. INGILD, youngest son, who died in 718, the father of

209. EOPPA, who had

210. EAFA, who had

211. ALEMUND, the father of

Chapter 28

Page 178 212. EGBERT, called First king of all England. He was born about 775 and fled from his cousin Brethrick, taking refuge in the court of Charlemagne, where he stayed for about twelve years, serving as one of his captains. On the death of Brethrick, who was poisoned by his wife, Egbert returned to England. In 802 at Winchester he was crowned king of the West Saxons. He subdued West

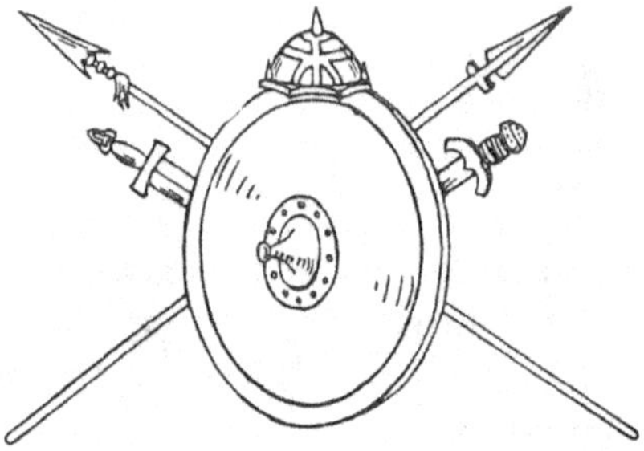

SAXON ARMS

Wales, or Cornwall, defeated the king of Mercia at Ellandune, annexed Kent and in 829 became overlord of all the English kings and gave the name of England to the whole realm. There are still in existence some coins struck by Egbert, though these are now extremely rare. In 835 Egbert defeated a formidable army of Danes at Hingston Down in Cornwall, when they attempted to invade England. He married Lady Redburga and dying in 839, was buried at Winchester. He was succeeded by his son

213. ETHELWULF, "Noble Wolf." During his reign the Danes miserably spoiled England, daring to winter there for the first time. In 851 Ethelwulf routed them at Okely in Surrey. By the advice of St. Swithin, Bishop of Winchester, he granted to the church the tithe of all his dominions. His first wife, the mother of Alfred, was Lady Osburga, daughter of Oslac, the royal cup-bearer. On a pil-
Pages 183 188 grimage to Rome in 855, Ethelwulf married as his second wife, Judith, daughter of Charles the Bald, see Chapter 29. When he returned home it is said that he made his son Ethelbald king of Wessex, and retained Kent for his own rule. He died 13 January 857, and was buried at Stamridge, his body later being removed to Winchester. Ethelwulf was succeeded by each of his four sons in turn, the fourth and youngest of whom was

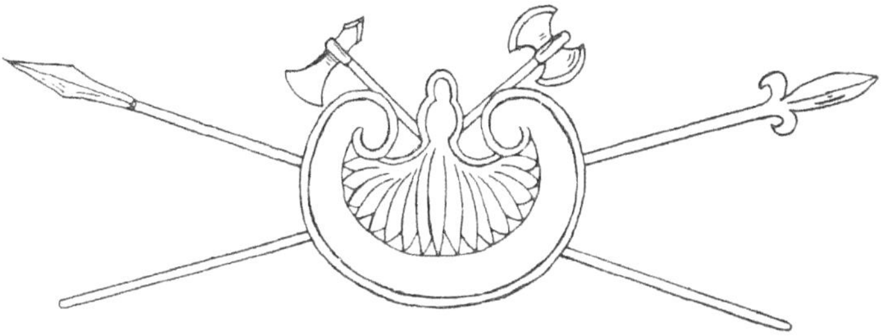

DANISH ARMS

214. ALFRED THE GREAT, the ablest king who ever sat upon the English throne. No name in English history is so justly popular as his. That he taught his people to defend themselves and defeat their enemies, is the least of his many claims to our grateful admiration; he did much more than this: he launched his people upon a great advance in civilization, and showed a horde of untaught country men that there were other and worthier pursuits than war or the pleasures of the table. He was indeed one of those highly gifted men that would seem to be especially raised up by Providence to protect and advance his people.

Alfred, the Founder of England's Civilization and Nationality, was born at Wantage, in Berkshire, in the year 849, ascended the throne in 871 at the age of 23, and reigned thirty years. Young Alfred, according to the historian Asser, Bishop of Sherborne, was a more comely person and of a sweeter disposition than his older brothers and consequently became the favourite of both his parents and was sent by them to Rome, while yet a child, in order that he might be anointed king by the Pope. But though Ethelwulf showed this especial instance of regard for his son, he altogether neglected his education, and the young prince in his twelfth year had not yet learned to read and write. But if he could not read for himself, he nevertheless loved to listen to the rude but inspiring strains of Saxon poetry when recited by others, and had he not been a hero and a statesman, he might easily have been a poet.

In 871, Alfred succeeded as king, at a period when the whole country was suffering under the ravages of the Danes, and the general misery was yet further increased by a raging pestilence, and the internal dissensions of the people.

Chapter 28

Alfred now for the first time took the field against these ruthless invaders with such skill and courage, that he was able to maintain the struggle till a truce was concluded between the combatants. Neither was this the worst of the evils that beset the Saxon prince. Any compact he might make with one party, had no influence whatever upon others of their countrymen, who had different leaders and different interests. No sooner had he made terms with one horde of pirates than England was invaded by a new force of them under Rollo; and when he had compelled these to abandon Wessex, he was attacked by fresh bands of Danes settled in other parts of England. So long, however, as they ventured to meet him on the open field, his skill secured him the victory; till, taught by repeated defeats, they had recourse to other tactics. That is, suddenly to land and ravage a part of the country, and when a force opposed them, they retired to their ships, and passed to some other part, which in a like manner they ravaged, and then retired as before, until the country, completely harassed, pillaged and wasted by their incursions, was no longer able to resist them. Then they ventured safely to enter and to establish themselves. Therefore Alfred, finding a navy necessary, built England's first fleet.

In the winter of the fourth year of his reign, pressed by the Danes, he was forced to flee his court and conceal himself for a time, disguised as a peasant, in the hut of one of his herdsmen who did not know his face. There the romantic incident of the burnt cakes is supposed to have occurred. The story is told by many of the old writers, but nowhere so fully as in the life of St. Neot. There we read:

Now it happened that on the Sabbath day, the herdsman, as usual, led his cattle to their accustomed pastures, and the King remained alone with the man's wife. She as necessity required, placed a few loaves, on a pan, with fire underneath, to be baked for their repast, on her husband's return.

While she was of need busied, peasant-like, upon other affairs, she went anxious to the fire, and found the bread burning on the other side. She immediately assailed the king with reproaches. "Why, man, do you sit thinking there, and are too proud to turn the bread? Whatever be your family, with such manners and sloth, what trust can be put in you hereafter? If you were a nobleman, you would be glad to eat the bread which you neglect to attend to." The king, though stung by her upbraidings, yet heard her with patience and mildness, and roused by her scolding, took care to bake her bread as she wished.

KING ALFRED MINDING THE CAKES

This tale has been variously told; some accounts making the disguised prince busy working upon his bow with arrows, and other instruments of war, while the woman gives vent to her indignation in rhyme:

> "To turn the burning cakes you have forgot,
> Prompt as you are to eat them when they're hot."

In a short time the king's hiding place became known to his subjects who flocked to him in numbers. He soon found himself able to carry on a sort of guerrilla warfare upon the nearest Danes. Growing bolder from the general success of these sallies, he at length determined upon more decisive measures; but before making the attempt, it was expedient to learn the actual condition of his enemy. With this view he assumed the costume of a Saxon minstrel, and ventured with his harp into the Danish Camp at Chippenham, about thirty miles distant from his stronghold amongst the marshes. In this disguise he went from tent to tent, and, as some of the chroniclers tell us, was admitted into the tent of Guthrun himself, the Danish leader, his quality of gleeman assuring safety even to a Saxon. Having obtained the necessary information, he returned to his former stronghold at Athelney, which he finally left on the seventh week after Easter, and rode to Egbert's Stone, in the eastern part of Selwood, or the Great Wood. Here he was met by all the neighbouring folk of Somersetshire, Wiltshire and Hampshire who, for fear of the pagans, had not fled beyond the sea. Once more he encountered his enemies and with marvelous success routed the Danes at Ethendune (Edington) in 878 with so much slaughter that they were glad to obtain peace on such terms as he chose to dictate. As merciful as he was good and brave, he then, instead of killing them, proposed peace on condition that they should altogether depart from the western part of England and that Guthrun should become a Christian, in remembrance of the religion which now taught Alfred, the conqueror, to forgive the enemy who had so often injured him. Thereupon Guthrun embraced Christianity and became the adopted son or god-child of Alfred.

Never before was there a king who was so completely devoted to the welfare of his people. Encouraging the arts and sciences, he founded Oxford University. He carried in his bosom a small book in which he noted things he wished to preserve, now a bit of family genealogy, now a prayer. He was equally great as a scholar, a patriot and a legislator, and he was a thorough business man and an able warrior. He made London the capital of England, fortified it in 886, and carried on a defensive war with the Danes from 894 until they withdrew in 897. He organized judicial and educational reforms, compiled a code of laws, rebuilt the schools and invited learned monks from the continent and from Wales to his court to teach the young men there. He was himself a man of much learning; he translated from Latin into Anglo-Saxon parts of the ecclesiastical writings of Bede and others. He was the author of the famous Anglo-Saxon Chronicle, the first history written in any modern language.

His Five Axioms have come down to us:

1. A wise God governs.

2. All suffering may be accounted blessing.

3. God is the chiefest good.

4. Only the good are happy.

5. The foreknowledge of God does not conflict with man's free will.

There are many things to the credit of King Alfred. He divided his time, setting aside definite portions for certain work. But how to accomplish this? He cut notches in candles, dividing time much as we do now, and to prevent the wind from blowing the candles out or burning unevenly, he had them put into cases formed of wood and white horn. These were the first lanterns made in England.

He was a great and good king and wherever the descendants of the Saxons of his day are, in Europe, or America, or elsewhere, the influence of Alfred's life goes on for good. After reigning thirty years, he died 28 October 901, aged 52. On his deathbed he spoke this message: "This I can now most truly say, that I have sought to live worthily while I lived, and after my life to leave to the men who come after me a remembering of me in good works."

Alfred married in 869 Lady Alswitha, who died 904, a daughter of Ethelred and Edburga of the royal house of Mercia, in the central part of England. Their second son was

215. EDWARD THE ELDER, "the Unconquered King." He reigned 24 years from 901 to 925. He was not, like his father, a legislator or a scholar, although it is said that he founded the University of Cambridge, but he was a great warrior. He gradually extended his sway over the whole island, in which project he was assisted by his sister the Lady of Mercia who headed her own troop and gained victories over both Danes and Britons. Tradition assigns to Edward an even wider rule shortly before his death. In the middle of the ninth century the Picts and the Scots had been amalgamated under Kenneth MacAlpin, the King of the Scots, **Page** *191*
just as Mercia and Wessex were being welded together by the attacks of the Danes. It is said that in 925 the King of the Scots together with other northern rulers, chose Edward "to father and lord." Probably this statement only covers some act of alliance formed by the English King with the King of Scots and other lesser rulers. Nothing was more natural than that the Scottish King, Constantine, should wish to obtain the support of Edward against his enemies; and it was also natural that if Edward agreed to support him he would require some acknowledgment of the superiority of the English King. After a prosperous reign, King Edward died at Forndon, Northamptonshire in 925. His eldest child by his third wife Lady Edgina, daughter of Sigilline, Earl of Meapham, was

Chapter 28

216. EDMUND I, MAGNIFICUS, born 922, the twelfth of his father's fifteen children. The first of the six Boy Kings, he reigned between the years 940 and 946. He had to meet a general uprising of the Danes of Mercia as well as those of the North. In the suppression of this he showed himself to be a great statesman as well as a great warrior. Little is definitely known about the policy of the Scots at this time but it appears that they joined the English whenever they were afraid of the Danes, and joined the Danes whenever they were afraid of the English. Edmund made it to be the interest of the Scottish King permanently to join the English. The southern part of the kingdom of Strathclyde had for some time been under the English Kings. In 945 Edmund took the remainder, but gave it to Malcolm on condition that he should be his fellow-worker by sea and land. The King of the Scots thus entered into a position of dependent alliance towards Edmund. A great step was thus taken; the dominant powers in the island were to be English and Scots, not English and Danes. Edmund thought it worth while to conciliate the Scottish Celts rather than to endeavour to conquer them. The result of Edmund's statesmanship was soon seen, but he did not live to gather its fruits. On 26 May 946 an outlaw named Lief, who had taken his seat at a banquet in his hall, slew him as Edmund was attempting to drag him out by the hair. He was succeeded by his brother Edred. By his wife, Princess Elgiva, "the Fairies' Gift," who died in 944, Edmund had a son Edwig, who became the third Boy King, and his brother

217. EDGAR THE PEACEFUL, the fourth Boy King. Born in 943, and ascending the throne in 959, he maintained order, with the help of Dunstan as his principal advisor. That versatile, able and accomplished arch-deceiver made himself the real ruler of the kingdom and Archbishop of Canterbury as well!

It is recorded that Edgar, while keeping his court at Chester, was rowed down the River Dee, the oars plied by eight kings of neighboring tributary states. The story, though probably untrue, sets forth his power not only over his own immediate subjects, but over the whole island. He had a well-trained army and a strong navy and his title shows that at least he lived on good terms with his neighbors. Edgar died 8 July 975, having reigned sixteen years. He was succeeded by his son Edward the Martyr who reigned from 975 to 978, when he was murdered by his father's second wife. She, whom Edgar had married in 964, was Elfrida, daughter of Ordgar, Earl of Devon, and widow of Ethelwold. By her Edgar had a second son

218. ETHELRED, born in 968, a boy of ten when he became king in 978, who reigned thirty-eight years. He was the last of the six Boy Kings. The epithet "The Unready" which is usually assigned to him is a mistranslation of a word which properly means the Rede-less, the man without counsel. He was entirely without the qualities which befit a king. Ethelred died 23 April 1016 in London, and was buried in St. Paul's. His second wife, whom he married in 1002, was Emma, "the Flower of Normandy," sister of Richard Duke of Normandy. She was the mother of Edward the Confessor. Page 111 Ethelred's first wife was Elfled, daughter of Earl Thorad. They were married in 984, and their eldest son

219. EDMUND II, IRONSIDE, was born in 989 and succeeded his father in April 1,016. In this year he fought six battles, but through treachery he was completely overthrown at Assandun, in Essex. He and Canute the Dane agreed to divide the kingdom, but the heroic Edmund died, having reigned only seven months, and Canute became King of England without a rival. Edmund's death took place at London, 30 November 1016; his body lies at Glastonbury. By his wife Lady Algitha, who died 1014, widow of Sigefrith the Dane, Edmund had a son

220. EDWARD THE EXILE, who fled the country and lived at the court of Hungary until recalled by his father's half brother, Edward the Confessor. He was never crowned king, as he died in London immediately after his return in 1057, and was buried at St. Paul's Cathedral. While on the continent he married Agatha, whose parentage is much in dispute. Edward was the founder of the House of Burgoyne and had one son Edgar Atheling, who married the sister of Malcolm III, King of Scotland, but died without issue, and two daughters, one Christiana, a nun, and the other, named Margaret, died 1093, became the wife of Malcolm III, Canmore, King of Scotland, see Chapter 30. Page 191

Chapter 29

Charlemagne

The following persons also may claim descent from the Emperor Charlemagne:

Mary Adelaide Jones Bush
Margaret Cornelia Hagan Cook
Margelia E. Mackey de Vou
Mary R. de Vou
Ellen Goode Rawlings Evans
Isobel DuBois Hill
Benoni Virginia Trigg Hodges
Ruth Frances Nuckolls Johnston
Anna Shepley Nagel
Howard Ross Nelson
Strobie King Oulla
Nina Gregory Jones Proctor
Grace Edna Vollnogle Phillips
Carolyn Heberton Plumer
Ruth Vail Sankey Ripley
Mary Lane Landis Scott
Belle Swan Tinkham
Gertrude Adelaide Reilly True
Prudence Sharpless Doyle Vollnogle
Thekla Fundenberg Weeks
Emma Huey Wister
Burkhardt Wurts
Ethel Denune Young

CHARLEMAGNE, No. 125 above, King of the Franks and Emperor of the West, was born 2 April, 742, probably at Aix-La-Chapelle. When only twelve years old we find him commissioned to receive and welcome the pontiff who came to implore his father's aid against the barbarians that threatened Rome. He probably accompanied his father in his campaigns at an early age, but the first time that we really see him in the field, is on the renewal of the war with the rebellious Duke of Aquitaine.

Upon the death of Pepin, in 768, Charlemagne and his younger brother Carloman succeeded to equal portions of one of the most powerful of European kingdoms, bounded by the Pyrenees, the Alps, the Mediterranean, and the ocean. But this would hardly have enabled the monarchs, even had they been united, to resist successfully the incursions of the barbarous tribes on the German frontiers of France, which had commenced with the first establishment of the Frankish dominion in Gaul; and which were kept alive by the constant pouring forth of fresh hordes from the overpopulated north. The situation of Charlemagne was rendered yet more perilous by the passive enmity of his brother, and the rebellion of Hunald, the turbulent Duke of Aquitaine. But fortunately Charlemagne had a genius equal to the difficulties of his situation; though his brother refused to aid him, he defeated Hunald; and no less illustrious by his clemency than by his valour and military skill, he forgave the vanquished rebel.

Desiderius, the King of Lombardy, had made large encroachments upon the states of the Roman Pontiff, whose cause was taken up by Charlemagne. This led to feuds, which Bertha, his mother, endeavoured to appease by arranging a marriage between her son and the daughter of the Lombard. But Charlemagne soon took a disgust to the wife thus imposed upon him, and repudiated her, that he might marry Hildegarde, the daughter of a noble family in Suabia.

CHARLEMAGNE and HILDEGARDE

In 771 Carloman died, and Charlemagne was elected to the vacant throne, to the exclusion of his nephews, whose extreme youth made them incapable of wearing the crown in such troublous times. Gilberge, the widow of Carloman, immediately fled, and sought refuge with Desiderius, the common retreat for all who were hostile to the Frankish monarch.

From that time, sole ruler during a reign of forty-three years, he waged incessant wars on all his borders, subduing rebellions, extending his domains and at the same time advancing Christianity. In 772 he began a thirty-year war with the determined Saxons, after the successful opening of which Charlemagne was called to the assistance of Pope Hadrian I against Desiderius, King of the Lombards. Charlemagne marched two armies over the Alps and conquered Lombardy in 774; returned and beat the Saxons again and hastened into Spain, in 778, to help the Arabian rulers of that country against the Osman Caliph of Cordova. It was in this war that Roland, the hero of romance, fell in the pass of Roncesvalles.

In 799 the Romans revolted against Pope Leo III, and were again brought into subjection by Charlemagne. In return, while he was praying on the steps of St. Peter's Church, he was crowned by Leo with the iron crown of the Western Empire, successor of the Roman Caesars, unexpectedly to him, as he pretended, on Christmas Day, 800, amidst the popular acclamations, "Long life and victory to Charles Augustus, crowned by God, great and pacific Emperor of the Romans!"

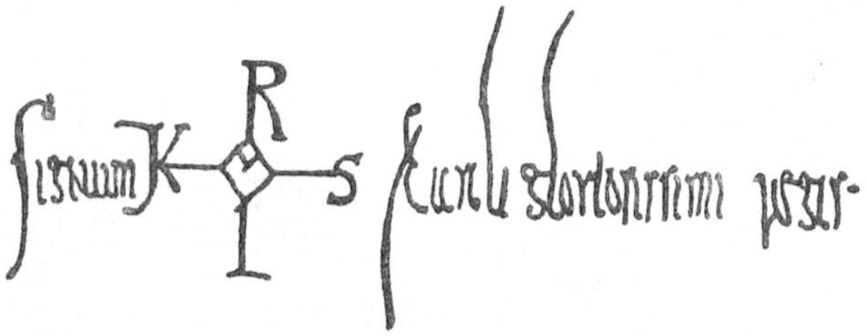

CHARLEMAGNE'S AUTOGRAPH

The extensive domain of Charlemagne was rendered secure only by ceaseless vigilance and warfare. The short intervals of peace which were allowed him, he employed in endeavouring to educate and civilize his people. He made a tour through his dominions, causing local and general improvement, reforming laws, advancing knowledge, and building churches and monasteries, Christianity being one of the chief means to which he trusted for the attainment of his grand objects. In this he was no less successful than he had before been in war. With the exception of the Eastern empire, France was now the most cultivated nation in Europe, even Rome herself sending thither for skilful workmen, while commerce, roads, and mechanics must have been much advanced, as we may infer from the facility with which marble columns and immense stone crosses were often carried through the whole extent of France upon carriages of native construction. Luxury, too, with its attendant arts had made considerable strides. Vases of gold and silver richly carved, silver tables highly wrought, bracelets, rings and table-cloths of fine linen, might be seen in the houses of the nobles. The people must have been dexterous in working iron, for their superiority in this respect is shown by the severe laws forbidding the exportation of arms.

Charlemagne drove back the Arabs, reduced the Huns, and effectually protected his long line of coast from the attempted invasion of the Northmen. It is said, that upon one occasion he arrived at a certain port just as the pirates were preparing to land; but the moment they learned of the presence of the monarch, they immediately fled in great terror at the mere mention of his name. Gazing on the departing vessels, tears came to his eyes. His nobles could not help showing surprise at such unusual emotion in the monarch; which being observed by him, he exclaimed, "I weep not, my friends, because I myself fear these miserable savages; but I weep that they should dare to show themselves upon my coast while I am living, for I foresee the evils they will bring upon my people when I am dead."

It was always an object of first importance with Charlemagne to support the papal authority, as holding out the only means of spreading Christianity, which he justly considered the most effectual instrument he could employ to enlighten and civilize the world. Two disappointed aspirants to the papacy, Campulus and Paschal, made an attempt to mutilate the Pope, and thus disqualify him for his office, but he escaped from their hands and brought his complaints before Charlemagne. The conspirators attempted to justify the deed, by accusing the Pope of atrocious crimes; and the King calling to his aid certain of the Roman prelates, proceeded to sit in judgment on him. The prelates, however, declared that by all the canonical rules they could not judge their superior; and Leo therefore was allowed, according to an old custom, to purge himself, by a solemn oath, of the crimes which had been laid to his charge.

Charlemagne securely laid the foundation of his empire. He was vigilant, sagacious, and energetic, both as a ruler and commander. He fostered agriculture, trade, arts, and letters with untiring zeal, clearing away forests, draining swamps, founding monasteries and schools, building cities, constructing splendid palaces, as at Aix, Worms and Ingelheim, and drawing to his court scholars and poets from all nations, being himself proficient in science, as well as all hardy accomplishments.

Charlemagne was tall and of a commanding presence, and could speak and write Latin as well as his native German. He is said to have written that stirring hymn of the ages

"Veni, Creator Spiritus"

"Creator Spirit, by whose aid
The world's foundations first were laid."

used extensively for centuries at the coronation of kings and ordination of bishops. He fostered all learning and the fine arts, studying rhetoric and astronomy. He reigned over France, half of Germany and four-fifths of Italy. "Excelling all men of the time, to all alike dread and beloved, by all alike admired," his fame spread far and wide. The Caliph Haroun-al-Rashid sent an embassy to the court of Charlemagne with gifts in token of good will.

Attacked with pleurisy he died after a short illness, in the seventy-second year of his age, and the forty-seventh of his reign, 28 January 814. Some years later Charlemagne was canonized by the church. His fourth child

526. PEPIN, son of wife Hildegarde, was born in 776 and died 8 July 810, before his father. He was crowned by the Pope in 781 King of Lombardy and Italy. He married Bertha, daughter of William, Count of Toulouse, and had

527. BERNHARD, King of Lombardy, who succeeded his father about the year 812. He was deposed by his uncle Louis, blinded and put to death about 818. By his wife Cunegonde he had

528. PEPIN, who was deprived of the throne of Italy by Emperor Louis, the Debonaire, and received a part of Vermandois and the Seigneuries of St. Quentin and Peronne. A lay abbot in 840, he was father of Herbert I, see later, and of

529. PEPIN de SENLIS de VALOIS, Count Berengarius of Bretagne, who was living in 893, the father of

530. LADY POPPA, puppet or little doll, who became the first wife of Rollo the Dane, first Duke of Normandy, see Chapter 31. Their son

Page 194

531. WILLIAM LONGSWORD was the father of

532. RICHARD THE FEARLESS, who was the father of

GEOFFREY, Count of Eu and Brionne in Normandy in 996, who had

GISLEBERT CRISPIN, Count of Eu and Brionne, whose eldest son, Richard FitzGilbert, see Chapter 5, was great great grandfather of Richard de Clare, the Surety.

Page 58

Richard the Fearless had another son

533. RICHARD II THE GOOD whose son

534. ROBERT OF NORMANDY became the father of

535. WILLIAM THE CONQUEROR, see Chapter 31. Page 195

---

528. Pepin, son of Bernhard and Cunegonde, above, was the father of

HERBERT I, Count of Vermandois, died 902, who married a daughter of Robert le Fort (and sister of Robert I, King of France) and had

HERBERT II, Count of Vermandois, died 943, who married Hildebrand and had

ROBERT, Count of Vermandois, whose wife was Adelaide de Chalons. They had

ADELAIDE de CHALONS, who died in 976, the wife of Geoffrey, Count d'Anjou, who died in 987, and they had

ERMENGARDE d'ANJOU, who was married to Conan I, Count de Bretagne, and had

JUDITH de BRETAGNE, who died in 1018, wife of No. 533, Page 194
Richard II, Duke of Normandy, who died in 1026. They had

534. ROBERT, Sixth Duke of Normandy, died 1035, who by Herleve de Falaise had

535. WILLIAM THE CONQUEROR, see Chapter 31.

Herbert II, Count of Vermandois, above, died 943, and his wife Hildebrand were the parents of

ADELA, whose husband was Arnulph I, Count of Flanders, son of Baldwin II and grandson of Baldwin I whose wife Judith was Page 170
daughter of Charles II the Bald, see above. They had

BALDWIN III, who died in 962, leaving a son

ARNULPH II, Count of Flanders from 965 to 988, when his son

BALDWIN IV inherited the title, and was Count until 1036. He had a son

BALDWIN V, who married Adela, daughter of Robert, King of Page 185
France. Their daughter

MATILDA, became the wife of William the Conqueror, see Page 199
Chapter 31.

LOUIS I, the Debonaire, No. 126 above, was the father of

LOUIS of Germany, born 806, died 876, married Emma, daughter of Guelph, Count of Andech, and Edith of Saxony, page 428, and had

CARLOMAN, died 880, married Litwinde of Carinthia and had

ARNULPH, died 899, married Oda, daughter of Theodore of Bavaria and had

EDITH of Germany, married to Otto, Duke of Saxony, died 912, and had

HENRY I the Fowler, born 876, died 936, married Matilda of Ringleheim and had

HEDWIGE, wife of Hugh, Duke of France, who died in 956. They had

Hugh Capet

Page 167

HUGH CAPET, King of France, born 938, died 996, whose wife was Adela, daughter of Otto I (some say daughter of William, Duke of Aquitaine) and they had

ROBERT THE PIOUS, born 971, died 1031, who reigned from 996 until the year of his death, a royal composer, chorister and poet, who might have ruled in Italy but preferred that his palace should be his cloister, where he lived in the enjoyment of melody and song. He used to conduct the matins and vespers in his royal robes. He was truly a devout man. He wrote that most beautiful hymn in Latin poetry: "Come, Holy Ghost, in love, Shed on us from above Thine own bright ray."

Robert the Pius

Robert the Pious married Constance, daughter of William, Count of Toulouse, and had

HENRY I, King of France, born about 1005, died 1060, who married, third, Anne of Russia (daughter of Jaroslaus, and granddaughter of Vladimir, first Czar of Russia.) They had

HUGH MAGNUS, who married Adelheid, daughter of Herbert IV, Count of Vermandois, and they had

ISABEL VERMANDOIS, known also as Elizabeth, whose first husband was Robert de Bellomont, made Earl of Leicester and Meullent. Her second husband was William de Warren, Earl of Warren and Surrey, see Chapter 31. A son of the first marriage was

ROBERT de BELLOMONT, second Earl of Leicester, died 1168, who married Amicia, daughter of Ralph de Waer, Earl of Norfolk, Suffolk and Cambridge, and had (beside

ROBERT de BELLOMONT, styled "Blanchmains," third Earl of Leicester, who died in 1196. His wife was Petronella, daughter of Hugh de Grantmesnil, and they had Margaret, wife of the Surety Saire de Quincey, see Chapter 21) a daughter

MABEL (HAWISE) BELLOMONT, married to William Meullent, second Earl of Gloucester. They were the parents of

AMICIA MEULLENT, died 1224/5, the wife of the Surety Richard de Clare, see Chapter 5. Page 59

Robert the Pious and his wife Constance, above, were the parents of

ADELA, who became the wife of Baldwin V, Count of Flanders and Artois, and had, beside Matilda of Flanders, wife of William the Conqueror, a son

BALDWIN VI, Count of Flanders and Artois, who married Richildis, daughter of Rainier V, Count of Hainault, which title was passed on to Baldwin, and their third son was

GILBERT de GANT, feudal Baron of Folkingham, co. Lincoln, who was an officer in the army of William the Conqueror. He married Alice, granddaughter of Hugh de Montfort, and had, beside Alice page 88, Emma page 110 and Agnes page 426,

FILIA GANT, wife of Ivo, Baron de Grantmesnil, who died on a pilgrimage to the Holy Land, son of Hugh, Count de Grantmesnil, living at the time of the Norman Conquest. Their son

HUGH de GRANTMESNIL, was feudal Baron of Hinckley, and lord high steward of England. His daughter

PETRONELLA was the wife of Robert de Bellomont, see above.

Hugh Capet and his wife Adela, above, were the parents of

HEDWIGE, whose husband was Raginerus IV, eleventh Count of Hainault, living in 977, and they had

BEATRIX, married to Eblo I, Count of Rouci and Reimes. They were the parents of

ADELA, Countess of Rouci, who was married to Hildwin IV, Page 128 Count of Montidier and Lord of Rouci and Ramere, and had

MARGUERITA, wife of Hugh de Clermont, second Count of Clermont in Beauvais, mentioned in Chapter 24, whose daughter

ADELIZA CLERMONT became the wife of Gilbert de Tonebruge, as stated in Chapter 5, and had Adeliza, grandmother of the Surety Robert de Vere, pages 58 and 128.

Page 185 Henry I of France and Anne of Russia, above, were the parents of

PHILIP I, King of France from 1060 to 1108, born 1052, died in July 1108 at Melun. By his first wife, Bertha, whom he married about the year 1071, daughter of Florent I, Count of Holland, he had

LOUIS VI, King of France, born about 1081, died 1 August 1137. In 1115 he married Alice of Savoy, daughter of Count Hubert II, and had

Page 212 LOUIS VII, King of France, born 1119, died 19 September 1180. His third wife was Adelaide, daughter of Theobold II, Count of Champagne, and they had

PHILIP II, AUGUSTUS, King of France from 1180 until 1223, who was born 21 August 1165 and died 14 July 1223. He married, first, Isabella, daughter of Baldwin V, Count of Hainault, who died in 1189, leaving a son

LOUIS VIII, born 5 September 1187, died 7 November 1226, King of France for only three years, from 1223 to 1226. His wife was Blanche, daughter of Alphonso VIII, King of Castile. They were married in 1200. Their third son, Robert, Count of Artois, married Maud, daughter of Henry II, Duke of Brabant, and had Blanche, wife of Edmund Crouchback, see Chapter 31. The successor of Louis VIII was his son Page 203

ST. LOUIS IX, King of France from 1226 to 1270. He, who was born 21 September 1215, died while on an expedition in Tunis, Africa, 25 August 1270, having married in 1234 Margaret, daughter of Raymond Berenger, fourth Count of Provence. They had

PHILIP III, The Bold, King of France from 1270 to 1285. He was born 30 April 1245 and died 5 October 1285. He married, first, in 1262, Isabella, daughter of James I, King of Aragon. She died in 1271 and Philip married, second, in August 1274, Mary, daughter of Henry III, Duke of Brabant, by whom he had a daughter Page 215 Margaret, wife of Edward I, King of England, see Chapter 34. By his first wife, King Philip had a son

PHILIP IV, The Fair, King of France from 1285 to 1314. Born in 1268, he died 29 November 1314, having married in 1284 Jeanne, daughter of Henry I, King of Navarre, and they had Page 287

ISABELLA, born about the year 1292, died 22 August 1358. She became the wife of Edward II, King of England, see Chapter 34.

King Louis VI of France, above, had also

PETER, Prince of France, Lord of Courtenay and Auxerre, fifth son, who married Elizabeth, daughter of Reginald, Lord of Courtenay, and had Page 202

ALICE, who became the wife of Aymer de Taillefer, Count of Angouleme. They were the parents of

ISABELLA TAILLEFER, wife of John, King of England, see Chapter 27. Isabella's second husband was Hugh le Brun, Count of Marche, and they had

ALICE le BRUN, whose husband was John de Warren, seventh Earl of Surrey, see Chapter 31. Page 205

LOUIS I

Page 178

Charlemagne's fifth child by his wife Hildegarde was

Page 167 LOUIS I, le DEBONAIRE, or the Gentle, No. 126 above, Roman Emperor from 814 to 840, was born at Casseneuil in 778. He succeeded his father 28 January 814 and three years later yielded to the wishes of his sons and gave each of them a share of his dominions, which caused complications he was incapable of managing, and which resulted in the dissolution of the Empire. He died at Ingelheim 20 June 840, and was buried at Metz. His youngest child by his second wife Judith, was

CHARLES II, the Bald, born 823, King of France 840, Emperor 875, who died in 878, having married in 842 Hermintrudis, daughter of Eudes, Count of Orleans. She died 6 October 869. By Page 170 her King Charles had a daughter Judith, born 844, wife of Ethelwulf, see Chapter 28; and a son

LOUIS II, the Stammerer, King of France, born 1 November 846, died 10 April 879. By his second wife Adelheide, daughter of Ludolph, Duke of Saxony, he had

CHARLES IV, the Simple, born 879, died 7 October 929. He became King of France in 893 and on 7 October 918 married as his third wife, Edgina, died 948, daughter of Edward the Elder, King Page 175 of England, see Chapter 28. Their son

LOUIS IV, d'Outremer, so named because he had visited England in his infancy, was King of France, born in 920 and died 10 September 954. During his reign a war was waged with Hugh, the father of Hugh Capet. In 939 he married Gerberga, born 913, died 969, widow of Gislebert, Duke of Lorraine, and daughter of Henry I, the Fowler, Emperor of the Germans. They had

CHARLES, who was born in 953. Having been excluded from

the throne of France, he became Duke of Lower Lorraine and, while waging war for the French throne, with his cousin, Hugh Capet, was taken prisoner and confined until his death in 993. He married, second, Agnes, daughter of Henry, Count of Vermandois and Troyes, and his wife Princess Edgina, granddaughter of King Alfred the Great, see Chapter 28. Charles and Agnes had Page 171

GERBERGA, Duchess of Brabant, who became the wife of Lambert Barbutus of Lorraine, first Count de Mous, who died in 1015 They had

MAUD, wife of Eustace, Count of Bologne, and they had

LAMBERT who had

JUDITH, who was married to Waltheof, beheaded in 1073, son of Syward the Saxon. They had

MAUD, wife of Simon de St. Liz, Earl of Huntingdon and Northampton. Shortly after the year 1100 he made a pilgrimage to the Holy Land and died in 1115 at the abbey of Charity in France. Their daughter

MAUD ST. LIZ, as widow of Robert de Tonbridge, became the wife of William d'Albini, feudal lord of Belvoir Castle, grandfather of the Surety of the same name, see Chapter 1. Page 40

Charlemagne's seventh child by his wife Hildegarde was

LADY BERTHE, born 779, died 853, whose husband was Angilbert, Governor of Ponthieu and Abbe of St. Richaire. They were the parents of

NITHARD, Governor of Ponthieu in 814, father of

HELGAUD, Governor of Ponthieu, who had

HERLUIN, Governor of Ponthieu in 864, whose son

HELGAUD II, Governor of Ponthieu, died 925/6. His son was

HERLUIN II, first Count of Montreuil, who died in 945, leaving a son

ROTGAIRE, Count of Montreuil, died 957, who had

WILLIAM I, Count of Montreuil, father of

HAUDOUN de RAMERU, Count de Rouci, living in 1033. His daughter

MARGUERITA, was the wife of Hugh, Count de Clermont, see above. Pages 128, 186

Chapter 30

The Scottish Kings

Arms: Or, a lion rampant gules within a bordure counter-floury of the second.

Page 162 KING COLE, Coel or Colius I, son of Marius (D), see Chapter 27, who married the daughter of Boadicea, was not only the father of Athildis, No. 101 above, but also the great grandfather of

401. AIOFE, who married Fiacha Strabhteine, 120th Monarch of Ireland, died 322, and had

402. MUREDACH TIREACH, the 122nd Monarch, who had

403. EOCHAIDH MUIGH MEADHOIN, the 124th Monarch, who had

404. NIALL MOR, known as Niall of the Nine Hostages, the 126th Monarch, father of

405. EOGHAN, or Owen, who had

406. MUREDACH, who had

407. FERGUS MOR MAC EARCA, the 131st Monarch, who in A.D. 498, with five of his brothers, went into Scotland with a complete army to assist his grandfather Loarn, King of Dalriada, in overcoming his enemies, the Picts. Upon the King's death, Fergus was unanimously elected king, and became the first absolute king of all Scotland, of the Milesian Race. He had

408. DONART, who had

409. EOCHAIDH, father of

410. GABHRAN, who had

411. EDHAN, who had

412. EOCHAIDH BUIDHE, from whose name that of the Boyd family is derived. He was the father of

413. DONALD BREAC, who had

414. DONGART, died 673, who had EOCHAID II, died 698, had EOCHAID III, died 733, who had

415. AODH (or Hugh) FIONN, who had

416. EOCHAIDH RINNAMAIL, father of

417. ALPIN, who died in the year 834, leaving a son

418. KENNETH MACALPIN, who died in 854. His son Page 175

419. CONSTANTINE, died in 878. He was the father of

420. DONALD, who died in 903. His son was

421. MALCOLM I, who died in 958, leaving a son

422. KENNETH, died 994, the father of

423. MALCOLM II, who died in 1040. He had no sons. Of his two daughters, the younger, Doda, became the wife of Synel, lord of Glammis, and had a son MACBETH, who died in 1057. The elder daughter

424. BEATRICE, was married to Crinan, lord of the Isles, and by him had

425. DUNCAN, King of Scotland, slain in 1041 by his cousin MacBeth, local chief of Moray.

> "Duncan is in his grave;
> After life's fitful fever, he sleeps well;
> Nor steel, nor poison, malice domestic, foreign levy,
> Nothing can touch him further." Page 168

426. MALCOLM III, King of Scotland, son of Duncan, called Canmore because of the large size of his head. He was born in 1024 and became king at the time of his victory over MacBeth in 1057, remaining so until his death in 1093. He was buried at Icelmkill. His widow, whom he had married in 1068 as his second wife, was Princess Margaret, daughter of Edward the Exile, see Chapter 28. Page 177 She died at Edinburgh Castle, of grief at the death of her husband, 16 November 1093, and was buried at Dumfermline. In 1250 Margaret was declared a saint and on 19 June 1259 her body was taken from the original stone coffin and placed in a shrine of pine-wood set with gold and precious stones near the high altar. In Scotland the grace cup is called St. Margaret's blessing. When Scotland became Protestant the remains of St. Margaret and her husband

were carried to Spain and placed in a chapel in the Escurial built
Page 200 in her honor by King Philip II. Their only daughter was

427. MATILDA, who became the wife of Henry I, King of
England, see Chapter 31, and they were the parents of

537. MATILDA of England, wife of Geoffrey, surnamed
Plantagenet, No. 69, see Chapters 27 and 31. Page 168

Malcolm III and his wife Lady Margaret had a son

ST. DAVID I, hallowed by the people but never canonized, who
was born in 1080, died at Carlisle 24 May 1153. He was King of
Scotland from 1124 until his death. David was a wise and just king.
In 1113 he married Matilda, who died in 1131, daughter of
Waltheof, Earl of Northumberland, and Judith, his wife, a niece of
William the Conqueror. King David and Matilda were the parents of

HENRY, Prince of Scotland and Earl of Huntingdon. He died
in 1152, before his father, to the universal grief of all Scotland. His
Page 112 wife, whom he married in 1139, was Ada Warren, daughter of
William de Warren and his wife Isabel Vermandois, see Chapter 31.
Henry, who was also ninth Earl of Northumberland, and Ada
Warren were the parents of Margaret, wife of Humphrey de Bohun,
Page 52 see Chapter 4, and of

DAVID, Earl of Huntingdon, younger brother of Malcolm and
William, Kings of Scotland, knighted by King Henry II in 1170.
On 26 August 1190 he married Maud, eldest daughter of Hugh de
Kevelioc, Earl of Chester. He died 17 June 1219 at Yardley, in
Northamptonshire and was buried in Sawtrey Abbey. Their daughter

ISABEL became the wife of Robert Bruce, fourth Baron of
Annandale. He was the son of William Bruce, third Baron, and had
large estates in both England and Scotland. He died in 1245 and
Isabel died in 1252. They had

ROBERT BRUCE, born in 1210, and died in 1295, who con-
tested unsuccessfully for the throne of Scotland, King Edward I,
the arbitrator, deciding in favor of John Baliol. His first wife was
Page 62 Isabel Clare, daughter of Gilbert de Clare, the Surety, see Chapter 6. ★
Their eldest son was

ROBERT BRUCE, born 1243, died 1304, married 1271, Marjorie, daughter of Neil Carrick and his wife Margaret, daughter of
Walter, high steward of Scotland, and they had ten children, the
eldest of whom, as on page 65, was

King Robert Bruce

KING ROBERT I, The Bruce, born 11 July 1274, died 7 June 1329. On 27 March 1306 he was crowned King of Scotland. During the reign of King Edward II, Bruce gradually reduced the English hold upon Scotland, until the English army in 1314 finally withdrew at the battle of Bannockburn. From time to time war with England continued until a truce was signed in 1323 and finally, after Edward III had been King of England for a year, in 1328, Robert Bruce was formally recognized as King of Scotland. His first wife was Isabel Mar, daughter of Earl Donald, and his second wife was Elizabeth, daughter of Richard de Burgh, see Chapter 13. Page 93 By his first wife he had

MARJORY BRUCE, wife of Walter Stewart, who had Page 66

KING ROBERT II, born 2 March 1315, died 13 May 1390, and had by his first wife Elizabeth Mure, an eldest son

KING ROBERT III, born 1337, died 4 April 1406, married Annabella Drummond, and had

KING JAMES I, born in 1394, died 20 February 1437, married Joan Beaufort, the daughter of John Beaufort, son of John of Gaunt, son of King Edward III, page 218.

William the Conqueror

Chapter 31

The Normans

See also Pedigree C, page 421.

ROLLO THE DANE, first Duke of Normandy, called also Rolf the Walker because, being so tall, he preferred to go afoot rather than ride the little Norwegian horses. Originally a Norse viking, he was noted for strength and martial prowess. In the reign of Charles II, the Bald, he sailed up the Seine and took Rouen, which he kept as a base of operations. He gained a number of victories over the Franks, and extorted the cession of the province since called Normandy. By the famous treaty which Charles and Rollo signed the latter agreed to adopt the Christian religion. He died in 932 and was buried in the Cathedral at Rouen, where his figure cut in the stone may still be seen. Rollo married Lady Poppa de Page 182 Valois, No. 530 above, and had

531. WILLIAM LONGSWORD, who succeeded as second Duke of Normandy. Everywhere could be seen the striking figure of the young Duke, carrying his great sword, the symbol of order and peace, resplendent with its golden hilt and long shining blade. William was also Duke of Aquitaine and died in 942, slain by Arnulf of Flanders with whom he had in good faith gone to confer. His wife was his cousin Espriota, daughter of Hubert, Count of Senlis, and they had

532. RICHARD THE FEARLESS, see Chapter 27, third Duke Page 164 of Normandy, who was born about 933, and died 996, having reigned fifty-five years. He married No. 63, Lady Gunnora of Denmark, who died in 1031, and they had, beside Archbishop Robert, the ancestor of Simon de Montfort, another son

Page 168 533. RICHARD II, the Good, fourth Duke of Normandy, died 1026. He married Judith, died 1018, daughter of Conan I, Count de Bretagne, and his wife Ermengarde d'Anjou. They were the parents of

534. ROBERT THE MAGNIFICENT, also known as Robert the Devil, sixth Duke of Normandy, died 1035, a combination of Page 168 much good and evil. By Herleve, also called Arlotta, daughter of the tanner, Fulbert de Falaise and his wife Doda, Duke Robert had

535. WILLIAM THE CONQUEROR, born at Falaise in 1027. Page 183 His mother afterward became the wife of Herlouin de Conteville, and is ancestress of Eleanor of Aquitaine, King John's mother. Page 202

The poet Wace, writing in the 12th century, has much to say of William, and of the signs which early indicated his future greatness. One of the stories is that of the infant William who, at the time of his birth, reached out upon the floor and filled both hands with the straw and rushes. The midwife, seeing in it an omen, predicted that the boy would be a king. "What a great lord wilt thou be! Much wilt thou conquer and obtain."

At his father's death he became Duke of Normandy, and by 1063, having conquered Maine, he was secure on his southern frontier and was able to turn his attention to England.

Another forewarning that he was destined to change the whole course of Western Civilization is recorded in the Anglo-Saxon Chronicle, which states that in May 1066 "There was over all England such a token seen as no man ever saw before. Some men said it was the comet-star, which others denominated the long-hair'd star. It appeared first on the eve called Litaina major, that is, on the eighth before the calends of May; and so shone all the week." Some thought that it foretold changes in the kingdom. This visitor was Halley's comet, which reappears every 77 years, and which was last seen in May 1910.

Duke William claimed the English throne not only as a son of the Confessor's first cousin, but more particularly because of a definite promise made to him by Edward the Confessor, the last Saxon king whom he had acknowledged. This promise was solemnly confirmed by Harold, who later declared his enforced oath was not binding. William was therefore compelled to fight for the crown. He was by no means a stranger when he invaded England.

Edward the Confessor died at Westminster late in 1065, or early in the following year, and his brother-in-law Harold, who had practically governed the kingdom for fourteen years, immediately upon Edward's burial seized the throne, and was crowned king, but his rule lasted only nine months and nine days. When Harold refused to honor his right to the throne William had no alternative, and after careful preparations, including the assembling of 896 ships, a loyal company of about sixty thousand men, after many delays, as soon as the winds were favorable, set out from St. Valery 27 September 1066, and on St. Michael's Day landed at Pevensey Bay. William's flag ship was given to him by his Duchess Matilda, and was named "Maura." It was ornamented with the gilded figure of a boy holding an ivory horn to his lips and with his right hand pointing toward England. From this ship William landed upon English soil, ahead of all his troops, and as soon as all had gone ashore the order was given to burn all the vessels, that there might be no turning back.

One account states that as William stepped ashore his foot slipped and to recover his balance, he sunk the other more deeply into the sand. A soldier noticing it said, that although the Duke had nearly lost his footing on English soil he had now gained a firm hold upon it, and he saluted him as King. The Chronicle of Battel Abbey says that he fell upon his face when alighting from the ship, causing his nose to bleed, and that he grasped the earth with both hands. Fitz-Osborn then cried out "Cease men to interpret this as a misfortune, for by my troth, it is a token of prosperity; for lo! he hath embraced England with both hands, and sealed it to his posterity with his own blood; and thus by the foreshowing of Divine Providence is he destined effectually to win it."

The Norman army marched to Hastings, where a wooden castle was hastily erected, and where they remained for two weeks, depending for food for the men and horses upon what they could plunder.

The incidents connected with the Norman invasion are set forth in pictures embroidered upon the famous Bayeux Tapestry, a linen or canvas roll 20 inches high and 214 feet long, containing in all 1512 figures. It was at first thought to have been the workmanship of Queen Matilda and her ladies, but later authorities attribute it to the half brother of William the Conqueror, Bishop Odo, and his followers. In it Harold is depicted as a usurper, while William is shown as the long-suffering and rightful claimant to the English throne. The Tapestry had been concealed in the Bayeux Church and was not found until 1724, and in 1803 Napoleon had it conveyed to Paris.

Harold had hastened north upon hearing of an invasion there by the Danes, and was in Yorkshire with his army celebrating recent victories with a great feast when he received word of the arrival of the Normans, and thus was not on hand to greet them when they landed. At once he hurried back to London with his exhausted army, covering 200 miles of bad roads in five days, and continuing from London southward for 57 miles in three more days.

Three times, we are told, William offered to fight alone with Harold in single combat to avoid the great loss of life which he knew would result from open battle, the victor to have the kingdom. Harold's brother Gyrth asked that he might take the challenge, but all these proposals Harold stubbornly refused. Elated by his victories in the north, he disregarded warning and advice. He sent spies into William's camp to learn the enemy's forces and position. They were captured and taken to the Duke, who instructed that they be shown everything and returned unharmed to Harold.

The Saxon preparation for the battle was all made on the day before, and it is said that, either through recklessness or desperation, they caroused the whole night long, the woods echoing with their shouts and songs. By morning they were plainly out of control. The Chronicle records that the Normans in their camp, only a mile away, spent the night in confession and prayer. William vowed that if he should be victorious on the morrow he would erect upon the place of battle a free monastery. Bishop Odo administered the Communion in the morning and doffing his church vestments, immediately replaced them with battle attire and marshalled his men-at-arms. William "committed himself trustfully to his Creator in every matter and had given no heed to omens; neither had he ever loved sorcerers."

Both Harold and William claimed Saturday as the day of their birth, and thus a propitious day for battle. It was Saturday, 14 October 1066, when the armies met on the Sussex hill at nine o'clock in the morning.

Harold brought with him from twelve to fifteen thousand men and, curiously enough, no horsemen, although he must have been aware of the numbers and the equipment of the enemy.

During the greater part of the day the fighting was furious, with little advantage to either side. At last the Duke realized that he must resort to strategy. Feigning a rout, the Normans pretended to flee. The Saxons broke ranks and jubilantly started in pursuit, driving the Normans into a great fosse, or ditch, with so great slaughter that it became level full with slain and wounded men and horses. With sword, spear and battle-axe thousands of men were butchered on both sides. Through the entire battle it does not appear that William received any wound, although several horses were killed under him.

The Norman archers shot arrows into the air in such a way that they fell upon the faces of the Saxons. Toward evening, as Harold was encouraging his men, an arrow pierced his right eye. Striving to pluck it out, he unfortunately broke it off instead, and though dizzy and blinded, he remained at his post, whereupon four knights rushed upon him, in cruel manner despatching him with their swords. With their king slain and most of the nobles dead, the Saxons took to flight under cover of darkness. The Normans remained on the field until morning, and oh! what a spectacle presented itself by daylight. No wonder they called it Senlac, "Sangue lac," lake of blood!

The victor marched to London from his camp on the Thames, and on Christmas Day, 1066, was crowned at Westminster. The Norman soldiers on guard, mistaking the shouts of "Yea, Yea," for protesting voices, set fire to the wooden buildings around the church, causing great panic, but the service continued and the Conqueror was crowned William I, King of England.

Peace and order were restored. William even attempted, though without success, to learn the English tongue, that he might personally administer justice in his courts. His policy in regard to England exhibited the most profound statesmanship. He declared that he did not propose to change the English customs but to govern as had Edward the Confessor.

William was their king, their supreme landlord, and their military commander-in-chief. He introduced into England the feudal system in which the land is all owned by the king, though let to tenants and sub-tenants, who for rent render various commodities and services. The Anglo-Saxon Chronicle states "The king had mickle thought and very deep speech with his witan about this land, how it was set, and by what men." The result of this conference was the Great Survey of English lands and their holders. The record of it was called the Domesday Book, because there was to be no appeal from its dooms or judgments. It covered every shire and district of the kingdom and was made with great thoroughness, as the Conqueror intended it to be the basis of taxation and military service.

The Chronicle continues "so very narrowly he let spear it out, that there was not a single hide nor a yard of land, nor so much as—it is shame to tell, and it thought him no shame to do—an ox nor a cow nor a swine was left that was not set on his writ. And all the writs weer brought to him afterward."

With a strong will he reigned for 21 years, and it was at the siege of Mantes in the autumn of 1087 that William met his death. While destroying the city, he rode about encouraging his men, when a burning brand fell before his horse. The horse shied at it, or stumbled, pitching William forward upon the high pommel of the saddle, causing a mortal injury. In great pain he dictated his will to the notaries, providing for the disposition of his lands and wealth. When after suffering for about three weeks, death came to him 9 September 1087, no member of his family was present, each having selfishly hurried away to look after his own legacy. As soon as he was pronounced dead the servants rushed upon the furnishings and money, carrying off everything, even the linen from the bed and the king's clothing, tossing his naked body out upon the floor. "On the floor he was born, to the floor he was now returned, William the Conqueror."

Finally a knight named Herlouin, at his own expense, had the body prepared for burial and sent to Caen, to the abbey of St. Etienne which William had founded. There, during the funeral procession, fire broke out and everyone except a few monks fled. Later, as his body was being placed, a knight rushed forward demanding payment of the amount the king owed for the land before he would allow him to be buried there. When that matter was settled, it was found that the stone coffin provided was too short and too narrow, and received the body with great difficulty. With great haste the interment was finally accomplished. Page 183

By Matilda his wife, sometimes called Maud, daughter of Baldwin V, Count of Flanders, a descendant of the Emperor Charlemagne, see Chapter 29, William the Conqueror had eleven children, recorded as follows:

Robert, Duke of Normandy.

Richard.

William Rufus, his favorite son, King of England from 1087 to 1100; killed by an arrow shot by an unknown hand. No issue.

Henry I, Beauclerc, King of England, of whom below. Page 200

Cecilia, Abbess of Caen.

Constance, wife of Alan, Count of Brittany.

Adelaide, died young.

Adela, wife of Estienne, Count of Blois.

Agatha, died without marrying.

Matilda.

Gundred, wife of William de Warren, of whom later.

Concerning Gundred's father there has been much uncertainty. Freeman thinks she was the daughter of Gerbod, Matilda's first husband. The tomb of Gundred and her husband was discovered in 1845. Phillips Russell, 1933, places her as the youngest daughter of the Conqueror.

Chapter 31

Henry I

536. HENRY I, Beauclerc, was King of England from 1100 to 1135. He was born at Selby, co. York, in 1070 and died in France, 1 December 1135. His only son William, died without issue in a shipwreck described below, and Henry's nephew Stephen succeeded Page 192 him. Henry's only daughter, by his first wife, Matilda of Scotland, No. 427 in Chapter 30, daughter of Malcolm III, was

537. MATILDA of England, called also Maud, born in 1102, died 30 January 1164. In 1114 she became the wife of Henry V, Emperor of Germany, who died without issue 23 May 1125. Her second husband, to whom she was married 3 April 1127, was No. 69 Geoffrey, surnamed Plantagenet, Count d'Anjou, born 1113, died 1151. The friends of Geoffrey were unaware that their playful nickname for him of Plantagenet would live through the years. The story is told that while disguised in battle, and to make himself known to his followers, he leaned from his horse and grasped a sprig of "plante de genet," the common broom corn which grew thickly on the heath, and thrust it in his helmet. Thus he derived his popular title.

A noble person was Geoffrey, one of the most powerful princes of France, with "elegant and courtly manners and a reputation for gallantry in the field." His alliance with England came about in consequence of the great tragedy of the sinking of the famous White Ship. When it struck the hidden rocks off the coast of France, young William, Duke of Normandy, the heir apparent to the English throne, and three hundred others, were drowned in the freezing November waters, the Butcher of Rouen alone being saved.

King Henry I of England, in despair over the loss of his only

Pages
168, 192

son, sought the aid of Geoffrey Plantagenet and personally invested him with the order of Knighthood. Approving the marriage of his daughter Matilda with Geoffrey, King Henry expressed the hope that all Englishmen would give them full allegiance. The Barons took the oath to uphold the succession of Matilda and Geoffrey and their children after them. When, therefore, the sons Henry, Geoffrey and William were born, their grandfather thought the succession to the throne secure. However, "King Henry was no sooner dead than all the plans he had labored at so long crumbled away like a hollow heap of sand." Yet eventually, on 19 December 1154, Geoffrey's eldest son was crowned as King Henry II, and thus Geoffrey heads the line of English Kings which bear his Plantagenet name.

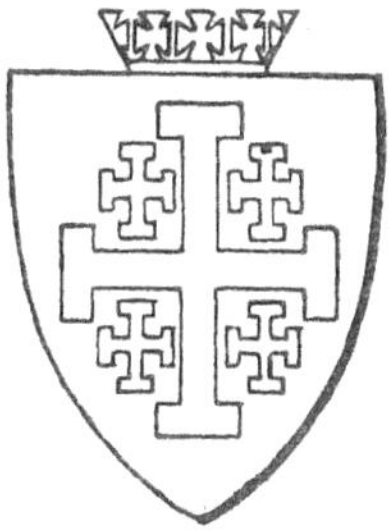

JERUSALEM

As eldest son of Fulk V, King of Jerusalem, and his wife, Ermengarde, daughter of Helias, Count of Maine, Geoffrey was of the House of Angevin Kings which had been prominent for three centuries. His noble character adds prestige to this illustrious background and merits the recognition given it by the formation of The Plantagenet Society, early instituted to commemorate these important historic events. Geoffrey and Matilda were the parents of

Chapter 31

See also Pedigree G, page 423.

70. HENRY II, who was born at Le Mans, 25 March 1133, and
Page died at Chinon, 6 July 1189. In 1152 he married Eleanor of
195 Aquitaine, former wife of King Louis VII of France, and daughter of William, Duke of Aquitaine. She survived King Henry nearly three years, dying 26 June 1202. Both were buried at Fontevraud,
Page in Anjou. Their daughter Eleanora became the wife of the elder
211 Alphonso IX, King of Castile, see Chapter 33; their eldest son William died at the age of four years, in 1156; their second son was Henry, born 28 February 1155 who, on 15 July 1170, by command of his father was crowned King of England, but died before his father, 11 June 1183. Their third son, Richard the Lion Hearted, died without issue 6 April 1199. Their fourth son, Geoffrey, Duke of Brittany, had a son Arthur, who was murdered in 1203, see page 6, leaving as successor to the throne of England

71. KING JOHN, Lackland, the fifth son of King Henry II and Queen Eleanor, born at Oxford 24 December 1166, died at Newark Castle, Notts, 19 October 1216, see page 22, and was buried at Worcester Cathedral. His first wife, whom he married 29 August
Page 1189, was Isabel, daughter of William, Earl of Gloucester. He mar-
187 ried, second, in 1200, Isabel, daughter of Aymer de Taillefer, the swordsmith, see Chapter 29. She was the mother of all his children. Their eldest son was

72. HENRY III, King of England, born 1 October 1207, at Winchester, died 16 November 1272, at Saint Edmundsbury, and was buried at Westminster Abbey. He was only nine years of age when his father died, and was crowned king, 28 October 1216. On 14 January 1236, he married Eleanor of Provence, whose ancestry

Page 206

Henry III

is set forth in Chapter 32. After his death Queen Eleanor took the veil at Ambresbury in Wiltshire and died there 24 June 1291. Their elder sons John and Henry died young and their third son became EDWARD I, King of England, No. 73, see Chapter 34. Their fourth son was Page 213

EDMUND, styled "Crouchback" because he habitually wore a cross on his back. He was born 16 January 1244/5 in London and died at Bayonne, while besieging Bordeaux, 5 June 1296, and was buried at Westminster Abbey. His first wife was Aveline, daughter of William Fortibus, but all his children were by his second wife, Blanche, widow of Henry, King of Navarre, and daughter of Robert, Count of Artois, son of King Louis VIII of France, see Chapter 29. They were married shortly before 29 October 1276, and his widow died in Paris 2 May 1302. They were the parents of Page 109

HENRY PLANTAGENET, Earl of Lancaster, who was born about 1281, died 22 September 1345, and buried with great ceremony on the north side of the high altar of Newark Abbey, Leicester. About 2 March 1296/7 he married Maud, daughter of Patrick Chaworth and his wife Isabel Beauchamp. Lady Maud died before 3 December 1322, and was buried at Mottisfont Priory, of which she was patron. One of their daughters, Eleanor, became the wife of Richard FitzAlan, see Chapter 24. Another daughter was Maud, wife of William de Burgh, page 94, and another was Joan, page 109, wife of John de Mowbray. Page 132

Maud Chaworth was a descendant of the family of Beauchamp as follows:

HUGH de BEAUCHAMP, the companion in arms of William the

Conqueror, obtained large estates in Hertford, Buckingham, and Bedfordshire, and was the founder of the illustrious house of Beauchamp. His third son was

WALTER de BEAUCHAMP of Elmley Castle, co. Gloucester, married Emeline, daughter of Urso de Arbitot, and was succeeded, in his estates and in the royal stewardship, by his son,

WILLIAM de BEAUCHAMP, Sheriff of four counties, this powerful feudal lord married Maud, daughter of William Lord Braose, of Gower, and was succeeded by his son,

WILLIAM de BEAUCHAMP who married Joane, daughter of Sir Thomas Waleries. He was succeeded by his son

WALTER de BEAUCHAMP. He married Bertha, daughter of William Lord Braose, and died in 1235, and was succeeded by his elder son,

WALCHELINE de BEAUCHAMP, who married Joane, daughter of Roger, Lord Mortimer. He was succeeded by an only son,

WILLIAM de BEAUCHAMP, feudal Lord of Elmley. He married Isabel, daughter of William Mauduit, of Hanslape, co. Bucks. He died in 1268, leaving a son

Page 49

WILLIAM de BEAUCHAMP, Baron of Elmley and Earl of Warwick. He married Maud FitzJohn, widow of Gerard de Furnivalle. Their daughter

Page 132

ISABEL BEAUCHAMP became the wife of Patrick de Chaworth. He died in 1382 and she married secondly Hugh Lord Despencer. Her only daughter by Patrick de Chaworth was

MAUD CHAWORTH who as stated above became the wife of Henry Plantagenet, Earl of Lancaster.

Geoffrey Plantagenet, No. 69 above, was the father of

Page 44

HAMELINE PLANTAGENET, brother of King Henry II of England, died 7 May 1202. He married in 1163, Isabel de Warren, widow of William de Blois. She was descended from the Earls of Warren and Surrey, as follows:

WILLIAM de WARREN who came from Normandy, called a

near kinsman of William the Conqueror, received large grants of land in recognition of the distinguished part he took at the battle of Hastings. King William Rufus made him Earl of Surrey. He married Gundred, according to the chroniclers, a daughter of William the Conqueror, and had Page 199

WILLIAM de WARREN, second Earl of Warren and Surrey, whose wife was Isabel Vermandois, see Chapter 29. They had a daughter Ada, wife of Prince Henry, Earl of Huntingdon, see Chapter 30, and a son Page 185

WILLIAM de WARREN, third Earl of Surrey. In 1147 he assumed the cross and accompanied Louis of France to the Holy Land against the Saracens. From this unfortunate enterprise he never returned but whether he fell in battle or died in captivity has never been ascertained. He married Adela, daughter of William de Talvace, son of Robert of Belesme, Earl of Shrewsbury, and by her had an only daughter

ISABEL WARREN, who married Hameline Plantagenet, aforesaid. They had a daughter, Isabel Plantagenet de Warren, wife of Roger Bigod the Surety, see Chapter 2, and a son

WILLIAM PLANTAGENET de WARREN, Earl of Warren and Surrey, who died in 1240. By his second wife, Maud, daughter of William Marshall, the Protector, he had a son

JOHN de WARREN, Earl of Warren and Surrey, a man of violent and imperious temper. He married, first, in 1247, Alice, daughter of Hugh le Brun, Count de la March, and died in 1304. Their only son Page 187

WILLIAM de WARREN, was killed in a tournament at Croydon, 12 December 1285, having married Joan, daughter of Robert de Vere, see Chapter 24. Their daughter

ALICE WARREN, became the wife of Edmund FitzAlan, Earl of Arundel, see Chapter 24. Page 131

FRANCE

Chapter 32

The Ancestry of

Eleanor of Provence

Wife of King Henry III

Arms: Azure, three fleur-de-lis or.

Page 165 CLOVIS, King of the Franks, and his wife St. Clotilde, see Chapter 27, were the parents of

CLOTHAIRE I, born 497, died 561, who married Ingolde and had

CHILPERIC I, born 523, died 584, married Fredegonde, born 543, died 598. They had

CLOTHAIRE II, who was born in 584 and died in 628, having married Bertrude, who died in 618. They had

CHARIBERT II, born 608, died 631, married Gisela, daughter of Amaud of Gascony and had

BOGGIS, Duke of Aquitaine, who died in 688. He married St. Oda and had

EUDES, Duke of Aquitaine, died 735, who married Valtrude, daughter of Valtrude and her husband Walchigise, Count of Verdon, son of No. 120 St. Arnolph, Bishop of Metz, died 641, and Dodo his wife, see Chapter 27. Eudes and Valtrude were the parents of

HUNOLD, Duke of Aquitaine, died 774, who had

WAIFAR, Duke of Aquitaine, who died in 768. He married his cousin Adele, daughter of Loup I, Duke of Gascony (son of Hatton, son of the aforesaid Eudes and Valtrude) and had

LOUP II, Duke of Gascony, died 778. He had

ADELRICO, Duke of Gascony, who died 812. His son

XIMENO OF GASCONY, died 816, leaving by his wife Munia a son

INIGO ARISTA, first King of Navarre, whose wife was Iniga Ximena. They had

GARCIA II of Navarre, who married Urraca of Gascony, daughter of Sancho II, a cousin, and they had

SANCHO I, who became King of Navarre in 905. He married his cousin Toda, daughter of Aznar Galindez, Count of Aragon, and they were the parents of

GARCIA III, who succeeded his father in 921 and died in 970. He married Teresa Iniquez of Aragon, daughter of Endregota Galindez, and had

SANCHO II, Abarca, died 994, whose wife was Urraca Clara, daughter of Fortuno Ximenez of Navarre, his second cousin. They had Page 209

GARCIA V, King of Navarre, who died 999, having married Ximena, daughter of Consalo, Count of Asturias, and his wife Teresa. They were the parents of the earlier of the two kings both called Sancho III (page 211 for the other) this one

SANCHO III, King of Navarre from 1000 to 1035. Through his marriage with Munia, daughter of Sancho of Castile, who died 1017, see later, this king united the two important Houses of Castile and Navarre, to which that of Aragon was later added. Of their four sons, Garcia was King of Navarre, the second, Ferdinand I, King of Castile, will be considered later, and the fourth

RAMIRIZ I, founded the kingdom of Aragon. He was killed in battle with the Moors, 8 May 1063. His son by his wife Gisberge, daughter of Count Bernard Roger, was

SANCHO-RAMIREZ, died 4 June 1094, King of Aragon. He married first, in the year of his coronation, 1063, Felice, died 14 April 1086, daughter of Hilduin, Count of Rouci. They had

RAMIREZ II, King of Aragon, a monk in the Monastery of St. Pons de Thomieres when he was made King in 1134. Three years later he preferred to leave the throne to his daughter and re-enter the Monastery where his death occurred, 16 August 1147. His wife was Agnes, daughter of William IX, Duke of Aquitaine, and their daughter

PETRONELLA was only two years of age when her father abdicated the throne in her favor. He had arranged that Raymund Berenger V, Count of Barcelona, see later, should govern the realm as Prince of Aragon, and that he should, at the proper time, marry Petronella. This was accomplished in accordance with his wish and Petronella, dying 18 October 1172, left four children, the eldest of whom was

ALPHONSO II, King of Aragon, born 1151, died 25 April 1196. He married his cousin Sanchia who was descended as follows:

KING SANCHO III (Navarre) and his wife Munia, as stated above were the parents of

FERDINAND I, King of Castile from 1033 to 1065, who died in battle 27 December 1065. In 1035 he married Sanchia, daughter of Alphonso V, King of Leon, and thus united the latter kingdom to his own. The second of their five children was

ALPHONSO VI, King of Castile and Leon. During his reign the city of Toledo was captured from the Moors. His wife was Constance, daughter of Robert, Duke of Burgundy, and they had

URRACA, whose first husband was Raimond of Burgundy, who died in 1108, after which Urraca became the wife of Alphonso I, King of Aragon. She died in 1126. Her only child, the son of Raimond, was

ALPHONSO-RAIMOND VII, who was born in 1103, and after capturing Cordova and other Moorish territory, died in 1157. By his first wife, Berenguela, he had two sons: Sancho III, the later, (called son of Alphonso) and Ferdinand II, King of Leon, died 1188, see Chapter 33. By his second wife, Richilda of Poland, he had

Page 211

SANCHIA, wife of Alphonso II, King of Aragon, as stated above, and they had

ALPHONSO II, King of Provence, who reigned from 1196 to 1209. He was the father of

RAIMOND BERENGER IV, King of Provence. He married Beatrix, daughter of Thomas, Count of Savoy, and they had Margaret, wife of Louis IX, King of France, and

ELEANOR OF PROVENCE, wife of Henry III, King of England, see Chapter 31.

Munia of Castile, wife of Sancho III, the earlier, (Navarre), son of Garcia V above, was descended from Clovis, as follows:

Page 207

CLOTHAIRE I, son of Clovis, above, married Ingolde, and had

SIGIBERT I of France, who married Brunchildis of Spain, daughter of Athanagildo and, dying in 575, left a daughter

INGUNDA. In 580 she became the wife of St. Hermengild, died 585, son of Leovigild of Spain. Their son

ATHANAGILDO, married Flavia Juliana and had

ARDEBASTO. She married Godo and had

ERVIGIO of Spain, who was present at the Council of Toledo and died in 687. He married Liubigotona of Spain and had

PEDRO, Duke of Cantabria. He had

FRUELA, Duke of Cantabria, died 760, whose son

RODRIGO FROLAZ, was Lord of Castile about the year 762. By wife Sancha he had

DIEGO RODRIGUEZ, Lord of Castile, who married Paterna. They had

URRACA of Castile, wife of Ramiro of Leon, whose son

RODERICK, about the year 850, was first Count of Castile. He had a son

DIEGO RODRIGUEZ, Porcellos, Count of Castile, who married Asura, daughter of Fernando Ansurez and his wife Nuna, and had

FERNANDO, Count of Castile about 910. By his wife Nuna of Amaya, he had

GONSALO FERNANDEZ, Count of Castile, who married his cousin, Nuna de Lara. They had

FERNAN CONSALEZ, first King of Castile, died 970, who married Sancha, daughter of Sancho I of Navarre and Toda of Aragon. They were the parents of

GARCIA of Castile, living in 974. He married Aba of Germany and had

SANCHO of Castile, died 1017, who married Urraca. Their daughter

MUNIA of Castile, as stated above, became the wife of Sancho III (Navarre).

Raymund Berenger V, who married Petronella, as stated above, was descended from Charlemagne as follows:

125. CHARLEMAGNE was the father of

126. LOUIS I the Debonaire, see Chapters 27 and 29, whose son

CHARLES II, the Bald, King of France, had by his wife Hermintrudis of Orleans, a daughter

JUDITH of France, born 844. The widow of No. 213, Ethelwulf, she became, in 862, the wife of Baldwin I, Count of Flanders. He died in 879. They had a daughter

WIDINILLE of Flanders, whose husband was Winifred I, Count of Barcelona, died 906. They were the parents of

SUNIAIRE, Count of Urgel, who died in 950, leaving a son

BORELO I, Count of Urgel, who married Leutgarde, and died in 993. Their son

RAYMUND I, Count of Barcelona, born 972, died 1017. In the year 1001 he married Ermensinde and they had

BERENGER, who died in 1035, having married Sancha, daughter of Sancho V, Duke of Gascony. Their son

RAYMUND II, died in 1076. His wife was Adelmode de la Marche, daughter of Count Bernard I, and they had

RAYMUND III, whose wife was Maud, daughter of Robert I de Hauteville. They were married in 1079, and he died in 1082, leaving a son

RAYMUND IV, called also Arnaldo, who died in 1131. He married in 1112 Aldonza, died 1190, daughter of Gilbert V of Milhaud and Gerberga of Provence. They were the parents of

RAYMUND BERENGER V, Count of Barcelona, who, as stated above, married Petronella, daughter of Ramirez II, King of Aragon.

Chapter 33

The Ancestry of

Eleanor of Castile

Wife of King Edward I

Arms: Gules, a castle or.

ALPHONSO-RAIMOND VII, as stated in Chapter 32, by his first wife Berenguela, (daughter of Raymund IV of Barcelona, and his wife Marie), whom he married about the year 1124, had two Page 208 sons: Sancho III, the later (called son of Alphonso) see below, and

FERDINAND II, King of Leon from 1157 until his death in 1188. In 1160 he married Urraca, daughter of Alphonso I, King of Portugal and Maud of Savoy. Urraca died in 1176, and they had the younger

ALPHONSO IX (Berengaria's husband), King of Leon, born 1166, died 1229. His second wife, whom he married before 1190, was his cousin, Berengaria, daughter of Alphonso IX, King of Castile, see below, and his wife Eleanor, sister of King John and daughter of Henry II, King of England, and his wife Eleanor of Aquitaine, see Chapter 31.

The elder Alphonso IX, (Berengaria's father), King of Castile, was son of the later Sancho III, (not Navarre), son of Alphonso-Raimond VII above.

Alphonso IX, King of Leon, and Berengaria his wife, were the parents of

FERDINAND III, born 1191, in whose favor his mother abdicated the throne of Castile in 1217. At his father's death twelve years later he became King of Leon. In the following years, until his death in 1152, Ferdinand greatly strengthened the Christian influence of Spain, reducing the Moorish nation to little more than a vassal state. By his second wife, Joanna, daughter of Simon de Dammartin Count d'Aumale, and his wife Marie, Countess of Ponthieu, see later, Ferdinand had

ELEANOR of Castile, who died in 1290. In 1254 she became the wife of Edward I, King of England, see Chapter 34. Page 213

Joanna Dammartin, wife of Ferdinand III, was descended from Charlemagne as follows:

WILLIAM I, Count of Montreuil, died 965, eighth in descent from Charlemagne, as set forth in Chapter 29, was the father of

HILDUIN, living in 981, whose son

HUGUES I, Count of Ponthieu, married Gisele, daughter of Hugh Capet and his wife Adela, see Chapter 29, and they had

ENGUERRAND I, Count of Ponthieu, who died in 1046, having married Adele, daughter of Arnulph, Count of Holland, and his wife Luitgarde of Cleves. Their son

HUGUES II, Count of Ponthieu, died in 1052. His wife was Bertha, daughter of Guerinfroi, Signor d'Aumale, and they were the parents of

GUY I, Count of Ponthieu who, dying in 1101, left by his wife Ada, a daughter

AGNES PONTHIEU, whose husband was Robert II, d'Alencon. He died in 1119. They had

WILLIAM III, Count of Alencon and Ponthieu, who died in 1172. He married Alice, daughter of Eudes I, Count de Bourgogne, whose wife Maud, daughter of William I, Count de Bourgogne, and Stephanie, was a first cousin once removed of William the Conqueror, as Alice was great granddaughter of Richard II, Duke of Page 194 Normandy and his wife Judith de Bretagne, who were grandparents of the Conqueror, see Chapter 31. William III and his wife Alice were the parents of

GUY II, Count of Ponthieu, died 1147, who by his wife Ida had

JEAN I, Count of Ponthieu, whose wife was Beatrice, daughter of Anselme, Count de St. Pol. He died in 1191, leaving a son

WILLIAM III, Count of Ponthieu, born 1179, died 1221, who Page 186 married in 1195 Alice, daughter of Louis VII, King of France, see Chapter 29, and his wife Constance, daughter of Alphonso VII of Castile and Berenguela his wife, see above. The daughter of William III and Alice his wife was

MARIE, Countess of Ponthieu, who died in 1251. In 1208 she became the wife of Simon de Dammartin, Count of Aumale, died 1239, and they had

JOANNA DAMMARTIN, mentioned above, second wife of Ferdinand III, King of Castile and Leon, and they had

ELEANOR of Castile as above, wife of Edward I, King of England.

Chapter 34

King Edward the First
King Edward the Second

Arms: Gules, three lions passant regardant or.

EDWARD, Longshanks, Earl of Chester, the third son of Henry III, King of England and his wife Eleanor of Provence, ascended the English throne as

Pages 168, 209

Edward I

KING EDWARD THE FIRST

He was born at Westminster 17 June 1239 and during the reign of his father took an active part in political affairs. He was taken prisoner at Lewes in 1264 but escaping, he defeated the Earl of Leicester. In 1272 he went on a Crusade as far as Acre, where his daughter Joan was born, and although he inherited the crown that year, he did not return to England until 1274, being crowned on 19 August. It is significant of the times that he was able to thus move in a leisurely fashion across Europe without fear of disturbances at home.

He fully accepted those articles of The Great Charter of King John which had been set aside at the beginning of his father's reign, and which required that the king should levy scutages and aids only with the consent of the Great Council or Parliament. The further requirement of the Barons that they should name the ministers of the crown was allowed to fall into disuse. Edward was a capable ruler, and knew how to appoint better ministers than the Barons were likely to choose for him. He was eminent not only as a ruler but as a legislator and succeeded in enacting many wise laws, because he knew that useful legislation is possible only when the legislator has an intelligent perception of the remedies needed to meet existing evils, and is willing to content himself with such remedies as those persons who are to be benefited by them are ready to accept. The first condition was fulfilled by Edward's own skill as a lawyer, and by the skill of the great lawyers whom he employed. The second condition was fulfilled by his determination to authorize no new legislation without the counsel and acquiescence of those who were most affected by it. Not until late in his reign did he call a whole Parliament together as Earl Simon de Montfort had done. Instead, he called the Barons together in any matter which affected the Barons, and the representatives of the townsmen together in any matter which affected the townsmen, and so with the other classes. In 1295 he summoned the "Model Parliament," so called because it became the form for future Parliaments.

Every king of England since the Norman Conquest had exercised authority in a twofold capacity: as head of the nation and as the feudal lord of his vassals. Edward laid more stress than any former king upon his national headship. Early in his reign he divided the Curia Regis into three courts: The Court of King's Bench, to deal with criminal offences reserved for the king's judgment and with suits in which he was himself concerned; The Court of Exchequer, to deal with all matters touching the king's revenue; and The Court of Common Pleas, to deal with suits between subject and subject. Edward took care that these Courts should administer justice, and dismissed judges and many other officials for corruption. In 1285 he improved the Assize of Arms of King Henry II, to assure national support for his government in time of danger. His favorite motto "Keep Troth" indicates the value he placed upon a man's oath.

Alexander III was King of Scotland in the earlier part of Edward's reign, and his ancestors had done homage to Edward's ancestors but, in 1189, William the Lion had purchased from Richard I the which Henry II had acquired by the treaty of Falaise. The Lion's successors, however, held lands in England, and had done homage for them to the English kings. Edward would gladly have restored the old practice of homage for Scotland itself, but to this Alexander had never consented. Edward coveted the prospect of being lord of the entire island, as it would not only strengthen his position, but would bring two nations into peaceful union. A prospect of effecting a union by peaceful means offered itself to Edward in 1285, when Alexander III was killed by a fall from his horse, near Kinghorn. Alexander's only descendant was his granddaughter Margaret, the child of his daughter and King Eric of Norway. In 1290 it was agreed that she should marry the Prince of Wales but that the two kingdoms should remain absolutely independent of each other. Unfortunately the Maid of Norway, as the child was called, died on her way to Scotland and this plan for establishing friendly relations between the two countries came to naught. If it had succeeded, three centuries of warfare and misery might possibly have been avoided.

Another death which happened in the same year brought sorrow to Edward's heart. His first wife, Eleanor of Castile, whom he had married in 1254, died 20 November 1290. She was the daughter of Ferdinand III, see Chapter 33. Her body was brought for burial from Lincoln to Westminster, and the bereaved husband ordered the erection of a memorial cross at each place where the body rested.

The years following were filled with wars with France and with difficulties in Scotland. Edward's second marriage took place 8 September 1299; he married Margaret, daughter of Philip III, King of France, see Chapter 29. King Edward died, during his third invasion of Scotland, at Burgh-on-the-Sands near Carlisle, 8 July 1307, and was buried at Westminster.

It was King Edward I who first conferred the title Prince of Wales, thus designating his fourth son, Edward, who was the oldest to survive, and who later became Edward II, King of England. **Page**

Margaret, the second wife of King Edward I, died 14 February 187
1317 and was buried at Grey Friars, London.

Chapter 34

Page 211 The children of King Edward I and his first wife, Eleanor of Castile, were:

John, died young.

Henry, died young.

Alphonso, Earl of Chester, born 24 November 1273, died 19 August 1284.

"The First English Prince of Wales"

Edward, Prince of Wales, became King Edward II, see below.

Eleanor, married first to Alphonso, King of Aragon, and second to Henri, Count de Bar. She died in 1298.

Joan of Acre, born in 1272, married first to Gilbert de Clare, see Chapter 6, and second to Ralph de Monthermer.

Margaret, married 9 July 1290 to John, Duke of Lorraine.

Mary, became a nun.

Page 55 **Elizabeth,** born in August 1282, married first to John, Count of Holland, who died without issue, and second to Humphrey de Bohun, see Chapter 4.

Page 187 By his second wife, Queen Margaret, Edward I had:

Thomas of Brotherton, Earl of Norfolk, born 1 June 1300, married first Alice, daughter of Roger Halys, by whom he had a son and two daughters. He married second Mary, daughter of William de Roos, but by her had no surviving children. He died in August 1338.

Edmund of Woodstock, Earl of Kent, born 5 August 1301, and in 1327 married Margaret, daughter of John, Lord Wake, by whom he had two sons who died without issue, and one daughter Joan, Page 232 "the Fair Maid of Kent." Edmund was beheaded 19 March 1329/30.

Eleanor, died young.

EDWARD, first Prince of Wales, mentioned above, ascended the English throne 23 February 1307 as

Edward II

KING EDWARD THE SECOND Page 168

He was born at Carnarvon Castle, in Wales, 25 April 1284. By charter dated 7 February 1301 he received a grant of the principality of Wales and the county of Chester. Incapable and pleasure loving, he reigned for twenty years, being advised at first by Piers Gaveston, whom the Barons disliked and murdered in 1312. In 1314 King Edward was defeated by the Scots at the Battle of Bannockburn. The Despencers later controlled the government; they too were disliked, and by the Queen in particular. She returned to her native France, taking her son Edward with her and refused to return while the Despencer family were in power. King Edward's followers deserted him and on 7 January 1327 he was deposed by Parliament. He was later captured, imprisoned at Kenilworth Castle and then at Berkeley Castle, where he was murdered 21 September 1327, and was buried at Gloucester. His wife, whom he married 28 January 1307/8 was Isabella, daughter of King Philip IV, The Fair, King of France, see Chapter 29. She died 22 August 1358. They had two sons and two daughters:

Page 218

Edward of Windsor, Earl of Chester and Duke of Aquitaine, became Edward III, King of England, see Chapter 35. Page 420

John of Eltham, Earl of Cornwall, born 25 August 1316, died in October 1336, never having married.

Joan, on 17 July 1328 became the wife of David Bruce, King of Scotland, and died without issue 14 August 1362.

Eleanor, married in 1332 to Reynald, first Duke of Gueldres, and died 22 April 1355.

EDWARD III

Chapter 35

King Edward the Third

See also Pedigrees A, R, S and T, pages 420, 430 and 432.

45 Generations from Boadicea

75 Generations from Aedd Mawr

Page 168 EDWARD of Windsor, Earl of Chester and Duke of Aquitaine, was born at Windsor 13 November 1312 and succeeded to the throne of England 13 January 1327, while his father, King Edward II was yet living. The Queen Mother and Roger de Mortimer governed in his name for a time, until he rejected their assistance and had Mortimer executed. His reign was filled with great domestic achievements and foreign wars. He renounced his right to Scotland in 1328, but to make good his claim to France in right of his mother, he invaded that country in 1339. He defeated the French at Crecy 24 August 1346. During his absence in France, the Scots invaded England. At the Battle of Neville's Cross, 17 October 1346, Edward took King David of Scotland prisoner. He took Calais on 3 August of the following year. In 1350 he defeated Page 217 the Spaniards at sea, and in 1356, winning the Battle of Poitiers, he took King John of France captive.

King Edward III died at Richmond, co. Surrey, 21 June 1377, and was buried at Westminster. His wife, whom he married Page 430 24 January 1329, was Philippa, daughter of William, Count of Holland and Hainault. She died 15 August 1369 and was also buried at Westminster. They were the parents of:

Edward the Black Prince, an original Knight of the Garter, see Chapter 36.

William of Hatfield, born in 1336, died young.

Lionel of Antwerp, Duke of Clarence, K. G., born 29 November 1338, died at Piedmont 17 October 1368, married first Elizabeth, daughter of William de Burgh, a descendant of the Surety, William ★ de Lanvallei, see Chapter 13. She died in 1363, leaving an only child, Philippa. Lionel married second, 28 May 1368, Violante, daughter of Galeazzo Visconti, Prince of Milan, but they had no children.

John of Gaunt, first Duke of Lancaster, K. G., King of Castile and Leon, born 24 June 1340, died 3 February 1398/9, married Page 225 first, 19 May 1359, Blanche, daughter of Henry, Duke of Lancaster, by whom he had Henry, who afterward became King Henry IV, Page 55 and two daughters, Elizabeth and Philippa. Lady Blanche died 30 September 1369 and John of Gaunt married second, in June 1371, Constance, daughter of Peter, King of Castile and Leon, and she, dying in June 1394, left an only daughter Katharine. John of Gaunt's third wife was Katharine, daughter of Payne Roelt, a native of Hainault, and by her he had three sons: John, Henry and Thomas, and a daughter Joan, married first to Robert Ferrers, a descendant of the Surety Saire de Quincey, see Chapter 21, and second to Ralph de Nevill, a descendant of the Surety John Fitz-Robert, see Chapter 7. Page 74

Edmund of Langley, first Duke of York, K. G., born 5 June 1341, died 1 August 1402, married first, 1 March 1371/2, Isabel, youngest daughter of Peter, King of Castile and Leon, who died 23 November 1392, having had sons Edward and Richard, and a daughter Constance. Edmund of Langley married second, 4 November 1393, Joan, daughter of Thomas de Holand, Earl of Kent, a descendant of the Surety Robert de Vere, see Chapter 24. She died without issue 4 April 1434.

Thomas of Woodstock, Duke of Gloucester, K. G., and Constable of England, born 7 January 1355/6, murdered 8 September 1397, married after 1374 Eleanor, daughter of Humphrey de Bohun, a descendant of the Surety Henry de Bohun, see Chapter 4. After her husband's death she became a nun, dying 2 October 1399. (Their children were Humphrey, Earl of Buckingham, and three daughters: Anne, Joan and Isabel).

Isabel, eldest daughter of King Edward III, was married 27 July 1365, to Ingelram de Couci, K. G. She died before 4 May 1379 and he died 18 February 1396/7. (They left two daughters: Mary and Philippa.)

Joan, died in 1348, not having married.

Blanche, died young.

Mary, married to John Montfort, Duke of Brittany, but died without issue.

Margaret, died without issue after 1 October 1361, having been married in 1359 to John Hastings, Earl of Pembroke.

King Edward III

Chapter 36

The Order of the Garter

When first this Order was ordained, my Lords,
Knights of the Garter were of noble birth,
Valiant and virtuous, full of haughty courage,
Such as were grown to credit by the wars;
Not fearing death, nor shrinking for distress,
But always resolute in most extremes.
He that is not furnished in this sort
Doth but usurp the sacred name of Knight,
Profaning this most Honourable Order.

—Shakespeare

On Saint George's day, April 23rd, it is said in the year 1344, or soon thereafter, the uncertainty in date arising from the early loss of all its original records, there was founded at Windsor by King Edward III, the most illustrious Order of British Knighthood, the Most Noble Order of the Garter. Indeed it is said of this distinguished Order of chivalry that "No Order in Europe is so ancient, none so illustrious, for it exceeds in majesty, honour and fame all chivalrous fraternities in the world." It has ever ranked as the highest dignity of knighthood.

The political situation of the time in which Edward III grew up led to his determination to restore the prestige of his beloved England, for the control of the crown had fallen into the hands of self-seeking and unscrupulous persons, and his father was powerless to stem the tide. Edward depended upon the nobility to assist in this task and, recalling the ancient traditions of King Arthur and his Round Table, he instituted the Order of the Garter to excite emulation among the knights, which resulted in the dawn of nobler days.

The members chosen, then as now, pledged themselves to support the laws of God and of the realm, and to promote all that is noble, just and true.

Edward's court was the most brilliant in Europe, his victories being celebrated with gorgeous tournaments. Gaities, festivities and honours prevailed. During his reign the fine arts, especially architecture and poetry, attained a great development. Geoffrey Chaucer flourished at this time, and in the sphere of religious reform stands out the noble and thoroughly English figure of John Wickliffe.

It was at a time when knighthood was in flower and when courtiers were most courtly. In the words of Hallam, this was a time when the court of England "was the sun as it were of that system which embraced the valour and nobility of the Christian world" when "chivalry was in its zenith, and in all the virtues which adorned the knightly character, none were so conspicuous as Edward III and the Black Prince."

The insignia of the Order are: the garter, a blue ribbon of velvet edged with gold and having a gold buckle, worn on the left leg below the knee; the badge, called the Great George, a figure of St. George slaying the dragon, pendent from the collar of gold, which has twenty-six pieces, each representing a coiled garter; the lesser George, worn on a broad blue ribbon over the left shoulder; and the star of eight points, of silver, having in the middle the cross of St. George encircled by the garter. The vesture consists of a mantle of blue velvet lined with white taffeta, a hood and surcoat of crimson velvet, and a hat of black velvet with a plume of white ostrich feathers, having in the center a tuft of black heron feathers. When the Sovereign is a woman, she wears the ribbon on the left arm.

The well-known motto appears on the insignia: "Honi soit qui mal y pense," "Dishonour to him who thinks ill of it," referring it is said, to the king's foreign campaign plans.

ST. GEORGE'S CHAPEL
WINDSOR CASTLE
THE SHRINE OF THE KNIGHTS OF THE GARTER

The Garter Chapel, erected more than a century later, was in recent years found to be in a state of great decay, and in grave danger of collapse. The fabric was so much weakened that, as the Dean of Windsor once remarked "we could find no scientific reason why parts of the roof should have stayed up at all." The reason, probably, is tradition: for tradition is precious to the English, and this Chapel seems almost sentient. The large sum needed for its restoration was provided and the necessary repairs were completed, made possible by the generosity of the King, the present day knights and others, including members of The Society of Descendants of Knights of the Most Noble Order of the Garter, which was instituted by the writer early in 1929, at the request of His Grace the late Duke of Somerset (Sir Edward Hamilton Seymour) and of which Society the Honorable William Howard Taft was Founder President.

Chapter 36

It was an event of great satisfaction when St. George's Chapel at Windsor Castle was reopened at a great thanksgiving service, in 1930, in the presence of King George, the Sovereign, Queen Mary, the only lady of the Order, and other members of the Royal Family, and the Garter Knights, to commemorate the Chapel's restoration. Inside the Chapel the clergy alone were splendidly robed. Yet the tradition of chivalry, the majesty and havoc of the past inspired the entire congregation.

The Dean and Canons of the Chapel robed in crimson, the Prelate of the Order (the Bishop of Winchester), and the Chancellor (the Bishop of Oxford), these last in their robes of dark blue velvet, met the King at the west door and escorted him and the Queen to their stalls under the organ loft, facing the altar. The Prince of Wales sat across the aisle at the King's left. The Knights were on either side. The choir advanced, singing, through the two nave aisles, meeting as they returned toward the altar, where the Dean stood, robed, a crimson figure against the golden light of the sacred plate, and offered a prayer for the King and Companions of the Order, that "they might likewise so dispose themselves in virtue and fortitude of mind and purpose that Thy law may be the better honoured, the Commonwealth the better served, and their fame remain to their posterity." And so, with fine music and simple, worthy words, thanks were given for the repair and renovation of the Chapel, "the gem-like shrine of the Cross and Faith of Christ." The organ thundered finally in the National Anthem. The King and his Knights departed, and a thousand shadows of vanished Knights, spurred and armed, and with hands resting on their swords, watched them go.

The Order, now as always, consists of twenty-five Knight Companions. The Sovereign by whom they are chosen is the head of the Order. In recent times there have also been included foreign princes as the King may designate.

The original Knights of the Garter, selected by King Edward III, are here listed:

1. Edward Plantagenet

The Black Prince

Born at Woodstock 15 June 1330

Age 14 at Founding? (No grandchildren)

Arms: Quarterly, France and England, differenced by a label of three points argent.
Badge: Three ostrich feathers encircled by a crown.
Motto: Ich dien (I serve).

Son of King Edward III and Philippa of Hainault, page 218.

He distinguished himself at age 16 when placed in command at the battle of Crecy 26 August 1346, wearing black armor, hence his name. He died in the lifetime of his father, 8 June 1376, and his body lies at Canterbury. He married his cousin Joan, the Fair Maid of Kent (widow of Thomas de Holand, No. 13 below) who died 8 August 1385, and was buried in the Church of the Grey Friars in Stamford, co. Lincoln. They had:

Edward of Angouleme, born 1365, died at age seven in Gascony.

Richard of Bordeaux, Prince of Wales, afterward King Richard II, who died without issue.

2. Henry Plantagenet

Duke of Lancaster

Born at Grosmont Castle, Monmouthshire, about 1300

Age 44 at Founding? (Issue)

Arms: The arms of England, differenced by a label of three points azure, each charged with three fleurs-de-lis or.

Son of Henry Plantagenet and Maud Chaworth, page 203.

A great commander, equally desirous of peace with honor, he fought in many engagements in France. In 1330 when his father became blind, he assumed responsibility in public affairs and served until 24 March 1360/1 when he died of the plague, and was buried at Leicester. After his death the Dukedom of Lancaster became extinct. His wife, Isabel Beaumont, whom he married about the year 1337, survived him. They had two daughters:

Maud, child wife of Ralph Stafford, and at the age of six years, his widow; married second, in 1352, to William, Duke of Bavaria, and died without issue 10 April 1362.

Blanche, born in 1346, became the wife of John of Gaunt, see Chapter 35.

Page 219

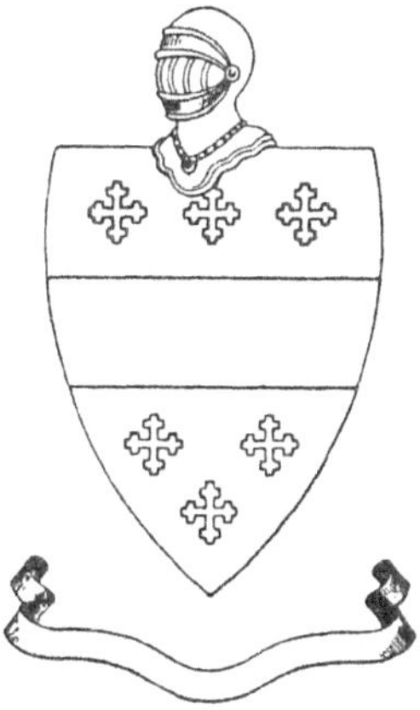

3. Thomas de Beauchamp

Earl of Warwick

Born in 1313

Age 31 at Founding? (Issue)

Arms: Gules, a fess between six cross crosslets or.

Son of Guy de Beauchamp and Alice Toni, page 327.

A descendant of the Sureties Roger and Hugh Bigod and Henry de Bohun, at the age of two years he succeeded his father as Earl of Warwick, and later took an active part in the wars in Scotland and in France. One of the chief commanders at the battle of Crecy, he distinguished himself at Poitiers, and was constituted marshal of England. His brother John is No. 10 below. Dying of the plague at Calais, 13 November 1369, Thomas "left not behind him his equal in warlike quality and fidelity. He and his wife Catherine Mortimer are both buried in a splendid tomb at Warwick, where their effigies may still be seen. Their sixteen children were:

Guy, married Philippa Ferrers; left issue.

Thomas, K. G., married Margaret Ferrers; left issue.

Reyburne, left an only daughter Alianore.

William, K. G., Lord of Abergavenny.

John, *Roger* and *Jerome*, all died without issue.

Maud, married Roger de Clifford; left issue.

Philippa, married Hugh Stafford; left issue.

Alice, married John de Beauchamp and died without issue.

Joan, married Ralph Basset; left issue.

Isabel, married first John le Strange and had an only daughter Elizabeth; married second William Ufford who died without issue.

Margaret, married Guy de Montford and later became a nun.

Alice, married first Mr. Cokesay and second Mr. Bardolf.

Juliana, died without marrying.

Catharine, became a nun.

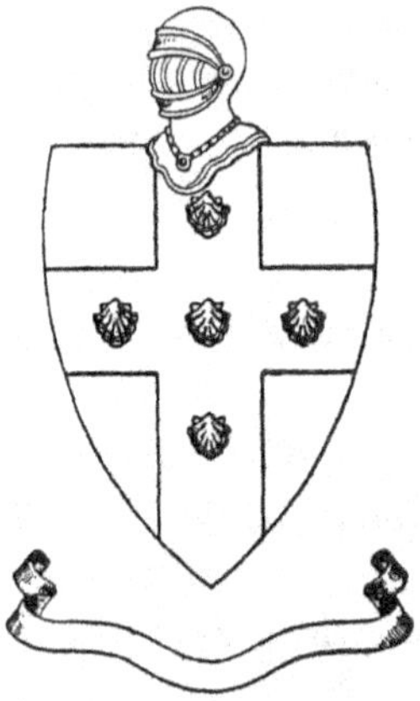

4. Jean de Grailly

Captal de Buch

Hereditary proprietor of a fort near Bordeaux, he was also Vicomte de Benauges

Arms: Or, on a cross sable, five escallops argent. Stall Plate at St. George's Chapel.

(No issue)

(Parentage not given)

In the battle of Poitiers, which took place 19 September 1356, he performed gallant service, and in later years was taken prisoner in battle, and confined in the tower of the Temple at Paris. King Edward made several offers for his exchange, but King Charles was willing to liberate him only upon condition that he would bind himself never again to bear arms against France. Declining to accept that condition he died in prison in 1377. In November 1350 he married Rose d'Albret, who died childless.

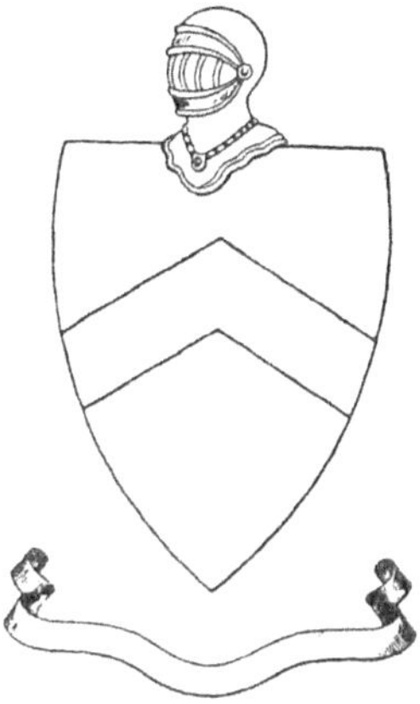

5. Ralph, Lord Stafford

Born in 1299

Age 45 at Founding? (Issue)

Arms: Or, a chevron gules.

Son of Edmund Stafford and Margaret Basset of Drayton.

One of the most esteemed of Edward's commanders, he distinguished himself in the wars in Ireland and in France; his long life being constantly employed in the King's service. He died 31 August 1372, and was buried in the priory of Tunbridge, beside his wife Margaret, and at the feet of her father and mother, Hugh Audley and Margaret Clare, see Chapter 6. They were the parents of:

Ralph, married Maud of Lancaster, but died without issue.

Hugh, married Philippa Beauchamp; left issue.

Beatrice, wife first of Maurice, Earl of Desmond, second of Thomas de Roos, and third of Richard Burley. Issue.

Joane, married John Cherlton; left issue.

Elizabeth, married Fulke le Strange.

Margaret, married John Stafford; left issue.

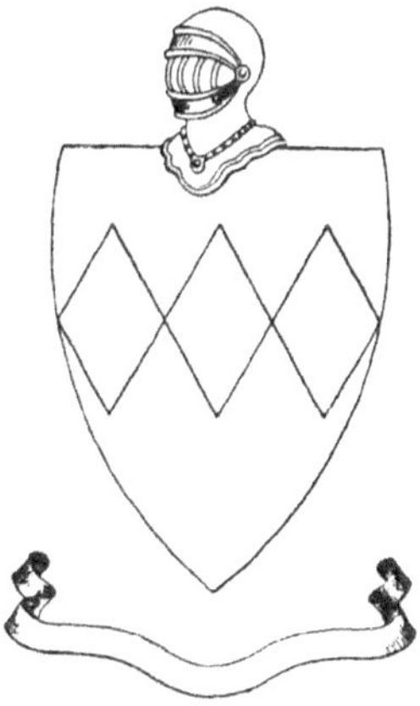

6. William de Montacute

Earl of Salisbury

Born 25 June 1328

Age 16 at Founding? (No grandchildren)

Arms: Argent, three lozenges conjoined in fess gules.

Son of William de Montacute and Katherine Grandison.

At age 22 he took part in the naval engagement with the Spaniards off

Winchelsea, and in 1356 commanded the rear of the English army at the battle of Poitiers. In 1376 he was made admiral of the fleet. He contended with the Earl of Warwick, in later life, as to which had spilled the more French blood. His entire life was spent in warfare.

The last survivor of the Founders of the Order, he died 3 June 1397 and was buried in the priory of Bustleham-Montacute in Berks, which had been founded by his father. His widow Elizabeth became a nun. She was the daughter of John de Mohun, No. 11 below. Their only child:

William, married in 1378 Elizabeth FitzAlan but died without issue when unhappily slain by his father in a tilting match at Windsor, 6 August 1382.

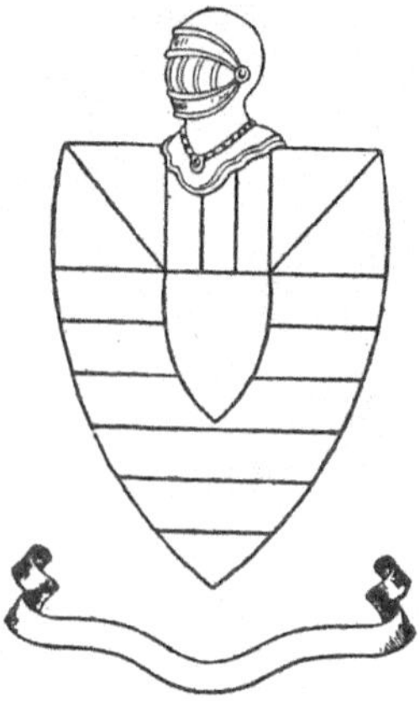

7. Roger Mortimer

Earl of March

Born at Ludlow 11 November 1328

Age 16 at Founding? (Issue)

Arms: *Barry of six, or and azure; on a chief of the first, two pallets between two base esquirres of the second; over all an inescutcheon argent.*

Son of Edmund Mortimer and Elizabeth Badlesmere, page 320.

A descendant of the Sureties Roger and Hugh Bigod, Richard and Gilbert de Clare, John de Lacie and Saire de Quincey, his personal courage and adroitness in the tournaments won for him a place among the Founders of the Order of the Garter. "Roger was a man of great strength, eager for the glory of battle, but prudent in counsel and praiseworthy for the goodness of his morals." He was Constable of Dover Castle and warden of the Cinque Ports. Dying at Romera in Burgundy 26 February 1359, he was buried at Wigmore. He married Philippa Montacute, sister of William, No. 6 above, and had:

Roger, died in his father's lifetime, leaving a son Edmund.

Edmund, married Philippa Plantagenet, daughter of Lionel of Antwerp, and had three sons and three daughters.

Margery, wife of John, Lord Audley.

8. John, Baron Lisle

(No known descendants)

Lord Lisle of Rougemont

Born about 1318

Age 26 at Founding?

Arms: Or, a fess between two chevronels sable. Stall Plate in St. George's Chapel.

Son of Robert de L'Isle who died in 1342.

He rendered valuable services at Crecy, Calais and elsewhere. Indeed the greater part of his life was spent in the French wars. He was sheriff of Cambridge and Huntingdon and governor of Cambridge Castle. Wounded by an arrow shot from a cross-bow, he died 14 October 1355, leaving by his wife Maud, daughter of Henry de Grey, whom he married in 1332, four children:

Robert, died in 1399, having married Agnes, and later Margaret, both of whom died childless.

John and *William*, died without issue.

Elizabeth, became the wife of William, Lord Aldeburgh, and had a son William, who died without issue in 1391.

9. Bartholomew, Lord Burghersh

Born about 1320

Age 24 at Founding? (Issue)

Arms: Gules, a lion rampant double queue or.

Son of Bartholomew Burghersh and Elizabeth Verdon, page 318.

A descendant of the Sureties Roger and Hugh Bigod, he was a close

Page 70 companion of the Black Prince and one of the most eminent warriers of his day, serving at Poitiers and elsewhere. He died 5 April 1369, and was buried in the Chapel of Walsingham, having married first, Cecily Weyland, by whom he had an only daughter:

Elizabeth, wife of Edward Despencer, K. G. Issue.

The second wife of Bartholomew Burghersh was Margaret Badlesmere, who had no children.

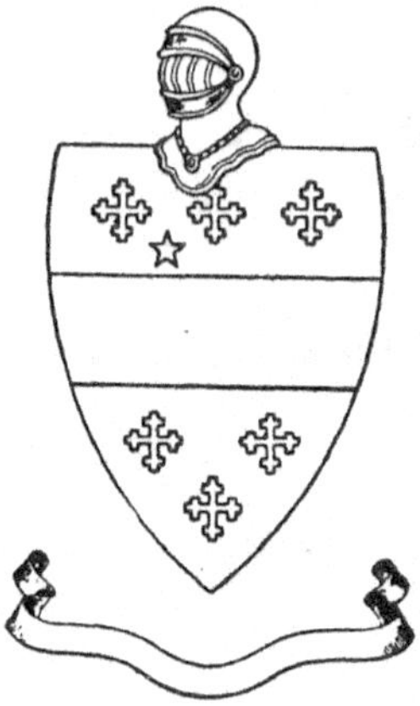

10. John de Beauchamp

Lord of Warwick

Born about 1315

Age 29 at Founding? (No issue)

Arms: Gules, on a fess between six cross crosslets or, a mullet for difference.

Son of Guy de Beauchamp and Alice Toni, page 327.

Descended from the Sureties Roger and Hugh Bigod and Henry de Bohun, he was a younger brother of Thomas de Beauchamp, No. 3 above, and he bore the royal standard at Crecy, having taken part in the naval victory off Sluys in 1340. He was appointed admiral of the fleet, constable of the Tower of London and warden of the Cinque Ports. Dying 2 December 1360, without issue, he was buried at St. Paul's Cathedral in London, where his monument may be seen.

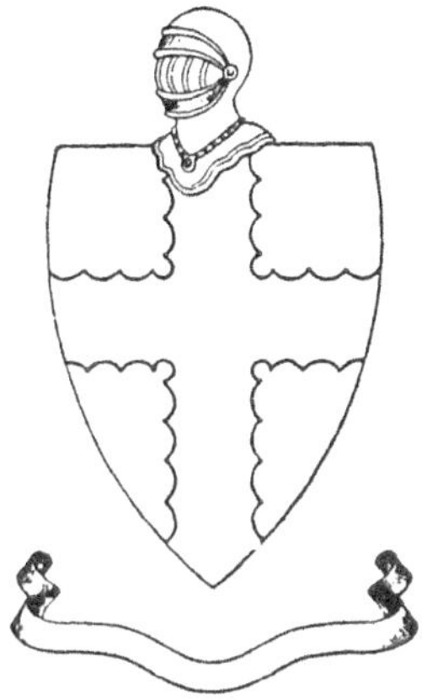

11. John, Baron Mohun

Born 1320

Age 24 at Founding? (Issue)

Arms: Or, a cross engrailed sable.

Son of John de Mohun who died in his father's lifetime.

Ninth in descent from William de Mohun of Dunster Castle, Somersetshire, and a descendant of the Sureties William d'Albini and Robert de Roos, he was in the retinue of the Black Prince and later in that of John of Gaunt, and performed many gallant services. He fought at Crecy and took part in the naval fight with the Spaniards off Winchelsea in 1350. His wife was Joan, sister of Bartholomew Burghersh, No. 9 above. They had three daughters:

Elizabeth, died in 1414, wife of William de Montacute, No. 6 above. No surviving issue.

Philippa, died in 1431, married first Walter FitzWalter, second John Golafre, and third Edward, Duke of York. She left issue which did not survive.

Maud, died in 1401, married John, Lord Strange of Knockyn, and had a son Richard, Lord Strange.

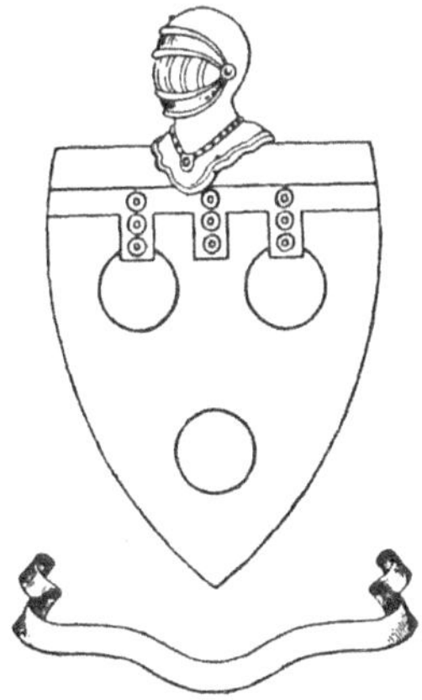

12. Hugh, Baron Courtenay

Earl of Devon

Born 22 March 1326/7

Age 17 at Founding? (No grandchildren)

Arms: Or, three torteaux, differenced by a label of three points, each charged with three annulets.
Stall Plate in St. George's Chapel.

Son of Hugh de Courtenay and Margaret Bohun, page 404.

He was descended from the Surety Henry de Bohun and accompanied his uncle, William de Bohun, at the siege of Calais, and dying before 2 September 1349, he was buried at Ford Abbey, Devonshire. By his wife Elizabeth, whom he married in 1341, he had an only son:

Hugh, who died after his father, but before his grandfather, having married Maud, daughter of Thomas de Holand, No. 13 below, and died without issue in 1377.

13. Thomas de Holand

Earl of Kent

Arms: Azure, semee of fleurs-de-lis, a lion rampant guardant argent.

(Issue)

Son of Robert de Holand and Maud Zouche, page 120.

Descended from the Surety Saire de Quincey, and of a family settled at Holand in Lancashire, he was one of the principal commanders at Crecy. His brother Otes is No. 22 below. In 1360 Thomas was appointed the king's lieutenant and captain-general in France and Normandy, but dying 28 December of the same year in Normandy, he was buried in the Church of the Grey Friars in Stamford, co. Lincoln. His wife, who was afterward married to the Black Prince, No. 1 above, and became the mother of King Richard II, was Page 216 Joan Plantagenet, the Fair Maid of Kent. They were married about the year 1339 and were the parents of three sons and two daughters:

Page 132 *Thomas*, married Alice FitzAlan; left issue.

Edmund, of whom nothing further is recorded.

John, Earl of Huntingdon, married Elizabeth Plantagenet; left issue.

Joan, wife of John, Duke of Brittany, K. G.

Maud, wife first of Hugh de Courtenay, No. 12 above, and second of Waleran, Earl of St. Paul.

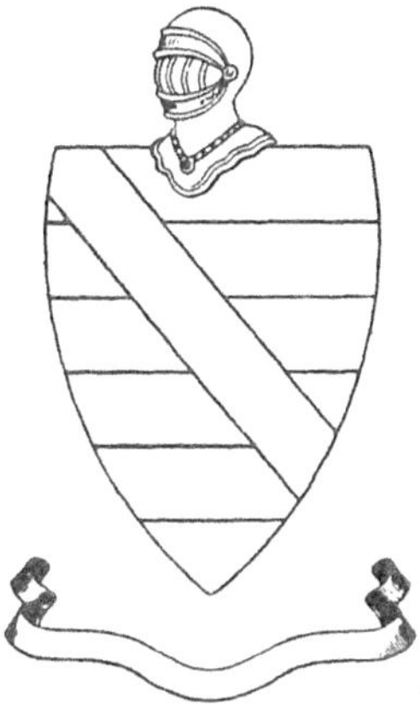

14. John, Lord Grey of Rotherfield

Born 9 October 1300

Age 44 at Founding? (Issue)

Arms: Barry of six argent and azure, differenced by a bend gules.

Son of John de Grey and Margaret Odingsells, page 80.

He was a descendant of the Surety Robert FitzWalter, marshal of the Baronial Army, see Chapter 8. He served in the wars in France, and died 1 September 1359, having married as his first wife Katherine FitzAlan, by whom he had:

John, married Maud Burghersh; had issue.

Maud, wife first of John de Botetourt and second of Thomas de Harcourt.

Lord Grey's second wife was Avice Marmion, and their two sons:

John and *Robert*, sometimes assumed their mother's name, Marmion. John died without issue and Robert had an only daughter Elizabeth, see page 80.

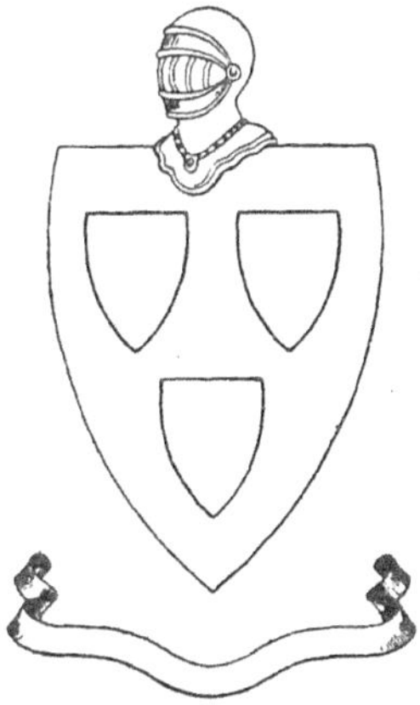

15. Richard Fitz-Simon

Arms: Argent, three inescutcheons, two and one, gules.

(Issue)

(Parentage not given)

In 1338 he was on the king's service under the command of Reginald Cobham. Like the other knights he too served in the wars in France, being employed in 1348 on the continent, under the Black Prince. He married Anne Conquest and had:

Adam, who married and left issue.

16. Miles Stapleton

Born in 1320

Age 24 at Founding? (Issue)

Arms: Argent, a lion rampant sable.
Stall Plate in St. George's Chapel.

Son of Nicholas Stapleton and Sibill Beaulieu.

"An expert soldier" he was chosen to march against the French, and in 1353 and subsequent years he was high sheriff of Yorkshire. He died 4 December 1364 and was buried before the high altar of the Church at Ingham, in Norfolk. His wife was Joan Ingham and their children were:

Miles, married and left issue.

Nicholas, who had Thomas (died without issue) and Elizabeth, wife of Thomas Meetham.

Gilbert, married Agnes FitzAlan and had two sons, Miles, and Bryan, K. G.

17. Thomas Wale

Born in 1303

Age 41 at Founding?

Arms: Or, a lion rampant gules.

(No issue)

(Parentage not given)

"A knight of great virtue and worthiness," he attended the King into Flanders in 1339 and had command in the expedition into Brittany in 1342. He died in Gascony 26 October 1352, leaving no issue by his wife Nichola. She survived him but died childless.

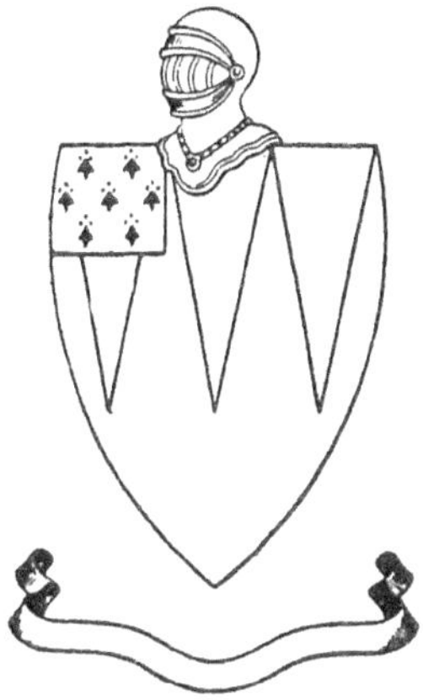

18. Hugh Wrottesley

Arms: Or, three piles sable, a canton ermine.

(Issue)

Of an ancient family long seated at Wrottesley, in Staffordshire, he served in Flanders and before Calais. His first wife was Mabel, daughter of Philip ap Rees, and he married second Isabel, daughter of John Arderne. His son by his first wife:

John, married and left issue.

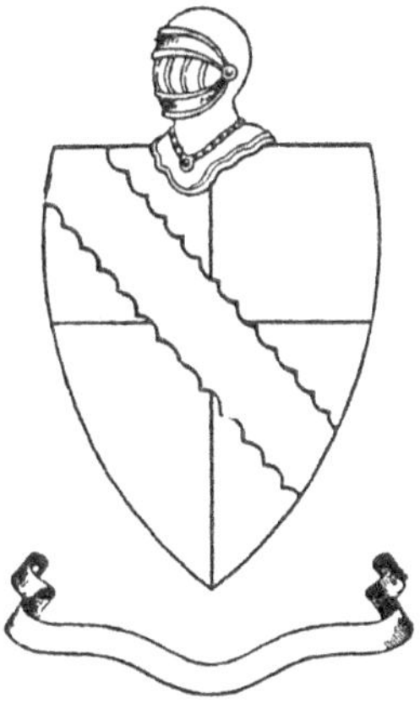

19. Nele Loryng

Arms: Quarterly, argent and gules, a bend engrailed sable. Stall Plate in St. George's Chapel.

(Issue)

He was of Chalgrave, in Bedfordshire. By his gallant conduct in the naval engagement off Sluys, 24 June 1340, he won the King's favor. In 1355 he attended the Black Prince into Gascony, and the next year at Poitiers he was appointed to attend the person of the Prince, being rewarded for his gallantry. After a life of great activity and devotion to the public service, he retired to his family estate at Chalgrave where he had, in 1365, obtained the royal license to enclose a park. He died 18 March 1385/6, and was buried in the priory of the Church of Dunstable, to which he had been a considerable benefactor. He married Margaret Beauple and had two daughters:

Isabel, wife first of William Coggan and second of Robert, Lord Harrington; left issue.

Margaret, wife of Thomas Peyvre; left issue.

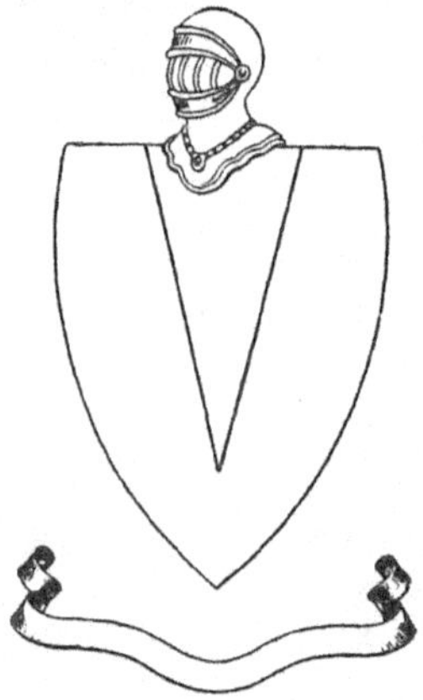

20. John Chandos

Arms: Argent, a pile gules.
Stall Plate in St. George's Chapel.

(No issue)

(Parentage not given)

Of Radborne, he has been called "the pride of English chivalry" and was renowned for innumerable feats of arms, gallant achievements in almost every martial expedition during a period of thirty years. Especially deserving of mention is the part which he took at Crecy and at Poitiers, and his personal friendship with the Black Prince. In the wars of Gascoigne he was slain at Lussac Bridge, 31 December 1369, without issue, never having married, and was buried at Mortemer. He appears to have been tripped by the long garment he wore over his armor and, his visor being open, he was stabbed by the enemy, bringing to a close the life of "a sweet-tempered knight, courteous, benign, amiable, liberal, courageous, prudent and loyal in all affairs, one who bore himself valiantly on every occasion."

21. James, Lord Audley

Arms: Gules, fretty or, a label for difference.

(No issue)

Son of James Audley of Stretton Audley.

He was not James of Heleigh, who died 1 April 1386, son of Nicholas, which supposition was followed by Sir Bernard Burke in his Dormant and Extinct Peerage but, as explained by Beltz, he was the son of James of Stretton Audley in Oxfordshire, and governor of Aquitaine. He took part at Poitiers where, with John Chandos, he was a chief advisor of the Prince, and was a commander at Calais, taking fortresses and garrisons. In 1369 he was seneschal of Poitou, and died in the same year at Fontenay-le-Comte, never having married. The Prince personally attended his funeral. "He was a prudent knight and gallant warrior, and the first assailant at the battle of Poitiers (where King John of France was defeated and taken prisoner) and on that day he was accounted the most brave of the whole English army."

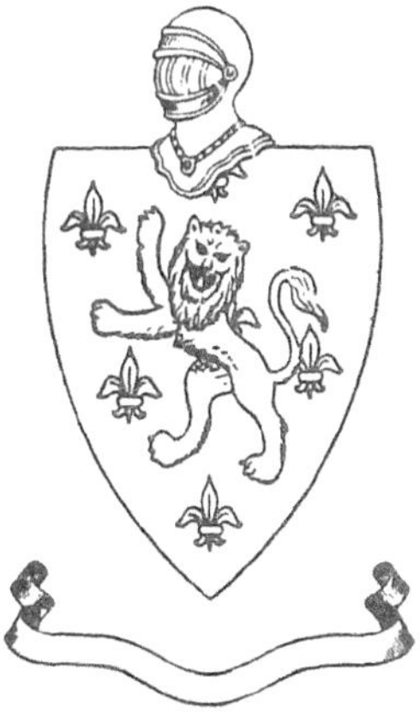

22. Otes de Holand

Arms: Azure, semee of fleurs-de-lis, a lion rampant guardant argent.

(No issue)

Son of Robert de Holand and Maud Zouche, page 120.

A descendant of the Surety Saire de Quincey and a younger brother of

Thomas de Holand, No. 13 above, he died without issue 3 September 1359 in Normandy. A person of great valor, he fell into disgrace through allowing the Earl of Eye, who had been committed to his custody, to go at large, armed.

23. Henry d'Enne

Arms: Party per fess, or and argent; issuant out of the center of a fess sable, a demi-lion rampant gules.

(No known descendants)

(Parentage not given)

The identity of this knight has not been fully proved, but it is believed that he died without issue shortly before April 1360.

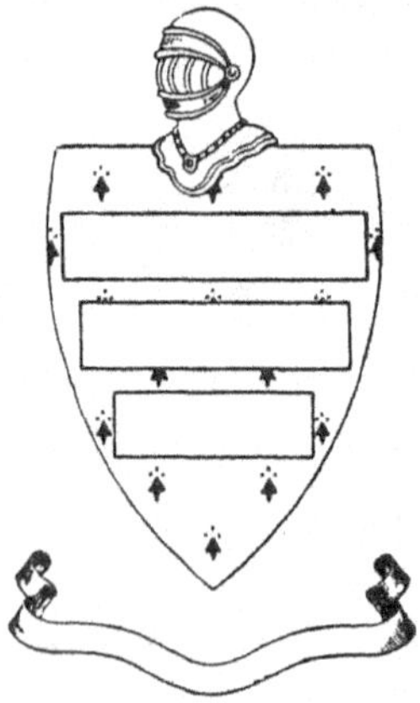

24. Sanchet d'Abrichecourt

Arms: Ermine, three bars humettee gules.
Stall Plate in St. George's Chapel.

(No known descendants)

(Parentage not given)

Of him scarcely any record has been preserved. He died about the year 1360. His father is presumed to have been Nicholas d'Abrichecourt, who graciously received and entertained Queen Isabel and her son Edward in 1326, at his castle near Bouchain in Ostrevant, for which Edward rewarded him in 1331.

25. Walter Paveley

Born in 1319

Age 25 at Founding?

Arms: Azure, a cross flory or.
Stall Plate in St. George's Chapel.

(No grandchildren)

Of ancient Norman ancestry, his family originally came from Pavilly, a small town near Rouen. His mother was Maud Burghersh and he appears to have been a first cousin of Bartholomew Burghersh, No. 9 above. He accompanied his uncle, Bartholomew Burghersh, Sr. and later King Edward, in the wars in France. In 1346 the Black Prince presented him with "a nouche adorned with pearls and diamonds" and when in Normandy the Prince gave him a swift war horse called Morel More, and allowed him to fish on his manor of Newport. In 1369 his cousin Bartholomew Burghersh bequeathed to him a standing cup gilt, his whole suit of armour for the jousts, together with his coat of mail and sword, and constituted him one of his executors. Paveley died 28 June 1375, and was buried in the Church of the Black Friars in London. The name of his wife has not been preserved; she is thought to have been of the St. Philibert family. They had two sons:

Edward, soon died without issue.

Walter, married Elizabeth, died without issue.

William the Conqueror's Burial Place
as described on page 199.

The Great Abbey of St. Etienne in Caen, France
built 900 years ago by William the Conqueror.
At the funeral it was discovered that he did not own the ground;
so his friends hurriedly bought it from the owner.
The price paid was 60 cents!

Mr. and Mrs. Harry Cyrus Holloway

Descent from King Edward III, Knights of the Garter, and from Fifteen Sureties for the Magna Charta of A. D. 1215

William d'Albini	John de Lacie
Hugh Bigod	William de Lanvallei
Roger Bigod	William Malet
Henry de Bohun	Saire de Quincey
Gilbert de Clare	Robert de Roos
Richard de Clare	Geoffrey de Saye
John FitzRobert	Robert de Vere
Robert FitzWalter	

*21. KING EDWARD III, whose biography appears on page 218 in the preceding Chapter, married Philippa of Hainault. Their third son was

*20. Lionel of Antwerp, K. G., page 218, married Elizabeth Burgh, descended as follows:

25. WILLIAM d'ALBINI the Surety, a record of whose ancestry and achievements appears at page 41, was lord of Belvoir Castle and ninth in descent from Louis IV, King of France, page 188. He married Margery Umfraville and died 1 May 1236. Their son

24. William d'Albini, page 42, married first Albreda.

23. Isabel d'Albini, married to Robert de Roos, descended as follows:

25. ROBERT de ROOS the Surety, a record of whose ancestry and achievements appears at page 122, was born in 1197 and died in 1226. He was 4th Baron of Hamlake Manor. His wife, Isabel, was daughter of William the Lion, King of Scotland, and they had

24. William de Roos, page 123, died 1258, married Lucia FitzPiers.

23. Robert de Roos as above married Isabel d'Albini.

22. William de Roos, page 124, married Maud Vaux.

21. William de Roos married Margery Badlesmere.

20. Thomas de Roos, page 124 and Chapter 52, married Beatrice Stafford.

19. Margaret Roos, wife of Reynold de Gray, died 1440, page 315.

18. Elizabeth (Eleanor or Isabel) Gray, married to Robert, 5th Baron Poynings, killed at the siege of Orleans in 1446.

17. Richard Poynings, died in his father's lifetime, 1430, married Alianore, daughter of John Berkeley of Beverstone.

16. Eleanor Poynings, married to Henry Percy, died 1461, descended as follows:

26. WILLIAM de LANVALLEI the Surety, whose biography appears at page 92, was governor of Colchester Castle and married Hawise Basset. He died in 1217, leaving an only daughter

25. Hawise Lanvallei, page 92, married to John de Burgh, died 1275.

24. John de Burgh, died 1279, married Cecily Baliol.

23. Margaret Burgh, page 93, married to Richard, son of Walter de Burgh.

22. John de Burgh, died 1313, married Elizabeth Clare, page 70.

21. William de Burgh, page 94, married Maud of Lancaster, page 203.

20. Elizabeth Burgh as above married to Lionel of Antwerp, K. G.

*19. Philippa Plantagenet, their only child, page 219, became the wife of Edmund Mortimer, page 320.

*18. Elizabeth Mortimer, married to Henry Percy "Hotspur," page 342.

*17. Henry Percy, died 1455, married Eleanor Nevill, page 348.

*16. Henry Percy as above married Eleanor Poynings.

*15. Henry Percy, K. G., who was confined in the Tower of London from 1461 to 1469 and was released by King Edward IV, to whom he swore allegiance. He was murdered 28 April 1489. His wife was Maud, daughter of William Herbert, Earl of Pembroke, and they had four sons and three daughters, among whom was

*14. Eleanor Percy, who became the wife of Edward Stafford, K. G., lord high constable of England in 1511. Like his father,

he was the victim of domestic treason and was decapitated on Tower Hill 17 May 1521. His baronial descent is as follows:

26. ROBERT de VERE the Surety, a record of whose ancestry and achievements appears at page 129, was hereditary lord great Chamberlain of England, and 8th in descent from Hugh Capet, page 184, and Pedigrees C and K on page 424. He died 25 October 1221, having married Isabel Bolebec.

25. Hugh de Vere, page 129, Earl of Oxford, died 1263, having married in 1223 Hawise Quincey, daughter of SAIRE de QUINCEY the Surety, a record of whose ancestry and achievements appears at page 112, who was Earl of Winchester and was born before 1154 and died 3 November 1219 on the way to Jerusalem. His wife was Margaret Bellomont (Beaumont).

24. Robert de Vere, page 130, 5th Earl of Oxford and 6th great Chamberlain, who died 2 September 1296. He married Alice Saunford.

23. Joan Vere, whose husband William de Warren, killed in a tournament at Croydon in 1285, was son of John, Earl of Warren.

22. Alice Warren, pages 131 and 205, wife of Edmund Fitz-Alan, Earl of Arundel who, without trial, was beheaded at Hereford in 1326.

21. Richard FitzAlan "Copped Hat," Justiciar of North Wales and Admiral of the West, married second Eleanor Plantagenet, daughter of Henry, Earl of Lancaster, page 203, whose ancestry appears also in Chapter 62.

20. Joane FitzAlan, page 132, married to Humphrey de Bohun, descended as follows:

26. HENRY de BOHUN the Surety, a record of whose ancestry and achievements appears at page 52, was Earl of Hereford and 5th in descent from MALCOLM III, King of Scotland, page 192. He died on a pilgrimage to the Holy Land in 1220. His wife was Maud FitzGeoffrey.

25. Humphrey de Bohun, page 53, Earl of Hereford and Essex, married Maud, daughter of Raoul de Lusignan, Count of Eu.

24. Humphrey de Bohun married first Alianore Braos.

23. Humphrey de Bohun, page 54, died 1298, married Maud Fiennes.

22. Humphrey de Bohun, died 1322, married Princess Elizabeth, daughter of KING EDWARD I, page 213.

21. William de Bohun, K. G., page 55, born about 1310, died 1360, married Elizabeth Badlesmere, page 68.

20. Humphrey de Bohun, K. G., page 55, lord high constable of England, died 1372. His wife as above was Joane FitzAlan. They had

19. Alianore, called also Eleanor, Bohun, page 55, whose husband was Thomas of Woodstock, Duke of Gloucester, 6th son of KING EDWARD III, page 218.

18. Anne Plantagenet, page 219, widow of Thomas and wife of his brother Edmund, 5th Earl of Stafford, K. G. and K. B., page 338, who was killed 22 July 1403. Her third husband was William Bourchier, of whom later. Edmund was descended as follows:

25. RICHARD de CLARE the Surety, a record of whose ancestry and achievements appears at page 58, was 4th Earl of Hertford, dying in 1217. His descent from Sveide the Viking is traced in Pedigree C, page 421. He married Amicia of Gloucester and they were the parents of

24. GILBERT de CLARE the Surety, page 61, who was born about 1180 and died 25 October 1230. His wife Isabella was one of the sisters of William Marshall the Surety, whose royal ancestry is recorded in Pedigree F, page 422.

23. Richard de Clare, page 66, married Maud, daughter of the Surety JOHN de LACIE, a record of whose ancestry and achievements appears at page 89, was 15th in descent from Alfred the Great and 28th in descent from Cerdic, Pedigree M, page 426, and married second Margaret, daughter of the Surety SAIRE de QUINCEY, of whom later.

22. Gilbert de Clare, page 69, Earl of Gloucester and Hertford, who died in 1295, having married second Joan of Acre (daughter of KING EDWARD I and his wife Eleanor of Castile, page 215).

21. Margaret Clare, page 70, wife of Hugh, died 1347, son of Hugh, Lord Audley.

20. Margaret Audley, page 338, married to Ralph, Lord Stafford, K. G., page 227.

19. Hugh Stafford, K. G., page 338, died 1386, married Philippa, daughter of Thomas de Beauchamp, K. G., page 225, whose ancestry appears on page 575.

18. Edmund Stafford, K. G., as above married Anne Plantagenet.

17. Humphrey Stafford, K. G., page 338, killed 27 July 1460, married Anne Nevill, page 348.

16. Humphrey Stafford, slain in the battle of St. Albans, 22 May 1455, having married Margaret, daughter of Edmund, Duke of Somerset, K. G. (who was son of John Beaufort, K. G., and grandson of John of Gaunt, K. G., page 219, 4th son of KING EDWARD III). They had

15. Henry Stafford, K. G., who was beheaded in the market place at Salisbury 2 November 1483. He married Katherine, daughter of Richard Widville, Earl Rivers, and they had

14. Edward Stafford, K. G., as above married Eleanor Percy.

*13. Mary Stafford who became the wife of George de Nevill, K. G., Lord Abergavenny, descended as follows:

22. JOHN FITZROBERT the Surety, a record of whose ancestry and achievements appears at page 72, and in Pedigree H, page 424, was high sheriff of co. Northumberland and governor of New-Castle-upon-Tyne, and married Ada Baliol. He died in 1240.

21. Roger FitzJohn, page 73, lord of Warkworth, died 1249, married Isabel.

20. Robert FitzRoger married Margaret Zouche.

19. Anastasia FitzRobert married to Ralph de Neville.

18. Ralph de Nevill, page 73, died 1367, married Alice Audley.

17. John de Nevill, K. G., page 74, married first Maud Percy.

16. Ralph de Nevill, K. G., married second Joan Beaufort, daughter of John of Gaunt, page 219, and granddaughter of KING EDWARD III. Their fourth son was

15. Edward de Nevill, K. G., page 348, who died 18 October 1476, having married Elizabeth Beauchamp descended as follows:

26. ROGER BIGOD the Surety, a record of whose ancestry and achievements appears at page 44, was Earl of Norfolk and Suffolk and 15th in descent from Sveide the Viking, Pedigree D, page 422. Born about 1150, he died in 1221, having married Isabella, daughter of Hameline **Plantagenet**. Their son

25. HUGH BIGOD was also a Surety, and Earl of Norfolk and Suffolk, page 46. He married about 1212 Maud, a sister of William Marshall the Surety, who was also 16th in descent from Sveide the Viking, Pedigree F, page 422.

24. Isabel Bigod, page 48, married first to Gilbert de Lacy, died 1230.

23. Margery Lacy, married to John Verdon.

22. Theobald de Verdon, died 1309, married Margery.

21. Theobald de Verdon, page 48, married first Maud, daughter of Edmund, Lord Mortimer of Wigmore. She died in 1315 and

their second daughter was

20. Elizabeth Verdun, page 318, died 1360, who became the wife of Bartholomew Burghersh, constable of Dover Castle who died 3 August 1355. They had

19. Bartholomew Burghersh, page 318, an original Knight of the Garter, page 229. He married first Cecily, daughter of Richard of Weyland, and had

18. Elizabeth Burghersh, born 1342, died 1409, wife of Edward Despencer, K. G., who died 11 November 1375. For his gallant conduct in the French Wars, Sir Edward was summoned to Parliament from 1357 to 1372. Their son

17. Thomas Despencer, K. G., beheaded 1400, married Constance, daughter of Edmund of Langley, K. G., page 219, son of KING EDWARD III. Their daughter and only surviving child was

16. Isabel Despencer who became the wife of Richard Beauchamp, Lord Abergavenny and Earl of Worcester, also of baronial descent. Their only daughter

15. Elizabeth Beauchamp inherited from her grandfather the barony of Despencer when his attainder was reversed in the year 1461. Her husband as above was Edward de Nevill, K. G. They had

14. George de Nevill who was knighted at the battle of Tewksbury 9 May 1471. He died 20 September 1492 having married first Margaret, daughter of Sir Hugh Fenne, treasurer of the Household to King Edward VI. She died 28 September 1485, leaving an eldest son

13. George de Nevill, K. G. and K. B., born July 1483, died 1536, as above married Mary Stafford and had

*12. Mary Nevill. She was married to Thomas Fiennes, Lord Dacre, born 1515, one of the jury at the trial of Anne Boleyn, 1536; he also bore the canopy at the funeral of Jane Seymour in 1538.

On the eve of May Day 1541, when less than 26 years of age, Thomas Fiennes, Lord Dacre, was unfortunately "tempted by his own folly or that of his friends to join a party to kill deer" in the park of an unpopular neighbor. They were seen by the foresters and a fray ensued in which one of the keepers was killed. The charge was indeed serious: manslaughter following deer stealing, which in itself was a felony. Both he and his friends were general favorites and the privy council hesitated long before they adjudged him guilty, being convinced that "if a poor man must be sent to the gallows for an act into which he might have been tempted by poverty, thoughtlessness could not be held as an excuse because the offender was a peer." King Henry, remaining true to his principles of equal justice, did not intervene and Thomas was hanged at Tyburn 29 June 1541, whereby it was considered that his honors were forfeited. He was buried in St. Sepulchre's Church near Newgate.

He had two sons: Thomas, who died at the age of fourteen, and Gregory, Lord Dacre, who died without issue in 1593, and a daughter MARGARET FIENNES, of whom later. These children happily were restored in blood, estate and honors by Queen Elizabeth. Thomas Fiennes, Lord Dacre, was descended as follows:

24. GEOFFREY de SAYE the Surety, a record of whose ancestry and achievements appears at page 126, died 24 October 1230, leaving extensive possessions in ten counties. His wife Alice was daughter of William de Cheyney and they had

23. William de Saye, page 126, died 1272, Governor of Rochester Castle.

22. William de Saye, page 126, died 1295.

21. Geoffrey de Saye, page 126, died 1322, married Idonea Leybourne whose ancestry appears on page 579. They had

20. Geoffrey de Saye, page 126, Admiral of the king's fleet, died 1359, married Maud, daughter of Guy de Beauchamp, Chapter 40.

19. Joan Saye, married to William Fienes, page 397, tenth in descent from John, Baron of Fiennes, kinsman and companion of William the Conqueror and sixth hereditary constable of Dover Castle and descended from Charlemagne and King Louis IV of France as follows:

38. CHARLEMAGNE, Emperor of the West, page 178, married Hildegarde of Suabia and they had

37. Louis I, le Debonaire, page 188, born 778, died 840, married second Judith and had

36. Charles II, the Bald, born 823, died 878, married Hermintrudis of Orleans. Their son

35. Louis II, the Stammerer, born 846, died 879, married second Adelheide of Saxony and had

34. Charles IV, the Simple, born 879, died 929, married third Edgina, daughter of Edward the Elder, King of England, page 175.

33. Louis IV, d'Outremer, page 188, born 920, died 954, married Gerberga of Lorraine.

32. Charles, Duke of Lorraine, born 953, died 993, married second, Agnes of Vermandois.

31. Gerberga, Duchess of Brabant, page 189, married to Lambert Barbutus of Lorraine who died in 1015.

30. Maud became the wife of Eustace, Count of Bologne, died 1049.

29. Eustace, Count of Bologne, died 1080, married Ida, daughter of Godfrey, Duke of Lower Lorraine.

28. Godfrey de Bologne, father of

27. Geoffrey de Bologne, married the daughter of Geoffrey de Mandeville.

26. William de Bologne.

25. Faramus de Bologne, who married Matilda.

24. Sybilla, wife of Ingleram de Fiennes, died 1189, great grandson of JOHN de FIENNES, who came to England with William the Conqueror and is said to have been his kinsman. He was made Admiral in 1084. Ingleram de Fiennes and Sybilla were the parents of

23. William de Fiennes, one of the Magna Charta Barons against King John, died 1241, father of

22. Ingleram de Fiennes, whose son

21. Giles de Fiennes, died 1293, a Crusader to the Holy Land with St. Louis and King Edward I. His wife was Sybilla and they had

20. John de Fiennes, died 1351, married Maud Monceux, heiress of Hurstmonceux (by some locally pronounced Horsemounces). She was descended as follows:

24. Waleran de Herst (de Monceux) died about 1207. The Saxon word Herst or Hurst denotes a thick wood or forest. He was owner of the Manor of Herst which, in the Confessor's time, was held by a priest named Edmer and which, after the Norman Conquest, was bestowed by the Conqueror upon his kinsman, Robert, Earl of Eu, who passed it to his son William. In 1264, Henry III spent the night at Hurstmonceux and in 1302 Edward I visited there. Waleran was father of

23. William de Monceux, constable of Pevensey Castle, who was father of

22. Waleran de Monceux, whose granddaughter

20. Maud Monceux inherited the Manor of Hurstmonceux from her brother John when he died without issue about 1320. As above she married John de Fiennes, in whose family its possession remained until 1708.

19. William Fiennes, son of John and Maud Monceux, as above married Joan Saye.

18. William Fiennes, sheriff of Surrey and Sussex in 1297 and again in 1300, is commemorated by an almost perfect brass in the chancel of Hurstmonceux Church. His wife was Elizabeth, daughter of William Battisford, and they had

17. Roger Fiennes, born in the Manor House of Hurstmonceux, baptized 14 September 1384, died 1484, treasurer of the household to King Henry VI. He married Elizabeth Holand and had Richard Fiennes, of whom later. Sir Roger was the builder of

HURSTMONCEUX CASTLE

in Sussex, about a dozen miles from the battlefield at Hastings. Begun in 1440, the building cost £3800, the equivalent of at least £70,000 today. To the already enlarged park he added 600 acres, bringing it to a total of several square miles of magnificent countryside, on rolling ground finely wooded with groups of forest trees, beech, oak and chestnut, surrounding broad acres of lawn, and clear pools, well stocked with fish. Two hundred deer roved the park, in which were also many herons and conies (rabbits). The Elizabethan garden was one of rare beauty. From Hurstmonceux the sea at Pevensey can be seen, but five miles away.

Though long deserted, there is still an air of feudal magnificence and solitary grandeur about the castle and grounds, which neither the havoc of time nor wanton destruction has been able to erase. There is an indefinable charm about the old Flemish brick walls, now covered with ivy, reminding one that in its glory it was the greatest house in all England, save only those occupied by the royal family. Its foundations measure about 210 feet square. The outer walls surrounding this area were secured by towers 84 feet high, used for look-out and signal stations. The lower 50 feet of the towers, which were built in three stories, contain loop holes for cross-bow defense. Below these and commanding the drawbridge are circular holes, built for the use of match-lock guns. The battlements were notched for the purpose of pouring boiling pitch or moulten lead upon assailants. Defense was thus the major consideration, and boldness and strength were tastefully blended with the richly ornamental qualities, which added to the charm of the castle.

On very principal window was painted an alant, or wolf dog, the emblem of the noble House of de Fiennes. There were known to have been "as many windows as there are days in the year, and as many chimneys as there are weeks."

Crossing the moat, long since dry, we enter the porter's lodge, the main entrance to the castle, under the gateway tower; it contains a huge fireplace. On the right is a winding staircase to the basement, one of the many curiously constructed stairways, built without wood entirely of brick. On the left of the porter's lodge is the guard room, made large for the stabling of the horses of the men at arms belonging to the household of the warrior. Here are two furnaces for the casting of bullets. Beyond the porter's lodge is the green court, now only a few crumbling walls richly overhung with ivy. In the center is an ancient holly tree, perhaps 400 years old. Its bare trunk remains, still alive and putting forth glossy green leaves. The green court was one of four courtyards which were open to the sky. Surrounding it was a cloistered porch.

Next beyond the green court was the great banqueting hall, with ceiling 26 feet high and a balcony for the musicians. Around the second floor were the bird, the yeomans and other galleries. Four large windows on each side gave light, and an immense fireplace provided heat. The outer rooms beyond the green court and the music hall were offices for the upper servants, register and steward, with lady's bower on the second floor. In this corner of the castle the basement of the tower was used as a dungeon, in which was a stone post with long chain attached. Over this were the Chaplain's quarters. Next along the outer wall came the Chapel, with stalls below and a balcony above and ornamented with stained glass windows. The tower of the Chapel was furnished with clock and bells.

Beyond the Chapel were the great and little parlors, the former being the chief reception room. Opposite its entrance was the grand staircase, which occupied a space 40 feet square, the steps themselves being ten feet wide. The light came from six large windows, between which were great mirrors reaching from floor to ceiling. Over the parlors were the best bedrooms, communicating with a large drawing room. What famous visitors and court beauties were entertained here! On two occasions at least, we know that the Monarchs themselves were house guests. Nearby on this upper floor were the castle's famous galleries, in which were displayed many pictures, tapestries and fresco paintings, and in the armour gallery might have been seen perhaps the suit worn by Sir Roger de Fiennes at Agincourt, or suits brought from the Holy Land by the Crusaders, Ingleram and William de Fiennes. In another corner of this floor were the Lord's and Lady's apartments: study, bedchambers, dressings rooms and library. It has been said that "the rooms on this floor are sufficient to lodge a garrison, and one is bewildered in the different galleries that lead to them."

The housekeeping quarters were equally spacious with dairy, larder and scullery, butler's pantry, confectionery room, distillery, a room for smoking meats, butler's court, chicken court and pump court, bake house, brew house, wine cellars and laundry. On one side was the great kitchen, rising to the whole height of the house, with three gigantic fireplaces. At the base of one of the largest towers was the famous oven, measuring 36 feet in circumference. It is said that on one occasion four-and-twenty women sat down in it to tea!

Also inside the castle was the gardener's room, convenient to the postern gate beyond which, in the gardens and orchards, he cultivated fruits, vegetables and flowers. For sanitation there were adequate underground passages, emptying at a distance beyond the moat into a running stream. An avenue of oaks led to Hurstmonceux Church, at the edge of the great park. Here is the font at which Sir Roger may have been baptized.

Thomas Fiennes, grandson of Richard who died in 1630, was the last of the family to own the estate. After lavishly embellishing it he fell into debt through extravagance and gambling and, in 1708, he sold the Castle and Manor of his ancestors to Mr. George Naylor for £38,000.

About 1780 the building was pronounced to be so dilapidated that it was judged expedient to demolish its interior, the materials being used for a modern dwelling called Hurstmonceux Place. The ancient tapestries, furniture and carvings were sold at public auction.

17. Roger Fiennes and his wife Elizabeth Holand as stated above were the parents of

16. Richard Fiennes, who became Baron Dacre in right of his wife, Joan, page 345, daughter of Thomas, Lord Dacre, of distinguished royal and baronial ancestry. They had

15. John (not Thomas) Fiennes, page 397, married Alice FitzHugh descended as follows:

24. ROBERT FITZWALTER the Surety, a record of whose ancestry and achievements appears at page 76, was the leader of

the Magna Charta Barons and their army and is shown to be 27th in descent from Pharamond, Pedigree P. He married first Gunora, daughter of Robert Valonies and had

23. Walter FitzRobert, page 77, eldest son, married Ida Longesepee.

22. Ela FitzWalter, page 79, married to William Odingells, died 1295.

21. Margaret Odingsells, page 80, married to John de Grey.

20. John de Grey, K. G., an original Knight of the Garter, page 233, married second Avice Marmion.

19. Robert de Grey de Marmion, page 80, married Lora St. Quentin.

18. Elizabeth Grey "Marmion," married to Henry FitzHugh, K. G.

17. William FitzHugh, page 352, born 1398, died 1452, married Margery, daughter of William, Lord Willoughby.

16. Henry FitzHugh, born 1430, died 1472, married Alice, daughter of Richard de Nevill, also of baronial descent.

15. Alice FitzHugh, page 352, as above became the wife of John Fiennes. They had

14. Thomas Fiennes, K. B., Baron Dacre, born 1472, died 9 September 1533, married about 1492 Anne, died 29 September 1530, daughter of Humphrey Bourchier, granddaughter of John Bourchier, K. G., and great granddaughter of Anne Plantagenet, No. 18 above, and her third husband William Bourchier.

13. Thomas Fiennes, died in his father's lifetime, 26 October 1528. In the chancel of Hurstmonceux Church was erected one of the finest examples of monumental architecture. Beneath its fretted canopy lie the effigies of No. 14 Thomas and No. 13 Thomas, "each clad in complete armour except for the head which is bare, their hands raised in supplication." Thomas Fiennes married in 1514 Jane Sutton, died August 1539, descended as follows:

25. WILLIAM MALET the Surety, a record of whose ancestry and achievements appears at page 96, was 24th in descent from Clovis, Pedigree L. He was sheriff of Somerset and of Dorset, and married Alice Basset, who survived him. They had

24. Mabel Malet, page 97, married to Hugh de Vivonia, baron of Chewton.

23. William de Vivonia de Fortibus, page 98, married Maud Ferrers of Kyme.

22. Cecily Vivonia, married to John de Beauchamp, died 1283.

21. John de Beauchamp, page 98, died 1336.

20. John de Beauchamp of Hacche, pages 99 and 364, died 1343, married Margaret.

19. Eleanor Beauchamp, as widow of John de Meriet, became the second wife of John le Blount, son of William of Sodington.

18. Walter Blount, renowned for his heroism in the wars of King Edward III, Richard II and Henry IV, slain at the battle of Shrewsbury 22 June 1403, married Lady Sancha de Ayala, died 1418, daughter of Don Diego Gomez de Toledo of Castile.

17. Constance Blount married to John Sutton, Lord Dudley, died 1407.

16. John Sutton, 4th Baron Dudley, K. G., died 1487, married Elizabeth Berkeley (widow of Edward Cherlton).

15. Edmund Sutton, died in his father's lifetime, married first Joyce, daughter of John, Lord Tiptoft (and his wife Joyce Cherlton).

14. Edward Sutton, K. G., died 1531, married Cecily, daughter of William Willoughby.

13. Jane Sutton (known also as Johanna) as above married Thomas Fiennes.

12. Thomas Fiennes, 9th Lord Dacre, hanged at Tyburn, as above married Mary Nevill.

*11. Margaret Fiennes, Baroness Dacre, born 1541, died 1611. In 1564, she was married to Sampson Lennard (Leonard)

He was M. P. for Sussex and sheriff of Kent, born about 1544, died 1615. Their home was at Chevening, co. Kent, 15 miles southwest of London, until perhaps 1594, the year of her brother's death, after which they were much at Hurstmonceux Castle, which they greatly embellished and where they entertained lavishly.

At St. Botolph's Church at Chevening is the stately alabaster tomb of Sampson Lennard and Margaret Fiennes. Effigies of the two figures are shown, the former in armour, and beside them are small kneeling effigies of their children: Henry, George and Thomas on the north, and Anne, Mary, Margaret, Elizabeth and Frances on the south.

Sampson Leonard and his wife Margaret Fiennes had children listed 1911 by the Marquis of Ruvigny as follows:

(a) Henry, 12th Lord Dacre, born 1570, married Chrisogona Baker. Henry accompanied the Earl of Essex in his memorable campaign and was knighted at the taking of Cadiz in 1596. He became Lord Dacre on the death of his mother in 1611 but only outlived her five years. The title descended to his son Richard who married Elizabeth Throckmorton. He died and was buried at Hurstmonceux in 1630.

(b) Gregory Lennard.

(c) Thomas Lennard, born 1577, according to tradition ancestor of the Taunton Leonards, of whom later.

(d) Anne Lennard, wife of Herbert Morley.

(e) Mary Lennard, wife of Sir Ralph Bosville.

(f) Margaret Lennard, wife of Sir Thomas Waller.

(g) Elizabeth Lennard, wife of Sir Francis Barnham.

(h) Frances Lennard, wife of Sir Robert More, M. P.

Sampson Lennard's ancestry is given by Burke as follows:

15. George Lennard (Leonard), Esq., was the father of

14. John Lennard, Esq., of Chepsted who married Anne, daughter of John Bird of co. Middlesex. Their son

13. John Lennard of Chevening, co. Kent, born 1479, died 1556, married Catherine, daughter of Thomas Weston of Chepsted and had

12. John Lennard of Knole and Chevening, born 1508, died 1591, married Elizabeth, daughter of William Harman of Cragford, co. Kent. Their three sons were: Timothy, who died without surviving issue, Sir Samuel, born 1553, and

11. Sampson Lennard as above married Lady Margaret Fiennes.

EARLY INTEREST IN IRON

It is interesting to note that his ancestors had for many years been interested in the manufacture of iron. There was early "a steel forge near Hurstmonceux Castle and, on this estate in 1574, an iron works." In 1626 patent rights for making steel were granted to Sampson's son, Richard Lennard, Lord Dacre (who married Elizabeth Throckmorton and who died at Hurstmonceux in 1630 and is buried at Hurstmonceux Church). There were also extensive iron works near Chevening, in the western part of Kent on the Sussex line, which gradually had to be abandoned. "Queen Elizabeth was one of those who urged persons acquainted with the iron business to go to Monmouthshire to develop the iron there. This may account for the Leonards of Kent and Sussex going to Monmouthshire to manage iron works."

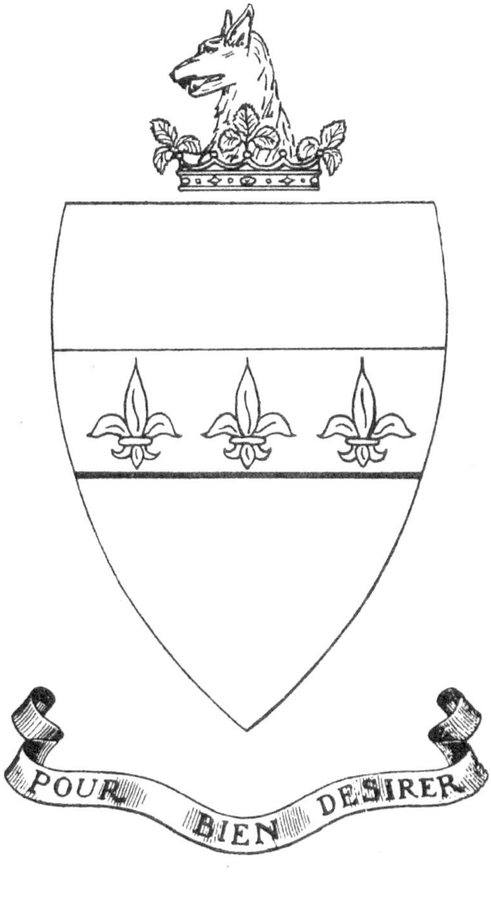

LEONARD

Arms used by the descendants of
Sampson Lennard of Chevening, co. Kent.

Arms: *Or, on a fess gules three fleur-de-lis of the first.*
Crest: *Out of a ducal crown or a wolf-dog's head.*
Motto: *Pour bien desirer.*

*10. Thomas Lennard (Leonard) born 1577, died 1638. He was engaged in the manufacture of iron at Pontypool, in co. Monmouth once belonging to Wales but, when the boundary between England and Wales was later changed, Monmouth became a part of England.

He married Lydia White and had

(a) Margery Leonard, married Henry Samson of Ireland.
(b) Joan Leonard, did not come to America.
(c) Sarah Leonard, died at New Salem.
(d) Henry Leonard, eldest son, called "the father of the American Iron Industry," since he persevered in that calling, and his foundries were perpetuated for centuries.

Henry Leonard was born at Pontypool, in 1618 we conclude, as in his deposition taken in 1655 he says he is aged 37 or thereabouts, being then of Hammersmith (Lynn).

The Leonards were the first skilled ironmasters to emigrate to America, and the family became so closely identified with the iron industry that there was a common New England expression: "Where you find an iron works, there you will find a Leonard." In the publications of the Genealogical Society of Pennsylvania, Volume XII, page 126, is described "An iron pot, the first casting in America, made at Saugus Iron Works by Henry Leonard in 1644." We think therefore that the four Leonard brothers were in America as early as 1642, coming perhaps soon after the death of their father Thomas. He did not remain long at Saugus (Lynn) as Adam Hawkes, from whose bog the ore was extracted, was contentious. "His suits for flowage of his lands put an end to the Lynn undertaking." James and Henry Leonard then went to Braintree.

Henry Leonard appears at Hammersmith in 1642, and in 1646 at Braintree, in 1650 again at Hammersmith, in 1652 at Raynham (near Taunton), where he and his brother James established the first forge in America. On the road from Taunton to Raynham, where the Old Anchor Forge stood, a tablet has been erected which reads: "Site of Taunton Iron Works, First in Old Colony."

At the Pilgrim Museum at Plymouth can be seen twelve wrought iron nails taken from the old Leonard House at Raynham, built in 1660. These nails were made at the Old Forge built at Raynham in 1652. In the possession of the writer is a piece of wood from the door frame of the first Leonard House at Raynham, which was obtained by the genealogist of the family, Elisha Clarke Leonard, when the house was demolished. Henry was at Lynn in 1655, at Topsfield and Taunton in 1656, and was a freeman in 1668 at Rowley Village, later removing to the Jerseys where, associated with Governor Lewis Morris, he built in 1674 at Tinton Falls near Shrewsbury, on a tract of 3540 acres, the first iron works in the Middle Atlantic States.

The Old Leonard House at Taunton, built in 1670 primarily for defense, was occupied by seven generations of the family and torn down about 1840. The ground with modern dwellings continued to be occupied by the eighth generation.

Henry Leonard and his sons often traded with the Indians and were on such good terms of friendship with them that, when King Philip's War broke out, the latter gave strict orders to his men never to hurt the Leonards. When both Leonard families were stricken with typhoid fever, Squaw Betty, niece of King Philip, gathered the herbs, prepared and administered the medicine, and nursed the patients back to health. Betty declined the wampum offered her, but did accept a red cloak, which she wore with pride and in which she expressed the wish to be buried.

King Philip resided in winter at Mount Hope, but his summer home was on the banks of the Two Mile River at Raynham, about a mile from the Forge, where he had his tomahawks and arrow heads made. As time went on he was unable to avert war and when he ordered the vicinity to be burned, he stipulated that the Leonard farms be spared. After much blood shed on both sides, an Indian guided the English to Philip's hiding place in a swamp at the foot of Mt. Hope, where he was surprised and killed while trying to escape. The head of King Philip was exhibited as a curiosity by Alderman, the Indian who shot him. Rescued and hid for a time in the cellar of the home of Henry Leonard at Taunton, the head was later sent to Plymouth and set on a pole as a public warning.

One of Henry Leonard's descendant's, George Leonard, Esq., visited in England and while there made investigations and was quite sure that his family was descended from the Lords Dacre. Some years later, in a letter to his cousin, Hon. George Leonard of Norton, Mass., written from St. John, N. B., dated 4 October

1798, he writes that he had "collected old records in England, at the Herald's Office, and among Lord Dacre's papers, who was very attentive to me . . . and who was very anxious that some of our family inherit some of the vacant titles."

Henry Leonard married at Lynn, 1650, Mary, whose last name has not been preserved. They were the parents of seven or eight children, probably all born in Massachusetts:

(1) Samuel Leonard, eldest son, born 1650, married Sarah Brooks.

(2) Nathaniel Leonard of Rowley, went to New Jersey.

(3) Thomas Leonard, married his wife in Virginia.

(4) Henry Leonard, born 14 June 1656, an incorporator of Christ Church, Shrewsbury, and sheriff of Monmouth County. His will, probated in New Jersey in 1739, mentions wife Lydia.

(5) John Leonard, married A. Almy. They were the parents of Judge Thomas Leonard who in 1757 built his residence in Princeton, N. J. This mansion, bought and occupied by Robert Stockton, next became the College Inn and later the Nassau Hotel.

(6) Sarah Leonard. There has been some confusion as to the place and date of her birth. Savage records that she was born in Lynn, 26 June 1663. Austin thinks she was born in Taunton, 27 May 1660, but it is apparent that the birth date should be 30 May 1660, as her gravestone at Christ Church, Shrewsbury, N. J., bears the following inscription: "Here lies the Body of Sarah, wife of Job Throckmorton, who Departed this life February the fifth Day, Annoq Domini one Thousand seven hundred forty three-four, Aged Eighty three years Eight months & six Days." She married Job Throckmorton. Their daughters Mary and Patience Throckmorton married respectively the pioneers Daniel and Amice GRANDIN.

(7) Mary Leonard, born 13 January 1666, died in infancy.

(8) Susannah Leonard, who married Thomas Morford, may have been a daughter in this family.

(e) James Leonard (second son of No. *10 Thomas), who we conclude was born about 1620, because living in Taunton, he is recorded as having died there before 1691, aged 70, of whom later, No. *9 below.

(f) William Leonard, remained in England.

(g) John Leonard, perhaps remained in England.

(h) Philip Leonard, who was at Marshfield in 1678 and afterwards of Duxbury, died in July 1708 at Taunton. He married Lydia, who died 13 November 1707, and they had an only daughter, Phebe Leonard, who was married 6 November 1694 to Samuel Hill of Duxbury.

(i) Thomas Leonard, who was drowned at Piscataway.

*9. James Leonard, second son, born in Pontypool, as we have said about 1620, was intimately associated in business with his elder brother Henry, was at Lynn 1651, at Braintree 1652, and the same year at Taunton. James Leonard, a captain, took an active part in King Philip's War, and defended a garrison in his own house.

James Leonard married first Mary Martin, mother of all his children; his second wife Margaret died without issue in 1700 or 1701. Children:

(a) Thomas Leonard, born 3 August 1641, some think in Pontypool, died 24 November 1713, town clerk, major and judge, married at Plymouth 21 August 1662 Mary Watson, died 1723 aged 81, probably daughter of George; ancestors of Harry Cyrus Holloway, of whom later.

(b) James Leonard, captain, born 1643, married first Hannah, and second Lydia Gulliver.

(c) Abigail Leonard, married to John Kingsley of Milton.

(d) Joseph Leonard, born 1655.

(e) Rebecca Leonard, born 1657, of whom later.

(f) Benjamin Leonard, married 15 January 1679, Sarah Thresher.

(g) Hannah Leonard, married 24 January 1678, to Isaac Deane.

(h) Uriah Leonard, born 10 July 1662, married 1 June 1685 Elizabeth Caswell.

(i) John Leonard, died at age 20.

*8. Rebecca Leonard, born at Taunton, Mass., 1657, died at Dennis, 15 March 1736, married 2 September 1678, Isaac Chapman, born at Marshfield, Mass., 1647, and was later of Barnstable. He died in 1737.

*7. James Chapman, born at Marshfield 5 August 1685, married about 1711, probably at Rochester, Mass., Mercy, who was born at Rochester in 1690 and died at Marshfield 21 December 1715.

*6. Mercy Chapman, born at Rochester in 1712, married there 17 November 1737 to Benjamin Raymond of Rochester, born there 7 December 1714 and died 2 October 1779.

*5. Joanna Raymond, born at Rochester 11 May 1740, baptized 27 June 1742, died at Barnard, Vt., in 1809. On 18 February 1759 she was married to Asa Whitcomb, born at Hardwick, Mass., 29 February 1735, died at Barnard, Vt., 31 March 1812. He served in the Crown Point Expedition in 1756; the following year marched to the relief of Fort William Henry; was at Ticonderoga in 1758. In 1774 he was a selectman at Woodstock, Vt., and was the second settler at Barnard, Vt., where he was selectman, justice of the peace, a representative and he was a member of the Vermont Constitutional Convention. Their son

*4. Anthony Whitcomb was born at Hardwick, Mass., 17 July 1766, and died near Cincinnati, Ohio, before 1809. At the age of 15 he served in the American Revolution and married about 1794 Lucy Wright, born 15 May 1774, died at Preble County, Ohio, 5 October 1821.

*3. Benjamin Raymond Whitcomb, born at Barnard, Vermont, 16 May 1798, pioneer merchant at Clinton, Indiana, where he died 23 April 1861. He married 16 July 1819 Anna, born 14 November 1804, died 20 May 1860, daughter of James Sutton, and they had

*2. John Whitcomb, born in Preble County, Ohio, 26 August 1821; member of the Indiana General Assembly 1856, died at Clinton, Indiana, 30 November 1891. He married twice: first, 29 February 1848, Margaret, died 1869, daughter of John Wright Whitcomb. Their five children:

(a) Charles Whitcomb, born 27 December 1848, married Emma Hill.
(b) Henrie Whitcomb, lived only 3 years.
(c) Clara Eunice Whitcomb, born 14 September 1853, married Dr. Samuel Beiler.
(d) Anna Cecilia Whitcomb, born 1855.
(e) Benjamin Howard Whitcomb, born 23 August 1857.
(f) Cora Leonore Whitcomb, born 7 November 1861, married Francis Wayland Shepardson. They had a son, John Whitcomb Shepardson.

John Whitcomb, above, married second 30 January 1870 Lydia Amelia Parks, born Sandy Hill, N. Y., 29 April 1840, died 4 May 1924. Their three children:

(g) Larz Augustus Whitcomb, born 26 March 1871, married Sarah Rogers.
(h) William Arthur Whitcomb, born 18 January 1873, married Grace Edna Merrall and had: Merle Whitcomb, John Merrall Whitcomb and William Arthur Whitcomb, Jr.

*1. (i) NEMA MARIA WHITCOMB, born at Clinton, Indiana, 24 May 1875, member of Coloney of New England Women, Daughters of Founders and Patriots, Sons and Daughters of the Pilgrims, Women Descendants of the Ancient and Honorable Artillery Company, Daughters of Colonial Wars, Daughters of American Colonists, Daughters of the American Revolution, U. S. Daughters of 1812; life member, The National Society Magna Charta Dames, Americans of Royal Descent; married 27 January 1904 Harry Cyrus Holloway, also a descendant as follows of James Leonard, No. 9 above, whose son Thomas married Mary Martin, and was father of

8. Mary Leonard, born 1663, married Joseph, son of John Tisdale.

7. Sarah Tisdale married Thomas Reed of Deighton.

6. Sarah Reed, born 1727, died 1798, married George Gooding.

5. Abigail Gooding married 1775 Peter Holloway, born 1751, died 1832, a soldier of the American Revolution.

4. Cyrus Holloway, born 1786, died 1842, married 1812 Permelia, daughter of Prince Tobey.

3. Frederick Madison Holloway, born 1815, died 1891, married 1837 Sybil Bacon Bassett.

2. George Allen Holloway, born 1839, died 1910, married 1865 Olive Melissa Tibbits, daughter of George.

1. HARRY CYRUS HOLLOWAY, born at Webster Grove, Missouri, 29 November 1874, husband of Nema Maria Whitcomb, No. *1 above. He is a member of the Sons of the Revolution and other literary, patriotic and historical societies and a life member of the Society of Descendants of Knights of the Garter. Their four children:

(a) John Whitcomb Holloway, born Chicago, Illinois, 30 January 1905, married Jane Dement.

(b) Ruth Whitcomb Holloway, born Cincinnati, Ohio, 17 July 1906, hereditary member, Magna Charta Dames, married Edward Tarr Herndon.

(c) George Allen Holloway, born Glencoe, Illinois, 17 August 1908, hereditary member, Society of Descendents of Knights of the Garter, married Betsey Paddock.

(d) Larz Arthur Holloway, born Glencoe, Illinois, 21 January 1910, married Ursula C. Kellner.

Charles Henry Browning

His portrait appears on page 1

Born in Cincinnati in 1846, Mr. Browning was educated in the classical school of Harcourt Academy, and at Kenyon College. It is rather remarkable that his tuition was paid for by the national government, but he was a "Foster Child of the Republic," becoming such when an infant orphan through two special, personal acts of Congress passed in honor of his father, Robert Lewright Browning, a naval officer, who lost his life accidentally while on special duty, being drowned off the coast of California in 1850; while his elder and only brother was appointed by the President an officer in the marine corps, and who was lost with the U.S.S. Levant in 1860. His grandfather was a Lord Mayor and a Member of Parliament.

Charles H. Browning, when of suitable age, was appointed one of his cadets-at-large to West Point by the President, but his guardian, Robert Buchanan of Cincinnati, decided that civil life was best for his ward. His start began at the Covington rail mill. Subsequently he became a partner in coal mines in the Kanawha Valley, and the president of two prosperous companies there engaged in shipping coal to Cincinnati and beyond. It was about this time that Mr. Browning "came out of the West" and eventually entered into journalism in the East, when his cousin, James Gordon Bennett, proprietor of the New York Herald, placed him in charge of his new Philadelphia office. Eventually he became the sole representative of the Herald in this part of the country.

As a diversion from newspaper work, Mr. Browning became interested in family pedigrees generally, and was widely known as a writer on genealogical subjects, and as the organizer of several hereditary societies. He was the editor of the American Historical Register and the compiler of nine editions of Americans of Royal Descent, and bulletins in which he corrected misapprehensions printed in the earlier volumes.

Mr. Browning was one of the first members of the National Society of American Authors, an original member of the Psi Upsilon Association, and in 1880 became a member of the Union League in Philadelphia.

BRITISH EMBASSY
WASHINGTON 8, D. C.

13th January 1945

Dear Mr. Wurts,

How very kind of you to send me Part III of "Magna Charta." I am very glad to have this as a companion to the first volume which you sent me nearly three years ago. They constitute, if I may say so, a very fine piece of historical research and one which will have lasting value.

Yours sincerely,

HALIFAX

John S. Wurts

His portrait appears on page 36

Lawyer, Author, Editor, born in Pennsylvania in 1876; a member of the Philadelphia Bar, admitted also to practice before the Supreme Court of the United States, specializing in organization and property management; he served for thirty-five years as Commissioner of Deeds, his initial appointment being made by President Theodore Roosevelt in 1902.

Since youth Mr. Wurts has had an absorbing interest in Colonial families, their pedigrees and traditions. He was for a time associated in genealogical compilations with each of the noted writers, Frank Willing Leach, Warren S. Ely and Charles H. Browning.

Mr. Wurts is widely known for his leadership in the Daily Vacation Bible School movement, of which he was a Founder in 1907 with Robert G. Boville and Floyd W. Tomkins, and succeeded the latter as President.

A Delegate repeatedly to The Indian Rights Conference, he has also actively served his own locality in Rescue Missions, Relief Societies, care of the aged, and local reform politics; a member for many years of the Executive Committee of the Pennsylvania State Y. M. C. A.

Pending the restoration of St. George's Chapel, the shrine of the Knights of the Garter at Windsor Castle, Mr. Wurts served as American Treasurer of The Garter Chapel Fund at the request of the Duke of Somerset. He is President, Descendants of the Continental Congress and a member of other historical societies and patriotic hereditary orders.

A POEM

Written for the November meeting, 1934.
By LLOYD HORD, Hereditary Member,
The National Society Magna Charta Dames.

THE MAGNA CHARTA OAK

At Runnymede a great oak stands,
   The Barons in its shelter tarry,
Sedate it smiles, and with gnarled hands
   Blesses the covenant they carry.[1]

The oak tree quivering, blessed this deed,
   Mankind and nature both united
In praise of those at Runnymede
   Who saw the torch of freedom lighted.

The oak has been a trysting place
   And freedom's sign the whole world over.
Beneath it one of Jewish race
   Made covenant with great Jehovah.[2]

That spirit born at Runnymede
   Crossed trackless seas and did not falter.
It rose to Hartford's mighty need
   And freed it from a monarch's halter.

The oak here played a different part
   From all the former roles assigned it,
It hid a Charter in its heart
   And King's men tried in vain to find it.[3]

Triumphant, held by Other Hands,
   Though men and nations pass unknowing,
Freedom, in Magna Charta, stands
   Like a great oak tree, ever growing.

---

[1] The venerable oak on the field at Runnymede, June 12-15, 1215.

[2] The Book of Joshua, 24th chapter, 26th verse.

[3] The Charter Oak at Hartford, Conn., October, 1687.

The Contrast between
AMERICANISM and GERMANISM
shown in two letters:

LINCOLN'S LETTER
1864

Dear Madam: I have been shown in the files of the war department a statement of the adjutant general of Massachusetts that you are the mother of five sons who have died gloriously on the field of battle. I feel how weak and fruitless must be any words of mine which should attempt to beguile you from the grief of a loss so overwhelming. But I cannot refrain from tendering you the consolation that may be found in the thanks of the republic they died to save. I pray that our Heavenly Father may assuage the anguish of your bereavement and leave you only the cherished memory of the loved and lost, and the solemn pride that must be yours to have laid so costly a sacrifice upon the altar of freedom.

THE KAISER'S LETTER
August 1918

"His majesty the kaiser hears that you have sacrificed nine sons in the defense of the fatherland in the present war. His majesty is immensely gratified at the fact, and in recognition is pleased to send you his photograph, with frame and autograph signature."

The woman to whom the above letter was sent has since become a beggar for food on the streets of Delmenhors-Oldenburg.

THE KAISER'S PHOTO

he German mother lost nine sons—
ll stalwart, young, upstanding Huns.
he wept beside her cottage door
or those who would return no more;
he burden of her grief and care
eemed greater than her soul could bear;
er face was wan, her eyes were bleak,
er hair grown snowy in a week.
ut now the postman comes and cries,
Here's something that will dry your eyes!
letter with the Potsdam crest—
ow may your woes go galley west!"
'ith awe the stricken mother takes
he missive, and the seal she breaks.
reat Wilhelm, ruler of the Huns,
as heard about her nine lost sons,
nd he has sent a work of art
o sooth and heal the broken heart;
is a photo of himself,
t for the mantel or the shelf;
Majestic, beautiful and grand,
Is autographed by his own hand.
The mother dries her scalding tears;
She and the postman give three cheers;
Their arms in ecstasy they lock,
And bunny hug around the block.
"Ach, himmel," cries the mother then,
"The world seems bright and fair again;
Who would not send a bunch of sons
Against the hungry, allied guns,
If thereby he or she might get
This photograph already yet?
I have a granddad in the house,
Two uncles and my worthy spouse,
And I shall send them forth to die;
Perhaps the Kaiser in reply
Will send a photographic view
Of Kronprinz Willyum Friedrich too."

—Walt Mason

KING JOHN

A Poem *by* Lydia H. Sigourney

There stands at Runnymede a king,
While summer clothes the plains,
The blood of high Plantagenet
Is coursing through his veins;
But yet a sceptred hand he lifts
To shade his haggard brow,
As if constrained to do a deed
His pride would disallow.

He pauses still; his faint eye rests
Upon those barons bold,
Whose hands are grappling to their swords
With fierce and sudden hold.
That pause is broke; he bows him down
Before those steel girt men,
And glorious Magna Charta glows
Beneath his trembling pen.

His false lip to a smile is wreathed,
As their exulting shout,
From 'neath the green, embowering trees,
Upon the gale swells out;
Yet lingers long his cowering glance
On Thames' translucent tide,
As if some deep and bitter thought
He from the throng would hide.

I know what sounds are in his ear,
When wrathful tempests roll,
When God doth bid his lightnings search,
His thunders try the soul:
Above the blast young Arthur's shriek
Doth make the murderer quake,
As if again his guiltless blood
From Rouen's prison spake.

But though no red volcano burst
To whelm the men of crime,
No vengeful earthquake fiercely yawn
To gorge them ere their time,
Though Earth for her most guilty sons
The festive board doth set,
The wine-cup and the opiate draught,
Yet say, can Heaven forget?

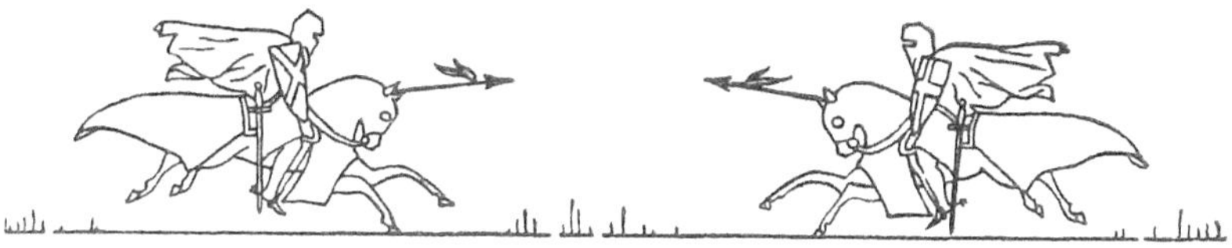

SUPPLEMENT and INDEX

MAGNA CHARTA by John S. Wurts
of "Hedgefield," Germantown, Pa.

Part I. The Romance of the Great Charter, pages 1 to 36.
Part II. Pedigrees of the Barons, pages 37 to 300.

To perpetuate the memory of the Barons of England who in or before the year 1215 rendered actual service toward securing, and who, after many defeats, finally did secure the articles of constitutional liberty, properly called Magna Charta, from their sovereign, John, King of England, which he ratified and delivered to them "in the meadow which is called Runnemede between Windsor and Staines," on the Thames, above London, on the 15th day of June, A. D. 1215.

To promote good fellowship among the descendants of those who compelled King John to grant Magna Charta.

To keep ever in mind the events connected with this most celebrated episode in the annals of the English race,

The wholesome emphasis the author puts on events that took place at Runnemede, seven hundred and twenty-seven years ago make his writing both startling and exhilarating reading. We have for so long accepted without thanks the stipulations that the Barons exacted from King John that for us to face a world that may ignore them at first seems fantastic and later becomes a challenge. Mr. Wurts' book is far more than a reference volume. . . . It is also a stimulating discussion of phases of English history that in a day of serious confusion may be reviewed by most of us with quickening results.

—The New York Genealogical and Biographical Record

Chapter 1. Continuing page 39, the following persons also may claim descent from Baron d'Albini and the Emperor Charlemagne:

Elisabeth Bailey Backus
Barbara Stowe Blatherwick
Lavern Bordwell
Charles Shepard Bryan
Henry Wurts Canfield
Eleanor Stickney Chapman
Charles U. Doolittle
Grace Bailey Dunklee
Sarah Minna Scott-Hyman
The Princess Kaplanoff
Margaret Elizabeth Layton
Charles Bispham Levey
Rebecca Lamb Bolling Littlejohn
Marion Drake-Smith Maltby
Henrietta Foster Morison
Mary Logan Orcutt
William Warren Orcutt
Jessie Jones Phillips
Fannie May Grossius Scoville
Anna Taylor Peirce Shewbrooks
Carolyn Beale Spelman
Charlotte M. Taylor
Ella Gertrude Holthoff Thayer
Benjamin Franklin Tillson
Philip Van Culin
Richard Wurts

Chapter 2. Continuing page 43, the following persons also may claim descent from Baron Roger Bigod and King Ethelred II:

Sarah Anderson Atherton
Ruth Wurts Burt
Eugenia Whyte Carton
Victoria Booth-Clibborn Demarest
Anna Jean Doan
Edward C. Donohoe
Walter Weston Folger
Anna Edkin Rhodes Hager
Eleanor Lewis Logan
Adelaide Newell Meek
Leonard Townsend Morse
Ellen L. Patterson
Tunstall Barker Perry
Mary Savage Schuh
Fannie May Grossius Scoville
Helen Cornwill Hill Sloan
Nell Escott Smith
Harold Turk Smutz
James I. Thorne
Mary Grace Murray Verner
Ellen Conway Howard Wilson
Bertha Crouch Wrightsman

Chapter 3. Continuing page 46, the following persons also may claim descent from Baron Hugh Bigod and the Emperor Vladimir:

Meribah Irwin Moore Bamber
James Culver Bierbower
Olive Jones-Whitmer Brown
Mabel Victorine Richardson Clement
Eleanor McGilton Connor
Margaret Lapham Lewis Courtenay
Clara Mary Harvey Deuble
Francis J. Doan
W. G. Donald Donohoe
Elizabeth Ridgely Dorsey Griffiss
Wilma Beard Harper
Margaret Elizabeth Layton
Norman Van Pelt Levis, Jr.
Albert Gallatin Matthews
Lucretia Wiley McAdams
Ellen Constance Walker Morse
Dorothea Stuart McGill Scott
Fannie May Grossius Scoville
Martha Reed Shoemaker
Julia M. Beale Spelman
Eleanor Randolph Thomas
Frances Hannah Whiting Turner
Mary Grace Murray Verner
Jane Pope Wilson

Chapter 4. Continuing page 51, the following persons also may claim descent from Baron Bohun and King David I:

Cora Belle Bailey Acosta
Francena Elizabeth Hanford Banker
Virginia Crittenden Brown
Charles Shepard Bryan
Vesta Miller Westover Channon
Laura Lee Seaman Christian
Georgie Shackelford Collier Comer
John Vinton Dahlgren
Charles Emmett Davidson
Valentine Sherman Doebler
Margaret Bradley Dykes
Leverett Farwell Eggleston
Ella Syrene Holbrook
Jessie May Tillson Link
Florence Harris Longman
Agnes Irene Richardson MacCain
Mary Logan Orcutt
William Warren Orcutt
Ellen L. Patterson
Mary Delia Smith Robinson
Antoinette Quinby Scudder
Helen Semple
Lillian Walker Thixton
Mary Grace Murray Verner
Lavinia Sophia Rose Wilson
Frances Blue Woodson

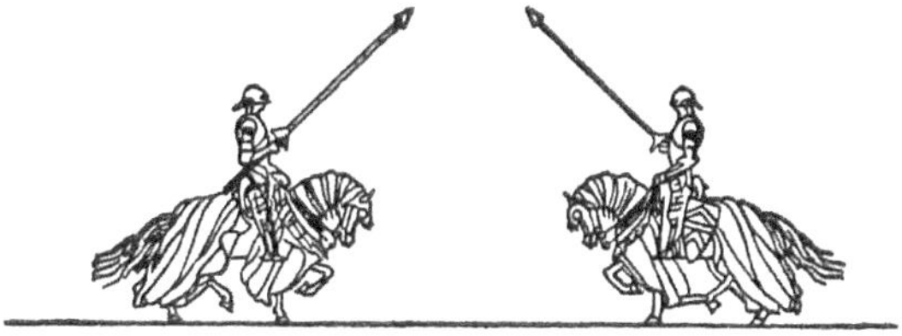

Chapter 5. Continuing page 57, the following persons also may claim descent from Baron Richard de Clare and King William the Conqueror:

Mary Selma Pyle Stalfort Beach
George J. Burnett
J. Irwin Doan
Julia Campbell Dulles
Hugh Kerr Fulton
Lula Edna Purdy Gilson
Louise Holly Goddard
Frances Cunningham Harper
Ella Syrene Holbrook
James Alexander Irwin
Anna H. Patterson Layton
H. Hobart MacCubbin
Hope Carson Randolph
Alberta Polk Pyle Roberts
Virginia Baines Schur
Caroline Triplett Taliaferro Scott
Sarah Pauline Johnson Sims
Rachel Cooper Reeve Spear
Elizabeth Ives Leete Stephens
Harry Wheeler Stone
John L. Tewksbury
Emma S. Underhill
Mary Grace Murray Verner
Ann Heron White
Martha Welles White
John S. Wurts

Chapter 6. Continuing page 61, the following persons also may claim descent from Baron Gilbert de Clare and King Louis I:

Zillah Bostick Agerton
Mary Stone Bush Berry
Martha Irwin Moore Braun
Hester Helena Beauregard Congdon
Francis Reeve Cope, Jr.
Martha Burge Courtenay
The Baron Decies
Clara Mary Harvey Deuble
Nellie Burnett Dickinson
Robert Webster Ferrell
John Giles Ferres, II
Hugh Kerr Fulton
Margaret Ellen Harper
St. Lo Earle Brunson Knight
Anna H. Patterson Layton
Harriet Janney Doan Lloyd
Electra Pearl Baker Long
Mabel Byron McClure
Mabel Overton Logan Monroe
Helen Petty
Grace Partridge Richardson
Dora Stuart McGill Scott
John L. Tewksbury
John Underhill
Mary Grace Murray Verner
Catherine Coryton White
Lavinia Sophia Rose Wilson
Susan Lillard Witherspoon

Chapter 7. Continuing page 71, the following persons also may claim descent from Baron Fitz Robert and the Emperor Hugh Capet:

Ione Sharpe Bell
Helen May Brown
Inez Hereford Brown
Helen Louise Potter Burns
Billie Anthony Carrington
Edna Arnold Copeland
May Lucinda Weller Curtner
The Rt. Hon. Lady Decies
Lettie Pate Evans
Marie Lovett Jewett
The Princess Kaplanoff
Susie Gibert Knowlton
Margaret Elizabeth Layton
Gladys Margaret Stowe Minahan
Howard Ross Nelson
Lillie Bell O'Donnell
Mary Logan Orcutt
William Warren Orcutt
Tunstall Barker Perry
Martha Venable Edmunds Rivers
Dora Stuart McGill Scott
Frederic Robert Scott II
Charles Lowrey Snow
Sexta Eavenson Strickland
Edwin James Taylor, Jr.
Benjamin Franklin Tillson

Chapter 8. Continuing page 75, the following persons also may claim descent from Baron Fitz Walter and King Cadwallader:

Cora Guthier Dahm
Grace Hawley Doyle
Emma Pearson Babb Glauser
Eloise Dexter Hunter
Harriett Cornelia Hunter
Anna H. Patterson Layton
John Lion Gardiner Lennig
Rebecca Lamb Bolling Littlejohn
William Butler McGill
Mary Logan Orcutt
William Warren Orcutt
Rollin Cobb Reynolds
Thomas Branch Scott, Jr.
Edwin John Scofield
Grace Emily Smith Scofield
Elizabeth Thorne Snow
Furman South, Jr.
Mary Grace Murray Verner

Chapter 11. Continuing page 84, the following persons also may claim descent from Baron Huntingfield and King Edward III:

William Le Roy Bates
Rebecca Lamb Bolling Littlejohn
Robert Malcolm Littlejohn
Anne Meech

Chapter 12. Continuing page 87, the following persons also may claim descent from Baron Lacie and King Malcolm Canmore:

Robert Webster Allen
James Culver Bierbower
Priscilla Bradley Cabell
Eliza Credilla Whyte Carton
Charles Emmett Davidson
The Rt. Hon. Lady Decies
Edward Francis Dickinson
Anita Lewis Frazer
Letitia Shelby Holloway Higgins
Ellen Newbold Cooke Jacobs
Effie Branch Bowles Kelley
Stanley Denmead Kolb
James Leonard Morse
Florence Walker Overstreet
Ellen L. Patterson
Tunstall Barker Perry
Charles W. Pettit
Julia Edwards Woodson Saunders
Virginia Baines Schur
Edwin John Scofield
Mary Delia Gregory Smith
Mary Grace Murray Verner
Camilla Boone Vogelgesang

Chapter 13. Continuing page 92, the following persons also may claim descent from Baron Lanvallei and King Duncan:

Ivanilla Dunham Ball
Catherine Mary Thomson Boyle
Frances Moon Butts
Byrdie Johnson Duffy Chapline
Josephine Twarling Clouser
Mary F. Glendinning Cooke
Richard Micou Daniel
Smith C. Daniell
Charles Emmett Davidson
Louise Crittenden Earll
Dana King Gatchell
Lola Peyton Kaiser
The Princess Kaplanoff
John Slack Keith
George Harrison Sanford King
Margaret Elizabeth Layton
Jessie May Tillson Link
Katharine Twining Moody
Mary Logan Orcutt
William Warren Orcutt
Anne Pratt Peck
Irene Hamilton Harness Rogers
Elizabeth Besson Rudolphy
Eleanor Brooke Stiefel
Effie Crouch Waite
Harriet Mullett Jenkins Yardley

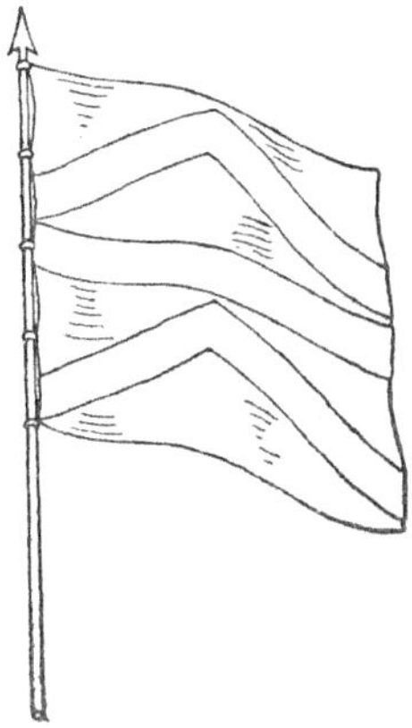

Chapter 14. Continuing page 95, the following persons also may claim descent from Baron Malet and King Clovis:

Connie Lee Andrea
William Ernest Brackett, Jr.
Leonardo di Andrea
Beulah Belle Bates Dickerman
Avis Stanbury Newcombe Fairbanks
The Princess Kaplanoff
Alice Warren Lambert
Rebecca Lamb Bolling Littlejohn
Anne Walker Morse
Lauretta Raymond Plumber Rogers
Benjamin Franklin Tillson
Baroness Katherine von Rosenberg
Mary Eva Woodward Woodward

Chapter 19. Continuing page 106, the following persons also may claim descent from Baron Mowbray and King Louis II:

Lulu Gray Auld
Myrtis Biddle Courts Baumann
Clara Augusta Pollard Blinn
Frances Moon Butts
Mary Ella Wright Cafky
Ouina Mary Pegram Childress
Charles Emmett Davidson
Martha Peters Donohoe
Sophia Norris Pitts Le Gendre
Anna Elizabeth Warren Leitch
Grace Ella Minot
Mary de Camp Banks Moore
Meribah Irwin Stearns Moore
Stella McGrath Moore
Ada Cora Park
Emma Railey
William Wright Shirk
Mary Randolph Peaseley Thomas

Chapter 21. Continuing page 111, the following persons also may claim descent from Baron Quincey and King Alfred the Great:

Ouina Mary Pegram Childress
Charles Emmett Davidson
Alice Louise Dwelle Dixon
Emma Dickinson Early
Mabel Julia Parsons Fay
Sumner Doane Fay
Sarah Woodbury Sylvester Hedge Godwin
Frances Elizabeth Warren Holt
Eloise Dexter Hunter
Harriett Cornelia Hunter
Margaret Elizabeth Layton
Edith Mabel Linsley Macke
Darrell Dwight Matthews
Mary Logan Orcutt
William Warren Orcutt
Elizabeth Otwell
Edna McClatchy Pearce
Tunstall Barker Perry
George R. Pond
Robert W. Pond
Ysobel Daisy Haskins Price
Emerson B. Roberts
Virginia Baines Schur
Margaret Fulton Slade Shattuck
Helen Matthews Shirk
Mary Grace Murray Verner
Mary Virginia Saunders White
Walter Harrison White
Sara Kathryn Wilcox
Davis Page Wurts

Chapter 22. Continuing page 121, the following persons also may claim descent from Baron Roos and King Donald I:

Philip Meredith Allen
Gillian Webster Barr Bailey
Frances Ranney Munro Ball
Frances Youmans Boothe
Jessie B. Bordwell
Marion McDowell Brackett
Francis D. Brinton
Charles Shepard Bryan
Margaret Bispham Levey
Mary Carolyn Logan McCullough
Clara Louise Brown Meech
Mary Logan Orcutt
William Warren Orcutt
Ellen L. Patterson
Arthur Carpenter Rogers
Ellsworth Marshall Rust
Grace Greenwood Cochran Sherard
Chester Peter Siems, Jr.
Rachel Witherington Stroud
Herndon Taylor
Benjamin Franklin Tillson
Charlotte Lansing Parker Wilson

Chapter 23. Continuing page 125, the following persons also may claim descent from Baron Saye and King Kenneth:

Nancy Larrabee Hill
Anna H. Patterson Layton
Robert Malcolm Littlejohn
Anna Hall Jones Parker
Alice Alden Rowland Steiner, II
Anna Virginia Wurts

Chapter 24. Continuing page 127, the following persons also may claim descent from Baron Vere and King Egbert:

Richard Carey Bierbower
Maimee Lee Robinson Browne
Alice Cushman
Charles Emmett Davidson
The Rt. Hon. Lady Decies
Elijah Dickinson
Marie Potter Froelich
Eloise Dexter Hunter
Harriett Cornelia Hunter
Mary Louise Shirk Kasson
Ellouise Baker Larsen
Anna H. Patterson Layton
Bertha Elizabeth Lloyd
Amelia H. Mangas
Ella Metsker Milligan
Gerald Griffin Morse
Mary Logan Orcutt
William Warren Orcutt
Tunstall Barker Perry
Frances Branch Scott
Stella Bigelow Sears
Mary Grace Murray Verner
Clare Harding Weber
Mary Greenleaf White
Julia M. Barker Wiggins
Marshall McDiarmid Williams
Mary Lyde Hicks Williams
Watt Ella Nevils Wilson

Chapter 29. Continuing page 178, the following persons also may claim descent from the Emperor Charlemagne:

Beatrice Burnett Armstrong
Royal Bruce Burnett
Edith Lewis Flack
Mabel Lyles Jaquiss Hadler
Alice Warren Lambert
Lillian Webb Naylor
Ardelle Schermerhorn Lynde Nutting
Ysobel Daisy Haskins Price
Mary Delia Smith Robinson
Dora Stuart McGill Scott
Benjamin Franklin Tillson
Mary Grace Murray Verner
Effie Crouch Waite
Bertha Crouch Wrightsman

Mr. John S. Wurts, who is president of the Descendants of the Continental Congress and who has been closely identified with numerous historical, patriotic and genealogical societies for many years, has prepared a volume relating not only the story of Britain's Great Charter but including the pedigrees of the Barons who met with King John at Runnymede to formulate and sign the famous document. This is followed with separate lists of those who may claim descent. . . . The material has been gathered from many sources and can be recommended particularly for the order and convenience of its presentation, a volume of interest and service to both genealogists and historians.

—Ray Baker Harris, in The New Age

To all interested in ancient and illustrious descent, this is the most valuable book published in many years. It opens with an address on Magna Charta delivered by the author before the National Society Magna Charta Dames at the New York World's Fair, October 10, 1939. This address, able and brilliant, is of exceptional worth, but the main interest of the volume centres in the pedigrees of the Barons, in connection with which are printed names of many living descendants, by no means all, but enough to be representative. Mr. Wurts, a foremost authority on the subject presented, has performed a notable service in the writing of this book and the publishers, on their fiftieth anniversary, have printed a volume worthy to endure.

—Rosa Pendleton Chiles

Let me congratulate you upon your "Magna Charta, Romance and Pedigrees." Nothing could be more timely than this publication. You have vividly portrayed the immortal Charter and the lives of the dauntless Barons in a scholarly and comprehensive style.

The book contains not only thrilling stories of the past, but it is of special interest as a book in which to go fishing, where one with a genealogical mind may find a real catch in its presentation of the marriages of the Barons and their descendants for several generations. I know of no volume to take its place. It fills a long felt want in a most concise and delightful manner.

The book should be in every library throughout England and America, including those of the Colleges and Universities. It should be available to all, since our noblest and our best are fighting to maintain the great principles therein set forth.

—Alice Elizabeth Trabue, President,
National Society Magna Charta Dames

I found your Magna Charta very interesting and instructive, and I again have occasion to admire your industry in the line of genealogical research and your power of lending romantic charm to an ordinarily dry topic.

—William L. R. Wurts, Yale '78, Editor and Columnist.

Knowing the thoroughness with which all your work is done, I am looking forward with great pleasure to reading your Magna Charta.

—Joseph Knox Fornance, Secretary,
Society of the Cincinnati.

Your treatment of the subject is most scholarly and interesting. The work you are doing is a valuable contribution to English and American History.

—Rev. Arnold H. Hord.

Your interesting article Magna Charta, Part I, I have read with interest, and want to send my thanks and appreciation. It is a good time for such a document to be passed around, and I wish that it could make a deep impression on some of the violators of its principles who have upset the whole European program.

—Richard M. Gummere, Professor, Harvard College.

America is vitally interested in the principles of Magna Charta, the foundation of all free governments, yet it is a depressing fact that the average American knows nothing about the history of his English ancestry, nor whence he has inherited his patriotism, courage and love of freedom. This book is therefore most appropriate at the present time.

—Col. Charles Shepard Bryan

Again I express my admiration for that most comprehensive volume, "Magna Charta" by John S. Wurts. I am tremendously impressed by it. How much "digging" it would have saved me! The book inspires implicit confidence regarding its accuracy, conveys very helpful historical data and, in brief, is a "joy."

—Alex. Galt Robinson

I have read with deep interest your "Magna Charta." It contains exactly the information that most persons ought to have about that all important document. You have done good service in publishing it.

—Josiah Harmar Penniman, Provost,
University of Pennsylvania

You have moved me deeply by this fine piece of work; especially is it to be valued in these days, when other tyrants, far worse than King John, are threatening the freedom of mankind throughout the world. The end of Part I is in the highest degree dramatic. It is a fine conclusion of a very fine thing.

—The Princess Pierre Troubetzkoy

A well known Philadelphia lawyer has taken time from a busy practice to make the necessary research. The lines of descent in this book may easily be connected with the genealogical papers of hundreds of American families.

—George Steptoe Washington

Nothing could be more timely than your witness to the great principles set forth in the Charter. I could not help recalling it when reading the Churchill address of Sunday last nor that of Mr. Willkie before the Senate Committee of Wednesday. May we of the present continue to enjoy the victory won by the English Barons!

—May Atherton Leach, Historian,
Genealogical Society of Pennsylvania

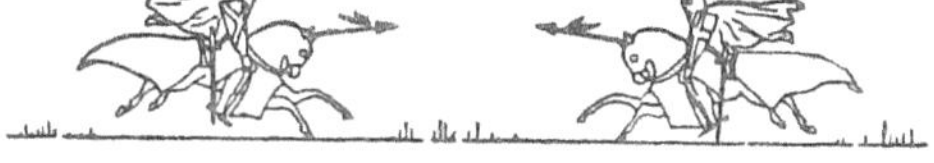

Compliments come from all directions for this book. . . . In Part II Dr. Wurts gives the pedigrees of the Barons. Here it seems is the popular appeal of the book. What genealogist has not traced through these long lists of historic and distinguished names to the founders of our liberties? The carefully prepared tables shown here go a long way to clarify those ancient lines we like so much to unravel.

—Roger Brooke, in the Virginia Historical Magazine

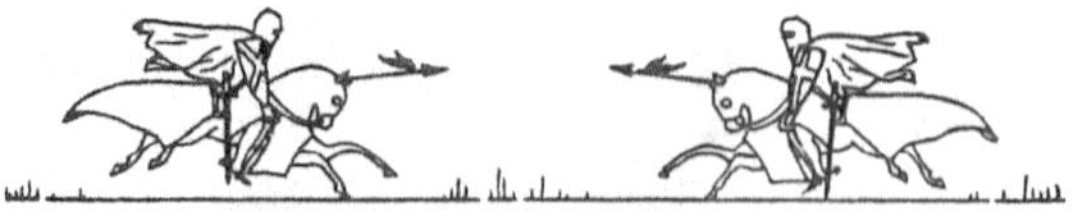

MAGNA CHARTA, PART I, ENTHUSIASTICALLY RECEIVED

I have read with deep interest your Magna Charta. It contains exactly the information that most persons ought to have about that all important document. You have done good service in publishing it.—JOSIAH HARMAR PENNIMAN, Provost, University of Pennsylvania.

It must have taken you a long time to make such a detailed analysis of Magna Charta, and an equally long time to assemble your material in such an interesting fashion. Your bibliography shows that details have been meticulously culled over while the manuscript contains only the material necessary for the reader's true concept of Magna Charta. Your understanding of psychology is shown in your character analyses so cleverly worked into the manuscript. The reader never experiences a dull moment.—GRACE L. BROOKE, Pennsylvania.

I have your handsome work on Magna Charta. I am calling this to Mr. McVey's special attention for the benefit of his course in English History, and shall see that a copy is placed in the school library.—RICHARD KNOWLES, Headmaster, William Penn Charter School.

I read it with much interest and relearned a lot of English history that I had forgotten. It helps one to realize the kind of stuff the English are made of and how they can stand the terrible bombing which has fallen to their lot.—PIERRE JAY WURTS, New Jersey.

We are reading it with interest and enjoyment.—BRITISH LIBRARY OF INFORMATION, New York.

Something every Magna Charta descendant should have. —MRS. HERBERT M. ADAMS, Rhode Island.

Most fascinating and valuable; it is both scholarly and vivid.—FRIENDS LIBRARY, Germantown.

We read your splendid address on Magna Charta aloud and enjoyed it and admired your logic and terseness of expression. I do not see how it could have been improved.—JAY M. WHITHAM, Maryland.

It is indeed a fine scholarly record and one which should be in great demand by all students and colleges.—MRS. WILLIAM WHITEHEAD ERWIN, Delegate, Magna Charta Dames.

Your "Magna Charta" just received, it is a most excellent account of this outstanding event . . . . It is especially pleasing to have this very fine exposition of the "Romance of the Great Charter."—JOHN BION RICHARDS, Honorary General President, Sons of the Revolution.

I found your Magna Charta very interesting and instructive, and I again have occasion to admire your industry in the line of genealogical research and your power of lending romantic charm to an ordinarily dry topic.—WILLIAM L. R. WURTS, Yale '78, Editor and Columnist.

You may well be proud of your work. The story is told graphically, yet with the reserve of the historian. I note that you give a tremendous bibliography, which infers authenticity. I am recommending your book to my own son . . . . from this, one can get a more dramatic picture of an important historical event than he would ever get from a text book. You have made it seem alive.—EVERETT S. KELSON, William Penn Charter School.

Nothing could be more timely than your witness to the great principles set forth in the Charter. I could not help recalling it when reading the Churchill address of Sunday last nor that of Mr. Willkie before the Senate Committee on Wednesday. May we of the present continue to enjoy the victory won by the English Barons!—MAY ATHERTON LEACH, Historian, Genealogical Society of Pennsylvania.

Most beautifully told, the story of our heritage is interesting and inviting. I am going to use it in our work here at Stevens School.—HELEN CHURCH, Principal, Stevens School for Girls.

In this very easy form for reading, it should be put where the public could have it.—MRS. JOHN CLAFLIN, New Jersey.

I congratulate you upon a piece of work so very well done.—JOHN LYMAN COX, Chestnut Hill.

I am glad to have your most charming book upon the Magna Charta. I have done enough research to realize what a tremendous amount of effort has gone into your work.—JEAN PENN-GASKELL HANCOCK, Philadelphia.

I am very glad to have had the opportunity to read Magna Charta, Part I, and glad to have it available as a reference for my two boys. We are living in a day when the history and importance of Magna Charta cannot be too greatly stressed, and every adult and child in the United States should be familiar with the beginnings and progress of the struggle for liberty.—MRS. HAROLD DEAN KRAFFT, Washington, D. C.

I must compliment you on a work so beautifully done and illustrated. It must have taken a long time to accomplish so much research and I consider it a most valuable possession. JOHN McARTHUR HARRIS, Architect, Germantown.

Knowing the thoroughness with which all your work is done, I am looking forward with great pleasure to reading your Magna Charta.—JOSEPH KNOX FORNANCE, Secretary, Society of the Cincinnati and Prominent Attorney.

Your treatment of the subject is most scholarly and interesting. The work you are doing is a valuable contribution to English and American History.—REV. ARNOLD H. HORD, Germantown.

Your book is a very valuable treatise on a most timely subject, expressed in a clear, appealing style. I have read it many times and with every reading it becomes greater. —MRS. JAMES BOONE RHODES, Texas

Your interesting article Magna Charta, Part I, I have read with interest, and want to send my thanks and appreciation. It is a good time for such a document to be passed around, and I wish that it could make a deep impression on some of the violators of its principles who have upset the whole European program.—RICHARD M. GUMMERE, Professor, Harvard College.

You have moved me deeply by this fine piece of work; especially is it to be valued in these days, when other tyrants, far worse than King John, are threatening the freedom of mankind throughout the world. The end of your book is in the highest degree dramatic. It is a fine conclusion of a very fine thing.—THE PRINCESS PIERRE TROUBETZKOY, Virginia.

And more than three hundred other lawyers, judges, educators, genealogists, book lovers, librarians, authors and historians have written unsolicited endorsements of this work. Among them are:

THOMAS S. GATES, President, University of Pennsylvania

JOHN MORIN SCOTT, Prothonotary Philadelphia Courts and Governor Pennsylvania Society Colonial Wars

H. BIRCHARD TAYLOR, Trustee, University of Pennsylvania and President, Americans of Royal Descent.

SAMUEL F. HOUSTON, President, Real Estate Trust Co.

CLARENCE C. BRINTON, President, Germantown Trust Company

ALICE ELIZABETH TRABUE, President, Magna Charta Dames

MRS. L. CARY SLAYTON, Connecticut

ALEX GALT ROBINSON, Kentucky

REV. HENRY W. FROST, Princeton

REV. ROWAN PEARCE, Christian Voices

MRS. THOMAS E. WARD, New Jersey

MRS. GEORGE CLAY FULLINWEIDER, South Dakota

MRS. H. A. KNORR, Arkansas

MRS. REED HOBART ELLIS, Maine

MRS. J. WENDALL KIMBALL, New Hampshire

MRS. BENJAMIN G. MILLER, Nebraska

MRS. SILAS ALLEN, Wisconsin

MRS. WILLIAM WARREN ORCUTT, California

DR. JAY BESSON RUDOLPHY, Pennsylvania

REV. HIRAM K. DOUGLASS, Alabama

MRS. MARGARET SCRUGGS CARRUTH, Texas

MRS. A. G. C. STETSON, Florida

MRS. SAMUEL A. MANGAM, New York

SUSIE de LORENZI, Florida

MRS. ROBERT H. WHITEHEAD, North Carolina

MRS. DAVID HAINES BALL, New York

MRS. WALTER C. WHITE, Ohio

MRS. JAMES M. WEAVER, Virginia

MRS. WILLIAM WALLACE, Massachusetts

HARRIETTE MILLER MALLEY, Connecticut

MAJ. WILLIAM A. CALLAWAY, South Carolina

MRS. JULIAN WOOD GLASS, Oklahoma

MRS. ARTHUR H. MERCHANT, Texas

MRS. WALTER S. WELCH, Mississippi

MRS. NORVILLE F. YOUNG, Ohio

MRS. KERN DODGE, Pennsylvania

DR. LESTER J. WILLIAMS, Louisiana

MRS. HARRY CLARK BODEN, Delaware

MRS. SALLIE HUME DOUGLAS, Hawaii

MRS. S. FAHS SMITH, Pennsylvania

MRS. OSCAR A. KNOX, Tennessee

REV. ALEXANDER MacCOLL, Philadelphia

THE PRINCESS KAPLANOFF, New York

MRS. GEORGE WOODWARD, Pennsylvania

MRS. E. PEROT BISSELL, Pennsylvania

WINTHROP COLE, Massachusetts

COL. CHARLES S. BRYAN, North Carolina

REV. HARLE WALLACE HATHAWAY, Philadelphia

MRS. H. L. KINNISON, Wyoming

MRS. BENNETT K. WHEELER, Kansas

MRS. OLIVE F. BOYER, Pennsylvania

MRS. ROBERT G. BOVILLE, New York

HARRIET F. B. STUART, Illinois

MRS. ANNA J. COTTON, Texas

ARTHUR McGEORGE, Delaware

MRS. QUINCY ADAMS GATES, Washington

MRS. ALTON BROOKS PARKER, New York

MRS. ALONZO L. McGILL, California

GEORGE CUTHBERT GILLESPIE, Historian

GARRARD GLENN, Professor of Law, University of Virginia

GEORGE STEPTOE WASHINGTON, Justiciar, Order of Washington

ARTHUR ADAMS, Professor, Trinity College

J. E. BURNETT BUCKENHAM, President, Colonial Society of Pennsylvania

ARTHUR deBERDT ROBINS, Vice President, New Jersey S. A. R.

ELIZABETH FISHER WASHINGTON, Regent General, Magna Charta Dames

BENJAMIN R. HOFFMAN, English Speaking Union, Philadelphia

MRS. A. A. MILNE, Minnesota

MRS. OSCAR H. RIXFORD, Vermont

MRS. J. FITHIAN TATEM, New Jersey

EDNA HAYNES McCORMICK, Texas

D. RALPH MILLARD, North Carolina

MRS. H. BELIN duPONT, Pennsylvania

DR. EGERTON L. CRISPIN, California

ALVERTA BIRD ELLIS, Colorado

MRS. EDWARD T. AGERTON, Georgia

MRS. CHARLES L. BUTTERFIELD, Idaho

MRS. WILLIAM JACKSON YOUNG, Indiana

MRS. GILBERT A. MACKENZIE, Iowa

MRS. CHARLES G. MAYWOOD, Michigan

MRS. FRANK H. BELOW, Missouri

MRS. ROBERT MOORE, New Mexico

MRS. A. EUGENE ROCKEY, Oregon

A. F. BENNETT, Utah

MRS. FRANK MATHER ARCHER, West Virginia

MRS. COURTNEY BOONE, Arizona

MRS. JOHN G. BROWN, Montana

RICHARD EARL GODWIN, Nevada

GEORGE NOBLE COOK, North Dakota

WASHINGTON STATE HISTORICAL SOCIETY

ERWIN CLARKSON GARRETT, Author, Germantown, Pa.

ROBERT T. McCRACKEN, Philadelphia Lawyer

COL. EDGAR ERSKINE HUME, President, Virginia Society of the Cincinnati

B. F. FACKENTHALL, JR., Pres. Bucks County Historical Society

THE NEW AGE

February-March 1945

"MAGNA CHARTA," Part III.

BY JOHN S. WURTS

Published by Brookfield Publishing Company, Mail Service Department, P.O. Box 4933, Philadelphia, Pa. Price $5.00

It is well for the reader to remember that this book is Part III of a series. Part I dealt with *The Romance of the Great Charter*, and Part II with *Pedigrees of the Barons*.

The present book continues the *Pedigrees of the Barons* and, in the Introduction and Chapter 37, packs a lot of history into eight pages. The story of the Crusades is a long and complicated one, yet the author has given an over-all account in what is a marvel of condensation. The succeeding 300 pages are devoted to genealogies. One of especial interest is a section in Chapter 55 devoted to the Genealogies of the Bible. In Chapter 60 are, among other pedigrees, those of Gen. Douglas MacArthur and Prime Minister Winston Churchill.

The book is carefully indexed and a page is given over to explaining the various calendars. One is impressed with the tremendous amount of research that must have been expended to produce this book and its predecessors. Not to be overlooked are the eight ruled blank pages at the rear of the book, so that the reader can keep his personal notations of the especial pedigree in which he is particularly interested. This is a novel feature and well-worthy of being copied by publishers of historical books. S. W.

ESSEX INSTITUTE
HISTORICAL COLLECTIONS

VOL. LXXXI APRIL, 1945 No. 2

MAGNA CHARTA. Part III. Continuing the Pedigrees of the Barons. By John S. Wurts. 1944. 619 pp., octavo, cloth, illus. Philadelphia, Pa.: Brookfield Publishing Company. Price, $5.00.

This volume is a continuation of Parts I and II. It contains additional pedigrees of the Barons, brief historical sketches of the events of the times, and biographical sketches of the ancestors with their occupations and personalities. Considering ancient sources "it is disappointing to find that the bards and monks and other contemporary historians do not agree in many of their details. Dates and places have often been too meagerly preserved to enable one now to form a fixed opinion as to the integrity of many early pedigrees." Mr. Wurts has selected the most logical items from this material. Coats-of-arms are well illustrated and described. There is an index.

THE NEW YORK
Genealogical and Biographical Record

VOL. LXXVI NEW YORK, JANUARY, 1945 NO. 1

MAGNA CHARTA PART III by John S. Wurts. 1944. 6½ x 9¼, cloth, illustrated, pp. 320. Price $5.00. Address: The Brookfield Publishing Company, P. O. Box 4933, Philadelphia, Pennsylvania.

This characteristically fine work continues Parts I and II of Magna Charta which covered The Romance of the Great Charter and Pedigrees of the Barons (Record 73:293) and brings down full Baronial Ancestry of certain New England, Pennsylvania, and Southern families through seventeen of the Barons to current times and to living descendants in such American lines as Throckmorton, Claiborne, West, Burnet, Bruen, Dudley, Randolph, Reade, Washington and others. There are chapters devoted to the Crusades, Biblical genealogies, Charlemagne, the Vikings, etc. The author has also examined and outlined the faults, virtues, interests, occupations, and human tendencies of the Barons which adds to the fascination and value of the book.

In the Foreword attention is drawn to the fact that "It is not important that these men were Barons, but it is important that they built a structure on which has been preserved our civil and religious freedom."

Spaces are provided thereon in which to set forth the names of all the ancestors one has in the most recent ten generations. If you desire to display your own ancestors, place your own name in the blank space designated "First Generation" which is in the lower middle portion of the chart. Directly above it, place your father's name in space No. 511, your mother's name in space No. 512, and thus continue working upward on the various lines of your ancestry.

The names of the two parents will always be directly over the name of their child. It will be seen, that at every odd number on this chart will be the name of a man. Any odd number plus one will be the name of that man's wife. Thus, every even number is for the name of a woman.

The system of numbering may at first seem confusing, but if one should wish to write the biographies of the forefathers and will use in a notebook a page for each pair of numbers (that is husband and wife), it will be seen that this system of numbering will be the most logical and satisfactory sequence in which the ancestors should be entered in the notebook.

For example: It is logical to begin with the family name of the person in question.

Going back ten generations on that name, the husband and wife will appear on the sheet as Nos. 1 and 2, and the page in the notebook on which their sketch is written, will be numbered "1 and 2." Their son through whom the line of descent comes will be No. 3 and his wife No. 4 therefore number this page "3 and 4." Before considering the next lower generation, No. 4's parents should be considered in order that they may not be overlooked. Thus No. 4's father is designated No. 5 and the mother No. 6. After their biographies have been set forth, the son of Nos. 3 and 4 can be taken, and he is designated No. 7 and his wife No. 8. Going next to the tenth generation of the new wife's surname (that is to her grandparents), these are designated Nos. 9 and 10, their son 11, his wife 12, and No. 12's parents would be 13 and 14. The general rule is: Whenever a new name is met with, proceed to the tenth generation of that name. In this way each family will be considered in its logical order and disposed of before a new surname is taken up for consideration. A blankbook in which all these biographies may be written will be found of great help toward obtaining a comprehensive survey of the whole array of more than a thousand ancestors of an individual for the most recent ten generations.

WE ARE REMINDED THAT IN ENGLAND:

Talbut is pronounced Tolbut.
Thames is pronounced Tems.
Bulwer is pronounced Buller.
Cowper is pronounced Cooper.
Holburn is pronounced Hoburn.
Wemyss is pronounced Weems.
Knollys is pronounced Knowles.
Cockburn is pronouneed Coburn.
Brougham is pronounced Broom.
Norwich is pronounced Norridge.
St. Ledger is pronounced Sillinger.
Hawarden is pronounced Harden.
Colquhoun is pronounced Cohoon.
Cirencester is pronounced Sissister.
Grosvenor is pronounced Grovenor.
Salisbury is pronounced Sawlsbury.
Beauchamp is pronounced Beecham.
Marylebone is pronounced Marrabun.
Abergavenny is pronounced Abergenny.
Marjoribanks is pronounced Marchbanks.
Bolingbroke is pronounced Bullingbrook.

CONCERNING THE LISTING OF DESCENDANTS: If you number among your ancestors at least one of the Barons for the Magna Charta, you may on request have your name listed in Part III, as for each book subscribed the Publishers have agreed to list the descendant's name under ONE Baron and King, as offered in the advance circular. You no doubt descend from several Barons.

IF ADDITIONAL LISTINGS ARE DESIRED they may be had on request to the Publishers, one listing for each book subscribed. (Some persons have thought it worth while to subscribe for sufficient copies to have their names listed under each Baron from whom they descend.)

As explained on page 37, where a name appears in print under only ONE Baron and King, it is NOT to be understood that such person is necessarily descended from ONLY that one, for as a matter of fact many of the persons listed are descended from several Kings and Barons.

Near relatives having the SAME pedigree will often be found intentionally listed under DIFFERENT Barons, as a means of recording a wider ancestry for the family in view.

You may be pleased to note that instead of finding YOUR name under a Baron already known to you, it appears under some other Baron, thus showing that your ancestry is wider than you may have been aware.

Calendar for 200 Years

Covering the Years from 1753 to 1952

Explanation—To ascertain your birthday or any day of the week, first look in the table for the year required and below (in the same column) find the number opposite the month required. This number refers to the corresponding figure at the head of a column in the table below. **Example:** Find the *day of the week* upon which Abraham Lincoln was born, the date being February 12th, 1809. In the table of years find 1809. Directly below, opposite February, is the figure 3, which directs us to column 3 below, which is a calendar for February, 1809. We there find that Lincoln was born on Sunday. *These tables give all the information that could be obtained from 200 yearly calendars.*

								LEAP YEARS						
	1761 1767 1778 1789 1795 1801 1807 1818 1829 1835 1846 1857 1863 1874 1885 1891 1903 1914 1925 1931 1942	1762 1773 1779 1790 1802 1813 1819 1830 1841 1847 1858 1869 1875 1886 1897 1909 1915 1926 1937 1943	1757 1763 1774 1785 1791 1803 1814 1825 1831 1842 1853 1859 1870 1881 1887 1898 1910 1921 1927 1938 1949	1754 1765 1771 1782 1793 1799 1805 1811 1822 1833 1839 1850 1861 1867 1878 1889 1895 1901 1907 1918 1929 1935 1946	1755 1766 1777 1783 1794 1800 1806 1817 1823 1834 1845 1851 1862 1873 1879 1890 1902 1913 1919 1930 1941 1947	1758 1769 1775 1786 1797 1809 1815 1826 1837 1843 1854 1865 1871 1882 1893 1899 1905 1911 1922 1933 1939 1950	1753 1759 1770 1781 1787 1798 1810 1821 1827 1838 1849 1855 1866 1877 1883 1894 1900 1906 1917 1923 1934 1945 1951	1764 1792 1804 1832 1860 1888 1928	1768 1796 1808 1836 1864 1892 1904 1932	1772 1812 1840 1868 1896 1908 1936	1776 1816 1844 1872 1912 1940	1780 1820 1848 1876 1916 1944	1756 1784 1824 1852 1880 1920 1948	1760 1788 1828 1856 1884 1924 1952
Jan.	4	5	6	2	3	7	1	7	5	3	1	6	4	2
Feb.	7	1	2	5	6	3	4	3	1	6	4	2	7	5
Mar.	7	1	2	5	6	3	4	4	2	7	5	3	1	6
April	3	4	5	1	2	6	7	7	5	3	1	6	4	2
May	5	6	7	3	4	1	2	2	7	5	3	1	6	4
June	1	2	3	6	7	4	5	5	3	1	6	4	2	7
July	3	4	5	1	2	6	7	7	5	3	1	6	4	2
Aug.	6	7	1	4	5	2	3	3	1	6	4	2	7	5
Sept.	2	3	4	7	1	5	6	6	4	2	7	5	3	1
Oct.	4	5	6	2	3	7	1	1	6	4	2	7	5	3
Nov.	7	1	2	5	6	3	4	4	2	7	5	3	1	6
Dec.	2	3	4	7	1	5	6	6	4	2	7	5	3	1

1	2	3	4	5	6	7
Monday 1	Tuesday 1	Wednsdy 1	Thursday 1	Friday 1	Saturday 1	SUNDAY 1
Tuesday 2	Wednsdy 2	Thursday 2	Friday 2	Saturday 2	SUNDAY 2	Monday 2
Wednsdy 3	Thursday 3	Friday 3	Saturday 3	SUNDAY 3	Monday 3	Tuesday 3
Thursday 4	Friday 4	Saturday 4	SUNDAY 4	Monday 4	Tuesday 4	Wednsdy 4
Friday 5	Saturday 5	SUNDAY 5	Monday 5	Tuesday 5	Wednsdy 5	Thursday 5
Saturday 6	SUNDAY 6	Monday 6	Tuesday 6	Wednsdy 6	Thursday 6	Friday 6
SUNDAY 7	Monday 7	Tuesday 7	Wednsdy 7	Thursday 7	Friday 7	Saturday 7
Monday 8	Tuesday 8	Wednsdy 8	Thursday 8	Friday 8	Saturday 8	SUNDAY 8
Tuesday 9	Wednsdy 9	Thursday 9	Friday 9	Saturday 9	SUNDAY 9	Monday 9
Wednsdy 10	Thursday 10	Friday 10	Saturday 10	SUNDAY 10	Monday 10	Tuesday 10
Thursday 11	Friday 11	Saturday 11	SUNDAY 11	Monday 11	Tuesday 11	Wednsdy 11
Friday 12	Saturday 12	SUNDAY 12	Monday 12	Tuesday 12	Wednsdy 12	Thursday 12
Saturday 13	SUNDAY 13	Monday 13	Tuesday 13	Wednsdy 13	Thursday 13	Friday 13
SUNDAY 14	Monday 14	Tuesday 14	Wednsdy 14	Thursday 14	Friday 14	Saturday 14
Monday 15	Tuesday 15	Wednsdy 15	Thursday 15	Friday 15	Saturday 15	SUNDAY 15
Tuesday 16	Wednsdy 16	Thursday 16	Friday 16	Saturday 16	SUNDAY 16	Monday 16
Wednsdy 17	Thursday 17	Friday 17	Saturday 17	SUNDAY 17	Monday 17	Tuesday 17
Thursday 18	Friday 18	Saturday 18	SUNDAY 18	Monday 18	Tuesday 18	Wednsdy 18
Friday 19	Saturday 19	SUNDAY 19	Monday 19	Tuesday 19	Wednsdy 19	Thursday 19
Saturday 20	SUNDAY 20	Monday 20	Tuesday 20	Wednsdy, 20	Thursday 20	Friday 20
SUNDAY 21	Monday 21	Tuesday 21	Wednsdy 21	Thursday 21	Friday 21	Saturday 21
Monday 22	Tuesday 22	Wednsdy 22	Thursday 22	Friday 22	Saturday 22	SUNDAY 22
Tuesday 23	Wednsdy 23	Thursday 23	Friday 23	Saturday 23	SUNDAY 23	Monday 23
Wednsdy 24	Thursday 24	Friday 24	Saturday 24	SUNDAY 24	Monday 24	Tuesday 24
Thursday 25	Friday 25	Saturday 25	SUNDAY 25	Monday 25	Tuesday 25	Wednsdy 25
Friday 26	Saturday 26	SUNDAY 26	Monday 26	Tuesday 26	Wednsdy 26	Thursday 26
Saturday 27	SUNDAY 27	Monday 27	Tuesday 27	Wednsdy 27	Thursday 27	Friday 27
SUNDAY 28	Monday 28	Tuesday 28	Wednsdy 28	Thursday 28	Friday 28	Saturday 28
Monday 29	Tuesday 29	Wednsdy 29	Thursday 29	Friday 29	Saturday 29	SUNDAY 29
Tuesday 30	Wednsdy 30	Thursday 30	Friday 30	Saturday 30	SUNDAY 30	Monday 30
Wednsdy 31	Thursday 31	Friday 31	Saturday 31	SUNDAY 31	Monday 31	Tuesday 31

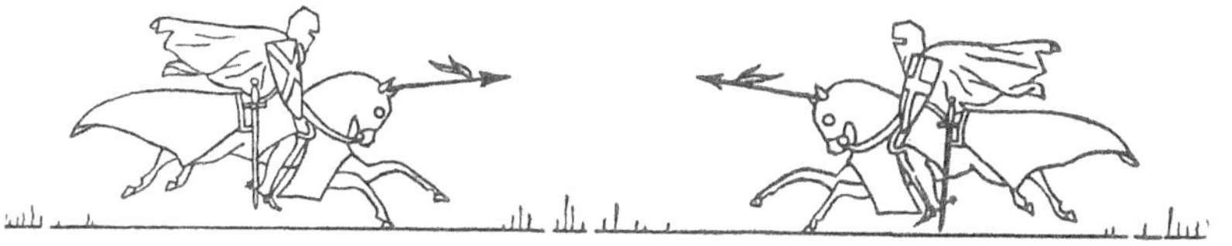

SECOND SUPPLEMENT TO PART II

MAGNA CHARTA
ROMANCE AND PEDIGREES

THE PARISH CHURCH OF RUNNEMEDE WHERE THE BARONS WORSHIPPED

MAGNA CHARTA

Printed in the U. S. A.

The Official Register of Royal Descent,

A Who's Who of Noble Lineage,

A standard reference work by

JOHN S. WURTS
of "Hedgefield"
Germantown, Pa.

Part III PEDIGREES OF THE BARONS CONTINUED for several more generations.

Some New England, Pennsylvania and Southern families are brought down to the present day. Other subscribers may yet have their lines from all their barons at once brought down in detail, generation by generation, to the present day, and to accomplish this the Publishers will on request arrange sufficient space and special terms.

This volume, illustrated and fully indexed, will be run on the press as soon as additional data are sent by descendants who wish to be included. It contains further lists of *living descendants,* and there is a place for YOUR NAME if your descent is available and you subscribe now.

IN ORDER TO BE INCLUDED you are not required to be a member of any of the various old world hereditary societies, but your descent from a king or a baron must be known.

If your family descent is such as should entitle you to be listed in "Magna Charta" and your name is not found therein, could it be because you did not request it to be put in? Or perhaps the request came too late for insertion. In the latter event your name will be printed in future lists.

As explained on page 37, where a name appears in print under only ONE Baron and King, it is NOT to be understood that such person is necessarily descended from ONLY that one, for as a matter of fact many of the persons listed are descended from several Kings and Barons.

Near relatives having the *same* pedigree will often be found intentionally listed under *different* Barons, as a means of recording a wider ancestry for the family in view.

You may be pleased to note that instead of finding YOUR name under a Baron already known to you, it appears under some other Baron, thus showing that your ancestry is broader than you may have been aware.

You may on request have your name listed in Part III, as for each book subscribed the Publishers have agreed to list the descendant's name under ONE Baron and King. You no doubt descend from several Barons.

IF ADDITIONAL LISTINGS ARE DESIRED they may be had on request to the Publishers, one listing for each book subscribed. (Some persons have thought it worth while to subscribe for sufficient copies to have their names listed under each Baron from whom they descend.)

It is part of the Publisher's plan that the representative families already included should be continued in place and their lineage brought on down to date, and to that end the Publishers are confident that if any former subscribers have not already sent their check $5.00 for Part III *to insure such continuance,* they will do so now.

In this volume, Part III, will be found many more ancestors, their faults and virtues, their interests, occupations and human tendencies; Richard de Clare, called Strongbow; the charming Arlotta, mother of William the Conqueror; King Cadwallader; Prince Llewellyn; Lady Godiva; the Guelphs; Peter the Hermit and the Crusaders.

The Descent of

HER MAJESTY QUEEN ELIZABETH

Through 73 Generations in 20 Centuries

Showing Kinship with Some Virginia Families

70. Boadicea, in Latin "Victoria", British Queen, d. A. D. 62, whose daughter, 69. name unknown, m. Marius (son of Arviragus, King of Britain, and his wife, 70. Venissa Julia, who was the daughter of 71. Tiberius Claudius Caesar, Emperor of Rome, son of 72. Antonia, daughter of 73. Mark Anthony, b. B. C. 83). Their son
68. Old King Cole, King of Britain A. D. 125, built Coel-Castra (Colchester) and his daughter
67. Athildis m. Marcomir IV, King of Franconia, d. 149, and had
66. Clodomir IV, King of the Franks, who died in 166, having m. Hasilda, and from them the line continues as follows:
65. King Farabert, died 186. 64. King Sunno, died 213. 63. King Hilderic, died 253. 62. King Bartherus, died 272. 61. King Clodius III, died 298. 60. King Walter, died 306. 59. King Dagobert, died 317. 58. Genebald I, Duke of the East Franks, died 350. 57. King Dagobert, died 379. 56. King Clodius I, died 389. 55. King Marcomir, died 404. 54. Pharamond, King of Westphalia, m. Argotta.
53. Clodio, the Long Haired, King of Westphalia, m. Basina.
52. Merovee, King of France, d. 458, m. Verica.
51. Childeric I, 436-481, King of France, m. Basina of Thuringia.
50. Clovis the Great, 465-511, King of France, m. St. Clothilde.
49. Clothaire I, 497-561, King of France, m. Ingonde.
48. Blithildes, m. Ausbert of Moselle, d. 570.
47. Arnoul, Bishop of Metz, d. 601, m. Oda de Savoy.
46. St. Arnolph, Bishop of Metz, d. 641, m. Lady Dodo of Saxony.
45. Anchises, d. 685, m. Begga of Brabant, d. 698.
44. Pepin d'Heristal, Mayor of the Palace, d. 714, m. Alpais.
43. Charles Martel, 689-741, King of France, m. Rotrude, d. 724.
42. Pepin the Short, 714-768, King of France, m. Bertha of Laon, d. 783.
41. Charlemagne, 742-814, Emperor of the West, m. Hildegarde, 757-782.
40. Pepin, 776-810, King of Italy, m. Bertha of Toulouse.
39. Bernhard, King of Lombardy, d. 812, m. Cunegonde.
38. Pepin, a lay abbot in 840, m. and had
37. Herbert I, Count of Vermandois, d. 902, m. and had
36. Herbert II, Count of Vermandois, d. 943, m. Hildebrand.
35. Robert, Count of Vermandois, d. 968, m. Adelaide de Chalons.
34. Adelaide, Countess of Chalons, d. 976, m. Geoffrey, Count d'Anjou.
33. Fulk III, Count d'Anjou, d. 1040, m. Hildegarde.
32. Ermengarde d'Anjou m. Geoffrey II de Gastinois.
31. Fulk IV, 1043-1109, Count d'Anjou, m. Bertrade de Montfort.
30. Fulk V, 1092-1144, Count d'Anjou, m. Ermengarde du Maine, d. 1126.
29. Geoffrey Plantagenet, 1113-1151, m. Matilda of England, 1103-1167, granddaughter of William the Conqueror.
28. Henry II, 1133-1189, King of England, m. Eleanor of Aquitaine.
27. Eleanor of England m. Alphonso IX, King of Castile, d. 1214.
26. Berengaria of Castile, d. 1244, m. Alphonso IX, 1166-1229, King of Leon.
25. Ferdinand III, 1191-1252, King of Castile, m. 1237 Joan de Dammartin.
24. Eleanor of Castile, d. 1290, m. 1254 Edward I, King of England.
23. Edward II, King of England, m. Isabel of France, d. 1358.
22. Edward III, King of England, m. Philippa of Hainault, 1313-1369.
21. Lionel, 1338-1368, Duke of Clarence, K. G., m. Elizabeth Burgh.
20. Philippa Plantagenet m. Edmund de Mortimer, Earl of March.
19. Elizabeth Mortimer m. Henry de Percy, K. G. called "Hotspur".
18. Henry de Percy, K. G., Earl of Northumberland, m. Eleanor Nevill.
17. Henry de Percy, Earl of Northumberland, m. Eleanor Poynings.
16. Margaret Percy m. William Gascoigne, d. 1486, Lord of Bentley Manor, co. Yorkshire.
15. Elizabeth Gascoigne m. George de Tailbois, Lord of Kyme Manor, co. Yorkshire.
14. Anne Tailbois m. Edward Dymoke, Lord of Scrivelsby Manor, co. Lincoln.
13. Frances Dymoke m. Thomas Windebank, Lord of the Manor of Haines Hall, co. Berkshire, knighted by King James I, 23 July 1603.
12. Mildred Windebank, 1584-1630, m. 1600 Robert Reade, of Linkenholt parish, Hants, d. 1626.
11. Colonel George Reade, b. in England 25 October 1608, came to America 1637, Acting Governor of Virginia 1638, d. in October 1674, m. Elizabeth Martian.
10. Mildred Reade, great grandmother of George Washington, m. Colonel Augustine Warner, 1643-1681.
9. Mary Warner m. 1680 Colonel John Smith of Purton.
8. Mildred Smith, b. 1682, m. 1700 Robert Porteus of Newbottle, Virginia, 1679-1758.
7. Rev. Robert Porteus, 1705-1754, Rector of Cockayne Hatley, co. Bedford, m. 1736 Judith Cockayne, 1702-1789.
6. Mildred Porteus, b. 1744, m. Robert Hudgson of Congleton, co. Chester, b. 1740.
5. Rev. Robert Hodgson, Dean of Carlisle, m. 1804 Mary Tucker.
4. Henrietta Mildred Hodgson m. 1824 Oswald Smith, 1794-1863, of Blendon Hall, co. Kent.
3. Frances Dora Smith, d. 1922, m. 1853 Claude Lyon-Bowes, later Bowes-Lyon, 13th Earl of Strathmore, 1824-1904.
2. Claude George Bowes-Lyon, 14th Earl of Strathmore, K. G., K. T., b. 1855, m. 1881 Nina Cecilia Cavendish-Bentinck, d. 1938.
1. Elizabeth Angela Marguerite, Her Majesty the Queen, b. 1900, m. 1923 His Majesty King George VI, b. 1895, succeeded 1936.

H. R. H. Princess Elizabeth, b. 1926.
H. R. H. Princess Margaret Rose, b. 1930.

Some Americans of Royal Descent

and Descendants of the Magna Charta Barons

Continuing pages 178 and 274, the following persons also (whose names will appear again, in Part III, under one or more Barons from whom each descends) may claim descent from the Emperor Charlemagne:

Horace Avery Abell
Anna Maria Stafford Anable
Sara Alma Anable
Robert Arthur
Robert L. Ashby
Lulu Gray Auld
Mary Travis Sarber Ball
Meribah Irwin Moore Bamber
Marion Brayton Barron
Katharine Geddes Benedict
Sallie Ward Beretta
Martha H. Allen Blackledge
Elaine Blackman
Martha Irwin Moore Braun
Edyth Clements Shipley Britton
Helen May Brown
Charles Shepard Bryan
Williamson Buckman
Mary Adelaide Jones Bush
Evelyn True Button
Frances Moon Butts
William Aylett Callaway
Rosa Pendleton Chiles
Winston Churchill
Virginia Marshall Clopton
Annie Crighton
Sally Daingerfield
Charles Emmett Davidson
Rufus Dickinson
Whittie Dickinson
Katherine Ireys Diehl
Allison Dodd
Valentine Sherman Doebler
Elizabeth Winslow Dulles
Ruth Larrabee Clay du Marais
H. Edward Dyer
Eliza Murphy Candler Earthman
Berenice Long Eckel
Anthony Eden
Jane Brooke Evans
Robert Brooke Dawson Wilson Evans
Charles Henry Faxon
Eleanor Alice Lawwill Felner
Cynthia Eaton Ferres
John Giles Ferres
Alice Urquhart Fewell
Mary Large Fox
Elisabeth Amelia Wheeler Francis
Nancy Washington Naulty Fuller
Henrietta Craig Dow Galey
Sallie Faison Peirce Gibson
Nettie Wilcox Glos
Florence Grandin
Josephine Brown Green
Richard Mott Gummere
Luteola Gibbs Hawley
Bertha Perez Lincoln Heustis
Edward C. Hoagland
Helen Penrose Hodge
Nema Whitcomb Holloway
Frances Elizabeth Warren Holt
Arnold Harris Hord
Estelle de Peyster Hosmer
Charles Lukens Huston
Frances Houston Irwin
James Alexander Irwin
Mary Rolfe Jackman
William Perry Johnson
Lola Estelle Rosborough Johnston
Mary Hannah Stoddard Johnston
Bruce Carr Jones
Charles Conway Jones
The Princess Kaplanoff
John Slack Keith
William Neely Keith
Edward Leland Kellogg
Laura Esther Halliday Kelsey
Gilbert S. King
Edna Caroline Laing
Hillyer Speed Lamkin
Mabel R. Landreth
Wilhelmina Shirley Lea
Mary B. Leidel
Rose Lawton Douglas Lewis
Samuel Bunting Lewis
Claudia Yewell Lindly
Augusta E. Muir Lippincott
George Eyre Lippincott
Sarah L. A. Evans Lippincott
Douglas MacArthur
Harriette Miller Hamilton Malley
Clara Clementine Chamberlain McLean
Daisy Brooke Merkle
David Ralph Millard
Florence Cooley Miller
Harry Oliver Moore
Meribah Irwin Stearns Moore
Howard Ross Nelson
Leah Post Norris
Dolores Nourse
Ella Foy O'Gorman
Mary Logan Orcutt
James Blenn Perkins
Tunstall Barker Perry
Nellie M. Darby Pettersen
Frances E. Pettit
Alexander Van Cleve Phillips
Grace Edna Vollnogle Phillips
Birdie Mildred Givens Pickle
Elma Celoa Moore Pollock
Avis Beatrice Wise Ramsey
Nellie Azora Pedersen Reddin
Etta D. F. Rees
Owen Rivers Rhoads
Lavinia Dandridge Richardson
Alex Galt Robinson
Elisabeth Besson Rudolphy
Jay Besson Rudolphy
Roberta McDonald Russell
Evelyn J. Salisbury
Henrietta Dawson Ayres Sheppard
Anna Taylor Peirce Shewbrooks
Amelia S. Douglas Howard-Smith
Georgine Northrop Wetherill Smith
Lewis Stone Sorley
Marguerite Drew Hall Stearns
Elizabeth Ives Leete Stephens
Eleanor Allen Carter Strickler
Ella Gertrude Holthoff Thayer
Eva Hanson Thornton
Benjamin Franklin Tillson
Alice Elizabeth Trabue
The Princess Troubetzkoy
Mary Vanuxem
Rose Genevieve Chatterton Van Wagner
Mary Grace Murray Verner
Prudence Sharpless Doyle Vollnogle
Rosalie Tarver Wade
Cleland A. Ward
Elizabeth Fisher Washington
George Steptoe Washington
Mary Lyde Hicks Williams
Lydia Anne Davison Woodhouse
Frederic Thomas Woodman
Davis Page Wurts
Edward Vanuxem Wurts
Robert Kennedy Wurts
Ethel Denune Young

ADDITIONAL ACKNOWLEDGMENT AND BIBLIOGRAPHY

Genealogical Tables. Hereford B. George. 1930.

Royal Genealogies. James Anderson, D.D. 1736.

Genealogy of the Most Illustrious Houses of all the World. Venice. 1743.

The Plantagenet Ancestry. W. H. Turton. 1928.

The Genealogists' Magazine. 1938, 1939.

The Genealogical Quarterly. 1934, 1935.

Yorkshire County Magazine. 1892, 1893, 1894.

Histories of the Counties of England.

The Royal Houses of Europe. Illuminated Genealogical Chart. 1854.

Americans of Royal Descent. Charles Henry Browning. 9 Volumes.

New Complete Peerage. Vicary Gibbs. 8 Volumes.

Peerage and Baronetage. Sir Bernard Burke. 1929, 1937.

Dormant and Extinct Peerage. Sir Bernard Burke. 1883.

Landed Gentry. Sir Bernard Burke. 1939.

General Armory. Sir Bernard Burke. 1878.

Irish Pedigrees. John O'Hart. 1892.

Dictionary of National Biography.

Memorials of the Order of the Garter. George Frederick Beltz. 1841.

The Register of the Order of the Garter. "The Black Book." John Anstis. 1724.

Garter Stall Plates. (1348-1485). W. H. St. John Hope. 1901.

SIR GEORGE CALVERT
Born 1580 — Died 1632

Knighted in 1617, in 1625 created 1st Lord Baron of Baltimore Ancestor of the distinguished American family of Calvert

The

CALVERT GENEALOGY

Lord Baltimore and his Descendants.

The American Calverts
set forth in their various branches

A new book by

ELLA FOY O'GORMAN

George, Cecil and Leonard Calvert were the active founders of Maryland. Several Maryland counties were named for members of the Calvert family.

Eleven Calvert men were Governors
of Maryland from 1634 to 1774,
and six were Lords Baltimore.

400 YEARS OF CALVERT HISTORY
1543 - 1943

This book fully indexed, and illustrated with portraits and coats of arms, is the most complete compilation of the Calvert Family yet undertaken. Featuring about 5000 known descendants of the 1st Lord Baltimore, continuing down 13 generations, this book contains also the known genealogy of more than 1200 additional persons, comprising a dozen family groups whose connection with the main stem has not yet been discovered.

The connection is shown for Royal descent, Magna Charta Barons, and kinship with Sir Anthony Eden. The full text is given of many wills, state papers and other documents.

BROOKFIELD PUBLISHING COMPANY — P. O. Box 4933, Philadelphia, Pa.

may prepare, bind and SEND to me:________________copies of THE CALVERT GENEALOGY, for which I will pay Ten Dollars per copy when informed that the book is ready.

NAME

ADDRESS

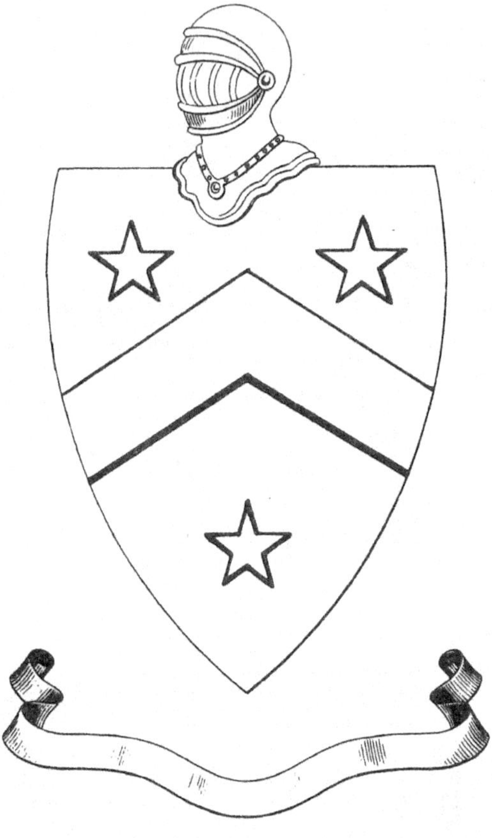

GRANDIN OF NORMANDY

An Ancient and Noble Family

Arms: Azure, a chevron d'or, between three mullets of the same.

Used by the descendants of Thomas Grandin, lord of Galonniere, living in 1330.

The Grandin Family in England and France

This family name appears early in England and in many parts of France, and was borne by members of the lesser French nobility, to whom coats of arms were granted at various times. The name of one Graundyn appears in Leland's list of those who came with William the Conqueror in 1066, and as early as 1227 Hugone Graundin is recorded as living near London. Thomas Grandin, lord of Galonniere in Normandy, was living in 1330. From him the New Jersey Grandins are believed to be descended. The French Graindorg or English Grandige may have been an earlier form of the family name. However, the present form has been used by the GRANDIN family for many generations and appeared in France long before any record of it was made on the Isle of Jersey, where this genealogy of the family begins.

THE ISLE OF JERSEY (in Latin "Caesar") has borne this name since the days of the Roman Empire. Charles the Simple, King of France, page 188, about the year 920 granted all the land on the seacoasts of Normandy and Brittany, including the Channel Islands, to Rollo the Dane, pages 194 and 421, and in that way the Dukedom of Normandy came into being.

When William the Conqueror, Duke of Normandy in 1066 became also King of England, he made the Islands a part of England's domain. In 1204, when King John lost Normandy forever, the Channel Islands, Jersey, Guernsey, Alderney and Sark, remained British, perhaps because overlooked by both contending parties, and they received their charter of liberties from King John, Lord of the Channel Isles, several years before Magna Charta was obtained by Englishmen. To this day their customs and their laws are Norman, and their language is principally French.

The Channel Islands have not belonged to France, but have been inherited from time to time by the Kings of England as successors of the Dukes of Normandy and are a part of the British Empire.

But never ask a Channel Islander if his Island belongs to England. If you do he will retort that England never conquered the Channel Islands, that on the contrary they played a prominent part in the conquest of England. The Islands helped to man William the Conqueror's ships. With their boats and their knowledge of the Channel they helped him to take an army across to England. As the Channel Islands are now all of Normandy which is left to the English Crown, the Islanders claim that they were the conquerors of England! Strange to say, the King of England is not recognized in the Channel Islands as such, but as the Duke of Normandy.

The Isle of Jersey is in the English Channel, 125 miles from England and 25 miles from France. On a clear day the spires of the French town of Coutances can be seen, as well as the white cliffs along the French shore. Jersey is a charming place, rugged cliffs along the north shore, sandy beaches prevailing along the south, and the center of the Island abounds in rich meadows and pleasant valleys. Its greatest length is twelve miles and its width is six miles.

Here sunshine is enjoyed in abundance. The climate is mild, snow being a rarity. With its wooded valleys, its winding lanes overarched with foliage, its orchards, its miles of glistening sand, its quaint old churches and picturesque granite farmhouses, all dominated by the magnificent ruins of Mont Orgueil Castle, Jersey exhibits unbounded prosperity and fertility. It is indeed a botanist's paradise. On Christmas Day one can gather as many as a hundred species of wild flowers, while the gardens are still bright with roses, geraniums and fuchsias.

The Channel Islands because of their position have long been a recognized place of refuge. To Jersey especially fled the persecuted Huguenots in the time of the Reformation. Among these refugees were families of the Grandin name.

Jersey's great feudal family of de Carteret, then the largest land owners in Jersey, remained loyal to Charles I and in 1646 the Prince of Wales found refuge in Jersey. When in 1660 he, as Charles II, the pleasure loving "Merry Monarch," was restored to the English throne, he was not ungrateful to the family which had befriended him in his exile. Among other privileges he granted to Sir George Carteret those lands in America which were named by him Carolina, after his royal master, and New Jersey (in Latin "Nova Caesarea") after his Island home. Carteret encouraged emigration to America, and a great many Jerseymen took advantage of the opportunity. It was the men he sent over to our New England shores who introduced to us the familiar dish of baked beans! Sir Walter Raleigh, who was Governor of Jersey in the days of Queen Elizabeth, linked the history of that Island with the American Continent by encouraging the Islanders' emigration to Newfoundland, and thus started the profitable codfish trade between North America and Europe. The justly famous Jersey cows are known the world over. The knitting of woolens also forms an important industry, and the garment popularly known as the "Jersey" found its origin here.

From the Ancient Rolls of the Royal Court in the Isle of Jersey this tragic item is quoted:

"MARIE GRANDIN, of the Parish of La Ternite, was apprehended on the 6th day of June 1648, and charged with sorcery. Upon her head a mark was found. It was piereced, first on one side and then on the other; one side bled but the other did not. Seventy or eighty persons passed before her, charging her with the crime of sorcery, therefore she was condemned by justice to be hanged and strangled, and her body to be broken and committed to the flames until it was reduced to ashes. She remained obdurate to the end, and confessed nothing. The execution was carried out on the 15th day of June, 1648."

About 70 years later, from this land of beauty, tragedy, mystery and charm, Daniel and Amice Grandin came to America and settled in East Jersey.

LE BROCQ

Arms: Gules, on a bend between two fleur-de-lis or, a lion passant gules, holding a weapon in his forepaw.
Crest: Issuing out of a crown or, a demi lion rampant, holding a weapon in his forepaw.

Arms used by the family of Rachel Le Brocq (Brook or Brock), mother of Daniel Grandin. He came from the Isle of Jersey and settled near Freehold, East Jersey, about the year 1717.

The arms were copied from a large seal used in America for many years on family documents and engraved on the silver service of some of Sarah Grandin's descendants.

The Grandin Family in Colonial Days

The earliest known acestor of the American branch of the Grandin family was

I. PETER GRANDIN. He lived on the Isle of Jersey and was the father of

II. ELIE GRANDIN, who was born about the year 1600. He lived in St. Ouen's Parish, in the western part of the Island. The church dates back to the year 1130. The following is a translation from the French of a part of the record of St. Ouen's Church:

"1662—A little before was buried Elie Grandin which was on the 18th July 1662 with a sermon preached by Mr. Gruchy and reading at the grave of the Book of Common Prayer of the Church of England."

He married, about the year 1630, JEANNE DUREL. The record continues:

"1662—The 27th August was buried Jeanne Durel, wife of Elie Grandin." They were the parents of

III. ELIE GRANDIN, born about the year 1631, and buried at St. Ouen's Church 21 January 1693/4. Prior to 1752 under English rule the year began March 25th. His wife, whom he married 27 November 1655 was ANN BARBIER. They were the parents of two sons, Elie and

IV. DANIEL GRANDIN, who was baptized 13 April 1656. His godfather was his grandfather Elie Grandin. Daniel seems to have died after 6 May 1711, when his son Rolin was baptized and recorded at St. Ouen's Church as "son of Daniel Grandin," and before 28 November 1719, when an entry was made regarding his son Rolin's death which describes him as "son of the late Daniel Grandin." According to the same record:

"1694—Sunday in the morning the 9th of September were married DANIEL GRANDIN, son of Elie, and RACHEL LE BROCQ."

The five children of Daniel Grandin and his wife Rachel Le Brocq, all baptized at St. Peter's Church, which dates back to the year 1167, were:

(a) DANIEL GRANDIN, baptized 3 January 1694/5. He later came to America.

A translation from the French of his baptismal certificate was given on 31 August 1931, by the Rev. Francis de Gruchy, the Rector of St. Peter's Church, Jersey, as follows:

"1694 January; Daniel Grandin son of Daniel, was presented for baptism by Amyce Grandin and his mother the 3rd day of January."

(b) ELIE GRANDIN, baptized 4 August 1700. Some of his descendants are still living on the Isle of Jersey.

(c) AMICE (Amyas) GRANDIN, baptized 29 March 1703. He came with his brother to America. A translation of his baptismal record was also given by Mr. de Gruchy as follows:

"1703 March; Amyas, son of Daniel Grandin, was presented for baptism by Amyas Grandin and his wife the 29th of March."

(d) PHILIP GRANDIN, baptized 7 April 1709, died 19 August 1722.

(e) ROLIN GRANDIN, baptized 6 May 1711. He died 28 November 1719, at which time the reference to his father's prior death was written.

In or about the year 1717, when AMICE was about 14, and DANIEL was about 22 years of age, these two brothers, apparently soon after their father's death, emigrated to America and settled in East Jersey.

AMICE GRANDIN, the pioneer (third son of Daniel and Rachel), was born as has been said on the Isle of Jersey and baptized at St. Peter's Church 29 March 1703. He married Patience Throckmorton (sister of his brother's wife Mary) by license dated 23 September 1732. She died before 27 March 1755, as her sister Sarah Nichols in her will refers to her as "my sister Patience Grandin deceased." Amice lived at Freehold, N. J., and later removed to Morris County. Their five children:

(a) Sarah Grandin, baptized at Freehold 11 May 1735.

(b) John Grandin, married Elizabeth Shepherd and had John Grandin, born 1781.

(c) Rachel Grandin.

(d) Amos Grandin, born about 1746. At Mount Pleasant Cemetery, Flanders, N. J., there is a gravestone with this inscription: "Here rests from his labors Amos Grandin who died Jan. 13, 1817, aged 71 years, 9 months. Whose Industry and Frugality, whose Honesty and Piety were long an example to the public. Rev. 14:13."

(e) Daniel Grandin, married Margaret.

DANIEL GRANDIN the pioneer (eldest son of Daniel and Rachel) was born, as has been said, on the Isle of Jersey, and baptized at St. Peter's Church 3 January 1694/5. He was a member of the Church of England. He came to the New World and settled at Colts Neck, Monmouth County, in the province of East Jersey.

On 23 September 1720, a deed executed by Richard Salter, was recorded in Book F, page 173, for the consideration of £113 8s 5d, conveying to Daniel Grandin forty acres of land "at Freehold in the County of Monmouth, in the late purchase called by the Indian name Passequenecka: Beginning at a black oak marked on four sides standing on the south side of Burlington Path, being George Corlies east corner tree . . . . bounded southerly by lands formerly of George Corlies, northerly by land late of John Powell, now Richard Salter, which is a part of said tract formerly patented to Robert Barclay, and by his attorney John Reid, Esq., sold and confirmed unto John Hamton, deceased, by deed bearing date 10 August 1688, and bounded westerly by Burlington Path, and easterly by Passequenecqua Brook."

Our knowledge of early real estate transfers is greatly limited owing to the fact that property owners too often failed to go to the trouble or expense of having their deeds recorded. Then too, many of the early deed books are now missing.

From various deeds recorded at Freehold we learn that portions of this tract of land were conveyed by Daniel Grandin as follows:

On 23 January 1729, a part to his sister-in-law Sarah Powell, nee Throckmorton; on 7 March 1731, a part to John Tenton; on 14 November 1734, a part to Jacob Mons. After Daniel Grandin's death his executors, William and Amy Grandin and Samuel and Sarah Cooper, conveyed on 3 June 1797, a part to Peter Wykoff. The same executors on 12 May 1804 conveyed a part to William Jackson who had married Rachel Grandin, sister of William and a granddaughter of Daniel, as was Sarah Cooper.

In the account of the recapture of Phil White, a prisoner under guard for participating with a party of refugees from Sandy Hook in the murder of John Rossell on the 30th of April, 1780, it is stated: "as White was being taken from Colts Neck to Freehold, when they reached a field next the woods between Daniel Grandin's the younger and Samuel Leonard's (or Lippincott's), he attempted to escape and was recaptured and killed by Lieutenant Rhea and George Brinley."

In surveys about the year 1755 recorded in the Proprietor's office, Perth Amboy, of land in what is now Brick Township, Ocean

County, "Grandin's Folly" is occasionally referred to as a landmark. No explanation is given of the origin of this term.

According to Hunterdon County records, Daniel Grandin was admitted to the New Jersey bar 6 June 1721 and continued to practice law until about 1739. Mr. Snell in his History of Hunterdon County, states that Daniel Grandin was also a Judge.

The will of Joseph Jewel, 12 April 1729, mentions debts to be paid to Daniel Grandine. On 24 November 1729, Daniel and his brother Amice both witnessed the will, which he may also have prepared, now on file at Trenton, of Dr. William Nichols who had married his wife's sister Sarah Throckmorton, widow of John Powell, upon which the signatures of both Daniel and Amice may be seen.

The library of Abel Morgan which was for many years kept in the parsonage of the Baptist Church at Middletown, N. J., and later moved to Peddie Institute, Hightstown, N. J., contains a book in which upon a blank leaf from time to time the following entries have been written:

"Samuel Grandin
Daniel Grandin
Bought of ye Rever'd Mr. Ch. Smith, pd. 16s.

Bought at a public vendue of Mr. Grandin's goods 1742, By Richard Mount who let me have this book for my use till he calls for it. —Abel Morgan

Daniel Grandin—his book, 1742."

The above memoranda may indicate that Daniel Grandin died during the year 1742 at which time he was about 47 years of age.

In 1719 or 1720, when he was about 25 years of age, Daniel Grandin married Mary Throckmorton. She was born 19 October 1695 and, according to the old family Bible, in possession of Prof. J. S. Kingsley, she "departed this life on wednesday the 26 day of september 1739 half an hour past 3 o'clock in the morning aged 44 years daughter of Job and Sarah."

Her father Job Throckmorton was born 30 September 1650 and died 20 August 1709. His gravestone may be seen in the ancient burying ground near Middletown.

Her mother SARAH LEONARD (page 258) was born 30 May 1660, and died at 10 o'clock at night 5 February 1743/4. Her gravestone may be seen at Christ Church, Shrewsbury.

Mary Throckmorton's sister, Patience, became the wife of Daniel's brother Amice Grandin.

The record of the children of Daniel Grandin and his wife, Mary

Throckmorton, is taken from two old Grandin family Bibles, one kept at Hamden, and the other in possession of Prof. J. S. Kingsley; from Sarah Nichols' will recorded in Book F, page 279, at Trenton; from records of Christ Church, Shrewsbury; and from tombstones in the Old Topanemus Graveyard on the farm of John Vandevere at Marlboro, about three miles northeast of the present town of Freehold.

Daniel Grandin and Mary Throckmorton had eight children as follows:

(a) (Judge) John Grandin, born 28 April 1721, married Abigail Lippincott.

(b) Daniel Grandin, born 11 May 1723, married his cousin Sarah Throckmorton.

(c) William Grandin of Trenton, born about 1724; died in the afternoon 1 October and buried 6 October 1747 at Christ Church, Shrewsbury. Of him nothing further is known.

(d) (Judge) Samuel Grandin, born about 1726, married Susannah Johnston.

Lewis Grandin. It may be that Lewis Grandin (who being "of full age" was granted a license on 16 November 1749 to marry Catharine Van Dyke, both of Staten Island, and who therefore was born about 1728 or earlier) was a brother in this family, but of this no proof is at hand.

On 5 August 1753, John Grandin, son of Lewis Grandin, was baptized according to records of St. Andrew's Church, Richmond. This church was built 1709.

[Letters of Administration on the estate of Lewis Grondine, mariner, deceased, were issued in Richmond County, on 13 August 1792 to John Grondine.

On the same day and place Letters on the estate of Samuel Grondine of Southfield were issued to Paul Micheau of Westfield.]

(e) (Major) Philip Grandin, born 14 August 1731; married Eleanor Forman.

(f) Mary Grandin, born Wednesday 20 October 1736. By New York license dated 7 October 1768, she married Matthias Swaine.

(g and h) Joseph and Job Grandin, twins born 19 September 1739 and both died on the same day as their mother, 26 September 1739.

Three American post offices have been named Grandin. They are located in Florida, Missouri and North Dakota.

(To be continued)

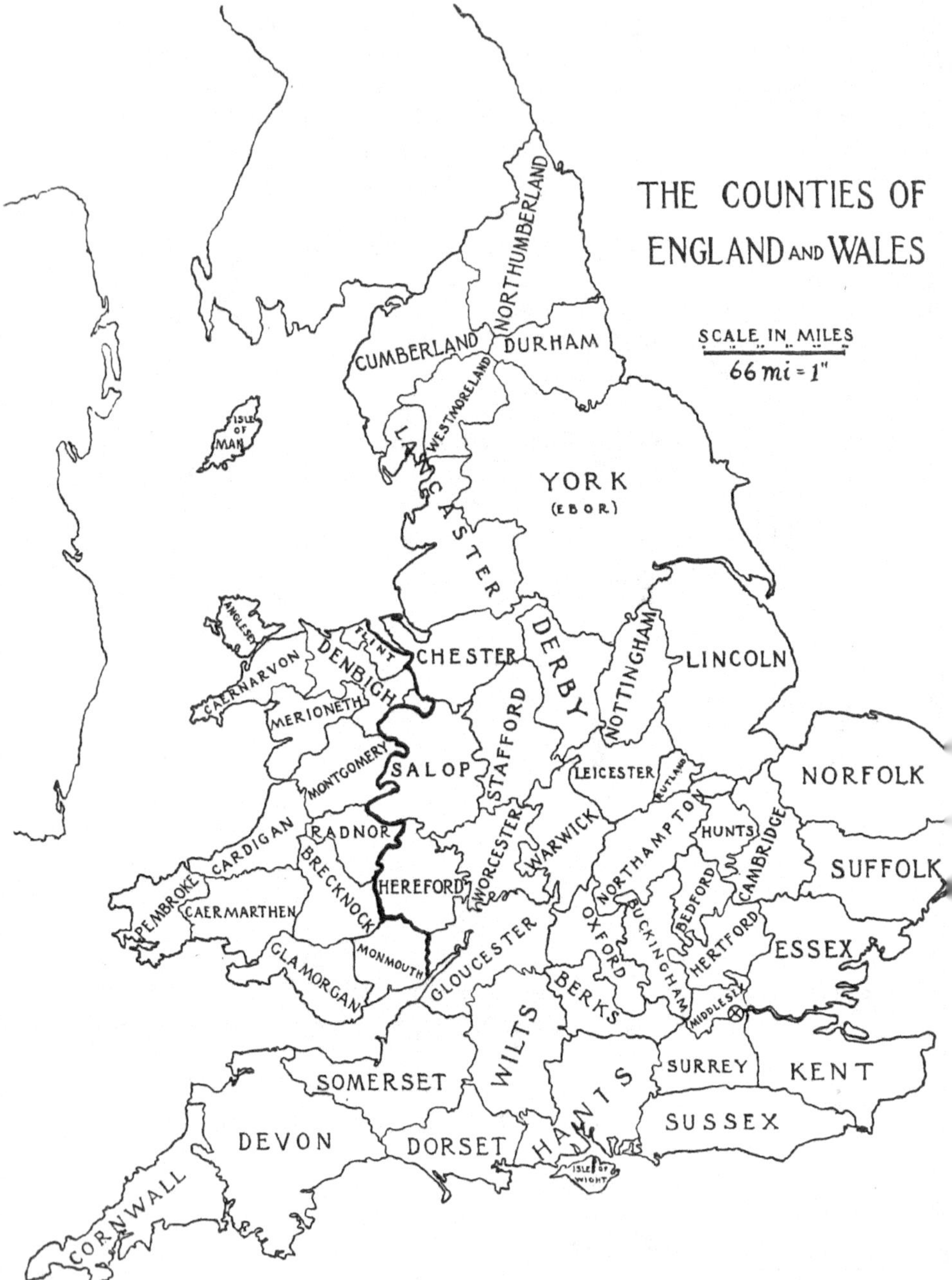
THE COUNTIES OF
ENGLAND AND WALES
SCALE IN MILES
66 mi = 1"
NORTHUMBERLAND
CUMBERLAND
DURHAM
WESTMORELAND
ISLE OF MAN
LANCASTER
YORK
(EBOR)
ANGLESEY
FLINT
DENBIGH
CHESTER
DERBY
NOTTINGHAM
LINCOLN
CAERNARVON
MERIONETH
SALOP
STAFFORD
MONTGOMERY
LEICESTER
RUTLAND
NORFOLK
RADNOR
WARWICK
NORTHAMPTON
HUNTS
CAMBRIDGE
SUFFOLK
CARDIGAN
BRECKNOCK
HEREFORD
WORCESTER
PEMBROKE
CAERMARTHEN
BEDFORD
OXFORD
BUCKINGHAM
HERTFORD
ESSEX
GLOUCESTER
MONMOUTH
GLAMORGAN
BERKS
MIDDLESEX
WILTS
SOMERSET
SURREY
KENT
HANTS
SUSSEX
DEVON
DORSET
ISLE OF WIGHT
CORNWALL

FIRST INDEX

The Surety Barons have been presented in alphabetical order. The Knights of the Garter are in the order of their initiation. The figures in this index refer to the pages of the book.

Abergavenny 226
Abraham 150
Abrichecourt 238
Acklen 92
Acre 216
Adams 51, 57, 106, 111
Aedd 158, 218
Agerton 61
Aiofe 190
Albini, 39-42, 108, 122, 123, 189, 231
Albret 226
Aldeburgh 229
Alencon 212
Alexander III 214
Alfred the Great 111, 171, 189
Allen 75, 92, 106, 111, 125
Allison 106
Alphonso 208, 211
Amorie 48, 70
Amos 127
Anable 111
Anderson, 57, 106, 121, 125, 127, 158, 160
Andrews 57, 111
Andrus 87
Angouleme 224
Anjou 164, 168, 183, 194
Anne of Russia 185, 186
Anthony 158
Antwerp 218, 228
Appleman 127
Appleton 92
Aquila 89
Aquitaine 195, 202, 206
Aragon 206, 208, 216
Arbitot 204
Archer 71
Arches 96
Arderne 235
Aregwedd 155
Argentine 130, 133
Arndt 92
Arnulph 183, 212
Arrington 121
Arthur 6, 163, 169, 202, 220
Artois 203
Artz 46
Arundel 132, 137
Arviragus 158, 162
Atherton 125
Athol 118
Atlee 95
Atyes 144
Aubigney 106, 107
Audenried 61
Audley 74, 227, 228, 237
Augsbury 43
Augustus 155, 160, 161
Auld 92
Aumale 82, 211, 212
Austin 95
Avenel 97
Avenne 47
Avery 75, 92
Aylesbury 86

Babcock 43, 111
Bache 106
Badger 106, 127
Badlesmere 55, 68, 113, 124, 230
Bahl 51
Baird 39, 121
Baker 46
Baldwin, 110, 125, 183, 185, 186, 210
Baliol 67, 73, 78, 93
Ball 95, 111
Ballentine 125
Bar 216
Baratta 39, 121
Barbour 39

INDEX

Barcelona 210
Barclay 46, 121
Bardolph 70, 226
Barnett 106
Barre 131
Barrett 57
Barrow 61
Basset, 47, 49, 86, 96, 118, 128, 129, 137, 226
Bates 51
Baton 71
Battle 127
Bavaria 225
Bayard 46, 87
Baylies 39, 51
Bayne 39
Beach 57
Beadleston 46
Beardsley 71, 87
Beatty 125
Beaty 106
Beauchamp, 49, 97, 98, 99, 108, 118, 126, 132, 203, 204, 225, 226, 227, 230
Beaufort 74, 193
Beaumont 59, 70, 133, 225
Beauple 236
Bechtel 57
Beck 46
Beebe 75
Behr 127
Beke 113
Belesme 205
Beli 159
Bell 127
Bellomont 112, 113, 185, 186
Below 57
Benedict 57
Benenson 127
Bennett 39
Bereford 133
Berengaria 211
Berenger 187, 210
Berkeley 114, 115, 119
Bermichan 94
Bethune 82, 103
Betun 59
Beutel 111
Bevan 46. 51
Bierbower 61
Bigelow 51, 87, 92
Biggs 61
Bigod, 7, 43-50, 56, 70, 93, 101, 103, 124, 126, 205, 225, 228, 229, 230
Biset 96
Biseth 42
Bissell 39, 51, 61, 87, 106, 127
Blackmer 61
Black Prince 218, 224
Blake 87
Bland 57
Blatchley 43
Blois 204
Blood 111
Boadicea 149, 156, 158, 162, 218
Boaz 158
Boden 75, 125
Bohun, 51-56, 68, 78, 79, 93, 97, 100, 114, 117, 125, 130, 132, 192, 216, 219, 225, 230, 231
Bolebec 129
Bonham 61
Bonquentine 133
Boogher 39
Boone 43, 125
Booth 92
Bordeaux 224
Boteler 133
Botetourt 119, 233
Botiller 50
Bourgogne 212
Boutros 57
Bowdry 71
Bowen 75, 125
Boyce 71
Bracebridge 81
Brackett 39
Bradley 57
Bramham 61, 87, 125
Bran 54, 155, 160
Braos, 45, 48, 53, 59, 60, 103, 109, 117, 119, 204
Bray 71
Brereton 57, 111
Bretagne 183, 194, 212
Brethrick 170
Brewer 43, 87

INDEX

Brinton 75
Brionne 182
Brittany 232
Britton 46
Brooke 111
Brown 43, 51, 57, 92, 95, 111
Browning 2
Bruce, 54, 62, 63, 64, 65, 93, 124, 192, 193, 217
Brun 70, 108, 115, 130, 187, 205
Brune 49, 103
Brunson 125
Bryan 95, 127, 133
Bryant 57
Brydain 158
Buch 226
Buchan 57, 111
Buck 92
Buckman 127
Bullard 92
Bulley 51
Bures 97
Burgh, 48, 50, 65, 66, 67, 70, 71, 72, 78, 92, 93, 94, 117, 135, 137, 193, 203, 218
Burghersh 229, 231, 233, 239
Burgundy 208
Burke 21
Burkhardt 167
Burley 227
Burnet 17, 47
Burnham 39
Burt 87
Busch 43, 111, 125
Bush 178
Buteville 42
Butler 56
Butterfield 39
Buttolph 75
Button 57
Byrd 57

Cadvan 162
Cadwalader 39, 121
Cadwallader 75, 160
Caesar 151, 153, 154, 159, 161, 162
Callaway 92, 95
Campbell 43, 65
Camville 90, 108
Cancelles 144
Canfield 92
Cantacuzene 125
Cantilupe 59, 90, 112, 128
Canute 177
Capet, 71, 167, 184, 186, 189, 212
Capp 51
Caractacus 160
Caradoc 155, 156, 158, 160, 162
Carew 132
Carloman 178
Carmine 46
Carpenter 43, 71, 127
Carrell 51
Carrick 64, 192
Carruth 111
Carter 46, 92, 125
Case 51
Cashman 127
Castile 202, 207, 209, 211, 215
Castle 71
Caswallon 154, 159, 162
Catherwood 46
Caunton 79
Cecil 71
Cerdic 169
Chandler 57
Chandos 236
Chapin 95
Chappell 51
Charlemagne, 25, 39, 112, 167, 170, 178, 188, 189, 209, 212
Charles II 210
Charlton 120
Chase 75
Chatterton 87
Chaumont 122
Chauncey 48
Chaworth 102, 203, 204
Cheney 72
Cherlton 227
Chesney 43
Chester 45, 114
Chetwode 98
Chew 51, 106
Cheyney 126
Child 127
Childeric III 166
Childress 71

INDEX

Childs 95, 106
Chiles 57
Chilperic 206
Christopher 125
Chubbuck 43, 46
Churchill 39, 92
Claflin 39
Clare, 44, 48, 49, 55, 57-70, 74, 89, 90, 94, 102, 103, 108, 110, 115, 118, 119, 124, 132, 167, 182, 185, 192, 227, 228
Clark 43, 75, 87, 125
Clarke 51, 57
Claudius 154, 156
Clay 92
Claypool 125
Clement 92
Clermont 58, 128, 186, 189
Cleves 212
Clifford 49, 68, 78, 115, 124, 226
Clinton 80, 81, 126
Clivedon 115
Clopton 121
Closson 57
Clovis 95, 165, 206, 209
Coel, see Cole
Coggan 236
Coil 121
Coit 92
Cokesay 226
Cole 111, 160, 162, 164, 190
Coleman 92
Coleville 59
Colgate 71
Colket 46
Collins 71, 121, 125
Collison 39
Comly 87
Comyn 63, 113, 123
Conable 87
Conaway 106
Condict 46
Condit 57
Confessor 136, 195
Conlon 61
Conquest 234
Constantine 163, 191
Conteville 195
Converse 71
Conway 51, 61
Cooch 127
Cook 106, 178
Cooke 121
Cooley 121
Cooper 92, 106
Cope 87
Corbet 57
Corbett 113
Corbin 61
Corner 43, 46
Cornman 39
Cory 95
Cotton 19
Couci 219
Coulson 111
Courtenay 46, 56, 129, 231, 232
Cox 75, 121
Coxe 75
Craig 87
Craighead 43
Cramer 111
Crane 46
Crary 39, 75, 87, 127
Crawford 51, 71
Cregar 46
Crerar 71
Cressi 129
Cresson 46, 127
Crispin 39, 96, 121, 182
Crissey 106
Crittenden 51
Crocker 95
Cromwell 50
Cron 57
Crosby 57
Croskey 127
Crouchback 187, 203
Cunynghame 64
Curry 125
Curthose 88
Curtiss 92
Cusack 49
Cygoyney 144
Cyllinus 160
Cymbeline 155, 162
Cymry 149, 158
Cynon 160

INDEX

Cynric 169
Cynvelin 155, 162

Dagworth 56, 79
Dammartin 211, 212
Daniel 92
Darcy 93, 124, 134
Darneal 39
Dart 46
Dashiell 125
Daubeney 137
Davenport 75
David 51, 113, 218
Davidson 43
Davis 87
Day 106
Deatrick 71
de Forest 57
de Groot 75
Deincourt 74, 124
Delano 106
Del Isle 78, 79
de Lorenzi 84, 121
De Mare 39
de Miege 125
Deming 43
Denbeigh 91
Denby 43, 91
Denison 51, 57
Denmark 164
Denton 95
de Peyster 127
Derby 55
Desiderius 179
Desmond 227
Despencer, 45, 47, 54, 55, 70, 109, 114, 118, 129, 132, 204, 217, 230
de Trampe 106
Devereux 133
Devon 231
de Vou 178
Dial 57, 87
Diaz 71
Dickinson 43, 46, 51, 57, 111
Dille 95
Dinefur 59
Dingley 71
Dixon 87, 111
Doak 57
Doan 61
Doane 39, 111, 127
Dobbins 106
Dodd 125
Dodge 92, 95
Dodo 206
Dolan 95
Domitian 156
Donald I 121
Donner 57
Doolittle 39, 121
Douglas 63, 92
Douglass 84, 95, 121, 127
Dover 80
Draper 71, 84
Drexel 87
Driscoll 43
Drummond 193
Duane 111
Dudley 46, 61, 75
Dulles 57
du Marais 57
Dunbar 63, 64
Duncan 92, 191
Dunklee 51
Dunn 61
Dunstan 61
du Pont 39, 121, 125
Dupree 87
Dutton 90, 91, 134
Duval 71
Dye 111

Earle 46
Earll 92
Eaton 39, 43, 111
Eckel 87, 111
Edenton 39
Edgar 176
Edmund 176, 177
Edward I, 54, 168, 187, 192, 203, 211, 213
Edward II, 63, 168, 187, 193, 213, 217, 218
Edward III 63, 84, 168, 193, 220
Edwards 57
Egbert 127, 170
Egger 61, 127

Elizabeth 39
Elliott 127
Ellis 51, 87
Eltham 217
Elwell 57, 75
Ely 71
Engaine 78, 85, 86
Enne 238
Ennis 71, 121
Enreux 102
Erskine 62
Ervien 57, 61
Ervin 61, 95
Erwin 127
Espec 121, 122
Essex 128
Estill 57
Esty 43
Ethelred II 43, 175, 177
Ethelwulf 170
Ettelson 57, 61
Eu 53, 58, 182
Eudes 206
Eurgain 160
Eurgen 162
Eustis 87
Evans 111, 178
Evereux 52, 164
Eye 238
Eyre 111, 127

Fairchild 43
Fairfax 106
Fairhaven 15
Faithorn 111
Falaise 183, 195
Faries 39
Fauconberge 123
Felner 46, 127
Fennell 121
Fenno 87
Fergus 190
Ferguson 111
Fergusson 43
Ferrers, 48, 54, 78, 97, 98, 103, 113, 114, 136, 219, 225
Ferres 127
Fewell 71
Field 95
Fiennes 162
FitzAlan, 55, 131, 132, 203, 205, 228, 232, 233, 234
FitzEustace 88
FitzGeoffrey 49, 50, 93
FitzGerald 15, 93, 137
FitzGilbert 58, 75, 182
FitzHerbert 99, 137
FitzHugh 80, 137
FitzJohn 49, 116, 204
FitzMaurice 68
FitzMorice 114, 116, 117
FitzNigel 72
FitzOsborn 196
FitzPayn 133
FitzPiers 53, 98, 100, 123
FitzRandolph 71
FitzReynold 99
FitzRichard 58
FitzRobert 44, 59, 71-74, 219
FitzSimon 233
FitzSwaine 104
FitzThomas 50, 94, 116
FitzWalter, 9, 12, 18, 56, 75-81, 93, 94, 105, 112, 117, 126, 133, 135, 231, 233
FitzWarren 134
Flick 106
Flitner 75
Fluker 111
Folger 51
Foliot 132
Forbes 39
Fornof 39
Forsythe 95
Fortibus 82, 98, 105, 203
Fortson 51
Foster 111
Fournoux 86
Fowler 51
Fownes 46
Fox 92, 106, 121
Foxcote 98
Franconia 164
Fraser 65
Freeman 95
Freiot 84
Frellsen 57
Frenes 90

INDEX

Frissell 75
Frye 95
Fuller 111, 121
Fullinweider 125
Fulstow 87
Fulton 57, 61
Furnival 48, 49, 74, 204

Gadarn 150
Gallaher 61
Galloway 137
Gam 62
Gand 110
Gant 88, 186
Garcia 107, 209
Gardner 125
Garner 57
Gascony 206
Gates 111
Gaunt 219, 225
Gaveston 54, 70, 109, 131
Gaylord 51
Geneville 49, 115
Geoffrey, see also Plantagenet, 6, 200
George VI 43
Gernon 60
Gerrard 132
Gerth 75
Ghent 128
Ghisnes 128
Gibbs 57
Gibson 127
Giddings 111
Gifford 42, 129
Gilbert 92
Gilbertson 54
Gilkey 95
Gill 61, 71
Gilpin 17, 71, 75
Glanville 85, 122
Glass 57, 61
Glenn 121
Gloucester 52, 55, 59, 219
Godley 61
Godwin 43, 111
Golafre 231
Goodman 111
Goodwin 111
Goodwin-Perkins 51
Gordon 57, 92, 121
Gordon-Smith 95
Gourney 107
Graham 64
Grailly 226
Grandin 39, 57, 75, 92, 121
Grantesmesnil 44, 112, 186
Grattan 127
Graves 71
Gray 75, 87, 106, 124
Green 84
Greene 119
Greenough 125
Greinville 85
Gren 125
Grenville 94
Greslei 93, 94
Gressinghall 84
Grey, 66, 80, 85, 117, 118, 130, 229, 233
Greystock 74
Gribbel 51
Griest 106
Griffiss 57
Griscom 75, 95
Groves 57
Grundy 87, 95
Gueldres 217
Guelph 167
Gunnett 61
Guthrun 174

Hacker 121
Hainault 167, 186, 218
Haines 43, 61, 127
Halifax 127
Hall 57, 61, 87
Hallowell 57, 61, 71, 75
Halys 216
Hamblen 61
Hamilton 64
Hamlin 75
Hammond 75, 121
Hampton 94
Hancock 61
Hanger 71
Hanna 127
Hannay 75
Harcourt 45, 112, 113, 119, 233

INDEX

Hardell 83
Hardwick 46
Hare 46, 61
Harmar 71
Harold 95, 195, 197
Harper 106, 121
Harrington 236
Harris 61, 75, 111
Harrison 43, 51, 57, 87, 95, 106
Hart 121
Hartman 46
Harvey 111, 127
Harwood 127
Hasbania 167
Hast 51
Hastings 44, 45, 59, 112, 219
Hatch 57
Hatcher 61
Hatfield 111, 218
Hauteville 210
Hawkins 121
Hawley 75
Hawthorne 87
Hay 43
Haya 85
Hayward 106
Hazen 111
Hebard 46, 71
Henderson 39, 92, 106, 121
Henry 39, 92, 95
Henry I 168, 192, 199, 200
Henry II 168, 193, 201, 202
Henry III 168, 202, 206, 208
Herbert 61, 182, 183
Heristal 166
Heron 93
Herrick 46, 75
Herrin 43
Hersey 43
Heveningham 131
Hewett 95
Heyl 106
Higgins 95
Higgons 95
High 121
Hightower 43
Hill 61, 95, 111, 127, 178
Hinshaw 87
Hires 127
Hoag 71
Hoard 111
Hobrugg 85
Hodge 111
Hodges 178
Hodgkins 51
Hoggett 95
Hohn 84
Holbrook 127
Holand, 120, 132, 219, 224, 232, 237
Holland 216, 218
Holloway 121
Holmes 46
Holt 43, 71, 111
Holton 95
Hooker 121
Hooper 125
Hoopes 121
Hopkins 111
Hopkinson 71, 75
Hord 43, 46
Hornor 39
Horton 61
Houston 106
Howry 92
Hugh Magnus 185
Hume 92
Huntingdon, 45, 52, 62, 112, 192, 205, 232
Huntingfield 77, 84-86
Hussong 111, 121
Huston 46
Hutchins 61

Ingersoll 39
Ingham 234
Irevy 62
Irvine 57
Isaacs 65
Ivy 61

Jacobs 125
James I 193
Jameson 127
Jarden 61
Jeanes 111
Jenkins 127
Jerusalem 201

INDEX

Jesus 161, 165
Jewett 71, 121
John 7, 13, 16, 22, 202, 211
Johnson 39, 43, 46, 92, 111, 127
Johnston 43, 106, 178
Jones 43, 46, 61, 95, 111, 127
Jost 111
Joy 43

Kains 75
Kaplanoff 39, 121, 127
Karlomann 166
Keim 87
Keith 57, 61, 64, 65
Kendal 17
Kennedy 61
Kenneth 125, 191
Kent 57, 75, 111, 232
Ketchum 61
Keveliok 113, 192
Kilbourne 87
Kimball 111, 121
King 46, 51, 75
Kinnison 71, 121
Kirk 106
Kirkhuff 111
Knight 71, 111
Knolles 79
Knorr 92
Knott 61
Knowles 127
Knox 46, 51
Knyvett 86
Kopperl 95
Kothe 51
Kouwenbergh 57
Kruger 46, 111
Kuhn 106, 111
Kutz 75

Lacie, 48, 51, 59, 68, 87-91, 105, 107, 113, 228
Lacy 43
Laigle 107
Laing 61
Laird 43, 121
Lammers 43
Lancaster 203, 204, 219, 224, 227
Landon 111
Lane 111
Langley 219
Langton 10, 15
Lansing 106
Lanterman 75
Lanvallei 50, 70, 78, 92-94, 218
Lathrop 43, 46, 51, 57, 61
Lathrope 51
Latimer 74
Laubach 125
Laud 16
Layton 51
Lea 92
Leach 111
Lear 160, 162
LeBoutillier 39, 121
Lednum 92
Leet 111
Leete 57
LeFavour 125
Lennig 75, 87, 92
Leon 208, 211
Leopold 46
Leslie 57, 64
Leupold 95
Levick 71
Levis 43
Lewis 46, 51, 87, 111, 127
Leybourne 50, 114, 126
Leycester 91
Lindsay 62
Lindsey 127
Link 84
Linus 160
Lippitt 43, 111
Lisle 57, 130, 229
Lisours 72, 88
Little 92
Littlejohn 39
Llewellyn 59, 69
Lloyd 39, 43
Locke 75
Lockwood 57, 111
Lohman 51
Long 57, 61
Longesepee 77, 90, 120, 136
Longsword 182, 194
Lorimer 46
Lorraine 216

INDEX

Loryng 235
Louis I 61, 167, 184, 188, 210
Louis II 106
Louis IV 188
Louis VI 186, 187
Louis VII 202, 212
Louis VIII 187, 203
Louis IX 208
Loundres 49
Lovain(e) 117, 133
Loveland 39
Lovering 75
Lowry 95
Lubbe 39
Luce 46
Lucius 160, 162
Lucy 94
Luke 43
Lutz 92
Lyman 111
Lyons 46, 95

MacArthur 57
Macbeth 191
MacCubbin 57
MacDonal 113
Macke 87
Mackenzie 46, 75, 111
MacLean 57
Macneil 127
MacPhiores 79
Maddock 57
Maddox 75, 87
Malcolm III, Canmore, 62, 87, 168, 177, 187, 191, 200
Malet 84, 95-99, 117
Malley 51, 71
Maltby 39
Maltravers 132
Maminot 125
Mancill 87
Mandeville 77, 100, 101, 125
Mangam 92
Mann 57, 95
Mar 62, 65, 193
Marble 75
Marc 144
March(e) 205, 210, 228
Marius 158, 162
Marmion 80, 233
Marsh 43, 46, 92, 111
Marshall, 12, 17, 23, 47, 52, 53, 62, 72, 82, 89, 102, 103, 108, 114, 137, 205
Martel 99, 166
Martin 57, 99
Martiny 144
Mary 46
Mathews 111
Matthew 8
Mauclerk 70
Mauduit 204
Mauley 41, 124
Maywood 84
McAdams 51
McArthur 111
McCain 43
McCall 127
McClinton 106
McCormick 95
McCoy 111
McCurdy 71
McDermott 87
McElroy 111
McGaw 125
McGee 46
McGill 46
McKaig 111
McKean 57
McKinney 61
McKnight 125
McPheeters 111
McPherson 51
McWatters 127
Meapham 175
Mears 51
Meek 46
Meetham 234
Megee 61
Meinill 93, 124
Menteth 62
Mercer 43
Merchant 92, 95
Meredith 61
Meric 158, 162
Merritt 39
Merz 43
Meschines 40, 58

Meullent 101, 185
Meyer 39
Meynell 78
Mielziner 106
Milan 218
Milham 57
Millard 61
Miller, 39, 46, 51, 71, 75, 87, 111, 121
Milne 43, 46
Milner 95
Mitchell 71
Mobberley 91
Moels 130
Moen 39
Mohun 79, 124, 228, 231
Monnette 39
Montacute 132, 227, 228, 231
Montalb 119
Montbegon 104
Montchensi 103
Montfichet 83, 105
Montford 226
Montfort 68, 130, 164, 194, 219
Montgomery 43, 51, 121
Monthermer 70
Montreuil 189, 212
Mook 57
Moore 46, 61, 95, 106, 127
Moreton 130
Morgan 61, 87, 92, 121, 152
Morley 79
Morris 39, 61, 111, 121
Morse 51
Mortimer, 48, 49, 68, 97, 115, 204, 218, 225, 228
Morton 95
Moulton 46, 60, 78
Mowbray 60, 62, 104, 106-109
Muir 43, 46, 125
Mulford 57
Multon 94, 109
Munia 207, 208, 209
Mure 193
Murray 57, 87
Muscegros 97, 114, 117
Musgrave 115
Myers 87, 106
Mylin 43, 87
Nagel 178
Napoleon 155
Narcissus 155
Naunton 134
Navarre 206, 208, 209
Neff 111
Neilson 71, 127
Nelson, 39, 43, 46, 51, 57, 61, 87, 95, 106, 111, 121, 127, 178
Nerford 131
Nero 156, 157
Nevill(e) 73, 74, 137, 219
Newcombe 71, 127
Niall 190
Northampton 55
Northen 87
Northwode 126
Norris 75
Norton 71
Norville 118
Norwich 86
Nott 43

O'Boyle 75
O'Brien 117
Odo 196
O'Gorman 51
Oliphant 65
O'Neill 51
Orcutt 46, 125
Ormonde 93
Otto 184
Oulla 178

Packard 71
Packer 106
Page 57, 61, 75, 92
Pagon 92
Paine 57, 127
Palmer 61
Pandulf 7
Paris 25, 40, 73, 77, 82, 89
Parish-Watson 57
Park 75
Parker 39, 51, 111, 127
Parrent 111
Parry 61, 71
Patterson 39
Patton 125

Paul 71
Paveley 239
Pedro 209
Pemberton 71
Pembroke 102, 114
Pembrugge 112
Pendragon 163
Penniman 43, 51
Pennypacker 43
Penrose 121
Pepin 166, 178, 182, 183
Pepper 46, 92
Percy 74, 78, 110
Perot 127
Perrow 71
Perry 43, 51, 71, 75, 125
Peshale 109
Peterson 87
Petronella 208, 210
Pettigrew 95, 127
Pettit 57, 61, 87
Peyvre 236
Philip 7, 22, 215, 217
Phillips, 43, 46, 51, 57, 71, 87, 95, 111, 127, 178
Pickett 71
Picot 96
Pinckeney 98
Pinckney 39
Pinkerton 46, 111
Pipes 71, 127
Pious 184, 185
Plantagenet, 44, 70, 83, 90, 94, 103, 109, 130, 131, 132, 168, 192, 200, 201, 203, 204, 205, 224, 228, 232
Plautius 155
Plumer 178
Poe 87
Polk 75
Pontfract 88
Ponthieu 189, 212
Poppa 182, 194
Porcher 61
Port 110
Porter 46, 75
Potter 75
Powell 127
Power 84
Powers 39
Poyntz 97
Praers 98
Prasutagus 156
Pratt 57
Preuss 39
Price 75
Pridgen 71
Prime 84
Probert 71
Provence 202, 206, 208
Pudens 156, 160
Pyle 57

Quincey, 10, 45, 52, 54, 66, 76, 89, 97, 111-120, 129, 219, 228, 232, 237

Radcliffe 92
Rader 57
Rainey 75
Raleigh 70
Randall 121
Randolph 43, 63, 64, 127
Rankin 57
Ransom 75
Redvers 129
Rees 235
Reeves 75
Reimers 39, 111
Rheinberger 51
Rhodes 75, 106, 125, 127
Rice 127
Rich 87, 92
Richard 6, 182, 194, 212, 232
Richards 39, 43, 75
Richardson 46, 51, 61, 121
Riddle 87
Ridgway 106
Riehl 57
Ringe 75
Ripley 178
Rippey 57
Risher 39
Ritchie 92
Rixford 51
Robbins 43
Roberts 39, 75, 111
Robertson 46, 92, 121

INDEX

Robins 39, 46, 51, 57, 87, 111, 121
Robinson 46, 75, 125
Rockey 71
Rockley 66, 119
Roelker 71
Roelt 218
Roger 11
Rogers 15, 57, 75
Rollo 182, 194
Rooke 121
Roos, 42, 67, 68, 121-124, 216, 227, 231
Roosevelt 61
Roppelay 137
Ross 61
Rouci 207
Rougemont 229
Rowe 46, 121
Rudolphy 51
Rundstrom 57
Rush 121
Rust 71
Ruth 158
Rutter 87
Ruxton 92

Safford 95
St. Arnulph 165
St. Boniface 167
St. Clotilde 165, 206
St. David 192
St. George 134, 221
St. Hillery 58
St. John 104, 130
St. Liz 40, 189
St. Maur 120
St. Neot 172
St. Paul 159, 160, 161, 232
St. Philibert 239
St. Pol 212
St. Quentin 80
St. Timothy 162
St. Walerie 59
Salisbury 120, 137, 227
Saluces 90
Sancho 207, 208, 209, 211
Sapp 106
Sappington 61
Satterlee 61
Satterwhite 57
Saunders 51
Saunford 130, 132, 133
Savage 51
Savoy 42, 208
Saye 53, 81, 100, 125, 126
Schermerhorn 95
Schoenfeld 111
Schwinbeck 51
Scot 113
Scott, 39, 43, 46, 51, 57, 61, 71, 92, 95, 106, 111, 121, 127, 178
Scoville 121
Scrope 80
Seamans 111
Sears 51
Segrave 117, 120
Selby 121
Selden 95, 106
Sellers 46
Semones 111
Senlis 84, 194
Separk 106
Sergeaux 132
Sexton 125
Seyburn 61, 127
Seydel 106
Shakespeare 7, 39, 94, 191, 220
Shelley 127
Sherard 95
Sherrerd 106
Shirer 95
Shirk 51, 127
Shoemaker 39, 46
Shrednick 121
Shrewsbury 205
Shryock 106
Sinkler 71
Sisson 111, 121
Skeel 111
Skeen 43
Slack 127
Slane 49
Slaughter 61
Slaymaker 51
Slayton 46
Smiser 106
Smith, 17, 39, 43, 46, 51, 71, 95, 111, 121

Smither 111
Snow 57, 61
Snowden 51, 92
Snyder 127
Solers 85
Somerset 222
Sorley 39
South 127
Spahr 39
Spain 127
Spalding 43, 106
Sparhawk 43, 127
Sparks 125
Spear 106
Speer 111
Spiney 122
Spining 111
Spofford 39
Sprague 111
Spring 111
Squire 57
Stackhouse 43
Stacy 39
Stafford 74, 124, 225, 226, 227
Stalfort 61
Stanhope 17
Stansfield 57, 111
Stapleton 234
Starin 127
Steele 111, 127
Steelman 46
Stein 43
Steinman 39, 121
Steinmetz 43
Sterne 111
Sterritt 57
Stevens 46
Steward 106
Stewart 39, 57, 62, 66, 193
Stiefel 71
Stilson 127
Stinchfield 106
Stiness 127
Stoll 92
Strange 90, 108, 132, 226, 227, 231
Strathbogie 65
Strawbridge 39
Strawn 106
Strong 46, 61
Strongbow 102
Stuart 39, 125
Sturdon 86
Stuteville 84, 107, 135
Sudler 106
Sudley 126
Suermondt 125
Sullivan 61, 95
Suppes 57
Surrey 204
Sutherland 65
Sutton 44
Sykes 95
Symmes 121

Tacitus 161
Taft 75, 222
Taggart 57
Taillefer 187
Talbot 57, 100, 111, 120
Taliaferro 61
Talvace 205
Tams 121
Tarver 61
Tarwater 127
Tatem 46
Tavistock 130
Taylor, 39, 43, 46, 61, 75, 92, 121, 125
Telford 111
Tempest 120
Temple 61
Tenuantius 162
Tennyson 128
Tertullian 153
Thiot 39
Thomas 43, 46, 61, 75, 95, 111
Thompson 51, 149
Thomson 39, 121
Thorn 95
Thornton 84
Throckmorton 92, 121
Thweng 123
Tibetot 68, 73, 124
Tierney 57, 87
Tilden 51
Tilghman 43, 71, 75
Till 87
Tillson 57

INDEX

Tilton 92
Tinkham 178
Todeni 39
Tonbridge 189
Tonebruge 58, 75, 128
Toni 53
Torrence 61, 92
Torreyson 106
Toulouse 182
Towles 121
Townsend 92
Townshend 75
Trabue 125
Troth 87
Troubetzkoy 92
True 111, 178
Trusbut 42, 122, 123
Tubman 51
Tull 39
Tunis 87
Tyson 135

Uerikon 167
Ufford 73, 132, 226
Ulcote 122
Ulster 120
Umfraville 42
Uracca 208, 209, 211
Urgel 210

Vail 127
Vail-Cloud 57
Val 88
Valence 45
Valentine 43
Valoines 77, 80, 121, 126
Valois 182, 194
VanCulin 39, 106, 121
Van de Mark 71
Vanderwerf 87
VanHeusen 125
VanRensselaer 92
Vanuxem 43, 71
Vaux 39, 124
Verdon 48, 70, 118, 206
Vere, 44, 55, 56, 68, 72, 78, 88, 112, 127-134, 205, 219
Vermandois 185, 189, 192, 205
Verner 43
Vernon 129
Verrill 51
Vesci 72, 135, 136
Viall 51, 127
Victoria 162
Vipount 49, 50
Vivonia 96, 97, 99
Vladimir 46
Vollnogle, 43, 46, 51, 57, 61, 71, 87, 95, 111, 127, 178

Wace 195
Wahul 97
Waite 51
Wake 113, 216
Walden 61
Wale 234
Waleries 204
Wales 51
Walker 39, 87, 111
Wallace 43, 71, 121
Waller 84
Wallingford 111
Wallis 106
Walsh 75
Walters 92
Wandel 106
Ward 111
Warde 78
Warder 39, 51
Waring 106, 121
Warre 94, 104, 109
Warren, 44, 75, 92, 108, 130, 131, 137, 187, 192, 199, 204, 205
Warrington 95
Warwick 225, 228, 230
Washburn 46, 51, 92, 111
Washington, 27, 39, 43, 46, 51, 61, 71, 87, 92, 95, 106, 111, 121, 127
Waters 106
Watmough 87
Watson 46, 125
Way 127
Wayne 95
Wear 51
Weaver 61, 87, 111
Webber 106
Weeks 178

Weightman 43
Weisiger 71
Welch 71, 95
Wells 95, 124, 136
Wendell 95
Werke 124
Westerlind 51
Weston 125
Wetherill 43, 46, 51, 61, 87, 127
Weyland 230
Wharton 75
Wheeler 87, 106, 111
Whitaker 39, 111, 127
White 43, 46, 51, 61
Whitehead 46, 75
Whitham 121
Whitney 95
Whitridge 127
Widener 46, 51
Wiener 87
Wiggin 95
Wiggins 127
Wightman 106
Wilberforce 61
Wilcox 43
Wilkins 111
William I, the Conqueror, 57, 168, 183, 195, 197, 212
William the Lion, 44, 112, 123, 124, 136
Williams 39, 43, 111, 125, 127
Williamson 106
Willing 87, 92
Wilmer 71
Wilson 39, 92, 95, 106, 111, 121
Winn 39
Winsor 92
Winter 39, 121
Wister 39, 121, 178
Witherspoon 61, 106
Wolfe 87
Wood 43, 46, 92
Woodbridge 111
Woodhull 127
Woodroe 75
Woods 95
Woodson 87
Woodstock 219
Woodward 92
Woolman 39, 75
Work 87
Worth 111
Worthington 61
Wright 95
Wrottesley 235
Wurts, 39, 43, 46, 51, 61, 71, 75, 87, 92, 95, 106, 111, 121, 125, 127, 178

Yarnall 75
Yeomans 71
Yorke 219, 231
Young, 39, 43, 46, 51, 61, 71, 75, 87, 92, 95, 106, 111, 121, 125, 127, 178

Zantzinger 127
Zouche, 70, 73, 80, 112, 113, 114, 115, 119

Browning 263
Grandin 293, 297
Halifax 264
Herndon 261
Holloway 241, 261
Hord 266
Le Brocq 296
Leonard 253
Lincoln 267
Sigourney 268
Whitcomb 261
Wurts 265

REMEMBER

December 7, 1941

In the beauty of the lilies, Christ was born across the sea,
With a glory in His bosom that transfigures you and me;
As He died to make men holy, let us die to make men free;
While God is marching on.

ADDITIONAL INDEX

Acklen 57
Acosta 270
Agerton 271
Allen 272, 274
Anderson:
Alice S. 106
Caroline T. 121
Cora M. S. 57
Emma W. 125
Helen G. B. 127
James 158, 160
Andrea 273
Armstrong 274
Atherton 270
Auld 273
Backus 270
Bailey 274
Ball 272, 274
Bamber 270
Banker 270
Bartlett 121
Bates 272
Baumann 273
Beach 271
Bell 271
Benedict 57, 121
Berry 271
Biddle 121
Bierbower 270, 272, 274
Blatherwick 270
Blinn 273
Boothe 274
Bordwell 270, 274
Bowen 75, 127
Bowie 39
Boyle 272
Brackett 273, 274
Braun 271
Brinton 274
Brown:
Cordelia A. 57
Florence B. M. 92
Helen C. 43
Helen M. 271
Inez H. 271
Juanita R. H. 111
Manning P. 51
Mary R. L. 95
Olive J. W. 270
Virginia C. 270
Browne 274
Bruer 121
Bryan 270, 274
Burnett 271, 274
Burns 271
Burt 270
Butts 272, 273
Cabell 272
Cafky 273
Canfield 270
Carrington 271
Carter 43, 46, 92, 125
Carton 270, 272
Channon 270

Chapline 272
Chapman 270
Childress 273
Christian 270
Clement 270
Clouser 272
Comer 270
Congdon 271
Connor 270
Cooke 272
Cope 271
Copeland 271
Courtenay 270, 271
Curtner 271
Cushman 274
Dahlgren 270
Dahm 272
Daniel 272
Daniell 272
Davidson 270, 272, 273, 274
Decies 271, 272, 274
Demarest 270
Deuble 270, 271
di Andrea 273
Dickerman 273
Dickinson:
Edward F. 272
Elijah 274
Louis A. 51
Nellie B. 57, 271
R. Clayton 46
Whittie 43, 111
Dixon 273
Doan 270, 271
Doebler 270
Donald I 191, 272
Donohoe 270, 273
Doolittle 270
Doyle 272
Dulles 271
Dunklee 270
Dykes 270
Earll 272
Early 273
Eggleston 270
Evans 271
Fairbanks 273
Fay 273
Ferrell 271
Ferres 271
Flack 274
Folger 270
Foote 71
Frazer 272
Froelich 274
Fulton 271
Gatchell 272
Gibson 61, 127
Gilson 271
Glauser 272
Goddard 271
Godwin 273
Graham 64, 95
Grandin:
Elizabeth 75
Elliot C. 121
Florence 57
F. Samuel 92
William J. 39
Gray:
Ada G. 75
Carl R. 111
Eleanor G. 87
Griest 111
Griffiss 270
Hadler 274
Hager 270
Harper 270, 271
Harrison:
Charles C. 43
Frances R. T. 95
George L. 87
Harry W. 51
John K. M. 57
John S. 106
Higgins 272
Hill 274
Holbrook 270, 271
Holt 273
Hugh Capet 184, 186, 270
Hunter 272, 273, 274
Hyman 270
Irwin 271
Jacobs 272
Jaroslaus 185
Jewett 271

Johnson:
Albert M. 46
Clara M. 43
Dolores N. 39
Howard C. 127
Jessamine S. 92
Katie E. F. 111
Jones:
Charles C. 43, 61
Franklin C. 46
Hilton I. 95
John C. 111
Livingston E. 127
Kaiser 272
Kaplanoff 270, 271, 272, 273
Kasson 274
Keith 272
Kelley 272
King 272
Knight 271
Knowlton 271
Kolb 272
Lambert 273, 274
Larsen 274
Layton 270, 271, 272, 273, 274
Le Gendre 273
Leitch 273
Lennig 272
Levey 270, 274
Levis 270
Link 270, 272
Littlejohn 270, 272, 273, 274
Lloyd 39, 43, 127, 271, 274
Logan 270
Long 271
Longman 270
Lusoriis 72, 88
MacCain 270
MacCubbin 271
Macke 273
Maltby 270
Mangas 274
Matthews 270, 273
McAdams 270
McClure 271
McCullough 274
McGill 272
Meech 272, 274
Meek 270
Miller:
Anna M. W. 46
Clara G. 75
Florence C. 39
Florence L. H. 111
Gertrude E. D. 87
Louise D. L. 71
Mary C. B. 51
Nathalie T. P. 121
Milligan 274
Minahan 271
Minot 273
Monroe 271
Moody 272
Moore 273
Morison 270
Morse 270, 272, 273, 274
Naylor 274
Nelson:
Flora E. S. 111
Gene W. 57, 106
Howard R. 39, 178, 271
Janet A. 127
Nero 156, 157, 161
Nutting 274
O'Donnell 271
Orcutt 270, 271, 272, 273, 274
Otwell 273
Overstreet 272
Park 273
Parker 274
Patterson 270, 272, 274
Pearce 273
Peck 272
Perry 270, 271, 272, 273, 274
Pettit 272
Petty 271
Phillips 43, 61, 178, 270
Pond 273
Price 273, 274
Railey 273
Randolph 271
Reynolds 272
Richardson 271
Rivers 271
Roberts 271, 273

Robins:
Arthur de B. 111
Edward 46
Ellis 39
George P. 57
Henry R. 87
Mary R. E. 121
William B. 51
Robinson 270, 274
Rogers 272, 273, 274
Rudolphy 272
Rust 274
Sadler 87
St. Swithin 170
Saunders 272
Scattergood 75
Schuh 75, 270
Schur 271, 272, 273
Scofield 87, 272
Scott:
Caroline T. T. 271
Carrie T. T. 75
Dora S. M. 43, 270, 271, 274
Dorothea S. M. 270
Elizabeth B. C. 71
Emma J. 57
Frances B. 274
Frances P. 43
Frederic R. 271
Helen I. C. 106
John M. 121
Mary L. L. 39, 75, 178
Randolph 39
Rose M. 39
Russell C. 46
Thomas B. 272
Scoville 267, 270
Scudder 270
Sears 274
Semple 270
Sexton 87, 125
Seymour 222
Shattuck 273
Shaw 87
Sherard 274
Sherrerd 87, 106
Shewbrooks 270
Shirk 273
Shoemaker 270
Siems 274
Simms 87
Sims 271
Sloan 270
Smith:
Claire D. E. 46
Ely J. 87
Flora P. M. 39
Helen K. 51
Hoxie H. 75
James S. 111
Katherine B. 51, 71
Laura C. 111
Lucy N. M. 17, 95
Mary D. G. 43, 272
Mary W. de M. 121
Mellcene T. 95
Nell E. 270
Vernon R. S. 121
W. Gregory 87
Smutz 270
Snow 271, 272
South 272
Spear 271
Spelman 270
Steiner 274
Stephens 271
Stephenson 75
Stiefel 272
Stone 271
Story 87
Strickland 271
Stroud 274
Sturr 75
Tassencourt 57
Taylor:
Ada L. 75
Alice R. 125
Anita M. S. 46
Charlotte M. 270
Clarice P. 125
Dorothy W. 43
Edith P. H. 121
Edwin J. 271
H. Birchard 43
Herndon 274
Joseph C. 92
Mary S. F. 61
Merritt H. 39

Tewksbury 271
Thayer 270
Thixton 270
Thomas:
Carrie F. B. 111
Eleanor R. 270
Leonard M. 75
Louise C. J. 43, 46
Margaret H. 95
Mary R. P. 43, 273
Nancy S. 61
Thorne 270
Tillson 270, 271, 273, 274
Turner 270
Underhill 271
Van Culin 270
Verner 270, 271, 272, 273, 274
Vladimir 46, 185, 270
Vogelgesang 272
von Rosenberg 273
Waite 272, 274
Washington:
Agnes H. 51
Anne M. 92
Elizabeth F. 39
Francis R. 106
George 27
George A. 95
George L. 61
George S. 121
Hannah F. 71
Lawrence 87
Martha 43
Samuel W. 127
Thomas 39
Thomas C. 57
Thomas R. 46
William L. 111
Wayt 57
Weber 274
Wetherill:
Abel P. 61
C. A. Heckscher 46
Edith B. 43
Francis M. 87
Giles P. 51
Samuel P. 127
Webster K. 57
White 271, 273, 274
Wiggins 274
Wilcox 273
Williams:
Cornelia D. 125
Donald H. 61
F. Churchill 39
Jane C. 111
Lester J. 43
Marshall M. 127, 274
Mary L. H. 274
Paul F. 43
Wilson 270, 271, 274
Witherspoon 271
Wolfe 57, 87
Woodson 270
Woodward 273
Wrightsman 270, 274
Wurts:
Albert 111
Anna V. 274
Anne B. 75
Burkhardt 43, 178
Charles S. 61
Courtney W. H. 71
Davis P. 127
Dorothy B. W. 43
Dorothy W. 121
Edward V. 39
John J. 121
John S. 125
Laura J. 46
Louisa V. 111
Lionel 92
Natalie D. 87
Norman 75
Pierre J. 95
Richard 270
Robert K. 106
Theodore M. 57
Thomas H. C. 92
Ulrich 167
Waldemar 51
William L. R. 87
Yardley 272
Young 57

www.ingramcontent.com/pod-product-compliance
Lightning Source LLC
Chambersburg PA
CBHW071836270326
41929CB00013B/2017
9780788430992